Gray Panthers

Gray Panthers

Roger Sanjek

PENN

University of Pennsylvania Press

Philadelphia

Published by
University of Pennsylvania Press
Philadelphia, Pennsylvania 19104-4112

Printed in the United States of America on acid-free paper

10   9   8   7   6   5   4   3   2   1

Library of Congress Cataloging-in-Publication Data
Sanjek, Roger, 1944–
    Gray Panthers / Roger Sanjek.
        p. cm.
    Includes bibliographical references and index.
    ISBN 978-0-8122-4137-2 (alk. paper)
    1. Gray Panthers—History. 2. Older people—United States. 3. Ageism—United States.
4. Kuhn, Maggie. I. Title.
HQ1064.U5S265 2009
305.26097—dc22

                                                                                    2008032914

For Lillian Rabinowitz and Frances Klafter,
and Maggie of course

Contents

Abbreviations

AAA	Area Agency on Aging
AARP	American Association of Retired Persons
ACTS	Aging Continuing the Struggle
ADA	Americans with Disabilities Act
AFL	American Federation of Labor
AGE	Action Group for the Elderly
AMA	American Medical Association
AOA	Administration on Aging
BANHR	Bay Area Advocates for Nursing Home Reform
BARF	Berkeley Anti-Reagan Festival
BORP	Bay Area Outreach and Recreation Program
CARD	Coalition against Registration and the Draft
CARIP	Coalition against Rent-Increase Pass-alongs
CETA	Comprehensive Employment and Training Act
CIL	Center for Independent Living
CIO	Congress of Industrial Organizations
COLA	cost of living adjustment
CNN	Cable News Network
C-SPAN	Cable-Satellite Public Affairs Network
CUNY	City University of New York
DFTA	Department for the Aging
DHEW	Department of Health, Education, and Welfare
DIA	Disabled in Action
DRG	Diagnostic Related Group
FEMA	Federal Emergency Management Administration
HMOs	health maintenance organizations
IDI	Issue Dynamics Inc.
IMF	International Monetary Fund
IRA	individual retirement account
JPAC	Joint Public Affairs Committee for Older Adults
MAD	Mobilization against Displacement
MAD	Mobilization against the Draft

MCHR	Medical Committee on Human Rights
NAACP	National Association for the Advancement of Colored People
NARFE	National Association of Retired Federal Employees
NCCNHR	National Citizens Coalition for Nursing Home Reform
NCOA	National Council on Aging
NCSC	National Council of Senior Citizens
NGO	non-governmental organization
NOW	National Organization for Women
NPR	National Public Radio
NSC	National Steering Committee
NSCLC	National Senior Citizens Law Center
NWRO	National Welfare Rights Organization
NYNAM	New York Network for Action on Medicare
NYNAMSS	New York Network for Action on Medicare and Social Security
NYPIRG	New York Public Interest Research Group
NYSARA	New York State Alliance for Retired Americans
OWL	Older Women's League
PBS	Public Broadcasting System
PhRMA	Pharmaceutical Research and Manufacturers of America
PIRG	Public Interest Research Group
PSC	Public Service Commission
PSS	Presbyterian Senior Services
RAM	Retirees Associated in Ministry
RCFE	Residential Care Facilities for the Elderly
RIMM	Retirees in Mission and Ministry
RPU	Retired Presbyterians United
SAFE	Seniors against a Fearful Environment
SASS	Seniors for Adequate Social Security
SDS	Students for a Democratic Society
SEIU	Service Employees International Union
SOCC	Save Our City Campaign
SOS	Save Our Security
SPAN	Stop Patient Abuse Now
SRO	single room occupancy
SSI	Supplemental Security Income
RPAG	Retired Professionals Action Group
UHCAN	Universal Health Care Action Network
UN	United Nations
UNA	United Neighbors in Action
U2K	Universal Health Care 2000
TA	Transit Authority

VISTA	Volunteers in Service to America
UCLA	University of California, Los Angeles
WHCoA	White House Conference on Aging
WTO	World Trade Organization
YWCA	Young Women's Christian Association

Preface

I will never forget my first Gray Panther meeting. It was held at the West Berkeley Library on a February afternoon in 1977. I was struck immediately by the voluble energy of some two dozen gray-haired women and men talking about political issues and the activities of their "network." I quickly realized, first, that I had never been in a room with so many older people before and, second, that whatever stereotypes of "senior citizens" I held had just flown out the window. I was thirty-two, and for Lani Sanjek and me the Gray Panthers transformed our notions of what our sixties, seventies, eighties, or nineties could be.

In the 1970s the elderly were still widely seen as "impotent, frail, disabled, demented, or dependent." They were expected to "disengage" (which was also a prominent gerontological theory), not enter the public sphere.[1] And because, like most people, they "conform[ed] to the institutional arrangements which enmesh them, . . . and which appear to be the only possible reality," most older persons remained "quiescent."[2] Throughout America's history, however, there have been "challenges" by political movements to "the rules laid down by . . . traditional authority," with public notoriety following when activists appear "out of place" from where cultural assumptions relegate them.[3] Women voicing political views in the eighteenth and nineteenth centuries were "out of place." So were factory workers sitting down on plant floors in the 1930s; African Americans sitting in at "white" eateries between 1957 and 1960; middle-aged female "displaced homemakers" picketing for job openings in 1974; and people in wheelchairs occupying federal offices to protest lagging civil rights enforcement in 1977.[4] The Gray Panthers similarly shattered dominant cultural expectations by appearing in locations and undertaking actions that were "out of place."

Lani and I had gone to Berkeley five months earlier for my one-year postdoctoral fellowship in quantitative anthropology and public policy at the University of California—mainly to escape threatened layoffs at Queens College in New York following that city's 1975 fiscal crisis. She had just completed the nurse practitioner program at Lehman College,

like Queens part of the City University of New York, and soon began volunteering at Berkeley's Over 60 Clinic, founded by the Gray Panthers. In
December she became the clinic's director. Though we intended to stay
in Berkeley for only nine months, Lani served as director for two years,
while I became an Over 60 volunteer applied anthropologist and then an
active member of the Berkeley Gray Panthers.[5] During our second year I
was awarded a fellowship in the University of California at San Francisco
medical anthropology program headed by Margaret Clark, a pioneer in
the anthropology of aging.[6]

Health care visionary and activist Lillian Rabinowitz, convener of the
Berkeley network, was our Gray Panther mentor. In Berkeley we also met
Gray Panther movement founder and leader Maggie Kuhn (pronounced
"koon"), whom we had seen on the Johnny Carson television show a few
times and who in 1981 was our houseguest on a visit to New York.

In 1978 I returned to New York and Queens College, where I taught
through 2008. In 1980 I joined the New York Gray Panthers in Manhattan and also established ties with the Gray Panthers of Queens, who met
near the college. In 1981 I was elected to the Gray Panther National
Steering Committee. The following year I organized a meeting of leaders of the seven Gray Panther networks in New York. This resulted in the
formation of an umbrella group, the Gray Panthers of New York City,
which I chaired from 1982 to 1987. Lani continued to work as a nurse
in community-based settings and also joined the New York Gray Panther
health committee. Meanwhile, I began a team fieldwork project on relations between established white and black Americans and new Asian and
Latin American immigrants in Queens, and this led to my appointment
as founding director of the Asian/American Center at Queens College
in 1987. The time demands of this position made it impossible to continue as convener of the citywide Panther group. While remaining dues-
paying members of the Manhattan network, by 1988 Lani and I were no
longer active Gray Panthers. That year she joined the staff of New York
StateWide Senior Action Council, a membership organization of older
activists, where she worked as a health care advocate and organizer until
retiring in 2006.

Through the 1980s and 1990s Lani and I kept in touch with Lillian
Rabinowitz during her visits to her sister Pearl in Queens. Over shared
meals Lillian gave vivid updates on activities in Berkeley, where the Gray
Panthers continued to flourish. In 1992 Lani and I attended the twentieth anniversary celebration of the New York Gray Panthers. Mirroring
the bigger picture nationally, their membership was shrinking and other
New York City networks were consolidating. In 1995 the movement's
founder, Maggie Kuhn, died at age eighty-nine. The following year I
spoke about my Queens research at a New York Gray Panther meeting,

and in 1998 Lani, who that year co-founded the New York Network for Action on Medicare (NYNAM), briefed members on threats to Medicare. By then only one Gray Panther network still existed in New York, and in 2000 it ended regular meetings.

I began this book in 1981–82 when I wrote first drafts of Chapters 2 and 3 covering the origins and first five years of the Gray Panther movement. I utilized eighteen boxes of organizational documents at the Presbyterian Historical Society in Philadelphia, which Maggie Kuhn and the Panthers' executive director, Edith Giese, arranged for me to visit; and I reviewed national office files with the cooperation of Gray Panther staff members Sherry Clearwater and Rosalie Riechman. I also interviewed Maggie about her pre-Panther life and the movement's beginnings. In 1982 I returned to Berkeley to interview Lillian Rabinowitz and work through that network's files. In 1983 I resigned from the Panthers' National Steering Committee after struggles between "National" and network-based factions (described in Chapter 6). Dispirited, I did not return to work on the manuscript until 1985 when I completed a draft of Chapter 4 on the Over 60 Clinic and Berkeley network. I planned to finish the book in 1986, but that year my father died and I made no further progress.

My three Gray Panther chapters remained on a back burner while I continued my Queens fieldwork project and completed a book about it.[7] In 1999 I read Maggie's autobiography, *No Stone Unturned: The Life and Times of Maggie Kuhn,* published in 1991.[8] Aside from personal details it contained relatively little about her career not found in previous writings and interviews, and surprisingly little about the Gray Panthers. In 1999 Lani and I also attended the twelfth biannual Gray Panther convention in Washington, D.C. In 2002 I returned to my Gray Panther manuscript. A 2003–4 John Simon Guggenheim Memorial Foundation fellowship and a 2006 Queens College sabbatical leave allowed me to revise Chapters 2, 3, and 4, add coverage of the Panther movement in New York City, and bring the national, Berkeley, and New York pictures up to date. As it turned out, the New York network resumed meeting in 2003, and while completing this book I became an active Gray Panther again. In 2004 we attended the thirteenth Gray Panther national convention in Seattle, and in 2007 I was a guest at the spring and fall national Board meetings. Lani and I also revisited Berkeley in 2007 and attended a meeting of the network where our involvement with the Gray Panther movement began three decades earlier.

I completed this book as I turned sixty-three, and many Gray Panther concerns look different to me now from when my consciousness about aging and ageism was raised in my early thirties. Sharing in hospice care for my father, Russell, who died from prostate cancer at age seventy (which is young to me now), and helping my mother, Betty, ninety-one, following her stroke and rehabilitation therapy in 2003 and subsequent falls and hospitalizations, plus frequent visits at her assisted living residence, color my understanding of health and long-term care issues. So have the lives of Lani's parents, James, who died at ninety-three in 2006, and June Morioka, ninety-three, both hearing aid users who aged in place at home with family members close at hand. Lani and I also remained close to a few activist friends as they entered their nineties, continuing to be inspired by their engagement with current politics and with life.

As a childless couple beginning our own retirement years, we remain concerned about war and intervention abroad and threats to Medicare and Social Security at home. It is the struggles waged by our 1960s political generation, plus the baby boomers who follow, that will help determine our future in a world we share with people on all continents and in a United States where by 2030 one in five persons will be age sixty-five and over.

Plan of the Book

In telling the stories of the national Gray Panther movement and its Berkeley and New York local groups, this book combines chronological and topical viewpoints. Chapter 1 briefly surveys the rise of old age poverty and retirement in the twentieth-century United States and the subsequent political responses by older people. It also presents biographies of six older Gray Panthers focused on their political activism from the 1930s onward, and biographies of two younger members who became activists in the 1960s and 1970s, before they joined the Gray Panther movement. Chapter 2 examines the pre–Gray Panther life of founder Maggie Kuhn and her creation of the movement in 1970 and its activities until 1972. Chapter 3 continues the national Gray Panther story through the group's first convention in 1975. It also introduces the theme of tension between national and local levels of the movement, which recurs in later chapters.

Chapters 4 and 5 shift to the local networks in Berkeley and New York City and their activities through 1985. Though the New York Gray Panthers started earlier, in 1972, I begin with Berkeley, where I first encountered the movement, and its origin in 1973. These chapters show what local Panther groups did in such areas as health care, nursing homes, housing, transportation, nuclear disarmament, and Social Security. They also deal with nuts-and-bolts aspects of how a social movement operates: committees and task forces, planning and conducting actions, links with other chapters, coalitions, interpersonal relationships, fund-raising.

Chapter 6 covers the national organization from 1975 to 1985, including Gray Panther responses to the presidencies of Jimmy Carter and Ronald Reagan. During this decade the Panthers formed an alliance with the National Senior Citizens Law Center, helped create the National Citizens Coalition for Nursing Home Reform, and achieved representation at the United Nations. As the local Panther networks rapidly grew to more than one hundred, initiated regional meetings, and formed umbrella organizations in California and New York, national-local conflict intensified during 1982–85. Biannual conventions occurred, and publicity expanded as Maggie became a national celebrity. In 1985 the Panthers opened a Washington, D.C., office.

Chapter 7 covers the period from 1986 to Maggie's death in 1995. As the founder grew increasingly frail and the movement faced closure in the early 1990s, new national leadership appeared. However, a loss of younger members to career demands, and older members to disability and death, diminished the number of networks as well as their activist ranks. Chapter 8 deals with the years after Maggie, 1996–2007, and efforts at the national level to mount national campaigns and to nourish the grassroots. Chapters 7 and 8 also trace events in Berkeley and New York from 1986 to 2007, when, despite setbacks, both networks continued to survive.

Four of the chapters use opening "time jump" vignettes, beginning with a key event in Gray Panther history that occurs at the end of the time period the chapter covers: Maggie's 1972 Denver press conference, which resulted in the movement's first national publicity (Chapter 2); the first Gray Panther national convention in 1975 (Chapter 3); the opening of the Panthers' D.C. office in 1985 (Chapter 6); and Maggie's passing in 1995 (Chapter 7).

The concluding Chapter 9 surveys the Gray Panther legacy. Here the movement's key contours over nearly four decades are sketched, and the principal accomplishments identified. Gray Panther ideology and tactics are delineated, and the later careers of several alumni, mainly younger members, briefly described. The book ends with discussion of how the Panthers' social justice agenda fares in the new century and how the Panthers may fare in the future. Readers wanting an analytic overview of the Gray Panthers might read this chapter first.

The book is written with a broad readership in mind, including Gray Panther members and alumni, other activists, students and scholars (in anthropology, American history, social movements, gerontology, health and social welfare policy, peace studies), and older people as well as baby boomers contemplating their own older years. Accordingly, references to sources and to academic discussions and theoretical concepts are restricted to endnotes.

Sources and Acknowledgments

This book is the work of a social anthropologist, yet it is not, strictly speaking, the product of ethnographic fieldwork like my writings about Brazil, Ghana, and Queens. In Berkeley I had no intention of writing anything about the Gray Panthers until shortly before returning to New York, when I addressed an anthropological audience about my experiences at the Over 60 Clinic.[9] And when beginning work on this book, I did not foresee including a chapter on the New York Gray Panthers and, as in Berkeley, recorded no fieldnotes. Consequently, the sections based on my participation in these two networks in the 1970s and 1980s are derived from newsletters, meeting agendas, letters, and other documents I kept in my files, sometimes with contemporaneous handwritten notations. These, of course, have been filtered and amplified by my "headnote" memories of events I witnessed as a participant.[10]

The chapter covering the national Gray Panthers in the early 1980s similarly draws upon documents and headnotes from my attendance at the 1981 national Gray Panther convention, National Steering Committee meetings in 1982–83, and interactions with national office staff and Maggie Kuhn during those years, plus "scratch notes"[11] recorded at the opening of the Gray Panther Washington office in 1985. Later chapters incorporate fieldnotes as well as printed materials from the 1999 and 2004 national conventions and a national Board meeting in 2007; notes on conversations with Tim Fuller and Charlotte Flynn in 2003, Susan Murany and Tim Allison in 2004, and Murany and Board members in 2007; and documents and fieldnotes from New York since 2004 and from our Berkeley visit in 2007.

Earlier and intervening Gray Panther events I did not observe were reconstructed from document files I consulted in Philadelphia, Berkeley, and New York in the 1980s and after 2003 and from additional information from my interviews with Maggie Kuhn and Lillian Rabinowitz. I also drew on documents from the New York Gray Panthers' early years conveyed to me by Hope Bagger in the 1980s and Lydia Bragger in 1992 and materials Charlotte Flynn sent me in 2003.[12] My "upstream"[13] (and downstream) understanding of these Gray Panther sources inescapably was influenced by my assessments of people I knew and my interpretation of events I participated in during 1976–78, 1980–87, 1992, 1999, and 2004–8. In reading these local and national documents, my "positionality" as a Gray Panther member thus animates and affects what I take from them. While I have attempted to employ an ethnographic sensibility and adhere to canons of validity I advocate,[14] this book admittedly is the story as one Gray Panther lived and sees it—part ethnography, part history, part memoir.[15]

This book has benefited from the reactions of several readers. I am fortunate that Shubert Frye and Cameron Hall read and commented on drafts of Chapters 2 and 3 in 1984. I also am grateful for responses to these chapters then from Steve McConnell, Sudie George, and Kit Scripps. Chapter 4 incorporates comments on a 1985 draft from Berkeley Gray Panthers Lillian Rabinowitz, Anne Squires, Tim Orr, Charlotte Knight, and Gerda Miller, and from Michael Cousineau and Marty Lynch. (I sent these three chapters to Maggie Kuhn but she never responded.) More recently, I am grateful to Randy Block, Glen Gersmehl, Maxine Lyons, Steve McConnell (again), Paula Mixson, Susan Murany, Margot Smith, Gene TeSelle, and Carla Woodworth for comments on various chapters and to Judy Lear for reading the entire manuscript. University of Pennsylvania Press readers Renée Rose Shield and Maria Vesperi offered numerous suggestions that improved the book.

Lani Sanjek read early and last drafts. More important, we have shared this life adventure together.

We've been aware of racism in our society for a long time. The women's liberation movement has helped to surface concern for the sexist elements of society. Probably the newest liberation movement is the group of older people who are fighting ageism. The subject of age affects everybody. We're all going to get old some day, but when we get to that place in life where we're no longer young we're immediately confronted with the fact that our society makes a fetish of being young. Now Gray Panthers are out to make old a beautiful thing, not something to be hidden, but something to be declared and affirmed. We have resources that no other group in our society have—for one thing, time, plenty of it. We have experience, plenty of it. We have wisdom, just the sheer wisdom of surviving. We have numbers.

The thing that we're up to is that life is a continuum and age is a period of fulfillment, of continued growth and creativity where the inputs, the experience of a lifetime can be related to the group of people who are coming into their creative productive years, and to our young people. The Gray Panther movement will ultimately affect every community where there are old people. What we're into is serious business. We're going to change things for ourselves, and we're going to make our neighborhoods, our communities, our state, our nation better, not just for us but for all human beings.

Older people are people; they're not a special breed set apart. Hopefully by organization of old people and young people we can help to change society and move it to a new sense of values—human-based values rather than thing-centered values. The potential results of our coalition have barely been glimpsed.

MAGGIE KUHN, 1972

Chapter 1
The Political Is Personal

In 1913 three thousand impoverished older people resided in New York City's Home for the Aged located on Blackwells Island (today's Roosevelt Island). They occupied "huge dormitories with the beds nearer than in the usual hospital wards. That people can sleep . . . so close together seems incomprehensible—for although the very poor have never been used to the luxury of real privacy there is a difference between sharing a room with two to four relatives—and a room with a hundred or so strangers." Married couples were separated by gender, Columbia University researcher Mabel Louise Nassau learned during her visit to the home, and "cleanliness and hygiene are big problems." She was particularly disturbed by "the lack of provision . . . for the keeping of personal effects. . . . Think of the tragedy of owning nothing more [than] a chair, . . . a bed, and the clothes on their backs." "All seemed to live such a hopelessly monotonous life," she observed. "People do get desperate and commit suicide or try to do so. . . . I hope some day other schemes for old-age provision will be found that do away with such gigantic institutions."[1]

Things would get worse before they got better.[2] In 1910 23 percent of Americans age sixty-five and older were "paupers," with inadequate economic resources to live on their own and little or no support available from children or kin. By 1922 33 percent of older Americans were impoverished. In 1930, as the Great Depression was beginning, 40 percent were poor, and by 1940 66 percent. This rising rate of old age poverty followed the transformation of the United States from a nation of self-employed farmers, craftspersons, and merchants to one where a majority worked for someone else in a marketplace of employees and employers, workers and bosses, labor and capital. With the growth of urban factory and bureaucratic employment, those older workers no longer able to work, or dismissed by employers at sixty or sixty-five, and without land, savings, or federal military pensions were on their own.

Public institutions like that on Blackwells Island housed only a small if rising number of the most vulnerable old—the physically and mentally incapacitated, kinless and solitary individuals, immigrants, and African Americans. Nassau found that elderly Manhattan residents resisted leaving their own quarters for such institutions, despite poverty or illness. Some received state poor relief or private charity. Others turned to children, many of whom, also part of America's expanding, mostly nonunionized working class, had insufficient incomes to support both themselves and their parents. Several states passed laws requiring children to provide for their aged parents, hardly a solution for either generation. And increasingly there were simply fewer adult children in relation to the growing number of older people. During the nineteenth century, the U.S. population over sixty-five grew from 2 to 4 percent. In the twentieth century it continued to rise, reaching 10 percent by 1970. Part of this was due to improved health and longer lives among the old, but mainly it resulted from falling birth rates. In the course of the nineteenth century, American women went from bearing an average of seven children to bearing only three. As families became smaller they became less "lateral"—with several adult children sharing family patrimonies and responsibilities—and more "lineal"—with fewer adult siblings per generation to care for elderly parents.

Older Americans and Political Activism

Older workers clung to jobs as long they could, but from the 1880s onward employers began adopting policies of mandatory retirement at a predetermined chronological age. A few U.S. companies awarded favored employees old age annuities, sometimes also used to "pension off" higher-paid and more workplace-savvy senior workers. Still, only 160 employers across the United States provided their workers pensions at the time of Nassau's Blackwells Island visit. When the Depression began sixteen years later, just one in eight U.S. workers could expect some, often meager, public or private pension benefit, and many of these plans soon failed. Government-administered universal old age pensions financed by compulsory employer and worker contributions began in 1889 in Germany and by 1924 existed in most of Western Europe. In the United States several state-level campaigns for publicly funded old age pensions arose in the 1920s but met resistance from employers and business groups.

California became a center of struggle, with its large number of retirees and network of "state societies" composed of older people relocated from states "back East." In 1933 the novelist Upton Sinclair's "End Poverty in California" movement proposed fifty-dollar monthly checks for each needy retiree. So threatened were government officials that after

Sinclair won the 1934 Democratic nomination for governor, party leaders supported the successful Republican challenger. The "Ham and Eggs" movement campaigned for "Twenty-five Dollars Every Tuesday" in dated money (which expired if not spent) to be issued to unemployed Californians age fifty and over. With mass marches, rallies, and radio broadcasts, the Ham and Egger vote elected a Democratic governor in 1938. The most far-reaching California movement began in 1933 when Dr. Francis Townsend of Long Beach faced mandatory retirement at sixty-seven. He proposed a monthly retirement benefit of two hundred dollars in dated money for all at age sixty, to be financed by a business transaction tax. This, he argued, would also be a means to reduce Depression-caused inventory backups through expanded purchasing power. Townsend clubs soon formed in every state, with hundreds of thousands of members in 1934.

Threatened by support for Townsend's Old Age Revolving Pension Plan, Congress passed President Franklin Delano Roosevelt's Social Security legislation in 1935 by a 371 to 33 margin. Intended to open jobs for younger workers among the fifteen million unemployed, as well as to allay old age poverty, it provided retired workers a check every month at age sixty-five. It also extended federal matching assistance to state-run relief programs for the elderly poor. Amendments in 1939 added spousal coverage and benefits for survivors of deceased workers. In 1940 Ida Fuller, seventy-six, of Ludlow, Vermont, received the first Social Security check. Over the next two decades Social Security coverage was expanded to nearly all workers, benefits were raised, disability coverage and early retirement options were added, and old age poverty was reduced. Though intended to be one leg of a "three-legged stool" with private pensions and savings, for most older people Social Security was the principal source of income. Old age poverty, still encompassing 35 percent of the aged in 1959, was "rediscovered" in the early 1960s.[3] At the end of that decade's "war on poverty" 25 percent of older Americans remained poor. With annual cost-of-living benefit increases beginning in 1972, and federalization of state-run old age assistance under the Supplemental Security Income (SSI) program, the figure dropped to 16 percent by 1974, though higher poverty rates continued among elderly women and African Americans.[4]

The supporters of Sinclair, Ham and Eggs, Townsend, and other pension advocates in the 1920s and 1930s constituted the first national political movement of older Americans. Like African Americans and women, older people were now a "second class" segment (or "reserve army") of the U.S. working class, excluded from full participation as income earners by, in their case, arbitrary employer assessments of their workplace efficiency or tractability or compulsory retirement because of age. Their exclusion became even more entrenched after Social Security helped make an exit at sixty-five obligatory in most workplaces. (In 1890 three-quarters of white men over sixty-five still worked; in 1920 60 percent did; by 1970 only one-quarter were employed, while a similar number preferred but were not allowed to continue working.) African Americans and women, who were further excluded from voting and other civil rights, had earlier organized movements for political and economic equality around the points of their exclusion, race or gender. As "the key determinants of the standard of living enjoyed or endured by the aged" became "national social and economic policies," older Americans organized to confront the state at their point of exclusion—chronological age—from the working class and its struggles[5] (now waged under more favorable circumstances as a result of New Deal legislation[6].)

In 1920 a contributory pension program at age seventy was inaugurated for federal employees, and in 1921 the National Association of Retired Federal Employees (NARFE) was organized to lobby in Washington to further member interests. The first local clubs and "senior centers" serving retired persons appeared in the 1930s and 1940s, and in 1950 staff members formed the National Council on Aging (NCOA), later including gerontological researchers and policy professionals as well as public and private service providers. In 1958 the American Association of Retired Persons (AARP) was created, both as a vehicle to sell older people insurance and as a nonpartisan lobbying voice for "senior citizen" interests in Washington, D.C.[7] During the 1950s labor union retiree caucuses sprouted, concerned in particular with health care coverage. Union retiree-liaison staffs expanded, with many later active in "Senior Citizens for Kennedy," part of Democratic candidate John F. Kennedy's 1960 presidential campaign. Potential voters over sixty-five that year amounted to 15 percent of the electorate, versus only 9 percent in the 1930s.

In 1961 newly elected President Kennedy convened the first White House Conference on Aging. Following this event the Democratic Party helped create the National Council of Senior Citizens (NCSC) and hundreds of local NCSC clubs to lobby for national health coverage; later the AFL-CIO (American Federation of Labor-Congress of Industrial Organizations) and several of its member unions provided leadership and financial backing. In 1961 a permanent Senate committee, the Special Committee on Aging, was established, followed in 1974 by the House Select Committee on Aging. In 1965 Kennedy's successor, Lyndon Johnson, signed a series of Great Society bills, with three directly affecting elderly citizens: (1) the Older Americans Act, which funded service and employment programs and launched the federal Administration on Aging (AOA); (2) Medicare, which provided hospital insurance and doctor bill coverage for the elderly and disabled; and (3) Medicaid, which provided health coverage for low-income persons of all ages and also fueled expansion of a commercial nursing home industry that housed one million older Americans five years later. By 1968 there were more than three hundred and fifty local union retiree chapters affiliated with the NCSC, whose *Senior Citizen News* reached four million readers. In 1970 the National Caucus on the Black Aged was founded, preceding the 1971 White House Conference on Aging, where NARFE, NCOA, AARP, and the NCSC played active roles, as they also did vis-à-vis Congress, the AOA, and other executive branch agencies.

In 1970 another new group, the Gray Panthers, appeared but went relatively unnoticed until receiving its first press coverage in 1972.[8] By the 1980s there were six to seven thousand members of more than one hundred local Gray Panther groups coordinated by a national office in Philadelphia, and the Panthers had sixty thousand financial supporters. The movement's vitality arose from intergenerational synergy between its older and younger members. The Panthers would make their mark by attacking mandatory retirement, critiquing ageist stereotypes, opposing the Vietnam War and nuclear weapons, demanding universal health care, calling for decent housing through the life cycle, defending Social Security and adequate incomes for all, and epitomizing an active and politically engaged old age. The Gray Panthers survived the death of their founder in 1995 and continue in 2009.

The People Who Became Gray Panthers

In the next chapter we will meet founder Maggie Kuhn (born in 1905) and her earliest Gray Panther cohorts, mainly fellow white, Northeastern, recent retirees from mainline Protestant religious bodies and social service professions. As the movement expanded nationally following media attention in 1972, the membership became more diverse, including older and younger members of varied occupational backgrounds, Jews and Catholics, and a few African Americans. Aside from some younger recruits, it was not involvement with senior citizen issues that brought most people to the Gray Panthers. It was rather lifetimes of engagement with labor struggles, civil and human rights, economic justice, health care, and peace—from the 1930s onward for the older Panthers and during the 1960s and early 1970s for younger members. Participants in a long American activist tradition,[9] they were persons for whom the political was personal—a part of daily thought and conversation—over years of organized action with others.[10]

Between 1976 and 1982 the national Gray Panther newspaper *Network* published thirty portraits of Gray Panthers, most of them leaders in the scores of local groups, also called "networks," that formed nationwide. Reflecting the movement's membership, twenty-two were old, five young, and three middle-aged (in their fifties). Two-thirds were women, and one-third men. One was African American, the others white. Their stories illustrate the new movement's roots.

Doris Mendes (born in 1907) acquired her social justice values as a teenager in a Methodist Episcopal church youth group in Omaha, Nebraska. In 1927 she arrived in Chicago and worked for eight years in the Methodist Board of Education's Young People's Department while living in a church-sponsored boarding school in an African American neighborhood. In 1935 she moved into the University of Chicago Settlement House, where she met community organizer Saul Alinsky, then working with youth in the Eastern European immigrant Back of the Yards neighborhood; later she moved to Hull House, founded by settlement house pioneer Jane Addams. While in Chicago Mendes attended a summer school for office workers; she then helped organize and became first president of AFL Local 20074, Stenographers, Typists, Bookkeepers and Assistants Union. In 1937 the AFL revoked her group's charter after members picketed in solidarity with the CIO-affiliated National Tea Workers. Mendes also joined a "modern dance with-a-social-conscience" group: "[We] sat on the gym floor in our leotards . . . and discussed jobs, discrimination, politics, war." In 1947 she returned to Omaha, where she worked as the University of Nebraska Medical School registrar and then in a fraternal organization's insurance program until she was forced to retire at sixty-five in 1972. Then "free . . . to do what I want to do, say what I want to say," she joined an older women's feminist group and, intrigued by a newspaper story about Maggie Kuhn, contacted the Gray Panthers. In 1974 she became founding "convener" of the Omaha Gray Panthers.[11]

As a child in the 1920s Frances Klafter (born in 1909) went door-to-door helping her father, a progressive Democrat and member of Oklahoma's first constitutional convention, to obtain signatures on ballot initiative petitions. At the University of Oklahoma she heard Socialist Party speakers and met her first husband, who as a graduate student traveled to Harlan County, Kentucky, to investigate conditions facing coal miners. "I began to read avidly about labor history, Emma Goldman and the Anarchists, the Sacco-Vanzetti Case, the Russian Revolution. I was angry that people were starving, and I wanted to learn why and what I could do about it. Our tiny apartment became a gathering place for radical intellectuals." In 1935 they moved to Washington, D.C., and Frances found work at the Federal Emergency Relief Administration, which distributed funds to states for public works employment, and later in the Public Housing Administration. She joined the CIO United Federal Workers, walked picket lines to support unionization drives, and served as union local president. In the later 1930s she joined efforts to aid the antifascist Spanish government and oppose Nazi Germany. During World War II her second husband, Ira Klafter, served overseas and she worked in Washington, D.C., as a writer and editor. Though not a Communist Party member herself, Frances had friends who were, and after the war she was unable to reenter federal government employment because of her support for progressive causes. In 1948 she backed the Progressive Party candidacy of Henry Wallace. During the 1950s and 1960s she worked for the Twentieth Century Fund as a researcher and editor while raising three children. Though McCarthyism "pretty much wrecked organized left-wing activity," she participated in campaigns to end racial segregation in suburban Prince Georges County, Maryland, where she lived, and with the League of Women Voters to register African Americans to vote. In the 1960s she joined an antiwar group and organized a large public meeting to protest the Vietnam War. In 1972 she retired voluntarily, but two weeks later Ira died in a swimming accident. After regaining equilibrium, she resolved to "enter the fray once more" and in 1974 joined the Metropolitan Washington Gray Panthers. In 1976 she became co-chair of the national Gray Panther Health Task Force.[12]

Raised near Jackson, Mississippi, by parents who were cotton sharecroppers, Angie Aker (born in 1911) attended black church-affiliated schools that ended at the eighth grade and was influenced by her independent-minded maternal grandfather, born during the last year of slavery, who owned land and was harassed by local whites. She married and remained in Mississippi through the 1930s. When the United States entered World War II she accompanied her husband to jobs at army camps, and in 1943 they moved to Kansas City, Missouri. He died in 1946, followed by two of their children, who succumbed to sickle cell anemia. Widowed, she did laundry at home to support her family and in 1949 married Rufus Aker, a hospital orderly, who died in 1971. Earlier she had joined "the PTA and did some community work," but now widowed again at sixty, she became active in senior citizen activities. She organized the Missouri AARP's "first black chapter," which grew to two hundred, including several professionals. She was appointed to the Governor's Advisory Committee on Aging, was a delegate to the 1971 White House Conference on Aging, and served four years in Missouri's "Silver-Haired Legislature." She also became active in the Missouri Association Against Sickle Cell Disease. In 1976 she founded a community organization funded by the Kansas City Area Agency on Aging to do home repairs and provide escorts for older people. Aker became a Gray Panther after hearing Maggie Kuhn at a 1974 conference in Kansas City. There she also met her third husband, Eri Fouts (born in 1906), a white, Roman Catholic cemetery landscaper who became her partner in Gray Panther activism until his death in 1978.[13]

As a boy Tom Moore (born in 1912) worked on his family's Texas farm while his father was employed "walking" an oil company pipeline. In 1929 he began college at Texas Tech in Lubbock just weeks before the stock market crash that precipitated the decade-long Depression. In 1934 he joined the Federal Emergency Relief Administration, working in Dawson County, Texas—"a population of 10,000 of whom 7,500 were on relief." He later moved to the Department of Agriculture headed by Roosevelt's Secretary Henry Wallace, and at age twenty-five became administrator for a colony of eighty Dust Bowl farm families resettled on a government-purchased sixteen-thousand-acre ranch. During World War II he served in the War Food Administration, recruiting and supervising U.S. and Mexican farm workers in seven Northwestern states, and also joined the Federal Workers Union. When Wallace broke with President Harry Truman over Cold War policy and was fired, Moore joined other Agriculture Department employees who resigned in solidarity, and in 1948 he served as a Progressive Party campaign official in Wallace's unsuccessful challenge to Truman. Five years later the farm supply business Moore founded closed when he was blacklisted following a House Un-American Activities Committee interrogation about his role in the Wallace campaign. For the next decade he worked as a truck driver and a union activist and pressed to open blue-collar union jobs to African and Mexican Americans. Leaving his home in Long Beach, California, where he led a branch of the liberal California Democratic [Party] Council and fought racial housing segregation, he moved to Sacramento in 1965 to direct an antipoverty program. Then between 1968 and 1978 he was an organizer of union-sponsored prepaid group health plans in California and Tennessee. In 1979 he joined the Sacramento Gray Panthers and was promptly elected convener. The following year he became founding president of the California Gray Panthers.[14]

Billie Heller (born in 1919) studied theater arts at the University of California, Los Angeles, until hepatitis forced her to discontinue. She then worked as secretary to singer Frankie Laine in the 1940s and married his manager Seymour Heller, who also represented bandleaders Tommy Dorsey, Glenn Miller, Guy Lombardo, and Lawrence Welk and after 1950 was the personal manager of pianist Liberace. In these years she enjoyed a glamorous social life in the entertainment world. In the late 1950s and early 1960s she had three children; spending more time at home, she experienced the rekindling of the political inclination instilled by her parents, both active Democratic Party members. She involved herself with the environmentalist Sierra Club and attorney Ralph Nader's Center for the Study of Responsive Law, founded in 1969, and embraced proconsumer, antinuclear, and National Organization for Women causes and issues. In 1972 she heard Maggie Kuhn speak, met with her at her motel, and became part of "the bedroom group" that organized the Greater Los Angeles Gray Panthers. Heller helped start eight Los Angeles area– Panther networks, with combined memberships of seven hundred. She also returned to UCLA to complete her education.[15]

Eddie Sandifer (born in 1929) lived in Louisiana and Mississippi during his childhood years, and by the time he was nineteen he realized he was gay. Open about his homosexuality and also critical of the anti- black racial prejudice of other whites, he experienced antipathy and threats at school and work. When drafted for the Korean War in the early 1950s he fought discharge because of his sexual orientation, and after two years of active duty he served five more in the Army reserve and National Guard. His military medical-unit training qualified him to work in nursing homes, which he did through the 1960s, and in 1971 he became a licensed nursing home administrator. Sandifer then orga- nized his facility's staff and residents to vote and join demonstrations and became a thorn in the side of the nursing home industry. He was also a consultant on male rape for the Jackson, Mississippi, Rape Crisis Center; joined the Mississippi Gay Alliance, National Citizen's Coalition for Nursing Home Reform, American Civil Liberties Union, and civil rights and welfare rights groups; recruited whites for confrontations with the Ku Klux Klan; and spoke at colleges and on radio talk shows. In 1975 he heard Maggie Kuhn at a Chicago conference and then organized the Jackson Gray Panthers.[16]

Daughter of a postal employee and a dressmaker, Leslie Kwass (born in 1949) lived in New York City to age fifteen. "My Dad was active in the Postal Workers' Union. . . . He often spoke to me of the racism in his work place and was adamant that . . . I grow up respecting the rights and talents of all people." Her Austrian immigrant grandmother resided in the Kwass household until she entered a nursing home. "It was a good home, run by a Jewish organization, [but] I was appalled by some of the things I saw there." In 1964 her family moved to Los Angeles, where she attended classes at UCLA during her high school senior year. In 1967 she enrolled at the University of California, Berkeley. "I opposed the [Viet- nam] war and participated in numerous street actions. . . . In 1969–70 the People's Park issue erupted and I found myself ducking beatings and arrests on the city streets. It became clear to me that we either had to go underground . . . or turn back into the system and work our way out." She entered Hastings Law School at Berkeley, held a two-year internship with the Senior Citizens Law Program in San Francisco, and graduated in 1974, whereupon she accepted a staff position with the law program. During the next four years she sued the state of California several times for failure to enforce nursing home regulations and became an active Berkeley Gray Panther.[17]

Ron Wyden (born in 1949) was the son of Jewish parents who as children both fled Nazi Germany. His mother became a librarian at Stanford University in California and his father a magazine editor and author. Wyden attended the University of California, Santa Barbara, on a basketball scholarship, completed his B.A. at Stanford, and graduated from the University of Oregon School of Law in 1974. During 1972 he worked in the unsuccessful senatorial nomination campaign of former Democratic senator Wayne Morse, who had voted against the 1964 Tonkin Gulf Resolution authorizing President Lyndon Johnson to expand the war in Vietnam. To Wyden, "Wayne epitomized . . . issues of social justice and economic fairness." He rejoined his mentor's 1974 antiwar Senate candidacy until Morse died unexpectedly less than four months before election day. At campaign events Wyden had been delegated to speak to senior citizen voters, and while in law school he began a legal clinic for the elderly. This attracted Ruth Haefner, eighty, a retired social worker and longtime activist who had met Maggie Kuhn in 1973. She contacted Wyden, twenty-five, in 1974 and invited him to attend a Gray Panther meeting with her in Chicago. After this they launched the Portland Gray Panthers. Wyden helped organize six more Oregon networks and became Gray Panther state coordinator. "We got tired of watching the politicians kiss seniors as if they were babies. . . . We have created a climate in Oregon where elected officials know that they're being watchdogged." In 1977 he was appointed head of Oregon's legal services program and a member of the State Board of Nursing Home Examiners, a gubernatorial nomination opposed as "too radical" by the long-term care industry.[18]

Chapter 2
The Road to Denver (1970–72)

The Gray Panthers first entered the American national consciousness on a May weekend in 1972. Margaret E. Kuhn was a last-minute stand-in at a press conference during the United Presbyterian General Assembly in Denver. What seized the reporters, and later their editors and television producers, were this elderly woman's persona and her words. The *New York Times* described a "slim 5-foot-3 militant [in] blue mididress, whose slit revealed her stylish boots." It added, however, "Margaret Kuhn would not be flattered if someone told her she looked younger than her 67 years." Maggie, as everyone called her, left no room on this score. "I'm an old woman. I have gray hair, many wrinkles, and arthritis in both hands."[1]

Such affirmation and realism about old age would be a continuing Gray Panther theme, but, equally important, Maggie's message in 1972 was not one of senior citizen interest-group politics. She did raise issues concerning older people: increased Social Security benefits, resident rights in nursing homes, the inequity of mandatory retirement, "asinine" activities in "those damned golden age clubs." Yet, the *Times* continued, "her major concern is with issues that transcend age: war, peace, poverty, hunger, racial justice." And Maggie's feminist credentials were on her sleeve when she stated, "Ageism is just as pervasive in our society as sexism." She added that her group, numbering about one hundred, included some two dozen younger members, and she emphasized "the curious and wonderful" empathy between older Panthers and the "cubs."

Maggie's words reverberated, and a celebrity was born. Taped radio spots were quickly broadcast. A Denver television station dispatched a reporter and camera crew and featured Maggie on 5 p.m. and 10 p.m. newscasts. Newswomen covering the Presbyterian assembly invited Maggie to a lunch and then filed stories. Eleanor Blau's *New York Times* feature, "Gray Panthers Out to Liberate Aged," was carried coast to coast, as was an Associated Press newswire release. A television interview with Frank McGee and Barbara Walters on the *Today* show quickly followed.

Time magazine carried a story about the Gray Panthers on the first page of its "Nation" section on June 5. Requests for interviews from *Life, Reader's Digest, Glamour,* and numerous newspapers and broadcast media poured in.

Maggie Kuhn Before

Maggie was born August 3, 1905. Her parents, Samuel and Minnie, were living in Memphis, Tennessee, where Samuel was posted as office manager by the Bradstreet Company (later Dun and Bradstreet), a credit rating agency. Of German ancestry, Samuel had little formal education but had taught himself Latin, Greek, and mathematics. He was also well versed in theology and was active in Presbyterian church affairs. Minnie Kooman Kuhn was of Dutch background. Though she went to business school, she never worked outside the home.

Both parents were northerners, but "my mother and father had different views of the south. My father as a businessman went along with it, the segregation and the prevailing view. My mother didn't like it, and she didn't want me to be born in the south. And that was why she undertook the journey two weeks before advent to go to Buffalo[, New York]." There Maggie was born in her maternal grandmother's house. Her earliest memories—gas lighting, horse-drawn trolleys, the arrival three years later of her only sibling, Sam—were set in that Buffalo house. And there during her holiday and long summer visits Maggie grew up surrounded by older people. "Three of my grandparents and two of my grandmother's friends died at our home. They were not segregated. They were cherished. My brother and I always had a lot of old people pay attention to us."[2] Another early influence in this "intergenerational household" was Pauline, her mother's older sister, who taught Maggie to read at age three. Widowed early, Pauline became active in the women's suffrage movement in Buffalo. "She marched, and demonstrated, and made speeches," Maggie recalled, "and she never married again."[3]

During the school year Maggie, her mother, and her brother resided with her father in Memphis. At Bradstreet's direction, the Kuhns later moved to Louisville, Kentucky, and then Cleveland, Ohio. Family life was stern. "Father was a tyrannical autocrat. 'Head of house' was his motto. My mother was never given an allowance. She always had to ask my father for all money. . . . This galled her." And Minnie's northern outlook persisted. "She was very concerned about having the cleaning woman who worked for us eat with us. And that was of course very daring . . . and her neighbors didn't like it."[4]

Maggie went to local public schools. When she graduated at sixteen in 1922 she hoped to get away from home, "but father didn't think I was old enough to leave." They compromised. Maggie stayed in Cleveland but moved into the dormitory of Flora Stone Mather College for Women (today part of Case Western Reserve University). "It was in college that I really protested a lot of the things my father felt—his attitudes. It got me started in what I've given my life to." Maggie majored in sociology and English, wrote for the college magazine, and helped organize a chapter of the League of Women Voters. "I was on the Dean's list all along. And I probably would have made Phi Beta Kappa. Then I had a very important love affair. And that threw my work very hard. I didn't work. I was just enjoying the experience."[5]

In college Maggie took teacher's courses. When she graduated in 1926, teaching jobs were scarce for all but top students, and her junior-year romance had lowered her grade average. Her father suggested she take a year off, and through a friend of her mother she secured a volunteer position with the industrial department of the Cleveland Young Women's Christian Association (YWCA). "That clinched it. I was hooked on working with groups." At the end of the year the YWCA hired her full-time.

The YWCA was very radical in those years. And I was involved in the early beginnings of the women's trade union movement. It developed because the men who were organizing would not admit women to their unions. The women's trade union movement brought together women who were working at very low pay in perfectly awful conditions. A good salary in those days was ten dollars a week—six-day week, 12 to 14 hours a day. My own salary was $900 a year. The YWCA was very influential in my life for its social criticism. It was a support system for young women who were miserably paid. Our job was to help organize them into clubs, and talk about their work. A couple of the women whom I met and worked with, who were my colleagues and bosses, were very radical Socialist types. This further alienated me from my father. He was very opposed to unions. I was helping to build them.[6]

While living with her parents in Cleveland, Maggie also joined "the Young Socialists League."[7] Then in 1930 the Kuhns moved to Philadelphia. Maggie attended a YWCA national convention that year and accepted a job offer from the Germantown YWCA in Philadelphia. Now, "I was more independent. I came and went." Still, her father "was very contemptuous of everybody that I ever went out with. He made [them] very uncomfortable and very angry because he treated them so horribly." Maggie never married and later reflected, "I was ahead of my time. I've had many great love affairs, which I don't regret. In many ways I was very lucky that I didn't marry any of the men that I was engaged to. Part of it was independence. Part of it was my work—in which I was very much interested."[8]

She continued to work for the YWCA through the 1930s. "I made it. I was on my way to the national staff." Then in her mid-thirties, she lived in New York City during World War II, her first experience away from her family.

> The YWCA was one of the member agencies of the United Service Organization. I was invited to . . . head the publication division of the USO. It was a big boost in responsibility and salary. I edited and wrote and worked with the program staff. And there I traveled widely. The YWCA's participation in the war effort was ambivalent. Many of us had come out of an anti-war, peace thing. But we were concerned about the women—in the war plants, in the camps, the army wives and children. And we, the YWCA, ran those operations.[9]

In 1947 Maggie left the YWCA and moved to Boston to join two former YWCA colleagues at the General Alliance of Unitarian Women. After a satisfying year and a half as program coordinator, she accepted a position with the United Presbyterian Church, and at forty-three returned to Philadelphia to care for her ailing father, who died in 1955 at eighty-six, and then her mother, who died in 1958 at ninety-one, both at home. She also assumed caregiving responsibility for her mentally ill brother Sam, who had entered a state hospital in 1938 and returned home in 1955.[10] Maggie's work for the Presbyterians involved writing, organizing, and traveling. She began at the Division of Social Education and Action, served as editor of *Social Progress* (later the *Journal of Church and Society*), and retired as coordinator of program in the Division of Church and Race in 1970. Much of her work involved preparing reports and program materials for classes and regional and national conferences. Here she developed contacts and knowledge about topics that would reappear as Gray Panther issues in the 1970s.[11]

A Social Justice Agenda

When the Presbyterians made their job offer in 1948 Maggie was earning $4,800 a year at the Alliance of Unitarian Women. The only other woman in the Presbyterians' Social Education and Action office "was getting $3,600 or $3,500, which was very low. I said I wouldn't come for that, and they raised it. And then I said, 'Well, what about her?' I wasn't going to be competitive with my colleague so they raised her salary too."[12]

Maggie soon formed close relationships with other women in the church bureaucracy. One, Margaret Hummel, headed a section developing curriculum materials for youth and had ten men working under her. (Hummel would later become a Gray Panther.) Maggie also joined a lunch group of five female colleagues in the Witherspoon Building, the Presbyterian headquarters in Philadelphia. "These were dear friends with grievances who gave each other support. This was the first time we really got our strategy together and talked about what our agendas were—and how we were going to deal with the men." Ordination for female Presbyterian ministers was approved in 1956, but "we were interested in the whole operation of the church. As a result of those luncheon meetings we took this matter to the Church and Society council meeting. They recommended to the General Assembly that there be a task force on the status of women. And this functioned for three years." Change came slowly as Presbyterian women's organizations, let alone the male hierarchy, resisted. "Some of the hard times we had were to get some of those women to listen. They did not feel oppressed, and they didn't see what we were fussing about. They liked it the way it was."[13]

In the late 1960s Maggie joined a church task force on sexuality and the human community. "I wrote a very controversial paper that got me into a lot of conflict, over the study of human sexuality. I wrote on the single woman, and I said [sex among unmarried adults] was o.k."[14] Her "Sex and the Single Woman" report drew on interviews she conducted with twenty single women ages twenty-two to sixty-three, as well as her own experience. She found that women "of *all* ages" desired association with men but that meeting unattached men was a problem for women in their thirties and older. Local churches were geared to families and showed little interest in single women and their concerns. Maggie raised topics for debate: extramarital sex, communal living, new forms of marriage. She concluded, "The church should point the way with compassion and wisdom to a way of life which enables those who are single to express their sexuality and to establish deep sustaining relationships with men who may or may not be married; to begin to experiment with ways in which particular members of a congregation may become an extended family. Such relationships between single women and married men might or might not involve coitus."[15]

When Maggie first joined the Social Education and Action staff she produced materials for a three-year racial and cultural relations program. "Racial justice was one of the key questions. There was great interest in those days—and we had huge classes. And we trained, we had cadres of people who could teach. Somebody said we did our work too well because there was a backlash when the fundamentalist mind-set, with much more conservative views, took over." In the early 1960s, when the civil rights movement was at the center of national attention, Maggie worked in the Office of Church and Society. "This was a very hard time for me, when the Commission on Race was formed. It was completely separated from the Office of Church and Society. And I was told to bug off, you know, get lost! All the things that I had been doing I had to stop doing. I've never been so outraged, or so hurt, or so alienated from some of my friends. I went to some of the marches—not as a Presbyterian—I just went because I cared."[16]

In the mid-1950s Maggie undertook a study of the cost of medical care, particularly for older people. "It was just a shock as to how much it runs." She persuaded the moderator of the United Presbyterian Church to hold a conference on the issue. "We invited the president of the American Medical Association (AMA), the president of the American Hospital Association, the president of Blue Cross-Blue Shield, and Nelson Cruikshank, a Methodist minister, who was working for the AFL-CIO, to take labor's point of view." (Cruikshank later became president of the National Council of Senior Citizens and an advisor to President Jimmy Carter.) By placing the question of linking health care benefits to Social Security on the conference agenda Maggie provoked "a real encounter with the medical establishment." Her report to the Presbyterian General Assembly called for the church to study health care financing. This was noted in the AMA newspaper, and telegrams from doctors opposing the study poured into Presbyterian headquarters. "There were some humdingers of letters that doctors addressed to me. Every doctor in Texas took me on."[17]

Maggie's next foray on health care occurred during the 1961 White House Conference on Aging, where she represented the Presbyterian Church. She helped develop momentum leading to passage of Medicare in 1965. "There was a strong recommendation out of that White House Conference for it, but it took four years . . . because the medical societies were fighting it so."[18] Maggie's advocacy on health care issues continued through the 1960s, and in 1971 the United Presbyterian General Assembly adopted a statement titled "Toward a National Public Policy for the Organization and Delivery of Health Services":

There [should] be comprehensive, coordinated planning and administration of health care with publicly disciplined participation of practitioners, support personnel, neighborhood ambulatory care units, general hospitals, medical research and teaching centers, and other specialized, formal, and folk resources. A national health agency [should] be empowered to provide leadership in developing and progressively refining objectives, standards, and methods of financing health care; and to regulate the financial operations of the health care system. There [should] be such public investment in financing health care services that every person may be assured quality comprehensive care, independently of ability to pay.[19]

In 1958 Maggie had moved with her mother and brother into two adjacent three-story stone and stucco houses in the Germantown section of Philadelphia. With her mother using a wheelchair and Maggie commuting to United Presbyterian Church headquarters in New York, she arranged for two University of Pennsylvania students to move into one of the houses, paying rent but also helping to care for Minnie Kuhn. Minnie died six months later but the students stayed. "Things worked out so well . . . that the idea of this kind of housing began to be more and more on my mind."[20] Her positive experiences with intergenerational shared housing would later become a key element in her Gray Panther speeches.

As Maggie saw it, the Presbyterian Church had long cultivated relationships with city planning agencies "to be sure that the master plan of the city would set aside sites for new church development. They didn't give a hoot about urban renewal, about housing policy, they just wanted to be sure that the church had the best place. . . . I worked with the planners on the basis of urban policy. For ten successive years [in the 1960s] we had a Church and Society seminar on housing and planning."[21] Maggie cultivated contacts in the University of Pennsylvania planning department that resulted in piggyback seminars for Presbyterian clergy and lay members during the American Institute of Planners annual meeting. Topics included community participation, equal opportunity in housing, relocation policy, and ecology.

During her years with the Presbyterian Church Maggie also planned seminars on peace and international issues. Some of these were held at the United Nations in New York City where in the late 1960s she served as alternate observer for the church. At the UN she became friends with Cameron Hall, a Presbyterian minister who worked for the National Council of Churches. Hall would later become a Gray Panther and bring his knowledge of disarmament issues to national Gray Panther meetings.[22] Other seminars Maggie organized were held in the nation's capital. "We had two or three every year. . . . I'd plan the seminars and lead them. It was one of the more popular things that the church did. People came at their own expense, in droves. We set up some very exciting people in Washington. Congressmen and Senators and staffers, people in the State Department."[23] When the American war in Vietnam escalated in the 1960s, Maggie also joined other protestors as a member of the Presbyterian Peace Fellowship.

Maggie's work was her calling but she managed to sandwich in other activities as well. In 1952 she worked in the Volunteers for [Adlai] Stevenson presidential campaign in Philadelphia and wrote him of her disappointment at his loss to Eisenhower. She took graduate courses at Temple University in Philadelphia and Union Theological Seminary in New York. She read widely and kept files of clippings, papers, and notes on political and social issues. In 1965, at the height of her dissatisfaction with exclusion from the church's civil rights efforts, Maggie was assigned to a three-year project on "renewal and extension of ministry. We made a report to the General Assembly and some things we identified have continued and some have died. Not much heard about it." Between 1968 and 1970 she shuttled between New York and Philadelphia. "Nobody really knew what to do with me. It was really a very frustrating time."[24]

Facing mandatory retirement on her sixty-fifth birthday in August 1970, Maggie was told in February, "Why don't you just take it easy. Before I was 65—that hurt me. They meant to be kind, but I thought—gosh! So while I still had a secretary and a Xerox machine we organized the Gray Panthers."[25]

From "Proposal" to Consultation

The origin myth of the Gray Panthers is "the meeting of the group of six." It was first recorded by Maggie in a typed "Gray Panther History" two months before the 1972 Denver press conference:

In March 1970 six of us who had reached retirement age met for lunch at the Interchurch Center in New York City. We came together to discuss a proposal written by Maggie Kuhn for the development of "a program to utilize the experience, wisdom, and skills of retired persons for action on public issues." All had worked for many years in national organizations and institutions. We had friends and working contacts with many groups all over the country, and many parts of the world. We were concerned about the survival of our planet and what we could do to make our troubled world more just and human. As we talked it was clear to each of us that old people could contribute a great deal to resolve complex controversial issues, that we had experience, time, and *freedom* to take risks and challenge the status quo without jeopardizing our families or losing our pensions and Social Security benefits. We concluded that first conversation by making a list of the retired people we knew in the Middle-Atlantic area, and setting up a larger meeting to consider further possibilities.[26]

This "meeting of six," actually held on Friday, April 17, 1970, was in fact arranged to discuss Maggie's "Proposal to the Board of Pensions concerning the Church's Ministries with Older Persons."[27] Maggie had drafted the proposal in March and sent it to Dr. Ron White of the Presbyterian Board of Pensions with a cover letter offering her services to recruit a "committee of 70" to implement it.[27] As this document underwent revision in meetings between 1970 and 1972, Maggie's and the emerging Gray Panthers' links with church institutions were filtered out, but many ideas broadcast nationwide at the 1972 Denver press conference were already in it.

The "Proposal" began: "Older persons in our society constitute a great national resource which has been largely unrecognized, undervalued, and unused. The wisdom, experience, and competencies of older persons are greatly needed in every sector of society and the church, and creative, resourceful ways have yet to be found to enable older persons to contribute to this new age, and to work together to deal with their own needs and self-interests." Maggie then asked the Board for "seed money" to launch "local cadres" who would undertake

recruitment and "refresher training" of retirees for new forms of community service and action in such fields as welfare, public education, housing, civil rights, community health, etc.; special ministries with older persons—counseling, visitation in nursing homes, retirement communities; special studies of existing services and "delivery programs" for new services; [efforts to] change prevailing attitudes about older persons held by society and by the aging themselves [including] the meaning of age, fiscal realities of age, the contributions and the needs of older persons, through such means as work with mass-media to correct current stereotypes about the aging; and [efforts to] establish meaningful relationships with youth.

The "committee of 70" would consist of retired Presbyterian ministers and laity. "Each participant would work in his or her own area as an enabler or catalyst in developing various elements of the program." Six members, plus twelve nominees from Presbyterian Church departments, would constitute an "advisory council of 18, administratively related and responsible to the Board of Pensions." After initial funding, "hopefully the program would be self-generating." Maggie proposed three acronymns for the new organization: RIMM (Retirees in Mission and Ministry), RAM (Retirees Associated in Ministry), and RPU (Retired Presbyterians United).

A week after the "Proposal" was sent to Dr. White, Maggie wrote to seven women friends to confirm "our plan to meet informally to ponder possibilities for mobilizing the power and experience of retired persons to work on social issues of the Seventies."[29] The April 17 noon meeting place was the cafeteria at the Interchurch Center at 475 Riverside Drive in New York, where Maggie worked, near Union Theological Seminary and Columbia University. Four days before this meeting Maggie sent another mailing with her "Proposal" to a list of male and female "Participants in Consultation on Church and Retirees" to confirm a second meeting on April 28 at the Witherspoon Building.[30] It is these two April 1970 meetings in New York and Philadelphia that mark the beginning of the Gray Panthers.

The New York meeting included Maggie, four of the women she had invited—Helen Smith, Anne Bennett, Eleanor French, Polly Cuthbertson—and Helen Baker. Their professional backgrounds were similar. Smith was director of the Division of the Laity, United Church of Christ. Bennett had worked in the Women's Strike for Peace and was a religious educator. French had been director of the Student Division of the National Board of the YWCA. Cuthbertson, the only Philadelphian other than Maggie, was director of the American Friends Service Committee College Program. Baker, a reporter at the UN, was former editor of *The Churchwoman*. "We were all in the same fix, having to retire, and wondering what in the world we were going to do about it. Our initial personal reactions to compulsory retirement were anger, shock, and a sense of loss—loss of friends, status, income and purpose in living. We had seen the lives of once vigorous colleagues trivialized and wasted in retirement. All of us were firmly against the war in Indo-China. That was one of the big issues in our lives."[31]

At their meeting the six women revised Maggie's "Proposal" to stress activism rather than person-to-person social service. The phrase "in extended ministries to other older persons" was replaced by "for action on public issues." The mission of the local retiree groups was changed from "efforts to deal with their own problems and needs" to "social action efforts." RIMM, RAM, and RPU as potential names were discarded for ACTS—Aging Continuing the Struggle. On April 22 Maggie mailed the jointly revised "Proposal" to the other five women and set another New York meeting for May 4 at International House at 500 Riverside Drive, four blocks from the site of their first gathering. She added that recruitment was on: "If you have any suggestions about others to add to our company of retirees and prospective retirees please invite and involve them."[32]

At the April 28 Philadelphia meeting the "Proposal" was also discussed and revised. Organizationally, this second meeting was more important to the emergence of the Gray Panthers. Among the fourteen in attendance were three ministers—Shubert Frye, Cameron Hall, and Al Wilson—who became Gray Panther stalwarts, each serving on the group's National Steering Committee to 1981. Here also an initial steering committee was formed comprising Maggie, Frye, Eleanor French from the New York meeting, and Elma Greenwood. As Hall recalled in 1984, "Maggie had a dream in her eye. I'd known her but I never saw that Maggie. We committed ourselves. We didn't understand what it was all about, but we did undertake to be supportive of Maggie."[33] While she remained at the center of Panther action, the other "group of six" members did not. Anne Bennett moved to Berkeley, California. Helen Smith moved to Ohio and died in 1971. French died that same month in New York. Helen Baker and Polly Cuthbertson joined the first Gray Panther National Steering Committee but served only to 1972 and 1974.

For the third meeting Maggie prepared a "Summary of Discussion of the Proposal," now no longer addressed to the Presbyterian Board of Missions. "Two streams of thought and strategy are emerging: Concerned older persons should work on the larger public issues—racial justice, poverty, war and peace, 1972 elections, national priorities. Concerned older persons should work on issues directly related to the particular interests and needs of the aging—taking advocacy roles on behalf of the aging, organizing older persons for dealing with their own problems; for example income maintenance, increases and adjustments in Social Security provisions, expanded pension benefits, better nursing care, housing and consumer protection." Maggie also placed on the agenda "planning and preparation for the White House Conference on Aging in November 1971" and "supportive relations and collaboration with youth groups, university students."[34] A mailing list of participants from the first two "consultations" was attached.

Fourteen people attended the May 4 "Consultation of Older Persons." Following Maggie's summary of the previous meetings and an airing of the "larger public issues" versus "needs of the aging" viewpoints, the group discussed the freedom from bureaucratic and job restrictions that retirees enjoyed, noting "the capacities of older people to take risks." As an example, Anne Bennett described her arrest the week before while participating in a peace vigil near the White House. The group also noted that they were relatively privileged compared to most older persons and that efforts to reach a broader base should be made. Some saw particular need "to react and interact with white suburbia, the 'frozen middle class.' " This was a response to President Richard Nixon and Vice President Spiro Agnew's characterization of the white "silent majority" as antagonistic to the social causes of the 1960s.[35]

Twenty people attended a fourth Consultation meeting in June at the Gilbert Beaver Conference Center in Yorktown, New York. A morning discussion of long-term care issues was led by Dorothea Jaeger, coauthor of *The Aged Ill*, a study of nursing homes in the New York metropolitan area.[36] The afternoon session returned to the "Proposal," with the group deciding "the paper should be rewritten in the first person plural as a manifesto." Their revised version now declared, "While the proposal has originated in the United Presbyterian Church, USA, we see the need to develop it on an ecumenical basis." It then outlined a possible structure. "Each member would be an organizer [to] encourage clusters of older persons living within particular metropolitan areas to organize locally for social action and influence public policy. These would be independent groups developing their own style of operation and agendas for action." Overseeing these groups would be a "planning and strategy committee with the present participants serving as the 'core group.' " This committee would "develop a communication network with interested older adults and groups of older adults concerned with action; identify innovative and socially useful action programs which could be models for other regions and groups; [and] maintain liaison with existing national groups concerned with older persons."[37] This vision well anticipated what the Gray Panther national movement would come to look like.

From Consultation to Gray Panthers

A month after her mandatory retirement in August 1970, Maggie, still a member of the church's Sexuality and the Human Community task force, was invited to speak about her "Sex and the Single Woman" study on New York's WPIX-TV program *The Council of Churches Presents.* On the way to the taping Maggie shared a cab with the program's producer, Reverend Reuben Gums, head of the New York Council of Churches' Department of Radio and Television.

Maggie was just retiring. I had heard about the group she formed—Anne Bennett had been on the program. I remember while we were waiting in traffic I told her people would be turned off by the name—the Consultation of Older Adults. Maggie had been talking about the need for militancy on the part of older people, and the need for them to organize for their own betterment. I've always felt a good name is important in public relations. I said, "Why don't you call yourselves the *Gray* Panthers." She practically fell off the seat, laughing. She liked it, and a few months later they were using it. The Black Panthers were active then—they had occupied a church in Harlem. They were getting attention beyond their numbers.[38]

The name came to Gums on the spur of the moment, and Maggie quickly shared it with Consultation members.

At the November 1970 Consultation meeting at Foulkeways, a church retirement home in Gwynedd, Pennsylvania, morning discussion concerned governance guidelines for church-related retirement homes. The afternoon was devoted to the war in Vietnam. Like many Americans, Consultation members had been shocked and outraged by National Guard shootings of student protestors at Kent State and Jackson State universities in spring 1970, and they were distressed that President Nixon refused to accept recommendations of the Commission on the Causes of Campus Unrest that he appointed following the incidents. Consultation member Polly Cuthbertson had arranged for four Haverford College and University of Pennsylvania students to share their thoughts on these topics with the older adults. "They all commented with intense feeling about the frustrations and despair that are evident among many, many students [and] the mood of rebellion against the 'established' ways of ordering society. . . . All the students stressed their eagerness to have opportunity to interact with older people [and] hoped we could get our peers as involved as we are." The expanded group also approved Cameron Hall's suggestion that the Consultation endorse the Campus Unrest Commission's recommendations and request a meeting with President Nixon to discuss their implementation. Late that afternoon commission member Joseph Rhodes joined the meeting. A Harvard fellow in political science and African American, Rhodes had been singled out as "unfit"

by Vice President Agnew. "Joseph Rhodes impressed us all with his suc-
cinct analysis of campus moods and issues. Alienation and despair are
spreading on campus. In some parts of the country [people] are arming
themselves out of fear. He urged us to see the President, and hold a full-
dress press conference if we couldn't."[40]

A few days later Maggie spoke to students at St. Joseph's College in
Philadelphia, affirming "this is an age of change, conflict, revolution
and *worldwide* struggle for freedom." (Her topic was "Why Men Ought
to Know about the Women's Liberation Movement.")[41] In December she
wrote on behalf of the Consultation to the chair of the Campus Unrest
Commission, fellow Pennsylvanian William Scranton, supporting its recommendations. She closed her letter: "We are a network of older persons in different parts of the country who are committed to engaging in
social action dealing with the larger public issues of peace and international concord, racial justice, freedom of oppressed minorities, and the
democratic participation of all persons and groups in the decisions that
affect their lives. One of our basic purposes is to support young people
in their efforts to change and make our society more truly human and
just. We find activity more energizing than Geritol."[42]

When the Consultation met again in January 1971 in New York they
discussed plans for an April conference in Washington and for the fall
White House Conference on Aging. They also heard a report from member Anne Bennett, one of three Americans who had visited U.S. prisoners in North Vietnam on Christmas Day. At the end of the meeting they
continued their ongoing debate over what to call themselves. Maggie
strongly favored "Gray Panthers." As she wrote a year later: "The name
has delighted most of the members of the Consultation [and] conveys
an immediate message to society and to old people ourselves. . . . At first
there was some disagreement about its effect on the people we are trying to reach. Then we decided if people are turned off by the name, we
should not try to change their minds. Obviously they are not ready for
action that creates a stir and changes things."[43]

Out of the Church and into the Frying Pan

A second meeting with students was held in March 1971. During the
morning ten Philadelphia-area students from Haverford, Bryn Mawr, Vil-
lanova, and the University of Pennsylvania caucused while the dozen and
a half older Consultation members considered their next steps. "It was
recognized that our interests and contacts are national and worldwide,
but at the present it is unrealistic to think of financing national meetings
or even a national steering committee. Rather a regional coordinating
committee should be responsible for overall planning, coordination of

strategy and action, and communication between local 'centers for action' in New York, Philadelphia, and Washington D.C."[44] Two more attempts at a name—beyond the Gray Panther "fun name"—were floated: NOA (Network of Older Adults) and O-PACT (Older Peoples Action). When the students joined them, discussion of the Vietnam War, the campus mood, and joint Consultation-student activity followed.

On April 20–21 the one-year-old Consultation went on the road in its first public activity. While the printed agenda read "Washington Conference of Older Adults," it was twelve older persons and twelve students who took part. On the first afternoon they gathered at the National Council on Aging to meet with Nelson Cruikshank, president of the National Council of Senior Citizens, Senator Frank Church, chair of the Senate Special Committee on Aging, and his committee chief of staff William Oriel, who briefed them on current aging policy and legislation. That evening they met with thirty Third World students at International House to discuss "Prospects for Peace in South East Asia." The second day began with updates on U.S.-Vietnam peace negotiations in Paris and legal cases against antiwar protestors. Next, Theodore Jacobs, director of Ralph Nader's Center for the Study of Responsive Law, spoke on "Organizing the Oldsters—Mature Militants," and a lunch with Karen Ferguson, coordinator of Nader's Retired Professionals Action Group followed. In the afternoon they visited congressional offices to voice opposition to the war and conferred with members of Vietnam Veterans Against the War encamped near the Capitol. (The following day John Kerry, one of this group's leaders, testified against the war before the Senate Foreign Relations Committee.)

With spirits high after Washington, the Consultation met in July 1971 to plan fall events and to hear Anne and John Bennett speak about their three-month trip to Southeast Asia and Janet Neuman, a member from Washington, D.C., report on her May visit with U.S. antiwar draft resisters and military deserters in Sweden. During the summer Maggie was busy leading a workshop at a National Welfare Rights Organization conference in Rhode Island, writing an article for the church magazine *Enquiry*, and completing her book *Get Out There and Do Something about Injustice*, published in 1972.

The *Enquiry* piece, "New Life for the Elderly: Liberation from 'Ageism,' " was later reprinted by the Gray Panthers. It situated the "militant elderly" within the liberation struggles of the 1960s and 1970s and drew parallels between racism and ageism: "Both deprive American society of the contributions of many competent and creative persons. Both result in individual alienation, despair, and hostility. To be eliminated, both will require mobilization and commitment of the national political process." For this struggle old people needed both "corporate strength" and "a new life style: accepting ourselves and our accumulated years with grace and authentic maturity of spirit and emotion; continuing to do useful work; maintaining interest in sex; democratizing and humanizing institutions serving the aged; and the capacity to be outraged about the state of misery, powerlessness, and poverty in the world."[45]

Get Out There and Do Something about Injustice was a guide to organizing church discussion groups and community projects. It blended biblical and pastoral themes with issues Maggie was grappling with in the Consultation: "the views of radical students about the war in Southeast Asia and the war-related research operations of the university"; "the Black power movement and the rise of a powerful, articulate, ecumenical body of black clergy and laity"; "the Women's liberation movement" and "Sisterhood is Powerful"; "voting power on governing boards for nursing home and retirement home residents"; and health care activists' "attack on the health empire." Heady stuff for Sunday schools and friendly visitors![46]

In September 1971 thirty Consultation members, including eight students, met in Princeton, New Jersey, where they reviewed fall plans and were briefed on two intergenerational Philadelphia projects. First, Margaret Hummel reported that, along with Bryn Mawr College and University of Pennsylvania students, several retired women from her "Committee of 65" group were being trained by Penn's Health Law Project to organize patients in Philadelphia nursing homes. Early in the summer project staffer Amy Boss, twenty, had uncovered patient abuse at the Sarah Allen home in West Philadelphia; she confronted the management, was barred from further access, sued, and reached an out-of-court settlement permitting project volunteers to organize a patients' rights committee in the home. Now efforts were being extended to other nursing homes. Next, Bryn Mawr student Leslie Sussan spoke about her work organizing an Elders Council at a senior center in Philadelphia's African American Kensington area. The council's first project was removing an abandoned, fire-scored church in their neighborhood, a symbol of decay. After determining the Presbyterian Church owned the property, Sussan contacted Consultation members she had met at the March 1971 meeting and remembered were Presbyterian ministers and staff members. With their prodding, the church agreed to demolish the building. Before adjourning, members set a five-dollar Consultation "non-dues," plus a one-dollar rate for students.

Ghost Ranch, Black House, White House

In October 1971 thirty older persons from Arizona, New Mexico, Colorado, and a few further points attended a week-long Consultation-sponsored seminar at the Ghost Ranch conference center in Abiquiu,

New Mexico. Maggie and Shubert Frye chaired the programs, and two students from the Consultation came with them: Leslie Sussan and Stanley Earley, both eighteen. Maggie encouraged the participants to "create a new public image of old age" and "help build 'new communities of concern,' supporting, encouraging, stimulating each other, [to] take the place of the old community of work."[47] Anne Bennett presented a history of the Vietnam peace movement since 1964. Her husband, John Bennett, newly retired from the presidency of Union Theological Seminary, spoke on international issues, reminding his audience that the United States was widely viewed as the "six percent of the people of the world who use forty percent of its resources." Two New Mexican Spanish Americans aged seventy and eighty-four recounted recent political and cultural struggles over land rights and education, and three young Chicanos from the Albuquerque Black Berets talked about moving from street gangs to political action. Finally, representatives of the Inter-Tribal Council discussed economic problems and federal Bureau of Indian Affairs paternalism confronting Native Americans in the Southwest.

In June 1970, while attending a gerontology conference at the University of Michigan, Maggie had met Hobart Jackson, the African American director of the Stephen Smith Geriatric Center in Philadelphia. Though both lived in the same city and were Presbyterians, they had never met before. "During the Michigan conference," Jackson later recalled, "she and I had the opportunity to talk several times and share some of our hopes about impacting society generally in order to achieve more social justice for the aging and aged, and in my case, of course, particularly the Black elderly."[48] In November 1970 Jackson founded the National Caucus on the Black Aged and invited Maggie to be part of its planning committee.

A year later in November 1971 the caucus sponsored a "Black House" conference on aging at the New York Avenue Presbyterian Church in Washington, D.C. Along with eight hundred African American organizers and senior citizens and a smaller number of Puerto Rican elders, Maggie arrived to assist with conference arrangements, accompanied by young Consultation members Amy Boss and Alan Grier of the University of Pennsylvania Health Law Project. The caucus planning community had assembled documentation on the conditions and needs of the black elderly, topics the upcoming White House Conference on Aging was neglecting. Black House panels focused on racism, poverty, and organizing, and conferees formulated a list of ninety recommendations for African American delegates to bring to the White House conference two weeks later.

On the second day of the Black House event its co-chairperson Fannie Jeffrey led seventy-five black older women, a few white older women including Maggie, and students in a march to the White House. They carried a list of ten demands that included an end to the Vietnam War and bringing the troops home. "The extraordinary mobilization of Secret Service, mounted police, and a bus load of patrolmen was frightening"; Jeffrey "was roughly and rudely treated by the White House Guards" and arrested and charged with disorderly conduct.[49] The marchers returned to the church, where motions of protest were directed to President Nixon and Arthur Flemming, chair of the upcoming White House conference. The participants voted that black delegates should boycott the White House conference unless Jeffrey was freed. Flemming, a friend of Maggie, intervened and the charges against Jeffrey were dropped.

The day the White House Conference on Aging opened, Hobart Jackson and Mrs. Jeffrey held a news conference, and Maggie, Boss, and Grier prepared a press release on the march and arrest. A WHCoA official confiscated copies, and Capitol District police tailed Maggie and her two colleagues for the rest of the day. Perhaps as a result of these events, however, the ninety Black House recommendations were incorporated into the WHCoA report. They also formed the initial policy agenda of the National Center on the Black Aged, which Jackson and the National Caucus established in Washington, D.C., in 1973.[50]

In addition to Ghost Ranch and the Black House and White House actions, there was other good news to share at the December 1971 Consultation meeting. Hummel's Committee of 65 was now meeting at Tabernacle Presbyterian Church near the University of Pennsylvania, and Rod Frohman, the young Tabernacle assistant minister working with them, reported that the United Presbyterian Women had made a grant of $2,000 to further their nursing home organizing efforts. Younger Consultation member Leslie Sussan spoke about her continuing volunteer work at the Kensington senior center and introduced three Elders Council members. Member Kris Ronnow announced the United Presbyterian Board of Missions would award $2,500 for "Consultation of Older Adults (Gray Panthers)" workshops and conferences to bring the group's message to older people and students beyond their East Coast nucleus and to begin a quarterly newsletter.

We Are the Gray Panthers (Almost)

Early in 1972 Consultation members received announcements of a February meeting in Philadelphia to focus on peace and international justice and an April meeting in New York to coincide with a "Mass End-the-War Action." On a cold, icy February day, twenty-seven members—twenty more had canceled due to weather—were briefed on antiwar activities by speakers from the Philadelphia Peace Action Coalition and Women's

International League for Peace and Freedom. They then turned to "We Are the Gray Panthers," a one-page statement of purposes and goals Shubert Frye had prepared. It encapsulated Consultation positions on ageism, retirement homes, peace, and racial justice, but its definition of who Gray Panthers were provoked debate. Frye wrote, "We are older persons in retirement. Our purpose is to celebrate the bonus years of retirement as a time for new contributions to the new age of liberation and self-determination. Our goals [are to] develop a network of regional groups of older persons." He identified "students and other youth" as coalition allies.[51]

What became known as "the cubs' revolt" followed. "There was vigorous protest from several students that the purpose did not make sufficiently clear that students and other young adults were also full-fledged members. Although they were not 'gray' they could identify with the name and purpose, and wished to do so—not as *one* among several coalescing groups, but as true partners in social concern." Frye's draft was referred to the steering committee, and the question arose about its lack of younger members. The topic had surfaced without particular urgency at previous meetings, but "it was evident that students and other young employed adults feel differently now and want to be part of the planning, coordinating group."[52] The "revolt" ended with the election of Leslie Sussan to the steering committee.

Some older Consultation members departed as the group's focus moved from retirees to intergenerationalism. Frye wrote to Maggie a week after the February meeting: "To revise our statement presented in Philadelphia, we will have to rewrite our history and original purpose so that the *we* is no longer older persons seeking to find fulfillment and purpose in retirement years, but rather younger and older persons seeking to express their common gifts of freedom for creative social initiative. . . . The experience of the younger people includes only their actual alliances with the older group. As Cam[eron Hall] and I said, if coalition means the full combination of several age groups into a social action body we become simply another social action group and we have lost our original unique position of older persons in action."[53]

The next meeting in April in New York began with discussion and provisional approval of a new statement of purpose, "Who We Are," drafted by Maggie and Sussan. It stated, "We are a group of people—old and young" and, with phrases from Maggie's original "Proposal" and other writings, listed parallels in the situations of the old and the young. Maggie and Sussan also distributed a mock-up of "The Network," a newsletter for the group. It featured a story "from the South West Region" about older people, some of them Ghost Ranch participants, forming a support group for a local barrio community clinic. Other articles were on Ralph Nader's Retired Professionals Action Group, the Philadelphia nursing home project, and a demonstration against Union Carbide over chrome purchases from white-ruled Rhodesia. A motion by Maggie was passed to employ student Consultation member Stanley Earley for ten weeks beginning in June to staff an office for the group in the basement of the Tabernacle Church. After a concluding discussion on corporate responsibility, several Consultation members stayed overnight in a rainy New York to join one hundred thousand peace demonstrators in Central Park the following day.

In the April meeting minutes Maggie referred to herself for the first time as "Convener." Three weeks later she flew to Denver for the Presbyterian General Assembly. Before she left, Frye wrote, "I was delighted that [another person] brought forward again and supported the use of 'Gray Panthers.' Maybe we can clinch this."[54] When Maggie faced reporters on May 18, 1972, the ingredients were in place. The Consultation membership list numbered ninety-six. A Philadelphia local group and a looser Southwestern one were in formation. The movement was intergenerational, even if older members far outnumbered "cubs" (a word soon to disappear in Panther usage.) Ageism was a special target, but activities on a range of issues, particularly peace, were also on the agenda. Funds were in the bank, an office ready to open, and a newsletter planned. Through her speaking, writing, and Consultation experiences Maggie's message had been refined. Now the organizing skills acquired during her working lifetime were about to be unleashed on a larger stage.

Chapter 3
The Road to Chicago (1972–75)

Peering over half-lens granny glasses, Maggie Kuhn opened the first national Gray Panther convention in October 1975 with a call to form coalitions with the disabled, environmentalists, and the women's movement. Her audience of more than two hundred Panthers from thirty-seven states had come to Chicago to give collective life to what was now a national movement. From California to Massachusetts to Arkansas, twenty-eight "networks" had affiliated with the national office in Philadelphia, and eight thousand people were on the Panthers' mailing list. Following Maggie, Shubert Frye told the assemblage, "We have known in our bones that some time we must meet one another face to face. So here we are in Chicago. Let's growl, prowl, and if necessary, scowl or howl, to make the best of this great occasion!"[1]

Frye spoke to the convention on behalf of the National Steering Committee, "women and men who struggle with putting the dream into some manageable form and order, trying desperately not to sacrifice the humaneness of the dream to the mechanics and weight of the structure." He reviewed the "long process" of growth from Consultation to Gray Panthers, from "old people, to a coalition of young and old, to affiliation of persons of all ages," and from "an informal, self-perpetuating, regional Steering Committee to a representative, national body operating under Articles of Agreement." Frye listed several accomplishments since 1972: merger with Ralph Nader's Retired Professionals Action Group; reports on the hearing aid and nursing home industries; advocacy for a national health service; protest against negative imagery of old people on television; and assistance to emerging Gray Panther networks nationwide. Yet money, he continued, remained an "ever present goal." A Gray Panther Project Fund had been incorporated to receive tax-deductible contributions, but with neither membership dues nor regular contributions from the networks it was individual gifts and church grants, and much volunteer labor, that sustained the Gray Panther office at its minimal level of operation. This financial gloom surprised many Panthers making contact with the national organization for the first time.

Following Maggie's and Frye's addresses, the program turned to workshops on housing, inflation and the economy, press releases and newsletters, nursing home reform, and "growing older female." There were also video presentations—journalist Studs Terkel's 1975 public television interview with Maggie, and a critique of the Carol Burnett television show's "Mama" character by Media Watch head Lydia Bragger. A plenary session voted on resolutions that solidified the Panthers' national platform: opposition to compulsory retirement on the basis of age; amnesty for Vietnam War resisters and deserters; multilateral disarmament; massive cuts in the defense budget; guaranteed annual income at an adequate level; radical tax reform; full employment; expanded housing options for older persons; support for rent control; more public housing and resident participation in planning; nonprofit community health centers; home health services as an alternative to nursing homes; support for the Equal Rights Amendment and displaced homemaker legislation; and opposition to cuts in federal student loans. Agreement on resolutions was all but unanimous, although one calling for "legalization of marijuana for person 18 years and older" provoked debate and a roll call vote. (A Pittsburgh Gray Panther quipped that selling marijuana might be a solution to the fund-raising quandary.) A "men's liberation caucus" constituted during the convention urged that "Gray Panthers must motivate and encourage more involvement of men, specifically older men, within the movement."[2] The active membership was largely female, but older males from labor union and college faculty backgrounds now augmented the original male cohort of retired clergy.

The new National Steering Committee (NSC) also met during the convention. Fifteen of its members were women and nine men; two-thirds were in their sixties and seventies, and the rest, none of them students, ranged from late twenties to fifties. Seven were from Philadelphia, five from New York, four from Washington, D.C., five from California, and three from the Midwest. In addition to church-related backgrounds, careers in journalism, social work, education, government, and health care were represented. Maggie was named a life member in the Articles of Agreement, but along with her only Shubert Frye, Cameron Hall, and Al Wilson remained from the Consultation days. Several local network leaders were members of the new NSC: Sylvia Wexler of New York City, Joe Davis and Lee Pikser of Washington, D.C., Alice Adler of Chicago, Cecilia Raske of Kansas City, and Billie Heller of Los Angeles. Some members were Jewish, and one, Thelma Rutherford of Washington, D.C., was black. As they introduced themselves and reviewed the funding picture, they also discussed questions raised by network conveners:

Should the NSC encourage regional coordination among nearby networks? Should Gray Panther activities originate at the network level or be set by "National"?

The convention energized and exhilarated the Gray Panther movement. Only Maggie in her constant travels had seen the national breadth now apparent to all. Frye observed, "There is a feeling of having come out of the woods of uncertainty into a clearing where we can take our bearings, begin to 'get it all together,' and push on toward our goals."[3] *Network* editor and new NSC member Chuck Preston wrote, "Emphasize the word *national*. We entered a new era of the Gray Panther movement in Chicago."[4] Press coverage of the four-day event included stories in Chicago newspapers, reports on the three television networks, and an appearance by Maggie on Phil Donahue's nationally syndicated television show. Weeks later Maggie wrote to her fellow NSC members, "What a spirited and profoundly moving experience it was to be together. As Boston Gray Panther Isadore Levitt said in Chicago, 'We are on a pilgrimage and a lark.' "[5]

The Summer of '72

When Stanley Earley began his Gray Panther summer job late in May 1972, the tiny Tabernacle Church basement office at 3700 Chestnut Street in Philadelphia contained a phone, a desk, and a file cabinet. There was already a backlog of two hundred letters precipitated by Maggie's Denver press conference, and calls and letters requesting interviews, membership forms, and help with personal problems continued to pour in. As Earley recalled, "Many of these people had the idea that the Gray Panthers were a large, well developed national organization with operating groups in most of the large cities in the country." Maggie tried to hold a steering committee meeting, but most members were unable to attend. In early June she, Earley, Margaret Hummel, and Rod Frohman, the Tabernacle Church assistant minister, met and agreed to add Leslie Sussan as a second employee. Arriving June 15, she was put to work on the newsletter. "For the rest of the summer the staff meetings consisted of these five people."[6]

The group prepared a form letter sent to persons writing for information, asking them to be patient. They also decided that the proper spelling would be "Gray," not "Grey," as usage until then had been inconsistent. On June 20 they met with an expanded group including steering committee members Shubert Frye and Polly Cuthbertson, Amy Boss of the University of Pennsylvania Health Law Project, Presbyterian Church staffer Kris Ronnow, and others from Philadelphia now volunteering at the office. After Maggie reviewed the Consultation's history and discussed how to avoid being overwhelmed by the "pounce of the media," they agreed that new members—though nobody could yet define "member"—should be encouraged to organize local groups, like the Committee of 65 Hummel was leading in Philadelphia.[7] Later in June Maggie and Janet Neuman of Washington, D.C., presented a Gray Panther statement to the Democratic Party platform committee calling for an end to "arbitrary and compulsory retirement solely on the basis of chronological age," immediate cessation of bombing in Southeast Asia, redirection of military funds to mass transportation and health care, and pension reform to assure reliability and portability from one employer to another.[8] (The Republican committee responded that it was not interested in Gray Panther testimony.) Maggie also talked with Jerry Rubin of the Yippies about a joint march of activist groups at the Democratic Convention, but no Gray Panther presence there resulted.

In July, volume 1, number 1 of the newsletter was ready. It included the first appearance of the Gray Panther motto "Age and Youth in Action" and featured articles on women's liberation, ending the Vietnam War, nursing home patients' rights, and property tax relief for older persons. It was mailed to all contacts as were the Kuhn-Sussan "Who We Are" statement approved at the April Consultation meeting. During the summer the Panthers received a second grant from the United Presbyterian Board of National Missions for $9,000, and Maggie participated in a Los Angeles conference with Ralph Nader staffers. When the steering committee met in August its members realized that the Gray Panthers were now a national organization and they reconstituted to include the office core of Maggie, Earley, Frohman, Hummel, and Sussan; continuing members Frye, Hall, Cuthbertson, and Elma Greenwood; and new members Amy Boss, Presbyterian minister and Consultation veteran Al Wilson, and Lydia Bragger, who was about to start a New York City Panther group.

During its August and September 1972 meetings the expanded steering committee produced a three-page manifesto titled "Rationale for Social Change," assigned priority for Gray Panther local organizing to Philadelphia, New York, Boston, the San Francisco Bay Area, and Santa Fe, and resolved that "if a person was in general agreement with the Gray Panthers' goals and principles, worked with the organization and considered himself [sic] a Gray Panther, then he was a Gray Panther."[9] By fall a new mail packet was ready; it included "Who We Are," "Rationale for Social Change" signed by the new National Steering Committee, "What We Are Doing," a list of conferences, Philadelphia projects, and work on national health issues by the New York Gray Panthers, and a "blue sheet" to be returned to the national office with check-boxes indicating whether the recipient wished to receive the newsletter and "meet other interested people in my area." The national Gray Panther mailing list totaled five hundred by October 1972, fifteen hundred by May 1973, four thousand by February 1974, and six thousand by July 1974, all deemed members. In December 1972 the last Consultation-style membership meeting was held, and from February 1973 to the 1975 Chicago convention responsibility for the Gray Panther movement resided with the fourteen-member National Steering Committee.

A Model for Local Gray Panther Action

Philadelphia events were as much on Maggie's mind when the Tabernacle Church office opened as were national Gray Panther developments, and these local activities would later give her a model to use in speaking and organizing efforts around the country. The University of Pennsylvania Health Law Project's work in Philadelphia nursing homes continued into 1972 and involved members of Margaret Hummel's Committee of 65, students, and also the Philadelphia Welfare Rights Organization. That spring Maggie kept in close touch while the project drafted a "nursing home bill of rights." And beginning in April 1972 Maggie was deeply involved with another local effort, the Action Group for the Elderly (AGE), an alliance of organizations in northwestern Philadelphia.

AGE's initial target was the First Pennsylvania Banking and Trust Company, the largest bank in Philadelphia. First Pennsylvania had branches in several neighborhoods with concentrations of older residents where, as Maggie pointed out, "Many old people who do not have checking accounts cash their Social Security checks the day they arrive. They pay their bills by foot and in cash and this makes us victims to holdups and muggers."[10] Moreover, like many banks, First Pennsylvania refused loans to older people unless they provided cash deposits or securities as collateral. AGE demanded changes in bank policy: free checking accounts for depositors over age sixty-five and acceptance of property as loan collateral, as was permitted bank customers under sixty-five. "Banks profited and grew," an AGE leaflet explained, "because of the great consumer activity in the last quarter century by the present generation of senior citizens. Banks have a social responsibility to provide service to the community; in this case to a community of older adults." After demonstrations at First Pennsylvania branches and a call to the bank president by Ralph Nader, who contacted Maggie about the campaign, AGE achieved victory. First Pennsylvania agreed to AGE's demands on collateral, to provide four free money orders per month for elderly depositors, and to form an advisory panel of older persons. Maggie was a key AGE negotiator in the "bank action," as she called it, and similar campaigns were later waged by Chicago, Washington, D.C., and Los Angeles Gray Panthers.

AGE's second target was securing a reduced senior citizen fare on Philadelphia buses and subways. After public pressuring and a Gray Panther threat to sit in on trolley tracks with canes and wheelchairs, the Southeast Pennsylvania Transportation Authority relented at a board meeting attended by Maggie and her AGE collaborators, the city's mayor, and Pennsylvania's governor. During fall 1972 Maggie and other Gray Panthers continued coalition organizing and in February 1973 more than 1500 people from 139 organizations attended the founding convention of the Action Alliance of Senior Citizens of Greater Philadelphia. Maggie was elected to its twenty-two member Delegates Council and was actively involved in later public hearings on utility rates.

Both the Gray Panthers and the Committee of 65 were charter members of the Action Alliance (which continues in 2009). Later in 1973 the Committee of 65 renamed itself the Philadelphia Gray Panthers. It began a newsletter that year and put much effort into proposals, none funded, for intergenerational housing. In 1974 the Philadelphia Panthers sponsored an organizing conference and in 1975 a thirteen-week FM radio series.

The Gray Panther–Nader Connection

In 1965 attorney Ralph Nader sent shockwaves through the automobile industry with his book *Unsafe at Any Speed.*[11] By the 1970s Nader and "consumerism" had become household words, and under his Public Citizen, Inc. umbrella, "Nader's Raiders" teams produced reports on occupational safety, the U.S. Congress, and health care issues, including *Old Age: The Last Segregation*, on nursing homes.[12] The Nader approach combined a populist critique of corporate power with muckraking research, local activism, and legislative reform, and soon Nader-inspired campus and statewide public interest research groups, or PIRGs, were forming across the country. In 1971 Nader launched the Retired Professionals Action Group (RPAG) to enlist retirees for work on social issues. With words recalling Maggie's original "Proposal," he announced, "Retired professionals generally have not only valuable experience—but sufficient leisure time, community contacts, financial security, few family obligations and a situation potential for free thinking unhampered by career ambitions or institutional restrictions."[13]

In 1972 Nader hired Elma Griesel, thirty-one, to coordinate RPAG. As an eight year-old Brownie in Yukon, Oklahoma, she made her first visit to a nursing home and felt "very sad because so many people seemed lonely and confused. It was a dreary place—an old converted motel." Later her mentally impaired grandmother arrived to live with Griesel's family, and her grandfather and an older neighbor moved to nursing homes, which

she visited. "Since I was little I have often been upset about discrimination . . . against other races, women, [and] older persons." At Oklahoma Central State University Griesel studied several nursing homes for
courses in sociology. For her master's degree in public health administration at the University of Oklahoma she specialized in gerontology and
long-term care. Her first job was with Oklahoma's health department,
where she was assigned to study its nursing home monitoring program.
"Since my report contained critical comments and recommendations for
change, two of my superiors were quite threatened. One physician (who
had been one of my college professors) said he would personally see to it
that my career in public health would be ended if I turned in the report
to the State Health Commissioner. I did turn it in and it upset several
people, with the end result that it was 'deep-sixed' and never used for
change."[14] In 1970 she moved to Washington, D.C., and a job with the
National Council on Aging.

Upon joining RPAG Griesel began a study of the $132-million-a-year
hearing aid industry. Two million Americans wore hearing aids, half
age sixty-five or older, and another eight million hearing-impaired persons who might benefit from hearing aids could not afford them. The
project began with eight Baltimore volunteers between ages sixty-eight
and eighty-two who received audiological evaluations at Johns Hopkins
Hospital and then, posing as customers, visited hearing aid dealers. In
nearly half their visits, dealers recommended hearing aid purchases to
persons whom the clinical evaluations indicated did not need them, and
no dealer tested any RPAG volunteer in a soundproof environment. During fall 1972 Gray Panther steering committee member Lydia Bragger
recruited volunteers in New York for the RPAG study, some of whom
joined that city's new Panther network. In all, Griesel and RPAG teams
in four states contacted more than one thousand hearing aid dealers and
manufacturers, hearing-impaired individuals, medical professionals, and
audiologists. They also obtained information from consumer groups,
state licensing boards and attorneys general, and federal Veterans Administration, Medicaid, and vocational rehabilitation offices.

In May 1973 a *Baltimore Sun* feature on RPAG led the National Hearing
Aid Society and the Hearing Aid Industry Conference to denounce Griesel's report before it was published. That summer they distributed a "Fact
Sheet" to all congressional offices and prepared press releases charging
that RPAG's conclusions were "not only factually wrong but materially
harmful to millions of Americans."[15] In September RPAG's 300-page *Paying Through the Ear: A Report on Hearing Health Care Problems* was released
by Nader's Public Citizen, Inc.[16] Griesel's team had found that 70 percent
of purchasers received hearing assessments from dealers only, with no
evaluation by medical specialists or clinical audiologists, and 60 percent

of hearing aid sales were made in customers' homes where soundproof testing conditions were absent. Hearing aid sellers frequently advertised inexpensive models and then pressured customers to buy more costly ones. They also claimed falsely that a hearing aid would prevent hearing loss or restore normal hearing, although hearing aids can only amplify sound. Advertising promoted smaller, in-the-ear or behind-the-ear models suitable for slight or moderate hearing loss even though larger, on-the-body models provided superior amplification. The use of white coats and phony medical-sounding titles by salesmen was also documented. And worse, less than one quarter of the nation's 15,000 hearing aid sellers had completed the National Hearing Aid Society's twenty-week home study course or subscribed to its voluntary code of ethics.

The RPAG report revealed a monopolistic industry in which four companies accounted for half of all sales, and the Federal Trade Commission had cited every major manufacturer for anticompetitive practices. It questioned the need for thirty-five brands and five hundred different models, which confused consumers, and markups from manufacturing costs of $75 a unit to retail prices of $350 to $400. *Paying Through the Ear* concluded that a publicly regulated hearing aid distribution system, modeled on that of the Veterans Administration, was needed, with mandated physician consultation and hearing evaluations by audiologists. It included a sample state licensing bill requiring examinations for dealers and banning in-home sales. RPAG sent the report to key public officials, including all fifty state attorneys general. More than three hundred libraries ordered copies.

Soon after the RPAG study began, Griesel met Maggie. In August 1972 they conducted a workshop at the University of Southern California for people who had written to the Gray Panthers or RPAG. Among the participants was Billie Heller, who would organize Gray Panther groups in Los Angeles and through her husband's show business connections arrange for Maggie's first appearance on the Johnny Carson show in 1974. In 1973 Griesel attended a Gray Panther National Steering Committee meeting with a proposal from RPAG, readily accepted, to make the *Network* newsletter a joint publication sent to both organizations' mailing lists. Later that year Maggie and Griesel presented a workshop on age discrimination, pension reform, and nursing homes at a United Presbyterian Health, Education, and Welfare Association meeting in Dallas. Maggie wrote to Nader about the Gray Panther–RPAG partnering and thanked him for arranging her second appearance on Phil Donahue's television program.[17]

Next Griesel proposed to Nader that RPAG merge with the Gray Panthers, and that Public Citizen, Inc. fund their activities for a three-year period. Nader liked the idea, and Griesel conveyed his offer to the Panthers of $12,500 if they could raise matching funds. The NSC accepted, and Maggie wrote Nader confirming that the hearing aid project would continue under Gray Panther auspices and that RPAG's files, library, and mailing list would be moved to Philadelphia. In December 1973 Nader's check arrived, and Griesel moved to Philadelphia—and into Maggie's house.

During 1974 Gray Panthers in Maryland, New York, and Pennsylvania lobbied for RPAG's hearing aid licensure bill and against industry-sponsored legislation, and Griesel assisted similar efforts by PIRGs in Iowa and Massachusetts. *Paying Through the Ear* sparked congressional hearings and a federal Department of Health, Education, and Welfare task force study. Griesel and Maggie met with the task force staff and were delighted when it issued proconsumer recommendations. Industry pressure on DHEW Secretary Caspar Weinberger, however, resulted in a last–minute "Supplementary Report" that overrode task force recommendations. The January 1975 issue of *Network* urged Gray Panthers to write DHEW in protest.

In 1976 Maggie wrote Nader outlining Gray Panther fund-raising successes of the past year: a $28,000 grant from the Women's Program of the United Presbyterian Church for a nursing home citizens' action manual, a smaller Peoples' Fund grant, and two reprintings of *Paying Through the Ear* that earned the Panthers $7,600. "We try to follow all the leads for funding, but we are also slowly building a base of support from our affiliates. We labor on and hustle!"[18]

Health Actions

The early 1970s was a time of ferment in health care activism. In 1968 a group of health professionals and planners had started the monthly *Health/PAC Bulletin*, which examined health politics in New York City, Medicaid, and private health insurance. In 1970 Barbara and John Ehrenreich collected Health/PAC's key articles in *The American Health Care Empire*, published by Random House.[19] In 1971 the Medical Committee for Human Rights (MCHR), formed in 1964 to aid civil rights workers in Mississippi, issued a position paper calling for a "neighborhood-based, community-worker controlled, progressively financed, non-discriminatory system which abolishes the profit motive from health care." It was included in *Billions for Band-Aids: An Analysis of the U.S. Health Care System and of Proposals for Its Reform* published in 1972 by the San Francisco MCHR chapter.[20] Prodded by Maggie, in 1973 the New York Gray Panthers announced an "alternative conference" to precede the American Medical Association's annual convention in New York City. They consulted Health/PAC and MCHR in planning the event, and their flyer read: "At a time when the health care situation in America is described as being in a 'crisis,' the AMA has chosen to devote all of the sessions of its conference to technical medical issues. Not one single workshop or address is devoted to the urgent changes that need to be made in our health system. In the absence of leadership from organized medicine on this vital issue, the Gray Panthers are presenting an alternative conference as part of their long-term goal of developing a national health service that will provide adequate health care to all Americans."[21]

More than two hundred mainly older persons attended the Panthers' "Do We Need a National Health Service?" conference. Marshall England, chair of the Harlem Health Alliance, delivered the plenary address, followed by more than twenty panelists including Elma Griesel, Allan Grier of the University of Pennsylvania Health Law Project, Judy Wessler of Mobilization for Youth Legal Services, and John Ehrenreich of Health/PAC. William Oriel, chief of staff of the Senate Special Committee on Aging, was in the audience and invited three of the speakers to testify before his committee: Sharon Curtin, a nurse and author of *Nobody Ever Died of Old Age*;[22] Dr. Herb Shulman, chair of MCHR's task force on aging; and Maggie, whose statement, prepared with New York Gray Panther Glen Gersmehl, concluded, "In our view, the only model is a *National Health Service*. It would provide for a single progressive system of financing to replace hundreds of insurance and governmental sources of funds. . . . The existing patchwork quilt of health programs—one for older people, one for the poor, one for children, etc . . . is completely inadequate. *Halfway steps* like National Health Insurance are not better. The people as a whole must own and through their representatives control the health system if it is to serve all of them."[23]

Gray Panther health activities blossomed in 1974. In January the New York Panthers held two more well-attended conferences. That month Maggie wrote the AMA to protest the demise of its committee on aging and its lack of attention to the 1971 White House Conference on Aging recommendations on health care. She also chided the AMA for its "Health Hints for Older Americans" pamphlet, which "ridicules the experience and wisdom older people have gained from years of living by suggesting that they need such information as, 'You can rid yourself of stomach gas by belching and intestinal gas by breaking wind,' or 'Constipation is one result of not chewing your food.' "[24] In April Maggie and Griesel were guests at MCHR's annual meeting, where Maggie was keynote speaker.

The June 1974 AMA convention opened with an address by Vice President Gerald Ford. Outside a Gray Panther picket line of two hundred, including nuns in habits and people in wheelchairs, distributed leaflets requesting the AMA to "have a heart" and reporters interviewed Maggie and Alice Adler, convener of the Chicago Gray Panthers. Then, in view of TV cameras and press photographers, a white van arrived and four Gray Panther "doctors" and "nurses" exited, announcing they were making a "house call" on the AMA. Another Panther impersonating the "sick AMA" was carried on a litter toward the "ambulance." The "doctors" tried to massage his heart but could not find it; only after pulling wads of fake dollar bills out of "the patient's" chest did they finally locate it. Using an MCHR press pass, Maggie entered the convention carrying a large scroll of Gray Panther demands for expanded home care, for mandated geriatric courses in medical schools, and for consumer representation in AMA deliberations. As she approached the podium she announced, "Mr. Chairman, I have a letter . . . from the Gray Panthers."[25] Before she could reach the microphone the AMA president escorted her off the stage. As he did, three MCHR doctors went to the microphone and began reading a joint Gray Panther–MCHR statement requesting the AMA to declare "an American health care crisis."

Four months after the Chicago AMA action, Representative Ron Dellums of Berkeley, California, introduced his proposal for a national health service in the *Congressional Record*. The plan had been drafted by the Coalition for Health Rights and Community Health Services, which included MCHR members. The January 1975 *Network* reported on Dellums's proposal and urged Gray Panthers to obtain copies. That month Griesel reported to the NSC that Gray Panthers had spoken at medical schools in Kansas City, San Francisco, Chicago, and Philadelphia, and that she and Maggie had addressed meetings of the American Nurses Association and several state nurses associations. She updated members on a new "Gray Panther Long-Term Care Action Project" funded by the Presbyterian Church. Linda Horn, twenty-seven, a nurse who led a nursing home monitoring program in Davenport, Iowa, was now working with Griesel on an advocacy manual for citizen groups, and she too was living in Maggie's house.

National attention to nursing homes was building. Reporter John Hess's 1974 *New York Times* series, one of fifty press investigations of nursing home abuses in the early 1970s, sparked New York State legislative hearings. And Senator Frank Moss, chair of the Senate subcommittee on long-term care, issued *Nursing Home Care in the United States: Failure of Public Policy*, a report detailing "cruelty, negligence, danger from fires, food poisoning, virulent infections, lack of human dignity, callousness and unnecessary regimentation, and kickbacks to nursing home operators from suppliers."[26]

In 1975 the Gray Panthers released Griesel and Horn's eighty-page *Citizens Action Guide: Nursing Home Reform*, which provided an overview of nursing home care in America. One million people resided in long-term care facilities. Their average age was eighty-two. Half had no close relative. Most would stay for two years. Eighty percent of nursing homes were profit-making enterprises in which little or no training was given to the aides who provided 80 to 90 percent of patient care and had a turnover rate of 75 percent a year. Nursing and medical staffs were in short supply. The public inspection process was inadequate. One DHEW regional director said his staff was instructed to regard themselves as "guests not as policemen," and nursing home operators were often given advance notice by state regulators. Griesel and Horn's main target was a reimbursement system that made nursing homes so profitable, to the neglect of more humane alternatives. "Our elderly have become the victims of a low-quality delivery system which was developed primarily by businessmen seeking to make the highest possible return on their investments. . . . We have made a tragic mistake in our society by failing to develop every possible program to keep people in their homes."[27]

The guide described the work of seventeen local groups whose activities ranged from individual patient advocacy to efforts to change state regulations and inspection systems. It provided would-be reformers with recommendations about what to look for and ask about in visits; how to obtain information on ownership, licensure, inspections, and state and federal regulations; how to use the press; and how to file complaints. It included information on the new federally funded nursing home ombudsman program and appended the *Federal Register's* "Provisions for Residents' Rights" in facilities receiving federal reimbursement. The *Citizens Action Guide* was sent to all Gray Panther networks and sold at cost to public agencies and citizen groups. Griesel and Horn also advised five Gray Panther networks and other long-term care advocacy groups on local projects. Ralph Nader helped generate attention, and speaking invitations multiplied. In June 1975 Griesel, Horn, and Maggie met in Washington, D.C., with leaders of fifteen nursing home reform groups and founded the National Citizens Coalition for Nursing Home Reform.

Maggie in the Sky

The growth from a loose Consultation band in 1970 to twenty-eight Gray Panther networks in 1975 was a mixture of serendipity and planning. Following Maggie's Denver press conference, requests for a Gray Panther speaker provided the chief organizing vehicle over the next two years. In addition to her radio and television appearances, Maggie was a featured speaker at national meetings of the Lutheran Church in America, the American Baptist Convention, the National Council of Jewish Women, the American Association of Homes for the Aging (comprising nonprofit nursing homes), and events in Boston, New York, Pittsburgh, Washington, D.C., Atlanta, St. Petersburg, Memphis, Cleveland, Kansas City, Omaha, Fort Dodge, Denver, Los Angeles, San Francisco, and Portland. Maggie made the most of her trips, visiting individually with potential "conveners" of new networks, meeting persons who had written to her, and cementing ties with active Gray Panthers. Maggie was the preferred Panther speaker, and she expressed concern about "the cult effect which develops with her as the only speaker."[28] She encouraged others to represent the organization. During 1973 and 1974 invitations from nearby churches, colleges, medical schools, and libraries were filled by several Philadelphia Panthers, and longer-range requests were met by Elma Griesel in Tennessee and Los Angeles, Shubert Frye in Texas, and Lydia Bragger in Massachusetts, Vermont, Ohio, Michigan, and Canada. Still other requests were relayed to the New York, Washington, D.C., Baltimore, Chicago, and Kansas City networks.

The new local Panther leaders called upon Maggie for personal advice, and by 1974 she maintained correspondence and telephone communication with Gray Panther leaders in Chicago, Kansas City, Dayton, Miami, Los Angeles, San Francisco, Berkeley, and the Southwest. Maggie wrote to these founding conveners about lessons learned by organizing in Philadelphia, and she offered suggestions on planning meetings, writing funding proposals, using the press, and obtaining information and allies on issues. The next step was putting Maggie's and others' ideas into a twenty-six-page *Network Organizing Manual* mailed to established and new network conveners beginning in December 1973. It defined what distinguished the Gray Panthers—social justice *and* problems of ageism; age *and* youth as comembers—and outlined steps for getting a network started. The manual reviewed "consciousness-raising" techniques Maggie used in organizing, discussed intranetwork conflicts, and included a detailed account by New York Panther Jane Wholey on planning the 1973 health conference.[29]

The Gray Panthers also organized their own conferences. In 1972 Maggie returned to Ghost Ranch with Consultation veterans Cameron Hall, Janet Neuman, and New York Gray Panther Lydia Bragger. Here two dozen older participants and two college students were brought up to speed on Panther developments and were trained by former National Council of Churches president Edward Dahlberg, eighty, on Vietnam War protest tactics. Two new networks were outgrowths of this second Ghost Ranch event. A *Washington Star* reporter interviewed Neuman upon her return and featured her in a Sunday front-page story. Calls poured in, and in 1973 seventy people attended the first meeting of the Gray Panthers of Metropolitan Washington, with Maggie and Neuman as speakers. The D.C. network immediately hooked up with RPAG, working closely with Elma Griesel until she moved to Philadelphia. And Ghost Ranch participant Ed Clark, a physician at the University of Kansas Medical School, helped organize the Gray Panthers of Kansas City. Maggie came to speak and received a key to the city. A third Ghost Ranch conference in 1973 was led by Maggie, Kansas City Panthers Ed and Cora Clark, and RPAG staffer Ethel Marquart, who spoke about pension issues. Three more Gray Panther networks resulted: Mildred Kreager began the Gray Panthers of Madison, Wisconsin; Penny Morgan helped start the Miami Gray Panthers; and four Arizonans became the nucleus of the Gray Panthers of Tucson.

A 1973 Gray Panther conference in Dayton, Ohio, was a direct response to the large number of queries the Philadelphia office received from the Dayton area. There Maggie recounted the history of the movement to an audience of fifty and coordinated her visit with a guest spot on the Dayton-based *Phil Donahue Show*. Later in 1973 Randi Koren, a work-study student in the Gray Panther office, organized an "Enabling and Equipping People Who Are Aging in the Church" conference at the Princeton Theological Seminary. Speakers included Maggie, NSC members Bragger, Hall, and Frye, and Philadelphia Gray Panthers Bobbi Granger, thirty-one, an urban studies graduate student, and Carol Hyde, seventy-three, a Universalist Unitarian minister ordained at age sixty after raising a family.

A joint national and Philadelphia network conference in 1974 attracted 125 Gray Panthers, the largest number to date. It featured presentations by Maggie, Griesel, Earley, Sussan, Bragger, Hyde, Granger, Hope Bagger of the New York network, and representatives from the Penn Health Law Project and the Action Alliance. A weekend conference that year included fifty Panthers from Washington, D.C., New York, New Jersey, and Philadelphia. The last preconvention conference was in Kansas in 1974 and brought together Maggie, Griesel, and Al Wilson with sixty-six Panthers. They included network leaders from Chicago, Omaha, Denver, and Cedar Rapids as well as Kansas City Panther activists Cecelia Raske, thirty-six, a future NSC member, and Angie Akers, who attracted a strong African American membership.

The whirl of Maggie's traveling and speaking, and the proliferation of new networks, led Cameron Hall to express concern that she not overextend herself. Overextended or not, Maggie was having great success. Her new life of Gray Panther speaking and organizing was what she had spent her working years doing, though never with the recognition her burgeoning movement was enjoying.

The National Steering Committee

From 1973 to the 1975 Chicago convention Maggie's Gray Panther home constituency was the National Steering Committee. Its core members were Shubert Frye, Cameron Hall, Al Wilson, Lydia Bragger, young members Stanley Earley and Leslie Sussan (during 1973–74), and Elma Griesel and Philadelphia Gray Panther Carol Hyde (during 1974–75). Another young member, Health Law Project organizer Amy Boss, attended a third of the eighteen NSC meetings during the three years, and student intern Randi Koren was a member for one year. Five older members of the Consultation steering committee did not continue, and three older Panthers active in local networks were NSC members for two years or less—Margaret Hummel of Philadelphia, Hope Bagger of New York, and Peg Diefenderfer of Bucks County, Pennsylvania. Meeting attendance averaged fifteen, including Philadelphia staff and occasional guests from East Coast networks.

The NSC faced three challenges during these years: securing funds for the national organization, defining Gray Panther positions on issues, and formalizing its relationship with the growing number of local networks. Although some NSC members had worked in large bureaucracies, the legal and financial aspects of managing an organization were new to them. With $9,000 in Presbyterian grants parked in a Tabernacle Church account at the beginning of 1973, the NSC needed to incorporate the Gray Panthers as an independent entity. Maggie and Hummel consulted a lawyer who prepared documents creating a "Gray Panthers Project Fund," a "charitable and educational" organization that could accept tax-deductible gifts and foundation grants but conduct only "insubstantial lobbying." In 1974 Al Wilson was elected fund president, Philadelphia Panther Bobbi Granger vice president, Maggie secretary, and Carol Hyde treasurer, with Elma Griesel designated to work on Project Fund grant proposals. Later Wilson reported that the lawyer preparing papers to copyright the name "Gray Panthers" informed him that "articles of agreement" defining the Gray Panthers' national membership were needed, as was a "convocation" of members to ratify them.[30] Late in 1974 the Project Fund's 501(c)(3) tax-exempt IRS certificate arrived, and existing funds were transferred from the Tabernacle Church to a Project Fund account.

During 1973 the Gray Panthers paid office expenses from a $23,000 in grants and donations from the American Baptist Convention, the Philadelphia Urban Coalition, Ralph Nader, and individual contributors. The following year they received the nursing home project grant, earnings from *Paying Through the Ear*, and $7,500 in donations and individual contributions. Maggie, Wilson, and Griesel explored private foundation prospects and submitted a $195,000 plan for regional conferences to the Edna McConnell Clark Foundation, but like other foundation proposals over the next two years it was rejected. By 1975 less than $8,000 remained in the Gray Panthers Project Fund, office expenses ran to $2,000 per month, and it was evident the Panthers would soon be in the red. The few thousand dollars in gifts and Maggie's speaking fees were not enough to forestall it.

In April 1975 the staff was laid off, and the national office relied on volunteer effort to the October Chicago convention. In the July *Network* a "Personal Appeal from Maggie Kuhn" for contributions was made to the national membership. Three months later editor Chuck Preston made another appeal: "The blunt truth is that this vital daily work is being shouldered largely by Maggie Kuhn and especially by Elma Griesel and Linda Horn. . . . Maggie said recently: 'Without sufficient full-time resources we may have to close the National Office."[31] The message was heard. Contributions that had been running at $300 per month before Maggie's appeal quadrupled after it. In September, $1,600 arrrived; in October, following Preston's editorial, nearly $3,000. A modest balance of $5,000 was in the bank by December 1975, and a monthly budget of $1,600 projected for 1976, now predicated on maintaining the mail donations stream.

In 1973 NSC members expressed dissatisfaction with media representations of their movement as a "senior citizen's organization." They admitted a decline in their student ranks and acknowledged it was mainly older people now joining because "a radical organization with old people in it can offer a feeling of hope and continuity of struggle."[32] A means to publicize their full spectrum of issues was needed. Randi Koren suggested a series of "Gray Papers" on topics like patients' rights, pensions, and youth advocacy, but nothing resulted. In 1974 they took a first step by formalizing a list of "Gray Panthers Major Issues": opposition to compulsory retirement and age discrimination in employment; participatory democracy for residents of institutions and recipients in social service programs; national standards for pension systems; amnesty for Vietnam War resisters and deserters; redirection of military expenditures to social needs; abolition of poverty through a guaranteed income, radical tax reform, and full employment; a national health service; a national housing program with a "cultural mix of age groups, income levels and racial backgrounds"; free or low-cost mass transportation; and educational opportunities for people of all ages.[33]

Griesel, now staffing the national office and dealing with mounting queries from the public and the networks about Gray Panther positions, drafted a hard-hitting memo to the NSC. "To be really creditable and effect change, it is not enough to continue to say only that we are for mass transit systems, against compulsory retirement, etc. We must offer facts and challenges for changing the system(s) or making structural reforms." She proposed: "Each steering committee member think seriously about researching and writing at least beginning working papers on issues which have been outlined as major concerns. . . . It would be ideal to have resource people who can . . . serve as liaison with other groups addressing the particular issue, help answer 'issue' letters which come to the office, testify at public hearings, review legislation and summarize it so we can get the information out to the networks, and write various legislators on behalf of the GPs."[34]

NSC members were not prepared to take this much responsibility. Instead, they decided to devote a day of each meeting during 1975 to an issue workshop. In January Linda Horn coordinated a session on health in which Glen Gersmehl and Alice Adler spoke about New York and Chicago Panther activities and guests covered national legislation and health care in China. The April workshop focused on nutrition, hunger, and food stamps. In May New York Panthers Gersmehl and Sylvia Wexler conducted a workshop on inflation, unemployment, the military budget, and economic priorities, and in June Washington, D.C., Gray Panther Thelma Rutherford led one on housing. No Gray Papers resulted but the focus on policy positions had an immediate result—three NSC members resigned. At the next meeting the continuing NSC members admitted that "as a process of self-education for the Steering Committee, the workshops have been successful, but little follow-up has occurred in the way of arriving at . . . official positions."[35] No organizational solution to defining Gray Panther positions would emerge until after the Chicago convention.

By fall 1972 the first two local networks were in operation in Philadelphia and New York. Stanley Earley observed, "There has been a change in purpose from a group of individuals working on their concerns to a national organization with local structures," and he asked "whether the structure should be more formal."[36] A request from a would-be convener for $5,000 to organize a network in 1973 led the NSC to formulate a "Policy on Gray Panther Groups":

All groups composed primarily of older and younger adults working for positive social change are encouraged to organize in their local areas and affiliate with the Gray Panther network by sending a description of their priorities, activities, and membership to the national Steering Committee and arranging to send a representative to a Steering Committee meeting. The National Gray Panthers do not, however, assume responsibility, either legal, financial, or other, for the actions and operations of local Gray Panther components or individual members. The use of the name "Gray Panthers" by any group assumes the group is operating in harmony with the philosophy and goals of the National Gray Panthers.[37]

During 1973 and 1974 Gray Panthers from the Philadelphia, New York, Bucks County, Washington, D.C., and Chicago groups did attend NSC meetings, but most of the sixteen networks in existence at the beginning of 1975 had no contact with the steering committee. Some NSC members were more troubled by this than others. The most persistent advocate for grassroots representation was Peg Diefenderfer, who urged the NSC to "meet with and be exposed to local groups in order to create dialogue" and suggested her own Bucks County network as a place to begin. Cameron Hall, not active in a network, spoke against the idea: "Members of the National Steering Committee [already] represent the interests, concerns, and flavor of local groups."[38]

In 1974 a committee on national-local relations, which included Washington, D.C., and New York Gray Panthers, suggested holding a "conference at the end of the year to reinforce communications and working relationships between Local and National," but the idea was tabled.[39] A report by Griesel synthesized questions the national office was receiving from the networks and concluded that they did not understand the composition of the NSC or how they were related to it. Diefenderfer added, "In reality each segment of the Gray Panthers has been working with minimum communication and isolated, more or less, from each other. Maggie as convener has labored hard to keep in touch with these various local groups as they developed and continue to grow. However, this cannot continue to be the sole responsibility of our convener."[40] She proposed four regional meetings of networks and steering committee members in 1975 and also that local networks be represented on the NSC. None of this was approved, and Diefenderfer resigned.

National Office, National Newspaper

The first Gray Panther office was a basement supply closet in the Tabernacle Presbyterian Church, a large gothic building near the University of Pennsylvania. The first staff members, Stanley Earley and Leslie Sussan, were paid $100 a week, with 30 percent contributed by the Gray Panthers and the rest from Haverford and Bryn Mawr colleges' federal work-study funds. During the fall of 1972 Tabernacle minister Rod Frohman was assigned to Gray Panther activities, and Earley and Randi Koren, a Princeton Theological Seminary student, worked part time, earning academic credit but no salary. The only paid staff member was Marian Koch, a retired secretary who was hired during the summer by Maggie to type *Get Out There and Do Something about Injustice* and who continued to work for her part time.

In 1973 the Gray Panther office moved upstairs to a four-desk, four-file-cabinet set-up at one end of a large assembly hall, and Oberlin College student Bernice Melton spent four weeks recruiting volunteers to join Earley and Koren in February. By June sixteen people were at work on various national and Philadelphia Gray Panther projects, and one, Susan Schacher, recorded her experiences in a report to her sociology instructor. "The Gray Panther office is staffed by volunteers, most of whom were recruited from local colleges. Since January 1973 the staff has consisted of ten people under 30, two between 30 and 60, and four over 60. The volunteers were trained by a student, Stanley Earley, who had been working with the organization for two years. Until the new staff felt sufficiently at home in the office to feel confident about making decisions, Stanley was consulted about everything. When Ms. Kuhn is in the office, then her judgment is deferred to."[41]

During 1973 Maggie established a personal Gray Panther office in her Germantown house where Koch typed correspondence and other writings and helped coordinate travel and press interviews. At the Tabernacle office Earley, Koren, and Melton worked full-time through the summer, but Earley then moved to New York to begin graduate school and student-run office operations ended. In the fall two of the older volunteers were hired under a Philadelphia Urban Coalition grant. Others continued to volunteer, including Jean Hopper, a retired librarian (and later national Gray Panther treasurer), who in 1974 created an office reference library consisting of Gray Panther files and RPAG materials transferred from Washington, D.C.

When Urban Coalition funds ran out in 1974, Griesel, then also beginning the nursing home project, took over. With hundreds of letters and telephone calls each month and increased communication with local networks, three office staff members were hired with money borrowed from the nursing home account. When these funds were exhausted in April 1975 they left and Robert McClellan, a part-time secretary for the nursing home project, was appointed office administrator. Conflict between McClellan and Griesel soon escalated, and he announced that everyone working for the Gray Panthers should be a volunteer and he would forgo his monthly salary. He constructed a lockable partition around the Tabernacle Church office and refused to give Maggie a key. Two NSC members met with him and learned he was discarding information about financial contributors and assigning volunteers unfamiliar with Gray Panther activities to handle press queries. After voicing resentment about work generated by Maggie's travels, he resigned in August. With the Chicago convention a month away, Maggie, Griesel, and Horn stepped in to run the office. After the convention Koch's daughter Edith Giese, thirty-five, was hired as full-time Gray Panther office administrator.

The transition from student and volunteer office to paid staff was paralleled by the evolution of *Network* from typewritten newsletter to printed national newspaper. In 1975 the first tabloid-size newsprint number of *Network* was published. National news appeared on the first few pages; "Food Stamp Cut Imperils Poor and Elderly," "Panthers Take Part in White House Summit," and "A.M.A. and the Elderly" were the front-page headlines. Coverage of national and local Gray Panther actions followed. Further inside were background features, on nursing homes and hearing aids in the first issue. The center pages were a round-up of network news. Shorter human-interest items came next—a story on Maggie's television appearance with Studs Terkel, a poem by Washington, D.C., convener Janet Neuman, coverage of Philadelphia Panther Carol Hyde's visit with a fifth grade class. A list of local network contact names and addresses completed the issue.

Network's guiding hand was Chuck Preston, sixty-four, who began his journalist career in the 1930s by turning down a *Wall Street Journal* job to work for *Pulse of the Nation*, a progressive magazine published in Indiana. There Preston got his "start in the radical movement by attending a meeting of the John Reed Club. These were a network of clubs across the nation of writers, artists, painters, poets, etc., who adhered to the philosophy of proletarian revolution to solve our problems of the Great Depression. They were started by the Communist Party USA, but you didn't have to be a Party member to belong to one."[42] Preston then worked for left-wing newspapers, including the *Anderson Auto Worker,* which covered the 1936–37 General Motors strike, and later for the *Indianapolis Times* and, near Philadelphia, the *York Gazette and Daily*. In the 1960s he was a public relations specialist for the Jobs Corps and sided with a contingent of protesting youth in a campaign against their director. After finding the Gray Panthers and feeling at home, Preston produced *Network* on a tiny budget. To contain costs it was laid out in York, printed in Lancaster, and mailed in Philadelphia, with Preston ferrying everything from one place to the next.

Ideology in Process

Most Gray Panther materials available to the networks and public in the early years were neither authored by Maggie nor contained much written by her. The only work by Maggie distributed by the national office before 1977 was a reprint of her 1971 article "New Life for the Elderly." The first Gray Panther brochures, "Who We Are" and "Rationale for Social Change," were collective statements from the steering committee. Volunteer Beth Yolton wrote most of the 1973 *Organizing Manual.* The initial *Network* newsletter in 1972 had a story by Maggie on property tax relief for the elderly, but the opening editorial was by Leslie Sussan, and during the next two years Stanley Earley, Carol Hyde, Margaret

Hummel, Susan Schacher, Elma Griesel, Randi Koren, and others contributed to it. After Chuck Preston became editor, Maggie wrote a few
stories but never had a regular *Network* column. Other publications from
the national office were the nursing home manual by Griesel and Horn
and a brief Gray Panther history authored by Earley in 1973.[43] Overall,
these documents played a minor role in the growth of the Gray Panther
movement. The new local networks were set in motion by something
that people responded to, but almost exclusively in the early years that
something was Maggie Kuhn herself and the message she articulated. If
Gray Panthers read publications from the national office it was usually
after listening to Maggie in person or on television or reading or hearing
about her.

The formation and dissemination of Maggie's message was for her a
social process. This is not to slight the power of her intellect or her ability to reach a conclusion and announce it, but what deserves emphasis
is how she arrived at her pronouncements. First, she was an avid reader
and an eager listener. She especially enjoyed putting together people
with background knowledge and strong opinions and listening to the
encounter and debate. She continuously absorbed new ideas and synthesized them with old ones—in one of her favorite expressions, she
liked to "try things on for size." She also constantly offered her own ideas
for response in conversations, drafts, speeches, panels, conferences, and
question-and-answer sessions. This interactive process marked the transformation of the "Proposal" through a half-dozen versions as the Consultation defined its direction. Between 1972 and 1975 the NSC and office
staff and volunteers were important sounding boards in crystallizing the
message Maggie took on the road. But so was the road. Maggie would
pick up new ideas, perspectives, and facts in one place and add them to
what she enunciated about a particular topic in the next.

During these years the most important articulation of Gray Panther
ideology was Maggie's public speeches, talks, and testimony. While they
had strong impacts on those who heard them, no one but Maggie was
aware of their range of issues and topics. Three of Maggie's addresses
prior to the Chicago convention were later reprinted (two in obscure
publications)[44] and others exist in typescript or as handwritten notes.
They were never collected in a "Little Gray Book" presenting the broad
range of issues about which Maggie spoke. The 1977 book *Maggie Kuhn
on Aging*, edited by Dieter Hessel, records a conversation with a religious audience and includes Maggie's views on only a few Gray Panther
causes.[45]

Maggie's talks and speeches often expanded on themes from her
"New Life for the Elderly" article and mentioned ongoing Gray Panther
actions, projects, and coalition partners, particularly in health care. A

speech to the Baptist Ministries Life Cycle Project included her famous criticism of senior centers,

the so-called Golden Age Clubs which I call glorified playpens. It is assumed that old people are like children and that what we really need in order to feel contented and cared for is a place to play. Golden Age Clubs run by mayor's offices funded by governor's commissions on aging are run by well-meaning professionals who are not old and who seldom consult their clients as to what they need or want. Consciousness-raising should prepare us to function as effective members of boards, committees and agencies that provide the services. If we really take seriously the goal of self-determination, what is required is that old people residents of an old people's home or retirement village, for example ought to have the controlling vote on the board. They should be determining the policy that prevails in the program, and should be monitoring the performance of staff.[46]

A speech to the American Nurses Association stressed that few health care professionals graduate with any personal experience of death and dying:

Students should have extensive opportunity to learn and practice skills in caring for the gravely ill and dying, of being advocates and enablers of the dying to die with dignity. . . . As an old person I have found in many of my peers a large degree of acceptance and calm readiness about death itself, but great anxiety about loneliness, disability, and abandonment—things that precede death. Universally we hope and pray we can die on our own terms, with as much control as possible over the situation. . . . Increasing numbers of us want to die at home without those tubes, respirators and transfusions that keep us alive, often not as persons but as vegetables. . . . The right to die, we reaffirm, is the right of the person to terminate his or her life in whatever way is appropriate. We believe that there is a time to die, and the right to terminate life when this time comes cannot be abrogated.[47]

"The Radicals of the Seventies," Maggie's 1974 speech at the Chautauqua Centennial in upstate New York, described her movement-building strategy. "We have identified particular groups of people who already know how to organize for action and social change: the union organizers of the 1920s and 30s, when they fought goon squads and police on the picket lines; the war resisters and older members of such groups as the Fellowship of Reconciliation and Women's International League for Peace and Freedom; the former members of the Socialist-Labor party; women who were active in the Suffrage movement; retired social workers with experience in community organization who know how to fight City Hall and raise hell in the State House; retired gerontologists and other professionals in related fields."[48]

A few days later Maggie told a Los Angeles audience, "People working in our movement . . . do not wear *Senior Power* buttons or think of ourselves as special pleaders for the cause of old people and old people's campaigns." Addressing "Power and Advocacy for the Elderly from Nader to Kuhn" at the University of Southern California Andrus Gerontology Center, she explained,

Our goal is to use our freedom, our experience, our knowledge of the past, our ability to cope and survive, not just for free bus fares and tax rebates for people over 65, although we need these benefits. We want to work as advocates for the larger public good, as public citizens and responsible consumers. As elders we are concerned not only for self interests and well being, but the well being of those who will live after us. We see our needs and losses, our lack of power and place as exaggerated forms of the need and lacks of a sick society; we also see them as a powerful judgment and social criticism of the dehumanizing forces created by our galloping technology, and the priority we give as a nation to profits and productivity, the billions we allocate to the Pentagon and pax Americana.

Maggie's constituency, she made clear, would not include all older people. "There are a number of rich old people who do have power and access to power—particularly men who serve on powerful boards of directors of corporations and banks involved in making decisions that have far-reaching social consequences. But these affluent powerful elders (by and large) do not identify with their peers who are not rich and powerful. They do not consider themselves to be old, or see themselves as advocates of old people. As I have analyzed this lack of identification, the divisions seem to be on the basis of social and economic class."

Her Los Angeles speech also included a dose of the individual "consciousness-raising" she used as a starter mechanism.

Many of us have resigned ourselves to a society which we feel has no place for us. Some have "copped out" and have tried to escape change and social involvement. We are not elders of the tribe but wrinkled babies. Some of us are so brain-damaged by society and its age barriers that we hate ourselves and our aging bodies. We will not admit that we are old. We keep trying in vain to look young. The first step in preparing us for advocacy roles is our personal liberation from the ageism of society. Liberation is both personal and social. This involves the acceptance of old age with grace and an authentic maturity, without self-hate or self-deceit. We have to feel differently about our being old—or young. Our sick society has afflicted us with this self-deceit—feeling flattered when told how young we look. The second step is awareness and analysis of our experience and appreciation of how we have coped with change and survived. Anyone who lived through the depression of the thirties and survived it has a valuable tool for dealing with the economic deprivations that all alienated minorities suffer today, including old people. . . . Old people must resist all efforts and pressures to put us on the sidelines.

Maggie urged her older audience members to engage in consciousness-raising with other old people. Yet, "as advocates for change and social justice for society as a whole, we recognize that we cannot hope to motivate everybody over 65 to join our movement. We have modest goals and hopes for the enlistment of small numbers of wrinkled radicals who are fully committed people, willing to engage in controversy and take the risks involved." Gray Panthers, therefore, were taking a further step by forming "groups of old people and young people [to] build a new community of support for change."[49]

The Media Watch the Gray Panthers, the Gray Panthers Watch the Media

Press, radio, and television were critical in spreading early word about the Gray Panthers, and after the first flurry of media attention in 1972 Maggie was not forgotten. In 1973 she appeared twice on the *Phil Donahue Show*, reaching more than fifty stations, on David Susskind's television interview show, and on many local television and radio programs during her travels. Newspaper reports and interviews following her speaking engagements frequently were reprinted and used as organizing tools by Gray Panther networks, which added their phone number or meeting place and time. After Maggie became even more a national celebrity following her first appearance on the *Tonight Show Starring Johnny Carson*, newspaper announcements preceded her talks and attracted potential Gray Panther recruits. Local organizers capitalized on media interest in the movement. Washington, D.C., New York, Philadelphia, and San Francisco Bay Area Gray Panthers appeared on television and radio during 1973, and in the following years more Panther networks entered the media lists.

Four visual documentaries about the Gray Panthers were produced between 1972 and 1975. The first, shown nationally in October 1972 by the ABC network religious series *Directions*, included scenes at an NSC meeting in Princeton, the Tabernacle Church basement office, a nursing home that Philadelphia Gray Panthers were helping to organize, and the First Pennsylvania site of "the bank action." *A Matter of Indifference*, a fifty-minute documentary featuring Maggie and New York Gray Panthers, was filmed in 1973 and screened in New York and at a Gray Panther conference in Philadelphia. The best-known production, *Maggie Kuhn: Wrinkled Radical*, was a Studs Terkel interview with Maggie aired in February 1975 on his *Assignment America* television series. The half-hour show was vintage Maggie—political, personal, persuasive—and included a sequence with a Cedar Falls, Iowa, Lutheran minister who had organized a Gray Panther nursing home task force. The similarly titled *Gray Panthers: Wrinkled Radicals*, a 1975 film strip and accompanying text produced by the Franciscan Communications Center, consisted of fifty-four striking still photographs of Maggie and other Panthers, with scenes from the Chicago "house call" on the AMA. The *Directions* film and both "wrinkled radical" documentaries were used by local networks and shown at the 1975 Chicago convention.

A noteworthy Gray Panther effort at public consciousness-raising was its national Media Watch, which monitored portrayals of older people in television programs and advertising. Led by Lydia Bragger and a New York City–based group, it distributed forms for home-based viewers to record objectionable television fare, noting station, date, time, and sponsor. "Watch for media stereotypes on aging: ads and programs that say being younger is better or that it is somehow bad to look or act older, and programs that picture older people in narrow ways. For example if a TV show only pictures older people as cranky, or useless, or senile, we would pick one of the worst examples, describe it to the station and sponsor and suggest that they show older people in a different way in the future."[50]

By 1975 the Media Watch was receiving fifty reports a month from Gray Panthers nationwide, ammunition for Bragger and Maggie to use in criticizing the media. In addition to glorification of youth in advertising and products to cover up gray hair and wrinkles, Panther media watchers documented jokes about older people being forgetful, or showing an interest in sex, in the comedy of Cher, Dick Van Dyke, and Johnny Carson, all of whom presented campy portrayals of old people. They also pointed to older characters in television series portrayed in negative fashion—Mother Jefferson as meddlesome, Redd Foxx as crotchety. But overall, the Media Watch found that few old people even existed in televisionland. In 1975 older characters accounted for only seven roles of any significance on the entire prime time network menu. This amounted to less than 2 percent of such roles, well below the 10 percent of Americans age sixty-five or older.

The Panther critique went far beyond calling for proportional representation in television series, though that was desirable. Millions of older Americans objected to seeing age peers presented in derogatory and stereotyped fashion. As a California Media Watcher put it, "I'm wheelchair-bound and my only enjoyment is watching television. But I only get frustrated and depressed when I see the way they make us elderly look." For young viewers such portrayals reinforced the distance between old and young, contributed to ageist attitudes, and provided a biased and unappealing view of what their own aging would entail.

In 1975 Bragger made a presentation with videotapes and transcripts at a National Association of Broadcasters meeting. Her arguments led the association to amend its program code to add "age" as a category where sensitivity was needed. The Media Watch agreed to consult and read scripts in an effort to improve the situation, and this led to a meeting with CBS department heads and producers in which Ted Swofford, vice president for programming practices, told the Panthers that he had not been conscious of age discrimination on television before their meeting. "Nobody is saying that never again will an older person be portrayed as constipated or fatigued, but we promise not to be insensitive."[51] Network television's consciousness had been raised—a little.

Meeting President Ford

It was a sign of growing Panther prominence that following the resignation of Richard Nixon they were among national aging organizations invited to a White House meeting in August 1974 by his successor, Gerald Ford. The event opened with a photo opportunity where, surrounded by older people, Ford signed the Employment Retirement Income Security Act (ERISA), under which the federal government assumed responsibility to pay benefits if an ERISA-covered private pension plan went bankrupt. Maggie knew she was being used but decided to make the most of the occasion. She arrived with a press release and letter to Ford critiquing ERISA: "The law will do nothing for the thousands of retired people who have already lost their private pension opportunities [or] anything about the 50 percent of the private work force not covered by pension plans. . . . In the near future we must reduce the number of years needed to qualify for a pension; allow for the transfer of pension credit in recognition of the extreme mobility of the American work force; increase the dollar amount of the pension received; and *extend* private pension coverage to include all those employed in the private sector."[52]

Ford was unaware of the letter when he met the group of organization leaders. As he acknowledged Maggie across the table, he said, "Young lady, do you have something to say?" Indeed, Maggie did. "Mr. President, I'm not a young lady. I'm an old woman."[53] Her message on ERISA then followed.

Ford's overture to the Gray Panthers was intended to bolster his legitimacy before he pardoned Nixon and launched his "Whip Inflation Now" button campaign. The Panthers would support neither. In September Maggie telegrammed Ford, "Your act of pardon for Richard Nixon affronts justice and undermines the confidence of the people which you had begun to receive, and fails to expunge his abuse of power."[54] In October the Gray Panthers were guests at the White House Summit Conference on Inflation. Phyllis Robinson of the Washington, D.C., network represented them, and like many in the audience she was aware that older people on fixed incomes were particular victims of inflation. The meeting began with the President's Council of Economic Advisors chair, Alan Greenspan, "inform[ing] the participants that those hurt most by inflation were the Wall Street brokers. Greenspan's remarks were greeted with incredulous gasps and scattered jeers from his audience. The speech was widely discussed during the session breaks, and was taken to reveal the true mentality of the Ford Administration." Robinson arrived with a Panther press release that "pointed out that the Department of Health, Education and Welfare controlled only 16 percent of the federal budget for 1975, while the Department of Defense controlled 59 percent. In our speech we insisted that immediate and substantial cuts in military spending were required to combat inflation and to control government spending. This recommendation found almost universal agreement among the conference participants."[55]

Preparing for the Chicago Convention

In January 1975 the NSC began drafting Articles of Agreement. The meeting agenda was full, however, and after ideas were aired members were requested to submit proposed language to Maggie. Her draft was ready for the April meeting, where, during a nine-hour session, the Articles were adopted by an expanded group of twenty-two. Maggie, Frye, Hall, and Amy Boss of the original 1972 steering committee were present, as were Griesel, Diefenderfer, and Hyde of the later NSC members. The others included Linda Horn, office staff members, and network representatives Doris Campbell from the South Jersey Gray Panthers, Barbara Modica from Philadelphia, Alice Adler from Chicago, Bob Bernstein from Boston, Barbe Creagh from Cleveland, Thelma Rutherford from Washington, D.C., and Sylvia Wexler, Estelle Rib, and Mildred Sklar from New York. The Articles were published in the July *Network* and mailed to local conveners. A nominating committee for the new NSC slate was chosen, and the Chicago Panthers' invitation to host the first national convention accepted.

The five-page Articles provided a formal constitution to a movement increasingly burdened by its own success. Up to then its governing body, the NSC, had no bylaws, election procedures, or lines of accountability to the membership. Too much of the organization was in people's heads, and answers did not exist to questions the networks were asking about NSC and local responsibilities. People had wanted things to work, and with financial and office staff crises looming, the Articles arrived just in time to carry the Panthers to their October convention.

The document began with a proclamation of "Purpose and Goals":

1. To develop a new and positive awareness in our culture of the total life span of all persons as a continuing process in maturity, self-fulfillment and social responsibility.
2. To strive for new life-styles and opportunities for older and younger

people which will challenge and help eliminate, in our institutions
and elsewhere, all forms of paternalism, discrimination, segregation, and oppression based solely on age—which makes "ageism,"
like racism and sexism, a socially destructive force.

3. To act as advocates for those who are powerless to throw off discrimination and oppression because of their age.

4. To build a new power base in coalition with other movements to
bring about social change in order to achieve justice, human dignity, and self-fulfillment for all people regardless of age, sex, race
or economic status.

5. To reinforce and support each other in our quest for liberation and
to celebrate our shared humanity.

Acceptance of the Articles was now the basis for joining the Gray Panthers. Individuals could affiliate directly, and so could groups of five or
more. Each local group would be autonomous in formulating its activities but had to send an annual report to the national office. Gray Panther policy would be set at a national convention every two years where
affiliated individuals could vote, as could networks represented by one
delegate for each twenty-five members to a maximum of four. Affiliates
would elect by mail ballot a new National Steering Committee of from
fifteen to thirty members who would serve two-year terms and could be
reelected twice; candidates would be selected to reflect the geographi-
cal distribution of members by an elected nominations committee or
nominated by petition from fifteen affiliates. The duties of the NSC included accreditation of networks and individual members, supervision
of the national office staff, fund-raising, and development of a national
program in conjunction with the local groups. It was also empowered to
create "task forces to work on priorities for action as established at the
national convention," with each task force chairperson to be an NSC
member. Maggie was named a lifetime NSC member.[56]

The NSC met again in June to review the convention agenda, and
Maggie, Griesel, and Horn then took over preparations. The old NSC
met for the last time in September to approve a packet of amendments
sent to the networks with the nominating committee's slate of eighteen
names, plus six added by petition from Los Angeles, Long Beach, and
Philadelphia. Remaining plans went smoothly, and so did the convention. Maggie's "dreaming and scheming" and five and a half years of
hard work had paid off. In Chicago a national movement discovered
itself.

Chapter 4
The Gray Panthers in Berkeley, California (1973–85)

The following two chapters shift focus to the local networks. This chapter looks at the origin and activities to 1985 of the Gray Panthers of Berkeley, California, where I first encountered the movement and became an active member during 1977–78. Like others, this network was the creation of a remarkable first convener, Lillian Rabinowitz. Lillian was an inspired speaker and organizer, a dedicated advocate for a "continuum of care" for the elderly, and an engaging, dynamic personality. With grace and good spirit she made the transition from founder to member, using the network's health committee as a vehicle to continue her activism. When Berkeley mayor Gus Newport declared March 18, 1981, "Lillian Rabinowitz Day" it was in recognition for her work of the previous eight years, but she wasted no time in pushing ahead to her next project.

Getting Started

The spring of 1973 was a busy time for Maggie Kuhn. The national office's move upstairs at the Tabernacle Church was followed by the first meeting of the Philadelphia Action Alliance, a Gray Panther conference in Dayton, and kickoff meetings for new networks in Kansas City and Washington, D.C. A New York Gray Panther health conference was just weeks away when Maggie arrived in Berkeley to speak at the Pacific School of Religion, and as usual she was on the lookout for potential network conveners. Lillian Rabinowitz, sixty-two, was in the audience and found Maggie "an extraordinarily charismatic person. Also a lot of what she said about ways of viewing old age was in line with my own thinking."[1] Lillian sat next to her at lunch, and during their conversation Maggie suggested Lillian visit her in Philadelphia when next traveling east to see family members.

Born in New Haven, Lillian graduated from the University of California in Berkeley in 1944 and returned to live there in 1955, raising three children. Following a divorce at age fifty she went back to school for a teaching degree and then taught for five years in New York and Oakland, California, public schools. In 1971 she went to work as a social worker for the Jewish Family Society of Alameda–Contra Costa Counties. "I began to see elderly persons as having a rough time in their 'golden years.' There were generic problems that had to do with the way society in general and the government viewed old people."[2] She was appointed to the Berkeley Commission on Aging by city councilmember Loni Hancock. As Lillian reflected on her new experiences, including eye-opening visits to Berkeley nursing homes, it dawned on her that the elderly were not someone else. "Good God! It was me!"[3]

A few weeks after their meeting Lillian wrote to Maggie that she would be in New York during the summer and suggested "perhaps it might be possible for me to flip down to Philadelphia for . . . the joy of a brief lunch-meeting with you."[4] The two women met at Maggie's house in August 1973. "At the end of the day she asked me if I would think about organizing a Gray Panther unit in Berkeley. I didn't have to think about it; I'd already decided."[5] As Maggie recalled the day, "Sitting back on the front porch we realized we were two kindred spirits."[6]

That summer Maggie heard from another member of her Berkeley audience, Tish Sommers, fifty-nine, of Oakland. "I heard you and talked to you in Berkeley. It was a real turnon for me. I was just beginning to become involved with older women's specific problems, and your presentation shoved me along the way." Sommers became coordinator of the National Organization for Women's Task Force on Older Women in 1971 and was developing materials for local NOW chapters. With grants from a Methodist women's association and the Women's International League for Peace and Freedom she also had formed the Women's Action Training Center in Oakland focused on "special problems of women between menopause and Social Security."[7] Maggie sent an appreciative response urging Sommers to help start a Bay Area Panther group. Lillian and Sommers met "to explore ways to bring a Gray Panther group into existence,"[8] and in September they were joined by Anne Bennett, one of Maggie's original "group of six" who had moved to Berkeley in 1971, and by Isabel Van Frank, seventy-six, a prominent advocate for the elderly. Van Frank had founded the East Bay Legislative Council for Senior Organizations in the late 1950s, fought for reduced transit fares for older people, and was named California Senior Citizen of the Year in 1972.

That fall the four women met Leslie Kwass, twenty-three, a law student intern at the Senior Citizens Law Program in San Francisco, who briefed them on California's new nursing home licensure law. Lillian wrote to Maggie, "Our Gray Panthers have decided that we wish in some way to make ourselves into a local watchdog to obtain the best possible enforcement of this law."[9] Meanwhile, Lillian was elected president of the Berkeley Commission on Aging and spoke before the city council in support of a door-to-door, minivan transportation program for the homebound elderly. By the beginning of 1974 the Gray Panther group had expanded to a dozen, including Eugenia Hickman, a retired social worker who had moved from New York to Berkeley and become supportive services coordinator for a program providing federally funded lunches to Alameda County senior centers. Lillian and Hickman, one white and one black, together lobbied the City of Berkeley to institute flexible work hours for city employees, a policy particularly helpful to women. "There were titters about our name, Gray Panthers, because they had never heard that before."[10]

The first meeting of the Berkeley network was in January 1974 at the University Avenue senior center. The group quickly added members, among them Ann Squires, twenty-eight, a student at the Pacific School of Religion. One of Squires's teachers, Anne Bennett's husband, John, suggested that she attend, and Squires brought other young persons. Members of the Gray Panthers of the East Bay were soon speaking in classes at the University of California medical school in San Francisco and planning a course for older students at a community college in Oakland. They also began a study of Berkeley's eight nursing homes, using evaluation forms from the University of California School of Nursing and funded by the federal agency ACTION. Lillian, Squires, and others collected the information, and Sommers's Women's Action Training Center conducted a parallel study in Oakland. The effort led to the closing of two Berkeley nursing homes.

Leadership of the network fell into Lillian's hands. The Bennetts moved to southern California. Van Frank remained a member but continued her involvement in other organizations. Sommers's energy went to a NOW "feminist guide" to Social Security and to the "We Should Live So Long Collective," a group of Oakland women between ages twenty and seventy-five who began a "Jobs for Older Women" project and were featured on a KQED public television program. After organizing a well-publicized demonstration in San Francisco for women's employment opportunities in 1974, Sommers lobbied for state and federal "displaced homemaker" (a term she coined) job training and placement legislation during 1975–77.[11]

Now convener of the Berkeley Panthers, Lillian wrote to the Philadelphia national office requesting the 1973 *Organizing Manual*, which she found "just common sense," and Gray Panther pins and stationery. During Maggie's visits to Berkeley in 1974 and 1975 she arranged for speaking venues, publicity, and press coverage. She attended the 1975

Chicago convention with Kwass, then a staff attorney at the Senior Citizen Law Program, where she remained until 1978. After two years Lillian felt fresh leadership was desirable, and Eugenia Hickman, sixty-eight, and Jenifer Rogers, in her forties and youth coordinator at the University of California YWCA in Berkeley, were elected co-conveners. Lillian remained on the network's steering committee and chaired its health committee.

In 1976 the Berkeley Panthers submitted a grant proposal to the San Francisco Foundation to open an office and hire staff and submitted a federal Comprehensive Employment and Training Act (CETA) application for a second staff position. Both were funded, and the network asked Lillian to become its "community organizer/administrator." She resigned from the Jewish Family Society and in July 1976 became a full-time Gray Panther. An office was rented at 2131 University Avenue in downtown Berkeley, Birute Skurdenis, nineteen, was hired as secretary, and the first monthly newsletter, prepared by Lillian and Squires, was published in August.

The Birth of the Clinic

While conducting their survey in 1974 the Panthers began to think about preventing nursing home placements before they occurred. Lillian, Van Frank, Hickman, Helene London, another retired social worker, and Teri Dowling, a young University of California public health student, met with Dr. Stuart Goldstein, director of the city's health department, to inquired about the lack of preventive care for the elderly, noting that such services existed for infants, pregnant women, and children. Goldstein explained that these programs were funded on a categorical basis but no such funding for the elderly existed. Soon afterward the Panthers learned the Alameda County Area Agency on Aging (AAA), which administered federal Older Americans Act funds, had issued a request for proposals for innovative health projects.[12] Young Gray Panther Squires consulted with others and submitted a proposal for a free preventive health program for older people in January 1975.

In April the Alameda County AAA announced the Gray Panthers would receive the grant. Lillian was astonished, and then scared: "Now we had to go ahead and do it." The network health committee first considered attaching their program to one of the four community clinics in Berkeley. They visited the Berkeley Free Clinic, which served a young clientele and ran drug abuse programs, and the Berkeley Women's Health Collective, focused on younger women's health concerns but not serving men. Next they went to the West Berkeley Health Center, serving mainly African Americans and Latinos but not the wider racial and ethnic mix the Gray Panthers hoped to reach. The George Jackson Clinic, run by the Black Panthers, was struggling to offer both local health care and services to prisoners in San Quentin federal penitentiary. The health committee concluded that none of these Berkeley clinics fit what the Gray Panthers envisioned.

They returned to Dr. Goldstein, asking for city sponsorship. He objected to their plan to augment paid staff with volunteers, who he said would not provide continuity, and to the lack of a doctor, since the Gray Panthers wanted the clinic to be run by a nurse. Over the course of six weekly meetings, solutions emerged. Volunteer training and minimal time requirements were established. If the clinic director was a nurse practitioner, the city health department could serve as medical backup. The clinic would have to use the city personnel department but the Panthers could publicize openings and participate in hiring decisions. Alameda County would issue checks to the Gray Panthers, who would endorse them to the City of Berkeley. At the county's insistence the clinic had to serve older persons in the adjacent communities of Albany, Emeryville, and north Oakland, and the Berkeley health department consented. The city also offered to assign Sylvia Brown, an experienced outreach worker, to the new facility. Kwass, the young Gray Panther lawyer, filed incorporation papers so that the Berkeley Gray Panthers were able to receive funds and launch the program.

Just as the contract was about to be signed the Alameda County Board of Supervisors stipulated the clinic must use a "means test" to limit services to persons below the poverty line. Although Older Americans Act funding did not require a means test, the county intended also to use federal Revenue Sharing funds, which did. "The means test was very destructive of the goals of the program," as Lillian saw it. "Persons at or below the poverty line were eligible for Medicaid services whereas those who were in the category of low income but above the poverty level were the persons most in need of such services—persons who had little income for private health assessment, and who would be economically and psychologically devastated by any major illness, which might be, perhaps, prevented by services such as we hoped to bring to them."[13] Lillian didn't want to lose the grant, so she signed the contract with the means test included, angering other Gray Panthers. Kwass and the county contract administrator then struck a compromise: if the clinic was located in a census tract with a large percentage of older people below the poverty line, it could be assumed that eligible people were being served and direct questions about income and assets could be avoided. The plan required approval by the board of supervisors; the Panthers organized the Coalition against the Means Test with other groups protesting the same restrictions and demonstrated at the board's November meeting. Kwass also threatened a lawsuit. The compromise was approved.

In January 1976 the Over 60 Clinic opened in a rented storefront at 2901 San Pablo Avenue in South Berkeley, a predominantly African American neighborhood. Berkeley Mayor Warren Widener, County Supervisor Tom Bates, the clinic's nurse practitioner Betty McKenzie, and nearly one hundred others attended as Isabel Van Frank cut the ribbon. Articles followed in Berkeley and Oakland newspapers, and Maggie sent congratulations.

Building a Constituency

The leaders of South Berkeley did not welcome the Over 60 Clinic when it opened. Sylvia Brown, the clinic's African American community outreach worker, was told more than once that this was a community of homeowners who did not look upon themselves as objects for anyone's charity. They had not been involved in planning its services or selecting its site, as they had with a Community High Blood Pressure Control Program located in their neighborhood. They saw the Gray Panthers as white people from "the hills" imposing something on black residents of "the flats." Berkeley's population of 116,000 was in large degree racially segregated by altitude. Most African Americans, some 23 percent of the city, lived in the flatlands adjoining San Francisco Bay, and the South Berkeley census tract containing Over 60 was 86 percent black. By contrast, the Berkeley hills were 85 percent or more white.[14] The clinic's first director, Betty MacKenzie, also was white. One Gray Panther clinic founder, Eugenia Hickman, was black but was a transplanted New Yorker.

During the first two months the older persons arriving for health screening included thirty-eight whites and seven blacks. Over the next months things changed, and by the end of 1976 the 618 older persons screened were 42 percent white, 40 percent black, 15 percent Asian—most from the East Bay Japanese for Action senior center visited regularly—and 3 percent Mexican American. By March 1977 a third of clinic clients were from South Berkeley. Local African American elders satisfied with Over 60 services had told others. Clinic staff, moreover, had developed friendly relationships with Leatha Phillips, proprietor of the Bus Stop Café next door, who lived a block away and was active in South Berkeley organizations. Outreach efforts by Sylvia Brown and Gray Panther Charlotte Knight, a white retired school teacher, at senior centers, churches, homes, and stores also softened community resistance. And Lani Sanjek, the director of Over 60 beginning in December 1976 after two months as volunteer nurse practitioner, was Japanese American, not white. By 1977 the score of clinic volunteers had also shifted from mainly white to include several African American South Berkeley residents who were users of Over 60 services.

A clinic visit included a health history interview, questions about diet and medications, a blood pressure reading, vision and hearing tests, a urine test for diabetes or kidney disease, mouth and foot examinations, joint and limb mobility assessments, and referral to doctors or other health care providers if warranted. Some clients used Over 60 only for these screening services specified in the AAA request for proposals and not covered by Medicare. Other clients began to use the Over 60 nurses, including Janet Peoples and Nancy Mackowsky, hired in 1977, as primary case managers, updating them about visits with doctors and other specialists. The nurses also became medical interpreters for clients when providers did not take sufficient time to explain things. As a man with diabetes put it after an explanation about the use and effects of insulin, "The doctors don't tell me anything. They never take the time to do this or explain anything." [15] Some clients dropped in without appointments for advice, follow-up care, referrals, or assistance with calls to doctors. Similar interaction occurred in "outclinics" at the five senior centers and elderly housing sites that Over 60 staff visited on a regular schedule.[16]

In 1977 services expanded to included ear cleaning, diet counseling, and teaching about prescription drugs, which 70 percent of clients used. Visits to homebound persons and arthritis exercise classes three mornings a week at Berkeley and Oakland senior centers were also instituted. Foot care and toenail cutting, difficult or impossible tasks for many with arthritis, obesity, vision or mobility impairment, and contraindicated for diabetics, was a growing concern, and the nurses arranged in-service training and backup with an Oakland podiatrist treating an elderly clientele. The clinic's referral file encompassed doctors, optometry clinics, podiatrists, and dentists. Transportation for visits to Over 60 or other health care providers could be arranged, and in a few cases staff members accompanied clients on referral visits.

Two-thirds of Over 60 clients during 1977 were women and one-third men. Their mean age was seventy-two, and one in six was in his or her eighties or nineties. They included former factory, port and railroad workers; retired clerks, household workers, and professionals; housewives, many of them widows; self-employed business proprietors, some still working; and a few single-room occupancy hotel dwellers and skid row alcoholics. Many were homeowners, others apartment renters, and still others lived in attractive or shabby senior citizen housing. They included native Californians as well as persons recently arrived from "back East" to live near adult children. Several of the whites were born in Europe. Many of the blacks knew scores of people from their Louisiana or Texas hometowns living in the Bay Area. Most Japanese were Japan-born

Issei. A few Mexicans, Chinese, Filipinos, and an Indian woman from Goa were also among Over 60's clients.

Susan Montero, eighty-four and born in Mexico, was a frequent dropper-in at the clinic.[17] Her Spanish-tinged English, sprinkled with "*Pero*, honey," was as delightful as her stories of the men and women she had known through her long life. Mrs. Montero lived a block and a half away, and some of the clinic staff invited to her home enjoyed performances by her trained birds and dog. On one occasion she fell in her kitchen and lay there for hours until Over 60 outreach worker Sylvia Brown discovered her.

Billie Johnson, eighty-two and African American, had worked many years in Chicago before moving to Berkeley. She dropped by to sell a church lottery ticket, show off a picture of herself, or talk about recent and past events in her life—she could recall precisely the day in her twenties when she stopped "worrying" about what other people say. Billie ate largely vegetarian fare—she used a blender to make carrot juice, and spinach salad with Kraft's dressing was one of her favorites. She regularly visited a 101-year-old nursing home patient to take her for a walk outside, "gave" one day a week at a senior center, and felt that older people, like herself, should be used in television ads "because the companies expect old people to buy their products." In 1985 when I visited Over 60 I learned that she was still a regular dropper-in at age eighty-nine.

The frequent visits of Mattie Taylor, eighty-two and African American, concerned her health status. She had recently moved to Berkeley, where she lived with a great-grandson. She was diagnosed with diabetes at the clinic, and with a nurse's help she began daily self-injections of insulin, a difficult process to begin at any age. Her experience illustrated how teaching clients to manage chronic conditions was increasingly supplementing screening tests and referrals. The clinic later helped Mrs. Taylor arrange cataract surgery and monitored her adjustment at home afterward.

Giuseppe D'Angelo, eighty-five and born in Italy, stopped by regularly for a blood pressure reading. He was an inveterate horse race bettor, and his stories of the track, including winning $5,000 in 1974, became part of Over 60 staff lore. Mr. D'Angelo insisted on "kissing all the girls" at the clinic, as he claimed he did before retirement when he worked at a movie theater. On one visit he complained he was having trouble receiving his Social Security check because of an incorrect zip code. As he left, he said, "I'm going to Social Security now, but I won't kiss *them*."

On arrival in the clinic's waiting room a warm camaraderie greeted clients as they snacked on granola, sipped herbal tea, and chatted with staff, volunteers, and other older people, including Gray Panther health committee members. Client interaction was cordial and sometimes conversations developed. One afternoon when I was the screening volunteer on duty, a white couple in their mid-eighties arrived for the wife's appointment. The husband, a retired military man, waited. He asked me about the clinic and I answered his queries. "No, we do not collect money on street corners. That's the Berkeley Free Clinic." Somehow the topic of America ceding Canal Zone sovereignty to Panama arose. Another client, sixty-two, black, and politically outspoken, joined the discussion. I feared they would take opposing positions but it turned out they were in complete agreement: the United States should get out of Panama and turn over money saved to social programs like the Over 60 Clinic.

A Gray Panther Health Clinic

Clinic volunteers, both old and young, were a key part of the Gray Panther vision. Following several Saturday training sessions they committed to work at least three hours a week for six months, doing intake interviews, screening tests, and outreach tasks. During 1976 white University of California students and Gray Panthers comprised most of the volunteer cohort, but the next year recruitment broadened to include white and black students from a wider range of institutions. Most planned to enter the health professions and appreciated the hands-on experience of recording health histories and taking blood pressures, and with the nurses' encouragement several registered for advanced first aid and cardiopulmonary resuscitation training. Three student volunteers also worked on a computer analysis of client records with me, a volunteer applied anthropologist.[18] They later surveyed local physicians to expand Over 60's list of providers who accepted Medicare and Medicaid patients or could accommodate non-English speakers. Volunteer Melissa Lagusis, a pre-medical student, wrote of her Over 60 experience: "The fierce competition for placement in professional schools has made pre-professional volunteer work essential. [Many], while not particularly concerned with the problems of the elderly when they began work here, soon discovered the importance of the geriatric field."[19]

The first older volunteers were Gray Panthers Charlotte Knight, Helene London, and Lorna Brangwin, and in 1977 they were joined by several Over 60 clients, most of them black South Berkeley residents. Laeeqa Muhammad, a retired nurse and a hearing aid user, became a screening volunteer and sensitized staff to communication skills in working with the hearing-impaired. Raymond Greene, a retired clerical worker, refiled client charts and became an integral part of office operations as well as a goodwill ambassador in his church and neighborhood. Ben Hinds, a retired commercial artist, did graphics for clinic flyers and brochures. Louise Palfini, a white South Berkeleyite, answered the telephone during Monday staff meetings. In addition, Gayle Schatz, a younger white real estate broker who spent hours in her car each day, gave rides to clients when her schedule permitted.

Several Berkeley clinics that the founding Gray Panthers visited in 1975 were members of the Alameda Health Consortium, an alliance of community clinics formed in 1973 after Joel Garcia, an attorney and director of La Clinica de al Raza in Oakland, read the new federal Revenue Sharing law and discovered that funds could be allocated to community-based organizations. Following a campaign by the newly formed consortium, then representing four clinics, the Alameda County Board of Supervisors agreed to provide Revenue Sharing support. With health expenditures mounting during the early 1970s, the supervisors understood that a primary care visit in a county-run health facility averaged $111, as compared with $38 at a community clinic. Moreover, a county-funded study stated, "Each of the [consortium] clinics has its origins in the efforts of various indigenous community groups to address unmet health needs of particular populations. What makes the medical service delivery offered at the primary care clinics unique is the cultural sensitivity of the staff, the small-scale decentralized setting, the availability of bilingual staff, the general absence of long waits, the comprehensiveness of services, and the flexible schedules under which the clinics operate. [The clinics] are key to shifting county health resources away from expensive, high technology acute hospital care and developing a preventive health care program oriented around health maintenance."[20]

When Over 60 opened, the Alameda Health Consortium invited Lillian Rabinowitz to attend its meetings, which she found "mind-blowing."[21] By then the consortium included clinics serving Latinos, African Americans, Asians, Native Americans, women, youth, and rural workers. With no doctor on staff, Over 60 was technically not a primary care facility; Lillian's request for membership was granted, however, and when Lani Sanjek became director she replaced Lillian as consortium representative. Membership benefits included information about Alameda County health care politics, clout as part of an alliance of thirteen clinics by 1978, and financial resources Over 60 could not secure on its own. In 1978 the board of supervisors accepted a recommendation from its health department to fund the clinics for six months with $250,000 beyond existing Revenue Sharing support. The consortium agreed to divide this money in equal shares, thus helping the smaller clinics in particular.

Maggie's dictum that in programs for the elderly "old people should be determining the policy that prevails and monitoring the performance of the staff"[22] was exemplified by the Gray Panthers who founded the Over 60 Clinic. But once it was in operation this was no longer the case; only two older members of the network's health committee were users of clinic services. In 1977 the committee resolved "to form a community advisory board which will eventually take over the functions of the Gray Panther Clinic committee. The board will consist of 2/3 or more members who are users of the clinic; other members may include key community representatives, including Gray Panthers, who might not be clinic users."[23]

That fall the staff planned a December holiday party as a first step to involve potential board members in Over 60 activities. Brown and Knight oversaw arrangements, and Ben Hinds designed an invitation mailed to nearly a thousand clients. Mrs. Phillips closed the Bus Stop Café on the day of the party and made its kitchen available for serving donated food and drinks. The party was scheduled for 2 to 4 p.m.; the first client guests arrived at noon and the last left after five. More than two hundred came, some in elegant long dresses, and forty clients and supporters contributed food, decorations, utensils, or cash. Al Morgan, president of South Berkeley's San Pablo Neighborhood Organization and an early opponent of the clinic, attended, as did founding Gray Panthers Lillian, London, Hickman, Squires, and Van Frank. With Alameda County in the midst of a bus strike, two auxiliary police spent the afternoon driving clients back and forth to the clinic; when one stopped for coffee and cake, he commented, "You people really know how to throw a party."

In January 1978 Helene London, a Gray Panther and Over 60 client, was elected chair of the clinic committee. Next month Raymond Greene and Laeeqa Muhammad, clinic clients and volunteers, attended, and in March Leatha Phillips and three additional clients came to hear Joel Garcia speak about La Clinica de la Raza's community board. The committee also discussed the feasibility of Over 60 becoming a free-standing clinic independent of the Gray Panthers and the City of Berkeley. But clouding these deliberations was a letter from Alameda County warning that the clinic might have to close if California's statewide Proposition 13 was approved that June. Four clients attended the May meeting, and plans to write bylaws for an independent Over 60 Clinic were approved. Twelve days later Proposition 13 passed.

The Clinic and Proposition 13

Proposition 13 was a voter referendum to roll back property assessments to 1975–76 levels, freeze tax rates at 1 percent of those assessed values, and allow reassessment to market value only after a property was sold. Promoted by antitax crusaders Howard Jarvis and Paul Gann, it offered residential and commercial property owners immediate tax reductions averaging 57 percent. The measure also was intended to force California governor Jerry Brown to expend the state's five billion dollar budget surplus to compensate county and city governments for Proposition 13–induced revenue losses. Opponents stressed that two-thirds of all savings would go to corporations and big landlords, that the tax burden would shift sharply from business to individual homeowners, and that renters, some 45 percent of California voters, would receive no benefit at all. They also warned that Proposition 13 would lead to cuts in social programs.[24]

The Gray Panthers campaigned against Proposition 13 but Californians voted for it two to one. Anticipating passage, Alameda County notified community-based Revenue Sharing recipients that their contracts might be canceled. For Over 60 this would mean losing one of its three nurses. In addition, the City of Berkeley would likely end support for a second CETA-funded nurse and for the clinic's community health worker.

The day after the vote Lillian briefed the Berkeley Gray Panther executive committee on Over 60's situation. The clinic would speed up plans to become independent, thereby preventing Berkeley health department workers with greater seniority from "bumping" Over 60 staff to claim their jobs. The committee voted to pay $750 for three months' clinic insurance coverage, and Leslie Kwass agreed to meet with the City of Berkeley attorney to sever the Panthers' legal and fiscal ties.

That same afternoon the Alameda Health Consortium clinic directors met and learned that the county planned to cut Revenue Sharing contracts by 60 percent. The consortium decided to press for full funding at the board of supervisors meeting the following day, countering that it was premature to make cuts when legislation to release the state surplus was likely. At La Clinica director Garcia's urging, the consortium notified the county that ending clinic funding would violate the State Health Facilities law requiring ninety-days' notice and a public hearing. Ironically, the consortium's ties to Alameda County had become closer in the year preceding Proposition 13. In 1977 the supervisors commissioned a year-long study of county hospitals that included a survey of the Consortium clinics. As part of a consortium workgroup, I compiled data from Over 60 client records and interviewed staff and clients. The workgroup's most significant finding was that consortium clinics accounted for 53 percent of all publicly funded primary care in Alameda County, and in the poorest area, the Berkeley-Oakland flatlands, they provided 61 percent.[25] Two months before the Proposition 13 vote, Alameda County invited the consortium clinics to submit a plan for $500,000 in additional support, but when the measure passed the offer was withdrawn.

On the evening of the day after the Proposition 13 vote, 150 representatives of community groups met at a church in Oakland's Chinatown to form the Alameda County Labor/Community Coalition and agreed to oppose all budget cuts. Led by Sherry Hirota, director of Asian Health

Services, a consortium member clinic, the next morning the coalition filled the board of supervisors' chambers to demand that existing resources be used to fully fund health and social service programs for three months, and that the supervisors lobby state legislators to release the surplus funds. Labor/Community Coalition members returned to press the supervisors many times during the summer of 1978, and they also organized demonstrations at the state capital in Sacramento calling for preservation of California's health and social service programs.

At the Over 60 Clinic three heady months followed passage of Proposition 13. A moratorium on new clients was instituted immediately. Next a letter was mailed to the 1,200 clients explaining the situation and possible closure; they were asked to come to the clinic to sign a petition of support and make a cash donation if able. By August 500 clients had signed the petition and nearly $1,400 in contributions was in a clinic bank account. The volunteer applied anthropologist became a volunteer paralegal and proposal writer. First I drafted articles of incorporation and bylaws for a free-standing Over 60 Clinic and deposited them in Sacramento. Then I applied for state and federal tax-exempt status and an employee identification number. After reviewing state medical facility regulations I prepared an application for a "free clinic" license to be filed that fall after expected passage of a new clinic licensure bill. When the legislature released state surplus funds to local governments in June, I submitted an Alameda County Revenue Sharing proposal for a three-month contract at 90 percent of the pre-Proposition 13 level (this was later extended to nine months). I prepared a request for additional Older Americans Act support, which I presented to the Area Agency on Aging, and I wrote and delivered funding proposals to two Bay Area private foundations, Vanguard and San Francisco. Finally, I drafted appeals to the City of Berkeley to renew CETA funding for a nurse and to keep community health worker Sylvia Brown at the Over 60 Clinic. As part of the lobbying effort for these two positions I assembled packets with letters of support and the 500-signature client petition and delivered them to each city council member. Miraculously, all these post–Proposition 13 proposals and requests met positive response.

A month after Proposition 13 the now independent Over 60 Health Clinic, Inc. had a staff M.D. internist on site two hours a week and available on call. A second mailing informed clients the picture looked brighter and invited them to an August meeting and party at a South Berkeley park three blocks from the clinic. There Al Morgan of the San Pablo Neighborhood Association welcome two hundred who enjoyed donated food and musical performances by two clients who were retired professional entertainers. Over 60 Clinic president Helene London introduced the fourteen members of the new board of directors, including six Gray Panthers. Their ages ranged from sixty-three to eighty-four. Nine were women and five men. Half were black and half white. Ten were clinic clients.[26]

During August Over 60's staff planned for a fall cohort of new student volunteers. Renovations to provide greater client privacy and more efficient use of clinic space were completed by September. I returned to New York that month and in November Lani Sanjek left Berkeley. At the end of 1978 the clinic had funds to add staff beyond the pre–Proposition 13 level. By 1981 its combined public and foundation funding of $290,000 was more than three times the 1978 budget. Two years later under director Marty Lynch the clinic moved to a larger site at 1860 Alcatraz Avenue and added dental services. When I returned to Berkeley in 1985 the staff numbered twenty and Over 60 nurse practitioners, physician assistants, and doctors were seeing more than 3,000 clients a year, including 250 in their homes.

Gray Panthers and Black Panthers

During their first two years the Berkeley Gray Panthers moved their meeting place to an African American church, then a senior citizen housing site with substantial black population, and finally to the West Berkeley library in a racially mixed neighborhood. These efforts did not attract black members as hoped, and the Berkeley Gray Panthers remained predominately white. Relations with African Americans and other people of color, however, emerged in coalitions.

One of the network's guest speakers in 1974 was from Project SAFE (Seniors against a Fearful Environment), an escort program run by the Black Panther Party of Oakland.[27] Troubled by the impact of teenage victimization of the elderly on both generations, Gray Panther Isabel Van Frank suggested the idea of protecting senior citizens from mugging on Social Security check day to Black Panther Bobby Seale during his unsuccessful 1973 Oakland mayoral campaign. The escort service was added to the other "survival programs" the Black Panthers operated in Oakland and Berkeley, which together contained the largest black population in California. Between 1974 and 1977, while Black Panther founder Huey P. Newton was a fugitive in Cuba, effort was devoted to the party's free breakfasts for children begun in 1968, the Oakland Community Learning Center school and the George Jackson Community Health Center, both founded in South Berkeley in 1971, and Project SAFE. Elaine Brown, a Los Angeles Black Panther who relocated to Oakland in 1971, was the group's most prominent spokesperson. In addition, the party was active in Brown's unsuccessful 1975 Oakland city council race and the 1977 campaign that elected the city's first black mayor, Lionel Wilson.

When in New York as a Jerry Brown delegate at the 1976 Democratic convention, Elaine Brown visited her hometown Philadelphia and met with Maggie Kuhn. Maggie promptly wrote Lillian about this Black Panther–Gray Panther encounter.

She is trying very hard to project a new and positive image. She is very much interested in a special school which she has been working in. She feels that it will encourage children in black communities to learn and develop their full human potential. At the present time I really don't know how we can cooperate in any kind of specific way. It needs to be considered by the National Steering Committee, and certainly your understanding of the situation in Berkeley and Oakland would be important to our decision. Many white liberals are concerned because we do not have any substantial numbers of black people in our movement. If there were a way of working in a constructive way with coalitions of black groups it would undoubtedly help us.[28]

Lillian responded that she had visited and donated materials to the Black Panther school. She added that she had another tie to the Black Panthers through the Over 60 Clinic. A George Jackson clinic staff member, "Joan Kelly, one of their important members,[29] and I are both delegates to a community health consortium. However, I feel that this is a very ticklish question, the way in which we relate to the Black community. I am not at all sure that we should do it by the mechanism of linkage with the Black Panthers, but not because of the intrinsic nature of what they do. As I am sure you are aware, large segments of the black community, both working class and middle class, reject the Black Panther movement as a meaningful solution."[30] This perception was reinforced at the Over 60 Clinic by outreach worker Sylvia Brown's observation that black people were wary of the Black Panthers after seeing "a lot of young black men getting killed" as a result of joining.

In September 1976 Lillian wrote Maggie to tell her she and Over 60 director Betty MacKenzie had met with the administrator of the George Jackson Clinic. "There is a strong possibility that we will move from our present location and rent property they own, right next door to them in Berkeley, and develop a synergistic relationship with them such that we will do our screening to include their elderly clientele and they will provide some kind of medical service through, probably, a once a week geriatric clinic."[31] Maggie responded, "If you can work it out in Berkeley, it would be a great strength to our entire movement."[32] The Berkeley Gray Panthers voted for the move, and during the first three months of 1977 Lani Sanjek negotiated arrangements with the George Jackson staff. Then in April the Black Panthers decided to use the empty space themselves, and discussion turned to joint George Jackson–Over 60 activities at the site. During the rest of 1977, however, the Black Panthers were occupied with efforts to bring Newton home from Cuba. The Gray Panther clinic committee decided to postpone further plans until Over 60's new client-majority board of directors was in place.

In 1978 discussion between Over 60 and George Jackson staff continued, but following Newton's return and Brown's subsequent departure from Oakland, the Black Panthers' community-based activities diminished. The George Jackson Clinic did not submit a proposal when county funds were offered to the Alameda Health Consortium clinics, and in 1980 it closed.

Age and Youth in Action

When Lillian became the Berkeley network's "community organizer/ administrator" in 1976 she could point to several accomplishments beyond the new Over 60 Clinic. In 1974 members monitored local compliance with a law requiring pharmacies to post prices for prescription drugs. In 1975 Lillian began a Gray Panther radio program on Pacifica station KPFA-FM in Berkeley with member Bea Frankel, who later continued it on her own. The first network newsletter in 1976 listed seven committees chaired by both older members—Lillian (health), Anne Kenin (adult day care), Gregory Bergman (consciousness-raising), Fancheon Christner (membership)—and younger ones—Leslie Kwass (nursing homes), Anne Squires (funding), Jenifer Rogers (housing). In 1977 dues-paying membership reached 95, and by 1982 380. Most were financial supporters. Active members—the Berkeley Gray Panthers who attended network meetings, joined committees, participated in marches and lobbying, and volunteered in the office and fund-raising—numbered perhaps fifty during the late 1970s and early 1980s.

Network meetings routinely included announcements of demonstrations, conferences, and public hearings, information from allied organizations, and committee and office staff reports. Featured speakers were announced in the newsletter and addressed varied topics: national health insurance and "Exploring Your Sexual Potential in Advancing Age" in 1976; rent control and discussion of the film *Maggie Kuhn: Wrinkled Radical* in 1977; the right to die, multiple prescription drug use, and utility rates in 1980; U.S. policy in Central America and European missile deployment in 1983. Guests included the director of Berkeley's Social Security office (who later joined the Gray Panthers), candidates for mayor and city council, and California Gray Panthers chairperson Frieda Wolff.

During these years Lillian's and Maggie's friendship grew closer. They saw each other several times a year: on Lillian's East Coast visits to see her two daughters and sister and brother-in-law; at meetings of the National

Steering Committee, on which Lillian served from 1978 to 1987; and on Maggie's visits to Berkeley, often twice a year during the 1970s, when, on occasion, she stayed with Lillian. Maggie's public appearances generated new network members and reinvigorated stalwarts, several of whom she knew from repeated visits.

Notwithstanding their friendship, Lillian was firm in presenting her network members' views to Maggie. In 1976 she wrote about their distaste for the new public television program *Over Easy* and urged Maggie to withdraw her endorsement. "One sees Phyllis Diller begin her segment of the show talking about how she had her face lifted not too long ago, thus reinforcing the idea that old is bad."[33] Maggie responded she did not intend her service on the program's advisory board "to be interpreted as sponsorship."[34] The producer of *Over Easy* was disturbed by the network's critique of the program, and Berkeley Panthers were invited to later *Over Easy* tapings in San Francisco, including a 1977 appearance by Maggie.

Unlike most networks, which were based in their convener's home, the Berkeley Gray Panthers had an office from 1976 onward. However, tension developed between Lillian and one work-study student, supported by co-conveners Jenifer Rogers and Gil Clark, who advocated a "collective" approach versus Lillian's businesslike manner. Lillian felt rejected and shared her disappointment with Maggie, who wrote to Rogers and Clark: "Your experiences are especially akin to what we have experienced in our national office. There were some people along the way who did not want any kind of structure or any agenda for action, but they found some other place to do 'their thing' and have left the movement. We have tried to work on a 'collective' basis; it proved not to be an effective way to get our work done."[35]

In 1977 job descriptions were written for staff positions, and the storm quieted. To broaden decision making the network reconstituted its steering committee to included the co-conveners, secretary, treasurer, and three members-at-large. Another dispute led to resignations before the situation stabilized under the next co-conveners, Leslie Kwass and Dan Trupin, a retired New Yorker who moved to Berkeley in 1972 to join adult children. (I was a steering committee member-at-large for nine months during this period.) In 1977 Lillian became "health consultant" to the network under a San Francisco Foundation grant and for several months enjoyed the volunteer office assistance of Helen Parsons, whose husband, sociologist Talcott Parsons, was a visiting professor at U.C. Berkeley. In 1979 network officers and committee chairpersons held a weekend retreat to clarify priorities; such retreats became recurring events. Lillian served as co-convener in 1979 and 1984 but most of her Gray Panther work focused on health projects. By 1985 fourteen Gray

Panthers had been co-conveners, seven older members and seven in their twenties or thirties.

In 1978 Rick Smith, a capable man in his early twenties, was hired to staff the Gray Panther office and remained for two years. When he departed other young people followed: Carla Woodworth, a former tenant organizer, and Tim Orr, who brought long-term care work and activist experience. Several students also interned in the office. Intergenerational friendships between young staffers and older Gray Panthers developed, mirroring those formed earlier between Squires and Kwass with Lillian, and by the Sanjeks with Lillian and London. Woodworth enjoyed the camaraderie of a handful of former Communist Party members and their stories about events in New York from the 1930s to the 1950s. Kate Feeney, a Pacific School of Religion work-study student who coordinated the monthly bake sale, was jailed for three weeks after a peace demonstration at Vandenberg Air Force in 1983 and wrote to the network: "Dear Carla, Tim, Joe [Guyon], Dan [Trupin], et al. I got them jailhouse blues . . . Sophie Trupin [whose impaired vision kept her homebound] really deserves lots of applause for the May sale—she made countless brownies. Give Sophie an extra special thanks in the Newsletter."[36]

Into the Political Arena

In its early years the Berkeley network developed tactics to influence the wider public and impact the political arena. First, Lillian formed an advisory board of human service professionals, academics, community organization leaders, clergy, and legislators, including Representative Ron Dellums, and called on them as speakers and allies on issues, for letters of support, and for student interns. Second, the network sponsored public forums to spotlight an issue or kick off a network project. Among early forums were "Medicine, Friend/Foe? Drug Abuse among the Elderly" with a panel of three doctors, "At-Home Health Care—Alternative to Nursing Homes," and "Day Health Care Centers for Seniors." A third tactic was participation in coalitions and conferences organized by others; for example, "A Working Conference on Human Security" featuring Dellums, city councilmember Loni Hancock, and Black Panther Elaine Brown listed Berkeley Gray Panthers as workshop participants.

Advancing legislation supported by Gray Panthers necessitated a fourth tactic, face-to-face negotiation and lobbying. The network's first foray was a "Right to Die" bill sponsored by state assemblymember Barry Keene. In 1976 four Panthers, including Lillian and Mollyann Freeman, a young sociologist, traveled to Sacramento to meet with Keene. After agreeing upon amendments, they publicly endorsed the bill, which passed and was signed by Governor Brown. Similar legislation had been introduced in twenty states but California was first to specify the language that a Right-to-Die declaration should include: "If at any time I should have an incurable injury, disease, or illness certified to be a terminal condition by two physicians, and where the application of life-sustaining procedures would serve only to artificially prolong the moment of my death and where my physician determines that my death is imminent whether or not life-sustaining procedures are utilized, I direct that such procedures be withheld or withdrawn, and that I be permitted to die naturally." The network held a public forum on the law with a physician, lawyer, and hospital chaplain, moderated by Freeman, and printed a sample living will in its newsletter. Briefed on the campaign by Lillian, Maggie discussed the California law in the book *Maggie Kuhn on Aging.*[37]

Next Lillian turned to mandatory retirement and asked Maggie for background materials. Neil Kobrin, a social work student on a six-month internship with the network, read them, reviewed bills pending in California, and wrote a network newsletter article affirming, "Compulsory retirement is an ageist, discriminatory process, for it is based on chronological age, usually 65, instead of a system based on competency. There is no evidence that a person's intellectual functioning declines with age or that everyone ages at the same rate."[38] Kobrin and other Gray Panthers lobbied in Sacramento for abolition of mandatory retirement, and victory followed when Governor Brown signed a law allowing employees to continue working irrespective of age as long as they met competence standards approved by the California Industrial Welfare Commission. While other states had similar laws for public workers, California was first to include the private sector.

In 1977 the Berkeley network cosponsored the Seventh Annual Senior Legislative Rally in Sacramento with ten other organizations. I joined twenty-two Berkeley Gray Panthers for the two-hour bus trip to the state capital, where Panther Van Frank was a rally speaker and "National Health Security," "Renters Relief," and "Increased Income for Seniors" were the day's slogans. Each year during this annual event Berkeley Panthers visited legislators to press their positions, and in 1983 network members entertained hundreds of rally participants with a guerilla theater skit. Though not solely a "senior" organization in theory or practice, the Berkeley Gray Panthers often worked with such groups. In 1977 they sent three delegates, two old and one young, to a founding meeting of the Congress of California Seniors attended by one hundred organizations. Several older Berkeley Panthers participated in mainline senior citizen activities; Van Frank was active in many groups, and in 1983 Joe Guyon ran for the Alameda County seat in the California Senior Legislature.

Lillian opened still another tactical front by bringing Gray Panther viewpoints to professional gerontologists when she cochaired a panel on

"Creative Life Styles" at the Western Gerontological Society meeting in 1977. Here a Gray Panther caucus representing Washington, Oregon, California, and Colorado networks championed a resolution supporting a national health service. Lillian and other Berkeley members would return to the "Western Gero" and other gerontology conferences, frequently staffing a Gray Panther information table and sometimes joined by Maggie. One result of their support for gerontologists pushing their profession toward advocacy was Lillian's friendship with Carroll Estes, a sociologist of aging at the University of California medical campus in San Francisco whose writing acknowledged the Gray Panthers.[39]

Berkeley Panthers were also visible on the streets in petition drives, tabling, and demonstrations. Ties with activist people with disabilities at Berkeley's Center for Independent Living, founded in 1972, began with the 1975 Coalition against the Means Test. In 1977 Gray Panthers joined a CIL demonstration in San Francisco demanding issuance of regulations to make all federally funded buildings accessible to disabled persons.[40] Other Panther protests during the Jimmy Carter years addressed U.S. investment in South Africa and the reimposition of the draft registration. After the inauguration of Ronald Reagan, action escalated. In 1981 a Panther forum on "El Salvador: Another Vietnam?" was held at Berkeley's Latin American community center La Pe–a, and over the next half dozen years members joined numerous demonstrations against intervention in Central America.[41] In 1982 the network worked to place a nuclear weapons freeze initiative on the state ballot and members spoke against proposed Social Security benefit cuts and eligibility restrictions. In 1983 Maggie joined Bay Area Gray Panthers at a Martin Luther King Jr. Day "Jobs, Peace and Justice" rally in Oakland, and later that year the Berkeley network helped publicize a United Farm Workers' list of boycotted food items. In a lighter vein, Berkeley Gray Panthers also participated in BARF, the Berkeley Anti-Reagan Festival, in 1982 and 1983.

Nursing Homes

Beginning with Lillian and Squires's 1974 survey, advocacy to improve nursing homes was a continuing concern of the Berkeley network. In 1975 California's new nursing home ombudsman held a training session for the Berkeley network at which co-convener Hickman reiterated the Panthers' commitment "to be a presence in Berkeley nursing homes; to observe conditions and visit with the residents. We hope to establish relationships with the managers and to be advocates. We also hope to upgrade the homes."[42] In 1976 Citizens for Better Nursing Home Care, founded by Van Frank and with Lillian on its board, inaugurated an

Alameda County nursing home ombudsman program with Squires as director.

In 1977 the Berkeley Gray Panthers and United Neighbors in Action, an Alameda County advocacy group operating a "nursing home hot-line," cosponsored a public hearing at Highland Hospital in Oakland.[43] Testimony was presented by nursing home employees, family and friends of residents, Leslie Kwass, chair of the Panthers nursing home commit-tee, and Charlene Harrington, director of the California health depart-ment's nursing home licensure division. A year earlier Kwass's Senior Citizen Law Program had sued the state for failing to issue regulations implementing its new nursing home law. In 1977 she sued again on be-half of the Panthers, UNA, and Marion Rogers, a nursing home resident, charging the state with refusal to sanction nursing homes for noncompli-ance with the state health code and failure to protect residents like Mrs. Rogers from management retaliation when they filed complaints.

Six weeks after Kwass's second suit, Harrington, who had vigorously pursued enforcement of nursing home regulations and closed the Shattuck-Carleton home in Berkeley, was fired. The action received wide press coverage, and the Berkeley network called for a public explanation of her dismissal. The Panthers enlisted support from state senator Nick Petris, a member of their advisory board, and testified for her reinstate-ment before the state commission that recommended the tougher en-forcement standards she had implemented. Later that year Harrington was a speaker at the Western Regional Gray Panther conference.

During 1978 the network's nursing home committee, now chaired by Winifred Thomas, a retired social worker, gathered information on Al-ameda County's ninety-one nursing homes with forms developed by the Urban Institute in Washington, D.C. The information was used by the county AAA to prepare a "consumer guide" for persons and family mem-bers selecting a nursing home. Thomas's committee next investigated non-English-language needs in Berkeley's nursing homes and board-and-care residential facilities. They found several instances of residents who spoke English during their adult years but reverted to their childhood language after being institutionalized. In all, one in twelve residents re-quired communication in a language other than English, with Italian most frequently needed. In 1979 Thomas's committee joined UNA, now organizing nursing home resident councils, to spotlight Oakland's Essex Convalescent Hospital where a fifty-nine-year-old patient died from in-adequate insulin monitoring; malnutrition, dehydration, and beatings were also documented. To draw attention, the two groups picketed the Essex owner's home in Carmel, an exclusive beachside community south of San Francisco.

In 1980 the Berkeley and Oakland Gray Panthers, UNA, and the Alameda County nursing home ombudsman formed the Coalition of Nursing Home Reform Advocates. Young Gray Panthers Rick Smith, Tim Orr, and Rick McCracken, a Columbus, Ohio, Panther who moved to Berkeley in 1978, led the effort with older member Joe Guyon, now chair of the Berkeley network's nursing home committee. The coalition testified at federal hearings on nursing home regulations in San Francisco in 1980 and participated with Maggie at the 1981 White House Conference on Aging forum on rights of nursing home residents. Once the Reagan presidency began, industry pressure to "deregulate" nursing homes intensified. The coalition opposed such efforts in the state capital, where Guyon spoke about staff and equipment shortages at a state assembly hearing. In 1982 the secretary of Health and Human Services, Richard Schweiker, announced repeal of federal nursing home sanitation and safety regulations and a reduction from annual to biannual inspections. The coalition obtained a meeting with federal officials in San Francisco and held an outdoor rally preceding it featuring Maggie, who was in town for a National Steering Committee meeting. Several NSC members, including myself, joined more than one hundred demonstrators who applauded the Coalition's "Bed Sores for Bonzo" guerrilla theater skit and sang along (to the tune "Mack the Knife"):

Oh, the Shark has wicked teeth dear
And he shows them pearly whites
And the Nursing Homes have a lobby
And it pleases Ron the Knife
If you're older or disabled
Big Business got you down
Your body's good for profits
Looks like Ronnie's back in town

Some Republicans also objected to nursing home inspection cuts, among them Senator John Heinz of Pennsylvania, who told the Reagan administration, "You have just about zero support."[44] Elma Griesel, director of the National Citizens Coalition for Nursing Home Reform, kept the coalition briefed on Washington developments, and, facing a storm of protest, the Reagan administration eventually backed off. In 1983 UNA folded and the Berkeley Gray Panthers and other supporters regrouped as Bay Area Advocates for Nursing Home Reform. The new organization conducted workshops and formed family support groups in a four-county area and began a nursing home information service that was computerized in 1986.

The Health Committee

In 1975 Anne Kenin, a retired social worker recently moved from New York City, began a Gray Panther campaign for an "adult day health center" to serve Berkeley's frail elderly. A few such facilities, like San Francisco's On Lok Center serving Chinese, Filipino, and Italian elderly (which several Berkeley Gray Panthers visited), were receiving Older Americans Act demonstration project funds to provide door-to-door transportation, rehabilitation services, physical and occupational therapy, nutrition counseling, medical and nursing supervision, and daytime respite for family caregivers. Kenin wrote in the Berkeley Gray Panther newsletter: "Day care for the frail elderly is more suitable to their survival, contentment and morale than the nursing homes into which they are placed because there is not suitable alternative care. Costs of the pilot projects seem to be no greater and are often less than nursing home care, and the day care centers entail far less human suffering."[45]

In 1977 Kenin and Teri Dowling, a young health educator in the San Francisco health department, became cochairs of the network's health committee and organized a "Day Health-Care Centers for Seniors" forum cosponsored by the Alameda County AAA, Berkeley's health department, and CIL. Kenin worked vigorously for legislation, passed later in 1977, that "define[d] carefully that a day health care center means an organized program of therapeutic, social, and health activities and services to restore or maintain optimum capacity for self-care, [and] to maintain a person in his own home. . . . Adult day health care centers must be community based, with . . . a governing board of which one-half shall be recipients of services or relatives, or community people."[46]

Gray Panther health committee members remained active on other fronts. Lillian and Dowling worked to have geriatrics courses added to California medical and nursing school curricula, to establish geriatric fellowships in teaching hospitals, and to add categorical funding for geriatric health services to the state budget. Beverly Bagozzi, a younger member, represented the Panthers in a coalition for expanded home health care funding and better training and pay for workers. The committee promoted the national health service bill introduced in 1977 by Representative Ron Dellums, though some members, particularly Van Frank, preferred the Kennedy bill for universal health insurance, which enjoyed greater congressional, union, and senior organization support.[47]

In 1978 Kenin underwent treatment for cancer. Bagozzi stepped in as health committee chair and with younger Panther Maxine Lyons and other members produced a series of newsletter articles comparing Britain's and Canada's national health programs with the Dellums and Kennedy approaches. Lillian also was treated for cancer in 1978, and again in 1979, and wrote in the newsletter about her experiences in Oakland's Kaiser Hospital. Her recovery went well and she was soon at work organizing a forum on "Medigap" insurance to supplement Medicare.

Anne Kenin died at the end of 1979 and the health committee was dormant during 1980. That year Lillian made a two-month study tour of geriatric health facilities in eight cities in England and Scotland. She visited acute and long-term care hospitals, day hospitals (the equivalent of adult day health care), senior centers, elderly housing, hospices for the terminally ill, and in-home service programs. After seeing in practice the "continuum of care" she advocated, Lillian returned with renewed commitment to create the remaining pieces in Berkeley. In 1981 she again became chair of the health committee and put adult day health care at the top of her agenda. After battles in Sacramento and opposition by the nursing home industry, in 1982 the nonprofit Community Adult Day Health Center serving Alameda County opened in an unused wing of Highland Hospital. The following year forty-five frail elders were receiving services.

The Berkeley Hospice

In 1978 the health committee first discussed hospice care for the terminally ill, and the following year a group of seven Panthers chaired by Joe Guyon formed a hospice committee.[48] A retired nurse who joined the Berkeley Gray Panthers in 1977, Guyon spent most of his career in hospitals and after retirement became a community organizer working in Appalachia with VISTA (Volunteers in Service to America), the domestic Peace Corps. While this new Gray Panther committee was organizing, Guyon attended a five-day retreat at the Hospice of Marin that outlined principles he would work to implement: defining the dying patient and their family as the unit of care; focusing on alleviation of pain rather than cure; coordinating home and in-patient care by a team of medical, psychological, and spiritual practitioners; providing services on a twenty-four-hour basis; and continuing work with the family after the patient's death. Guyon was convinced a Berkeley hospice should be a free-standing institution with a community-based board of directors and not operated by a hospital or for-profit health care agency. After researching hospice licensing and staffing regulations and surveying national legislation, and with the success of the Over 60 clinic as his model, he mapped a campaign to develop community support, write "seed money" funding proposals, and recruit like-minded volunteers.

By fall 1979 fifty people were attending Gray Panther hospice committee meetings, including nurses with experience caring for the terminally ill, physicians, lawyers, social workers, and clergy. In December the group affiliated with the National Hospice Association and submitted a planning grant proposal to Alameda County. In addition, $1,600 for the project was donated in memory of Anne Kenin. In 1980 the hospice committee's steering group voted to separate from the Berkeley Panthers, with Guyon the only dissenter. He reported to network members that while he was pleased with the interest his work had generated, he was dismayed that health care professionals on the committee did not share his free-standing, community-run vision

Within months both Herrick Hospital and Alta Bates Hospital in Berkeley announced intentions to establish hospice programs. Guyon reiterated, "A hospital is not a hospice and cannot become one merely by setting aside one wing or ward and assigning dying patients to stay there."[49] Dispirited, he resigned from the hospice committee, which then formed an alliance with the two hospitals and the Visiting Nurses Association. Guyon continued to speak about the hospice idea at conferences but shifted his activism to the network's nursing home committee. In 1982 the Community Hospice of the East Bay was incorporated in Berkeley by the hospital-led alliance. Soon it began community outreach along lines Guyon had suggested four years earlier at his initial hospice committee meetings.[50]

Housing Issues in Berkeley

An intergenerational housing committee formed in 1975 met little success in renting or buying a house to accommodate six to eight Gray Panthers ranging in age from their twenties to sixties or older. Tish Sommers's displaced homemakers group in Oakland and the CIL in Berkeley expressed interest, and Panther Anne Squires wrote an unsuccessful funding proposal, but by 1977 the group discontinued meeting.

Meanwhile Howard Hauze, a retired trumpet player, professional fundraiser, and lawyer, formed a Gray Panther housing committee in 1976 to focus on elderly Berkeley residents wanting to stay in their homes. As he saw it, "Housing for the elderly in Berkeley represents a bleak picture. The demand for purchase or rentals far exceeds the units available at a price within the means of the average citizen. . . . Taxes on property are at a high level. . . . Many elderly residents living on Social Security are in danger of foreclosure or being forced to sell. . . . Rental units in Berkeley are also 'out of sight' for many elderly on fixed incomes. Rent control legislation is a must."[51] Committee members gathered signatures for a Berkeley Housing Coalition rent protection ballot initiative and brought speakers pro and con to a network meeting. To their disappointment, the 1977 initiative lost. Although the Housing Coalition raised $5,000 for the campaign, the Berkeley Committee against Rent Control raised

$150,000 throughout California for direct mail, billboards, radio and newspaper ads, and voter phone calls to oppose it.

The committee turned next to defeating Berkeley Planning Commission proposals to ban rental units in single-family homes, allow no more than three unrelated persons to share accommodations, ease demolition permits of residential properties, and end public review of new apartment construction. On the evening of a city council vote on the plan, the Panthers arrived early to lobby councilmembers. The chamber was soon packed with hundreds of Berkeley residents. Sheryl Brown, a younger Gray Panther, argued that elderly homeowners depended on income from rental units in their homes and that their tenants made older persons feel safer and less isolated. Other speakers objected to restrictions on how many persons, related or not, might live together. Councilmembers well understood there were 6,000 or more technically "illegal" units in Berkeley homes, most of them in the hills. The council not only rejected the proposals but instructed the commission to report back on legalizing the rental units and ending the current limit of five unrelated persons who might live together.

In 1978 the entire network mobilized to defeat Proposition 13. As predicted, after its passage few landlords shared their tax savings with tenants, and this ignited pressure for rent control throughout California, where nearly half the state's three million elderly residents were renters. Chaired by younger member Susan Talcott, the Gray Panther housing committee campaigned for Berkeley Measure I, passed in fall 1978, which rolled back rent increases to June 6, the day Proposition 13 passed, and mandated that this "base rent" be reduced in 1979 by 80 percent of each landlord's Proposition 13 tax savings. Fearing these gains might be lost after Measure I expired, in 1979 Talcott and Gray Panther staffer Rick Smith met with CIL and the Berkeley Tenants Union to map a Berkeley Housing Coalition agenda eventually endorsed by forty organizations. The city council passed a coalition-sponsored rent freeze covering the first three months of 1980, but the coalition's vehicle for more lasting protection was Measure D, the Berkeley Rent Stabilization and Eviction Control Ordinance, which would create a rent board to approve future increases. Countering Measure D, however, was statewide Proposition 10, which would curtail local government power to regulate rents. California's real estate industry put five million dollars into a "Yes on 10" effort. In Berkeley the Gray Panthers and the Coalition mounted a "Yes on D, No on 10" campaign with network members staffing information tables throughout the city and on the University of California campus. They won on both, and defeat of Proposition 10 emboldened other California localities to pass rent ordinances.

While the rent control wars raged, Gray Panther housing committee members attended public hearings on land use, investigated protections for renters when buildings were converted to condominiums, and publicized federal Section 8 assistance for low-income tenants and Berkeley's free home repair service for persons over sixty. They testified before the new Berkeley rent board and with CIL sponsored a city council candidates' forum on housing. The network also joined Berkeley Consensus, a coalition of community groups opposing upscale housing at the vacated School for the Deaf and Blind site near the university campus and demanding instead new rental units for senior citizens, disabled persons, families, and university-related tenants. At the Senior Legislative Rally Day in Sacramento in 1980, housing committee cochair Gerda Miller, sixty-seven, cornered Governor Jerry Brown to back the Berkeley Consensus plan, and when Maggie visited Berkeley, Miller enlisted her to write Brown requesting endorsement.

Two campaigns to dramatize housing pressures on Berkeley's elderly and disabled were mounted during 1980. Rhoda Cutter, a wheelchair user, was evicted by her landlord after holding a tenant-organizing meeting in her apartment. The City of Berkeley and CIL intervened on her behalf, and after the Panthers, CIL, and the Berkeley Tenants Union picketed her landlord's home, the negative publicity brought Cutter a new lease. The Smiths were an elderly African American couple: Mr. Smith was disabled and Mrs. Smith handled the bills until she became incapable of managing paperwork. Despite the Smiths' twenty-five years of timely payments, the two companies holding mortgages on their home foreclosed after a missed payment, and it was sold to a realtor who initiated eviction. The Panthers and Berkeley Tenants Union picketed the new owner's office and met with city and state lawmakers sponsoring legislation to prevent similar occurrences.

Following visits to shared housing programs in south Alameda and Santa Clara counties, in 1981 the Berkeley and Oakland Gray Panthers began Project Share, "a free service [to bring] together mature persons who own homes with those seeking affordable housing. . . . It assists clients in meeting each other and working out their own living arrangements, and offers guidance before, during, and after each match is made."[52] Miller took a leave from the housing committee to work on this new project with several Gray Panther volunteers.

By 1982 the national crisis of homelessness arrived in Berkeley, and Miller briefed the network on a new East Bay Committee to Shelter the Homeless to which she was Gray Panther representative. That year the Panthers also joined other groups to challenge the Berkeley rent board's 9 percent increase. They were dissatisfied with the board's proposed increase for 1983 and supported a ballot initiative to make the board elected rather than appointed. After testifying before the rent board, the

Panthers were pleased when a zero increase was approved for 1984, but soon thereafter California's Court of Appeals gutted Berkeley's rent ordinance. Following lobbying by the Gray Panthers and Berkeley Tenants Union, the city council voted to appeal the ruling and permit the zero increase to go into effect. The Panther housing committee also joined a 1983 petition drive opposing acquisition of the School for the Deaf and Blind site by the University of California. They sponsored a forum on the site and urged the council to accept a plan for federally subsidized housing for elderly and disabled tenants proposed by the National Housing Law Project headquartered in Berkeley. The council approved and groundbreaking at the site began in 1985.

Other Gray Panthers

Berkeley was the first Gray Panther network in northern California but by the 1980s there were several groups in the Bay Area as well as a Gray Panthers of California umbrella organization in Sacramento representing two dozen networks. Many of the networks traced their origin to visits from Maggie, but Lillian also played a role in building the movement. In 1976 Maggie wrote to Lillian that she would be speaking to a new network in Sacramento, and while in Berkeley she asked Lillian to meet with the group's convener, who later visited Berkeley. Also at Maggie's request Lillian and young staffer Birute Skurdenis in 1976 helped launch a network north of San Francisco in Marin County, where Maggie previously had spoken at a college program for older people. The network did not flourish and only in 1981 did a lasting Marin Gray Panther group emerge.

A San Francisco network was started in 1975 by Dr. Alexander Riskin and his wife, and Lillian provided early advice. Then in 1976 the Riskins filed incorporation papers for a nursing home under the name "Gray Panther Health Foundation." The secretary of state's office notified Riskin that the Gray Panthers of the East Bay—Lillian's group—was already incorporated and any subsequent "Gray Panther" organization in California would need their permission. When Riskin called Lillian she told him that use of the name was a matter for the national organization. Riskin did not contact the Philadelphia office, and Alice Adler, chairperson of the National Steering Committee, wrote to him that since no information about the network's activities or membership had been received, "We shall be forced to oppose your use of the name 'Gray Panthers' and we shall no longer consider your San Francisco group to be an affiliate."[53] In 1977 a new San Francisco network began meeting and Lillian again was called for advice. The San Francisco and Berkeley Panthers worked together during 1978 to prevent closing of the Post Street nursing home in San Francisco.[54] Collegial relations continued, including a joint press conference to protest Medicare cuts in 1983.

Smoother starts occurred elsewhere. In 1976 Berkeley membership committee chair Fancheon Christner left to begin the Gray Panthers of Western Contra Costa County meeting in El Cerrito, a few miles north of Berkeley. In 1977 Rose Dellamonica, the succeeding membership chair, became convener of the new Oakland/Emeryville Gray Panthers. The following year Berkeley Panthers helped form a Santa Clara Valley network south of San Francisco, and in 1979 Lillian and Rick Smith helped inaugurate the Gray Panthers of Central Contra Costa County. That year the Gray Panthers of the East Bay changed their name to the Gray Panthers of the Berkeley Area. In 1982 the Oakland/Emeryville network with Tim Orr and Carla Woodworth of Berkeley helped launch the Gray Panthers of South Alameda County, bringing to eight the number of Bay Area Panther groups. Further north, the Gray Panthers of the North Coast began in 1982 following an organizing visit by Lillian and two young Berkeley members.

Communications from Berkeley to the Gray Panther national office included monthly contributions of five dollars in 1976, and ten dollars by 1978, as well as orders for Gray Panther pins, T-shirts, and written materials. Most Berkeley members' views of "National," including my own during 1977–78, were hazy. While many had heard Maggie speak, few regularly read *Network*, which was not mailed by the national office to all Gray Panthers until 1982. Berkeley, however, was well represented on the National Steering Committee. Leslie Kwass was elected in 1976, became chairperson in 1979, and remained a member through 1983. Lillian was elected in 1978 as was Ann Squires, who became national Gray Panther treasurer, although due to job commitments she resigned in 1980. The NSC met in Berkeley in 1979, and network members had an opportunity to meet their national leadership. Several Berkeley Panthers attended Gray Panther national conventions in Washington, D.C.—Lillian, Kwass, and Winifred Thomas in 1977, plus Squires, Guyon, Smith, and McCracken in 1979, and still others in 1981. In 1984 the convention was in San Jose, California, with many more Berkeley Gray Panthers participating.

Fund-raising

The Berkeley Gray Panthers maintained an office and paid staff continuously from 1976. This did not come easily. After initial grant and CETA support ended in 1978 the network adopted a "broad spectrum" approach to grassroots fund-raising. This produced nonmonetary rewards as member and staff ties intensified and the Panthers' public visibility in Berkeley was enhanced.

In 1976 Ann Squires attended a fund-raising course for Alameda County revenue sharing grantees. With expertise acquired there she obtained a San Francisco Foundation grant and a CETA contract. In 1978 the San Francisco Foundation informed the Panthers it would not fund a third year, and Rick Smith told members CETA funds would expire at the beginning of 1979. A fund-raising committee of Squires, Smith, Dan Trupin, and Howard Hauze was already meeting weekly and called for contributions for a Gray Panther garage sale. When they requested $375 to send Smith to a six-day fund-raising course for nonprofit organizations, the rest of the network steering committee was uneasy, but the investment proved well spent. Smith returned dedicated to making the Berkeley network self-supporting. Several small fund-raising events during 1978 were capped by the garage sale, which netted $1,450 and involved more than fifty network members. In December forty Panthers joined in a mailing party to send two thousand appeal letters to names in each member's address book plus a list of potential donors the fund-raising committee developed. Within four months the appeal produced $1,200, and a Vanguard Foundation grant brought another $1,500. With membership renewals, plus unanticipated CETA funding, Smith announced the network raised two-thirds of its 1979 budget. Small foundation grants filled in the rest and provided funds for work-study students.

New ideas proliferated from the fund-raising committee. Gray Panther dinners—one person cooked, the rest paid to attend—produced both money and intergenerational sociability. Holiday and office rent-raising parties charged nominal admissions that went into the network treasury. Gray Panther buttons were sold and in 1982 the Berkeley Panthers designed their own T-shirt. In 1979 a decathon committee chaired by Jenifer Rogers announced a ten-mile Gray Panther fund-raising walk through Berkeley. The cities of Albany and Berkeley both declared November 10 "Gray Panther Day," and Mayor Gus Newport of Berkeley and Representative Ron Dellums kicked off the walk with speeches. The event brought eighty old and young Panthers into the streets, and sponsors pledged money for each mile their designated Gray Panther completed. The event ended with a concert and foot-massage party.

In 1981 the network held its first raffle. Prizes were solicited from Berkeley merchants, Gray Panther members, and friends. The top prize was $100, and others included theater tickets, a free haircut, and one hour of clarinet music. Some 3,200 one-dollar tickets were sold, making the raffle a success. In 1983 first prize was a trip to Hawaii, and proceeds totaled $6,600. Monthly bake sales started in 1980 at flea markets and sites of political actions earned $1,000 a year by 1982. A score of members were involved as bakers, transporters, and sellers, and the bake sale table featured network newsletters, petitions, flyers, buttons, T-shirts, and raffle tickets. An additional source of funds was honoraria received by Lillian for speeches and university and medical school lectures. In a few cases they amounted to hundreds of dollars, and Lillian gave half to the network and half to the national office.

In 1980 the AAA funded the Berkeley Gray Panthers for an "advocacy training project" led by Rick Smith and Rick McCracken, now operating as R & R Associates, with workshops throughout Alameda County. Under a second AAA-funded project through 1985 trained volunteers worked three hours a week contacting frail or isolated older persons in Berkeley and connecting them with housing, food, health care, income, and transportation assistance. CETA funds for network office staff, and City of Berkeley funding after 1980, continued until 1982, when Reagan-era budget cuts reduced support to many Berkeley community organizations. By 1983 staff members Woodworth and Orr were working half-time. Only one quarter of that year's budget came from external sources, however, and membership dues, raffle proceeds, bake sales, and donations provided three-quarters.

Being a Gray Panther

To become a Berkeley Gray Panther was to make a commitment, of annual dues at the very least. For most, and certainly for active members, the commitment was also to the political messages of the movement. Those coming to meetings primarily for companionship were disappointed. Friendships might develop, but the ethos of engagement with political issues—whether nursing home reform, rent control, a national health service, or peace in Central America—was so powerful that anyone not sharing such commitments would be uncomfortable. Some members were recruited through previous involvement with Gray Panther issues; Lillian met Leslie Kwass in this way, as she did several younger members. More typically, however, a person, old or young, knew something about the Gray Panthers and learned their meeting place and time. The prospective member arrived and was greeted as existing members noted a new face. Many visitors never returned. Those who did might eventually decide to come to a Gray Panther committee meeting or attend a demonstration or conference with fellow Panthers. The new member then experienced a feeling of solidarity as veteran members welcomed his or her decision to become "active." Each additional activity added to the member's store of network memories and anecdotes. Eventually the new Gray Panther assumed the veteran role vis-à-vis a still newer member.

Acceptance by others in the Berkeley network accrued over time and had to be achieved. A new member at some point might be asked to represent the Panthers at an event, join or chair a committee, or accept nomination to network office. For older persons, earlier work or political experiences and skills were not automatic routes to network esteem. Younger Gray Panthers, on the other hand, often could trade on their age at first, since the older majority valued greatly the youth component in "Age and Youth in Action." Established members of all ages maintained their place in the network by participating in ongoing activities and recounting past actions. In election to positions of leadership, however, neither cumulative veteran status nor youth was sufficient, and willingness to participate in network meetings and projects was required.

Woe to the Gray Panther whose sense of self-importance was imposed on others and who sought leadership too quickly. Such persons rarely gained what they desired, but their disruptive presence might waste meeting time and force others to choose between democracy and network business. Occasionally a new member might prevail in winning a leadership post, unveil efforts at self-promotion, and provoke dissension and dampen spirits. But ordinarily a member would find a satisfying and effective role. Many committees in the Berkeley network were chaired by veteran Panthers who took on their current assignment after some time as a rank-and-file member.[55]

Personal details of work, family, tastes, or hobbies might be learned about fellow Panthers as friendships developed within the dyadic and small-group social glue holding the network together. People were not expected to recite their biography when they joined, and lengthy self-introductions by first-time attendees provoked foot-shuffling or ceiling-staring. In fact, many established members did not know all that much about each others' pre–Gray Panther history, even when they could readily recount shared network experiences. Close Gray Panther friendships included intergenerational as well as intragenerational ties. Lillian and Squires traveled in Europe together for three weeks in 1976, and young members Rick Smith and Rick McCracken formed their R & R partnership. Among older Panthers, experiences with illness or deaths were grist for conversations that might broaden to emotional support during health or family crises.

Composed of older members, the Berkeley network's consciousness-raising group was a forum for age-peer issues. The group formed in 1976 with Gregory Bergman as chair. Meetings were held in the hour preceding network meetings, with five to ten core participants always in attendance. Members were determined that the group would not become a rap session for personal problems or group therapy but would proceed via structured discussion around themes of common interest. The members would set the next meeting's theme at the end of each session, often agreeing on a common reading assignment. Meeting topics during the first year were "Widows as a Minority Group," stresses on retired people moving to Berkeley for the first time, and retirement and social security in other countries. Film showings produced larger attendance. One featured Gregory Bergman's effort in his mid-sixties to reconstruct his life following the death of his wife in an automobile accident, and his new career as a writer. Another was about an elderly politically active Berkeley resident and his philosophy of dealing with declining health.

In 1977 the consciousness-raising group was featured in a film, *Feelings about Death and Dying,* made by a Berkeley librarian. The following year at the urging of new chair Aimee Sumner, six members, including Helene London, Joe Guyon, and Dan Trupin, appeared before an audience of fifty at a Unitarian Universalist meeting to discuss "how we feel about aging and especially about the necessity of becoming aware of unrealistic, unfavorable stereotypes of age."[56] In 1980 the group discussed relations between "decision makers" and other members in the Berkeley network and suggested ways to improve meetings. Sessions were lively: "At one meeting, where the topic was ostensibly 'Enriching my life by discovering new areas of interest', we wound up laughing more than we talked!"[57] In 1983 plans began to bring discussions about aging to children in Berkeley public schools.

The death of a fellow network member was also part of being a Gray Panther. During Anne Kenin's last months in 1979 many Gray Panthers visited her. She sent the network "a heartfelt THANKS to you all who helped me and are still helping me through a most difficult period. All the Health Committee members were singly helpful, as well as the uncounted, beautiful men and women who took me to therapy and medical appointments over a long period, to go shopping, to do the numerous jobs I could not perform. Lillian Rabinowitz, in her own extremity, took time to write many consoling notes."[58] When Kenin died, the newsletter printed a remembrance and announced that contributions in her memory could be made to the Gray Panthers Hospice Fund. Dan Trupin, a fellow consciousness-raising group member, wrote a poem for Kenin printed next to the notice of her death. In succeeding years more tributes in the newsletter marked the passing of active members, often with requests by family members that donations be sent to the Gray Panthers.

Still, death notices were relatively few and the newsletter was testament to the affirmation of life by older Gray Panthers. It announced the holiday and summer parties and picnics and fund-raising activities that marked the life of the network beyond meetings and actions. It published poems selected or written by members, including several by Trupin and transplanted Philadelphia Gray Panther Rene Polard, for whom Trupin wrote an eightieth birthday tribute in 1985. (Both were members of "Mature Poets of Berkeley.") Trupin, a lawyer, had moved to California after he retired as a New York municipal employee, and he saw his Gray Panther activities assume an unexpectedly large part of his life. While no one registered the volume of speaking invitations or media coverage that Lillian did, Kenin, Van Frank, Hickman, Guyon, and others also addressed public audiences or the press about the Gray Panthers, aging, and health issues, and Trupin and his wife, Sophie, author of a memoir on Jewish settlers in the American west,[59] appeared on the *Over Easy* television show in 1981. Other Panthers could thus affirm Lillian's seventieth birthday comment about being a Gray Panther: "I'm in good health because I'm consumed with so much pleasure and interest in how I live. And anyhow, I think it's fun."[60]

Ten Years After

The Gray Panthers of the Berkeley Area began their tenth year in crisis. In January 1984 convener Winifred Thomas resigned for health reasons. Staff members Woodworth and Orr voluntarily resigned to avoid depleting a diminishing bank account, though Woodworth continued to coordinate fund-raising efforts as a volunteer. The fund-raising committee explained that a budget deficit would have to be filled and appealed to members to pledge five dollars a month. To complicate things, the nominations committee's officer slate announced their refusal to serve unless all four were elected. Passions and tempers rose in the network, but rallying had already begun.

Trupin stepped in to chair the consciousness-raising group. Miller began a new membership committee that organized a Gray Panther open house on the Cal campus attended by fifty, and she recruited members throughout Berkeley at tables where petitions on Panther issues were signed. In a few months the network roster increased from 350 to more than 400. A fund-raising dinner honoring city councilmember John Denton, who reappointed Lillian to the Berkeley Commission on Aging and supported network campaigns, raised $2,100. Bake sales and Gray Panther dinner parties continued, and the 1984 raffle netted $6,900. Orr and Woodworth, now working elsewhere, agreed to stand as officers. Woodworth was elected with three of the uncompromising slate who immediately resigned. Three steering committee members agreed to serve with Woodworth as officers until a new election. With new grants from the county AAA and Vanguard Foundation, Orr was rehired to reopen the office. After a "clear the air" retreat, Veronica Anthony, an older housing committee member, was elected convener, Lillian vice-convener, and former staffers Woodworth, Orr, and Skurdenis members of the steering committee. Reflecting on these events, Lillian wrote, "Our Berkeley Network has recently experienced a period of painful change; but we have survived. In looking back and thinking about what made us 'special' in the time of our organization's amazing infancy and youth, I think it was the fact that we were issue-oriented."[61]

Even while internal problems consumed energy, as 1984 began Bay Area Advocates for Nursing Home Reform (BANHR), with Orr as president, opened a new office in Berkeley, and the Panther nursing home committee lobbied with BANHR in Sacramento for the Nursing Home Patient Protection Act, which, though vetoed by Governor George Dukmejian, became law in 1985. Gray Panthers testified at city council hearings against evicting nursing home patients when personal funds were exhausted and they became Medicaid recipients, and the council voted to make the practice illegal in Berkeley. During 1985 the Panthers and BANHR cosponsored workshops for relatives and friends of nursing home residents.

The health committee turned its attention to health maintenance organizations (HMOs), which pledged to provide health care for a monthly premium; with AARP, the county AAA, the Over 60 Clinic, and the World Institute on Disability,[62] it sponsored a forum with public officials, academics, health care providers, and HMO spokespersons. On the housing front, Gray Panther Gerda Miller was elected to the Berkeley Rent Board in 1984 with the highest vote total among twenty candidates and joined a Panther-backed "Tenants' Rights Action Committee" board majority. The network conducted a "Gray Panther Walking Tour of Berkeley's Downtown Development" to spotlight an office-building boom, lack of low-income housing, and encampment of homeless persons living in cars near the city dump. The network's peace committee participated in demonstrations during the 1984 Democratic Convention in San Francisco and with the San Francisco Panthers hosted a reception for Maggie and Representative Claude Pepper. During 1984 and 1985 network members joined protests at the Oakland docks over trade with South Africa, and Gray Panthers were among forty-five arrested at a "Senior Anti-Apartheid Sit-In Demonstration" in San Francisco.

In 1984 the Berkeley network celebrated its tenth anniversary with Maggie as keynote speaker. Gray Panther ally Judy Heumann of CIL and the World Institute on Disability (and later Assistant Secretary of Education under President Bill Clinton)[63] was honored. Recognition was accorded to Lillian as founder and to veteran members Bergman, Hickman, and Squires, and the event raised $5,500 for the network. A celebration of the ninth anniversary of the Over 60 Clinic followed in 1985. Maggie was again in attendance, as were Representative Ron Dellums and five Gray Panther clinic board members: Lillian, now seventy-three; Lorna Brangwin, eighty-three; Eugenia Hickman, seventy-five; Charlotte Knight, seventy-three; and Helene London, eighty-two. Lillian's remarks captured the spirit of the evening. "The Over 60 Clinic was founded by a group of people, young, middle-aged and old, of diverse background and ethnicity, joined together by their perception of an unmet need and their vision of what had to be done. . . . For those of us continuing to serve on the Over 60 Board, the dream of dreams goes on apace: we would like to help create similar services in other community clinics throughout our Country."[64]

Chapter 5
The Gray Panthers in New York City (1972–85)

Four months after Maggie Kuhn's first 1970 meeting a handful of Consultation participants met to consider forming a local New York City unit. Among them were "group of six" members Helen Baker and Eleanor French, both Manhattan residents, and Presbyterian minister Cameron Hall from Long Island. The issues discussed reflected what was on the minds of these early Gray Panthers: the Vietnam War, government repression of the Black Panthers, and the fall congressional elections. Over the next two years Baker and Hall devoted their involvement to the Consultation steering committee (French died in 1971), and no further step was taken toward forming a network in New York.

Bagger, Bragger, and Gersmehl

Shortly before her May 1972 Denver press conference Maggie contacted Hope Bagger, eighty-one, who in March had convinced her assemblymember, Franz Leichter, to introduce a bill banning mandatory retirement in New York State. A union organizer in Detroit during the 1930s, Bagger moved to New York in 1934 with her naval officer husband and worked as a schoolteacher and then in the manpower industry until failing eyesight led her to stop at age eighty. "I had noted how hard it was for older people to get or keep jobs and I determined to work on that problem as a volunteer as soon as I retired."[1] During their telephone conversation Maggie learned that Hope had contacted members of the U.S. Senate Special Committee on Aging to urge a federal ban on mandatory retirement. The two women arranged to meet in Manhattan later that month.

Before their meeting the *New York Times* story on Maggie's Denver press conference appeared. Two days later another New Yorker, Lydia Bragger, wrote Maggie, "After reading the article I fairly shouted—Amen, Right-on, Beautiful," and suggested, "It will be wonderful to meet."[2] Bragger, sixty-eight, led Presbyterian Church youth groups while raising her children and during 1958–61 produced radio and television programs for the Rhode Island Council of Churches. After being widowed in 1964 she moved to New York City, operated a gift shop business, and then worked for *Christianity and Crisis*, a religious opinion journal whose editorial board was chaired by John Bennett, husband of "group of six" member Ann Bennett.

Late in May Maggie traveled to New York to meet each woman in person. First she had lunch with Lydia Bragger at the Interchurch Center building at 475 Riverside Drive, where Maggie had worked to 1970. During their meal she asked Lydia to come along to her meeting at Hope Bagger's 626 Riverside Drive cooperative apartment building twenty blocks uptown. There, after discussing Hope's efforts to ban mandatory retirement, Maggie asked her to organize a Gray Panther network in New York. Maggie then left for her Philadelphia train accompanied by Lydia. During their ride, Maggie invited Lydia to join the Gray Panther steering committee. Lydia agreed and attended the August 1972 NSC meeting in Princeton, New Jersey, which was videotaped for ABC television's documentary on the Gray Panthers.

Using Maggie's list of New York Consultation contacts, Lydia sent invitations to a September meeting at Presbyterian Senior Services on Broadway and 73rd Street on Manhattan's Upper West Side. Thirteen came, including Hope, NSC members Cameron Hall, Shubert Frye, and Leslie Sussan, two seminary students, and three of Lydia's female neighbors. After speaking about Gray Panther origins and the Ghost Ranch seminar in New Mexico that she would be attending with Maggie and Hall, Lydia asked about issues to tackle in New York. People mentioned national health care, compulsory retirement, housing, and Social Security, and a health care committee, headed by Hope, was formed at the meeting. Three days later Frye wrote to Lydia, "I came away with a good feeling of having made a very hopeful beginning. . . . I have a very strong feeling you are *destined* as the leader of the New York City group, at least provisionally."[3]

Hope saw things differently. She regarded Lydia, a dozen years her junior, as assisting her by handling administrative matters. Acting on the group's decision to address health care, Hope enrolled in a Community Council of Greater New York class where fifty participants studied national health plans in Sweden, Israel, England, France, and the Soviet Union. Although the topic of the U.S. health system was new to her, she quickly determined that the two-hundred-billion-dollar private health insurance industry must be excluded from any Gray Panther alternative.

The next few Gray Panther meetings were held at Lydia's apartment on West 66th Street, with a changing roster of a dozen or more each month. Hope missed the October meeting but in November she and five health committee members reported on their work. "Our idea is to gather material and find out what the operations are throughout the world on health programs. We plan to study and organize a health plan for ourselves, and when we know what we want, we can push for it in Congress."[4] She was followed by Glen Gersmehl, twenty-five, a recent graduate of Concordia University, a Lutheran school near Chicago, now working for the Church Health Action Committee in Manhattan. "Our aim is to have a really comprehensive national health program made available to everyone. The national health program may be 'the issue' of the 1970s."[5] In February 1973 Gersmehl attended his second Panther meeting and briefed the group on national health insurance legislation to be introduced by Senator Ted Kennedy of Massachusetts.

After the ABC Gray Panther documentary aired in October 1972, New York media interest and speaking invitations cascaded. Hope and Lydia both spoke on WNYC municipal radio, Hope was interviewed by conservative talk show host Barry Farber, and Lydia was a guest on the CBS television quiz show *To Tell the Truth*. Seeking members, Maggie joined both women at a West Side senior center meeting where the ABC documentary was screened, and all three spoke. In February 1973 Bagger and Bragger traveled together to address a group of Pennsylvania medical students. Hope also spoke at a National Association of Social Workers meeting at Fordham University, and that spring her bill to end mandatory retirement passed in the New York State Assembly. Friendship among Bagger, Bragger, and Maggie blossomed. Hope helped Lydia find an apartment in her cooperative building and wrote to Maggie, "We have a lot of fun together, and it will be even better when Lydia moves in here."[6] Maggie asked Hope also to join the NSC and over the next year she attended six meetings, five with fellow NSC member Lydia. In June 1973 Gray Panther stationery was printed listing Lydia Bragger as convener, Hope Bagger as co-convener, and the network's address as 626 Riverside Drive.

During this first year Hope cultivated New York legislators and organization leaders while Lydia's links to the national Gray Panther circle intensified. It was Lydia who Elma Griesel of RPAG asked to find New York volunteers for her hearing aid study. Lydia recruited nine participants, who visited twenty hearing aid dealers. And in March 1973 it was Lydia who Maggie requested to organize "something" for the American Medical Association Convention in New York that June. Bragger secured space for an "AMA Alternative Conference" at her church, Good Shepherd Presbyterian at West 66th Street, but asked Hope and her health committee to take charge of the program.

Hope was reluctant but Maggie prodded and came to New York to help plan logistics. Gersmehl pitched in with another young Panther, Jane Wholey of the Community Health Institute. They and Hope met each Sunday for five weeks before the June event, which they titled "Do We Need a National Health Service?," and they consulted experts "ranging from establishment types to radicals" at Health/PAC, the Medical Committee for Human Rights, and unions and recruited a score of panelists to follow Maggie's keynote address. Flyers were sent to the New York, Philadelphia, and Washington Gray Panther mailing lists and distributed at meetings in New York. Lydia prepared a press release, and a food committee organized a "homemade health foods" lunch of bean sprouts, yogurt, fresh baked bread, and apple cider.[7]

At the conference the New York Gray Panther health committee unveiled its "Health Policy Statement," drafted by Gersmehl, which demanded that health care be made universal, comprehensive, continuous through the life cycle, locally accountable, and financed by progressive income taxation.

Although we have the financial means, the medical knowledge and skill, and a productive capability second to none, the United States has failed to translate these strengths into a health system able to assure all our citizens good health service. Our present mechanisms for financing and delivering health care are so obsolete that a complete overhaul and restructuring of the present system is necessary. . . . We, the Gray Panthers, see our function in this effort as three-fold: to stimulate interest among the people, and action by the Congress to enact needed legislation promptly; to conduct research and to determine what structure and provisions in a national health care delivery system are the best; and to warn against, and prevent as far as possible, dangerous and costly mistakes in the planning, financing, administration, or control that might creep into a national health care plan. As the central motivating and driving impulse, the profit motive is as out of place in a system of health care as it would be in a system of education.[8]

Two hundred people attended, and *Village Voice* and *New York Post* coverage followed. Hope and other Panthers spoke about national health care on radio programs, and she and Lydia appeared with Maggie and Shubert Frye on the national David Susskind television interview show. In July Maggie testified before the Senate Special Committee on Aging, with Gersmehl helping write her presentation. That month the New York network met in high spirits; the Ethical Culture Society at West 64th Street offered meeting space, which the Panthers used for the next five years. Hope and Gersmehl announced a series of summer classes for national health service speaker-advocates that attracted thirty participants, including health care professionals who had attended the June conference. The curriculum consisted of fact sheets prepared by Gersmehl that detailed health care statistics, problems with Medicare, Medicaid, and private insurance, and the Panthers' alternative vision.

Bagger versus Bragger

In August 1973 tension between Hope and Lydia surfaced. As Lydia left for a vacation in Sweden, Hope sent letters to Maggie and four NSC members expressing her caustic opinion of Bragger and announcing, "I am not willing any longer to try to work with Lydia. Period." Hope's assessment of the New York Panthers praised younger members Gersmehl and Wholey, but otherwise the "Network has attracted a large number of interested bystanders and well wishers. . . . Among the elderly population we have acquired almost nothing in the way of trained representatives able and willing to take over any significant part of the work. We may—and must—be able to find an experienced, resourceful and energetic organizer for the N.Y. Network."[9] Hope intended to continue as a researcher and speaker but insisted that Lydia henceforth work under the auspices of the Philadelphia office, and outside New York City.

In September 1973 thirty people arrived at the Ethical Culture Society to celebrate the New York Gray Panthers' first anniversary. It was also the last network meeting Lydia would chair. She began by reporting on the situation of older persons in Sweden and then turned over the meeting to Hope, who summarized August's activities: her own radio editorials opposing mandatory retirement, requests for Gray Panther speakers at senior centers, and lobbying in Albany to kill pro-industry hearing aid legislation. Gersmehl reported on the national health service classes. "The first two weeks we talked about the faults of the [health care] system. The second two weeks were devoted mainly to politics: who holds the power in the system. Also we spent a whole session on economics. This week we will talk about what we want, and how we can achieve it."[10]

Hope's health committee now effectively became the New York Gray Panthers. She and Gersmehl prepared October and November newsletters announcing a second round of classes covering Gray Panther history, national health insurance bills in Congress, and a "media watch" to track "instances when older people are put down in TV and radio programs and commercials," using monitoring forms designed by Gersmehl.[11] On Super Bowl Sunday in January 1974 nine hundred people attended a "Health Care and the Aging" conference organized by the New York Gray Panthers, the Church Health Action Committee, the Medical Committee for Human Rights, and the Society for Ethical Culture. In a rally-like atmosphere Maggie challenged a "system that has been oppressive of the people it's supposed to serve" and demanded "a bill of rights for patients" and geriatric training in medical schools. Representative Shirley Chisholm excoriated "fee-for-service" medicine for making health care "available only to those who can afford it."[12] Two weeks later four hundred health care professionals and consumers returned for Saturday workshops covering nursing homes and home care, HMOs and patients' rights, participation on hospital advisory boards, and the differences between national health insurance and universal health care. Hope and Gersmehl were among the four opening speakers, and supporting groups included Health/PAC, MCHR, the Physicians Forum, the National Association of Social Workers, and several religious denominations. In February Gersmehl and Rhonda Kotelchuck of Health/PAC held a follow-up session on lobbying for health care legislation in Washington. Still more spin-offs came in April and May when Gersmehl conducted classes on health care politics in Forest Hills, Queens, and at the Society for Ethical Culture.

In March 1974 the newsletter announced that the New York Gray Panther mailing list had grown from sixty to six hundred, with another six hundred copies distributed in senior centers and venues where Panthers spoke. Led by Estelle Rib, who joined the Panthers through the hearing aid study, members had collected five thousand signatures for a petition demanding that Congress pass Kennedy's health insurance legislation. Individual members wrote to Congress urging expansion of Medicare to cover eyeglasses and prescription drugs and elimination of deductibles and co-pays. The *NBC Evening News* videotaped the March membership meeting, one of nine Gray Panther meetings or classes held each month.

Meanwhile Lydia worked with Maggie on press relations and spoke for the national Gray Panthers at conferences in several states. She advised the filmmakers of *A Matter of Indifference*, a documentary featuring residents of a retirement home and interviews with Maggie, Hope, and herself, which screened at the Museum of Modern Art and the Society for Ethical Culture. In February 1974 Lydia started a nine-week workshop for older persons and high school students at a Forest Hills, Queens, senior center whose director supported the creation of a Gray Panther network. Since it was outside Manhattan, Hope had no objection.

At the March 1974 NSC meeting the Bagger vs. Bragger conflict reignited. Lydia complained privately to several members about the letters Hope had written the previous August and she had now read. Trying to contain the situation, Maggie, Hall, and Frye met with Hope and proposed a New York organizing conference to recruit additional members from the Retired Professionals Action Group mailing list. Hope approved, saying, "To facilitate the change-over [to an expanded New York group], I think it will be helpful for me to resign immediately as coordinator of the New York local. . . . This tactic will get people used to the idea that I am entirely dispensable and will no longer have to run things."[13] Later that month she informed Maggie that the John Hay Whitney Foundation had offered to fund her antimandatory retirement and health care advocacy work for a year.

Maggie and Griesel scheduled an April conference planning meeting in New York with Hope, Gersmehl, and others Hope might invite. Three days before the meeting Lydia sent a memo to "Organizing people of N.Y. Gray Panthers" stating, "Since last September. . . . I have worked more or less in limbo, with no defined role. . . . To work responsibly and effectively it will be necessary for me to have complete responsibility for media relations and activities in N.Y.C."[14] Hope did not invite other New York Panthers to the meeting; upon arriving at the network's Ethnical Culture Society office she found Lydia, whom she did not expect, sitting with Maggie and Griesel. Aghast, Hope "felt my duty to the GP was at an end and I could not get out fast enough. I was too bitterly disappointed in Maggie. . . . The next day I told the Whitney people I would accept their offer."[15] Hope evidently had not seen Lydia's memo before the meeting and she later wrote a countermemo attacking it.[16]

The situation in New York deteriorated. The NSC budgeted $500 for Randi Koren, twenty-three, a work-study student and NSC member, to spend May and June in New York to help boost the number of active Gray Panther members. Hope boycotted the first two meetings Koren called, which Lydia attended, and refused to give Koren the New York network mailing list. Koren felt that the fifteen or so Panthers at these meetings were unprepared to absorb additional members. Her agenda for the third meeting was "multiple leadership." Hope attended this time, and Lydia did not, and the New York Panthers present, all Bagger loyalists, immediately gave Hope the floor. She explained that in July she would begin her Whitney grant, "severely curtailing the activities I would have at the disposal of the [New York] Panthers," and encouraged them to resist a Philadelphia "take over."[17] Members voiced uncertainty about what the Philadelphia Gray Panther office had to offer them but also reluctance to sever ties with the national movement. They reconstituted themselves "the New York Gray Panther Executive Board" and held a meeting without Koren, who wrote to them, "I have by my coming threatened the autonomy of the local group and gone against our principle of self determination. . . . Most people have encouraged me to leave."[18] And she did. Her final recommendation to the NSC was this: "Let the New York group alone for a few months and see if they are able to get beyond the point where they are now."[19]

Maggie's and Griesel's loyalty to Lydia persisted, along with their wish that a second New York Panther group might emerge under her leadership. In September 1974 Lydia received funds from the Central Presbyterian Church at East 64th Street in Manhattan to hold a conference aimed at organizing an East Side Gray Panther network. Koren coordinated this event at which Maggie gave the opening address to an audience of one hundred, and Griesel, Hall, and others spoke. No new group resulted, and it was the existing New York Gray Panthers, under new leadership, who returned to this church a month later to describe their ongoing activities for prospective new members.

Through the 1970s

The leadership vacuum following Hope Bagger's departure in 1974 was filled by Sylvia Wexler, a retired New York City Parks Department recreation administrator who joined the Panthers in 1973. As convener or co-convener, she would lead the network for almost six years. During this period the New York Gray Panthers added new causes and projects to their agenda, and the network became more visible in public testimony, coalitions, marches, picketing, forums, speaking venues, and press coverage.

In June 1974 five Panthers, including Hope and Gersmehl, testified at a Transit Authority public hearing. There the TA announced it would not include any of the newly available "kneeling buses," which could lower the front entry step to just three inches from the ground, in its upcoming federally subsidized purchase of 398 city vehicles. The Panthers protested that many elderly and disabled riders or mothers with young children found the existing model's sixteen-inch front step difficult to manage. The agency's new chairman invited the Panthers to TA headquarters to discuss and "test" a kneeling bus prototype. There Panther Syl Drago, who walked with crutches, demonstrated how she could more easily enter a kneeling bus from the street curb than step on to the standard model. In August the TA notified the Panthers that fifty kneeling buses would be included in the new city purchase. Not satisfied, they demanded that *all* new buses be kneeling ones, which even then would amount to less than 10 percent of the city's bus fleet. Returning to TA headquarters with ranks of elderly and disabled protesters, the Panthers declared victory in October when the TA announced that all new buses would have the kneeling technology.

In 1976 New York Panthers Jim and Peggy Coffey investigated how the new vehicles were faring. They discovered the kneeling technology was not being activated during rush hour because the TA considered it "too time consuming." Wexler joined the Coffeys in collecting rider complaint forms about drivers who refused to operate the mechanism. They presented the results at another meeting with TA officials where Coffey estimated that only 1 percent of drivers were actually operating the kneeling mechanism when requested. At the same time Gray Panther Rose Goldfarb was filmed by the *Prime of Your Life* television show in encounters with bus drivers who refused to use the kneeling mechanism or falsely claimed it was out of service. In 1978 the Panthers threatened legal action against the TA for noncompliance with a federal Urban Mass Transportation Act provision stipulating that service must be available to elderly and disabled riders. They also successfully pressured the TA to place large "Kneeling Bus" decals readable from a distance on the vehicles, which by that year numbered more than one-quarter of the city fleet. In 1979 Jim Coffey, Goldfarb, and others joined city councilmember Carol Greitzer at a City Hall press conference to protest continuing TA resistance to utilization of the kneeling machinery. (In 1980 New York Disabled in Action filed a lawsuit and began street protests to make city mass transit accessible to wheelchair users; eventually buses with rear-door platform lifts were phased in by the TA, and DIA then mounted its own campaign to make drivers use the new technology.)[20]

In 1975 Wexler and other Panthers testified against telephone rate increases before the New York State Public Service Commission. Four months later they returned to the PSC carrying large signs protesting a proposed 22 percent Con Edison electricity rate increase. On each occasion Wexler stressed "the plight of the elderly struggling on fixed incomes. An increase in utility rates would compound their fight for survival during this profit-ethic era."[21] The following year six Panthers attended another PSC hearing on a further Con Ed rate increase, and a cable television reporter interviewed Wexler. At a Department for the Aging (DFTA) public hearing in 1976 Wexler presented a five-page Gray Panther critique of how DFTA planned to allocate Older Americans Act funds, and at DFTA's 1978 hearing Gersmehl testified for the Panthers.

Wexler also brought the New York Gray Panthers into the streets on national and international issues. In 1975 they joined a coalition of fifty organizations and two thousand marchers on Fifth Avenue to celebrate the first United Nations International Women's Day. As a featured speaker alongside Representative Bella Abzug, feminist writers Gloria Steinem and Betty Friedan, and Beulah Saunders of the National Welfare Rights Organization, Wexler declared the Gray Panthers "are not meek little old ladies quietly accepting cuts in H.E.W.'s budget while President [Gerald] Ford continues to fight for millions more for an obsolete [Vietnam] war."[22] A month later network members carried a twelve-foot Gray Panther banner reading "What's an Economy For? Bread for the Elderly Poor, or Cadillacs for the Corporations?" in a Washington, D.C., march protesting President Ford's economic policies. They returned to the nation's capital in 1978 to join one hundred thousand urging ratification of the Equal Rights Amendment. They came again in 1979 to hear

Barry Commoner, Jane Fonda, Ralph Nader, and Maggie Kuhn call for shutting down nuclear plants during a mass demonstration following the Three Mile Island reactor accident in Pennsylvania.

Economic issues were a prime concern for Wexler, who joined five Panthers in an "Action Project on the Economy" study group led by Gersmehl. After consulting with "radical economists" at local universities they organized five evening seminars during April 1975 (the same month New York City went into financial default[23]), which resulted in *GP Special Report on the Economy*, a twenty-page booklet edited by Gersmehl that covered plant closings, corporate waste and greed, oil prices, and recession.[24] In 1977 the New York Panthers organized their first large conference in three years, "Who Is the Mugger?" The event presented the Panthers' work on economic issues—the "root causes of crime in our society"—with Wexler listing "aspects of life which are mugging older New Yorkers." Max Manes of Seniors for Adequate Social Security, founded in 1971, addressed income adequacy, and Rose Kryzak of New York StateWide Senior Action Council, formed in 1972, spoke about utilities.[25] Other speakers included senior center and youth program staffers, block association organizers, and representatives of the New York Police Department and Department for the Aging.

Convener Wexler repaired the network's ties to the national movement. In 1975 she replaced Hope Bagger as New York representative on the National Steering Committee. She participated in the NSC meeting during which the Articles of Agreement were hammered together and later that year, with five New York Panthers, attended the Chicago convention where she was elected to the NSC, to be joined in 1977 by Gersmehl. She and other New York network members participated at a 1978 Northeast Regional Conference attended by 125 Panthers from six states, and at follow-up meetings in 1979 and 1980. At the 1979 Gray Panther convention Wexler led a delegation of fifteen New York Panthers and chaired a workshop on "How to Work for Legislation at the Local, State and National Level." New York Panthers got to know Maggie during these events, and in 1979 several attended her talk about visiting China at New York's Fifth Avenue Presbyterian Church.

As convener, Wexler maintained a cordial relationship with Hope Bagger, who no longer attended Gray Panther meetings but continued to lobby in Albany as head of the network's Committee to Eliminate Mandatory Retirement. In 1977 city councilmember Miriam Friedlander introduced a local bill banning mandatory retirement; Hope and other New York Panthers testified for it, but, like the state effort, it failed to pass. In 1979 Wexler honored Hope at the New York Gray Panther winter holiday party, and the following year she presented Hope a plaque recognizing her as founder and Life Member.

In the meantime Lydia Bragger found a perch with the New York network's Media Watch. It met at the Council on Interracial Books for Children, whose director Brad Chambers helped Maggie and Lydia prepare the critique of prime time television programming that gained national attention in 1975.[26] Under Lydia's auspice the Media Watch became a national Gray Panther project. She also began a radio program on WBAI, New York's listener-supported Pacifica Foundation station, in 1977. Although she was the "voice" of the Gray Panthers in the city (her program continued into the 1990s), Lydia did not participate in Wexler's network, and when Hope was honored in 1980 she sent a terse note "to set the records straight" that she was the network's "founder."[27]

Health Care Issues

Health care, the principal issue for the New York Gray Panthers during their first two years, remained a key focus under Wexler. Her first co-convener, Estelle Rib, a retired Women's Trade Union League organizer, sent New York State lawmakers telegrams and wrote press releases opposing a hearing aid industry bill permitting practices criticized in Griesel's *Paying Through the Ear* report. She traveled to Albany to testify for alternative legislation passed in 1975 to strengthen regulation of the industry. A hearing aid user herself, Rib was chairperson of the New York League for the Hard of Hearing and remained an outspoken Gray Panther advocate on hearing health issues into the 1980s. She expanded the Gray Panther speaker's bureau, the network's main source of income, recruiting members who spoke on health issues and Gray Panther activism at up to one hundred senior centers, union retiree meetings, nursing homes, hospitals, medical and nursing schools, libraries, city agencies, colleges, and houses of worship each year during the later 1970s.

In 1977 the New York Panthers promoted the national health service bill sponsored by Representative Ron Dellums; as part of a national Gray Panther petition campaign, they collected four thousand signatures backing it. Two years later they held a "Political Action for Health" forum to spotlight the Dellums bill as well as health issues in that year's mayoral campaign, and in 1979 they organized a conference of national health service advocates, with Gersmehl a featured speaker. During the 1970s Gersmehl led a "Doctors Project" involving forty Gray Panthers and thirty student volunteers. It started as a practical effort to identify physicians willing to accept older patients on Manhattan's West Side, where many network members lived. Using a questionnaire developed by a Ralph Nader–inspired project in Maryland, a score of Panthers and allies from West Side senior centers launched the Doctors Project at a Channel 13 phone bank and were featured in a documentary on elderly activism aired by the station. By 1976 the project accumulated information about six hundred doctors, but after facing legal obstacles to publishing the results, the Panthers joined the New York Public Interest Research Group (NYPIRG), where Gersmehl now worked, in backing a "Physicians Statement of Practice" bill to make public each New York State–licensed M.D.'s fee schedule, hospital affiliation, and willingness to accept Medicare and Medicaid patients. Although six New York Panthers lobbied in Albany, and two dozen senior citizen, women's, labor, nurses', and religious groups supported it, the bill died in 1979.

The health care issue that produced the most Gray Panther recruits, old or young, was nursing homes. At the November 1974 organizing conference Elma Griesel discussed the advocacy manual she and Linda Horn were writing. This inspired Ann Wyatt, a social worker in her twenties, and other network members, including Peggy and Jim Coffey, to begin a Gray Panther nursing home action group. Their first activity was a meeting about governance issues with residents of the Isabella Nursing Home in Manhattan. Quickly the group swelled to two dozen and scheduled Saturday meetings with invited speakers. They began Project RE-MEMBER, which trained volunteers who visited nursing home residents newly transferred from the dozen New York City facilities closed for safety reasons by the state health department. Project members advised state officials about procedures to reduce deleterious health outcomes after relocation and met with administrators of the Village Nursing Home in lower Manhattan about initiating a volunteer visiting program. As co-chair Wyatt put it, "We feel strongly that the best antidote to the sort of crippling isolation which encourages poor patient care is active community participation in the life of nursing homes."[28] The action group moved into free office space at the Judson Memorial Church on East 62nd Street and merged their efforts with the New York City Medical Committee on Human Rights (MCHR) geriatric committee.

In 1975 Gray Panthers Wyatt and Pat LaMariana attended the founding meeting of Griesel's National Citizens Coalition for Nursing Home Reform in Washington, D.C. With their Panther action group's co-chair Irv Wiesenfeld, a former nursing home administrator and MCHR member, and the Coffeys, they lobbied successfully in Albany for legislation to correct the nursing home financial scandals and patient abuses detailed by John Hess in the *New York Times*.[29] Then just as the Panthers' visiting program at the Village Nursing Home was about to begin, the state health department ordered the home to reduce overcrowding by transferring one hundred residents to other facilities. Relocations did not comply with state regulations and the Panthers asked Legal Services for the Elderly Poor to sue to halt them. At this point the home's owner announced he would close it. Wyatt helped organize the Ad Hoc Committee to Save the Village Nursing Home, which over the next two years raised $275,000 to purchase the six-story brick residential facility.

In 1976 Wyatt launched Community Action and Resources for the Elderly, a foundation-funded nursing home watchdog group. On the day New York's most notorious nursing home owner, Bernard Bergman, received a lenient one-year prison sentence, Wyatt led a courthouse rally of one hundred Gray Panther and other protesters. "Abuses and neglect have been and continue to be a part of the pattern of nursing home 'care,' " she stated, but "neither money fines nor jail can atone for the crimes committed against our elderly and disabled."[30] The following year Wyatt became an administrator at the now not-for-profit Village Nursing Home. (She later worked for the New York City Health and Hospitals Corporation as associate director of the Office of Long Term Care, and as director of care management at Independence Care System, an agency providing home health care for people with disabilities.)

In 1975 Sylvia Wexler moved Gray Panther headquarters from the Ethical Culture Society to a free office at the Jewish Guild for the Blind on West 65th Street. Here volunteer network members answered the telephone, mailed the newsletter, and processed annual dues introduced in 1975. In 1978 network meetings were shifted to West Park Presbyterian Church on West 86th Street. Weekly meetings were held from 3:30 to 6 p.m., with a guest speaker or task force report following network business.

During 1979 Wexler devoted herself to her terminally ill husband and agreed, reluctantly, to serve another term as convener. She died in March 1980 (her husband died six days later). The network newsletter memorialized her "tenacity" and "ability to motivate people to work above and beyond their own desire."[31] Co-conveners Estelle Rib and Stella Murphy, who staffed the network office weekdays from noon to three o'clock (and continued to through 1998), filled in for the rest of the year.

Meeting the New York Gray Panthers

1980 was a presidential election year. A day before the Democrats met to renominate Jimmy Carter, eight female Gray Panthers led by Rib and Murphy joined a "People's Alternative" march to Madison Square Garden in Manhattan, site of the Democratic convention. Here Maggie stirred the crowd with a speech and "Put People First" chant, and the Panthers debuted a forty-inch-wide gray-on-yellow "New York Gray Panthers" banner. Later that month the banner reappeared when New York Panthers participated with Asian Women United, the National Coalition of Puerto Rican Women, New York Women against Rape, NOW, and writer Gloria Steinem in a women's rights march down Fifth Avenue. (The banner was still in use in 2008.)

I attended my first New York Gray Panther meeting in August 1980, in between these two marches. I introduced myself as a former Berkeley Gray Panther, though I doubt anyone saw me as more than another one-time visitor. Since returning to Queens College in 1978 I had spoken to academic audiences about my experiences at the Over 60 Clinic.[32] Now that I was launching a "Patterns of Aging" class I thought I should attend a local Gray Panther meeting before teaching about the movement.

The two dozen network members at my first meeting were friendly, and more so when I returned in September. I immediately felt I was back in the organizational world I had belonged to in Berkeley. Unlike Berkeley, however, there was no "Youth in Action" to complement "Age." Aside from me, then thirty-six, all were older people. Members often mentioned "Glen" Gersmehl, still working at NYPIRG, but after Wexler's death he attended no meetings before moving to California in 1981. Jane Wholey, Anne Wyatt, and other young Panthers had departed years earlier. That fall I attended network meetings, including one where Lydia Bragger spoke about media portrayals of older persons. I joined members at a Tenants Unity Day rally in support of state housing legislation, an evening network forum with health care advocate Judy Wessler, and a meeting of the National Steering Committee in New York, where Lani and I reconnected with Berkeley friends Lillian Rabinowitz and Leslie Kwass. We also helped distribute flyers for a New York Gray Panther evening talk by Tish Sommers, founder of the Older Women's League and our houseguest while in the city for the NSC meeting.

At the end of 1980 Lillian Sarno, seventy-one, was elected convener of the New York Gray Panthers. Over the next two decades she would be the network's leader, serving several times as convener, and its principal voice at city council hearings, on radio programs, and in college classes and other venues. With a law degree earned in 1931 and, after raising two sons, a masters in social work in 1960, Sarno had been a lawyer and a mental health center supervisor and had been active in PTA, Jewish women's, and pro-choice organizations. After joining the Panthers in 1976 she was co-leader of the speakers bureau and coordinator for women's issues. In 1979 she represented the Gray Panthers at a march to St. Patrick's Cathedral on Fifth Avenue, where Religious Leaders for Free Choice demanded dialogue with the Church on women's reproductive rights. When the Right-to-Life party achieved New York State ballot status in 1980, pro-choice supporters began annual Albany lobbying conferences to support continued Medicaid funding of abortions. Sarno organized a New York Gray Panther delegation to attend, and in 1982 I joined her and five other Panthers.

Sarno frequently insisted, "We don't consider ourselves a senior organization. We fight on issues that are important to all people."[33] Highly intelligent and quick to laugh, she followed city, state, and national politics closely and attracted a core group of active members. Among them, Sudie George, retired from the publishing industry, edited the bimonthly *Network Report* newsletter from 1978 to the mid 1990s. She joined the Gray Panthers as a member of the Media Watch and helped Lydia Bragger organize its 1981 conference where Maggie spoke. George also edited a 1983 Gray Panther guide for monitoring ageist media coverage. Doris Berk,[34] a former teacher and the network's recording secretary, focused on senior citizen housing and social services. She was active with West Side Seniors for Action in pressing the city's Department for the Aging to create a West Side "One-Stop Center" for income, housing, health care, and transportation benefits, opened in 1981. Retired science teacher Mildred Sklar was a member of the Gray Panther UN delegation before becoming chair of the network's health task force in 1980. She organized a campaign for the Dellums national health service bill, with presentations to senior centers and community groups.

Convener Sarno lived one block from the Gray Panther office, where she regularly met other active female Panthers. They went out together for coffee, dinner at a Chinese restaurant after meetings, or theater or classical music performances. Although several like Sarno were widows, their Gray Panther friendships were based in lifelong political commitments rather than a search for companionship.[35]

Gray Panther Males

And then there were the men. Occasionally I visited the Gray Panther office or joined a coffee or dinner group, but my primary attachment to the network was the bimonthly afternoon meeting. There the half-dozen men, most members of the network "economy task force," were more devoted to talk than to action. When Ronald Reagan's election in 1980 heightened concern, the male Panthers responded with wordy resolutions against "the total Reagan program" and attacks on convener Sarno for using meeting time to announce bills to oppose or locations of protest activities. They reflected the gap Maggie noted more broadly in the Gray Panther movement between "the women's movement . . . impact [with] more consensus [and] egalitarian leadership" and the "Old Left . . . kind of vigorous, male leadership."[36] Tish Sommers observed the same contrasts at Gray Panther conventions: "The men talk on and on, but the prime movers were overwhelmingly the women."[37] In the New York network this was about to change.

During the 1970s New York Panthers had opposed proposals by Gerald Ford and Jimmy Carter to cut Social Security benefits. To meet any funding shortfall, they advocated raising the upper limit on earnings subject to the payroll tax or using general revenues. Immediately after Reagan's inauguration in 1981 the network sponsored an evening forum, "Social Security under Fire," featuring James Durkin, sixty-nine, a retired actuary long involved in political causes and a new Gray Panther member. Closely following events in Washington, he outlined Reagan's Social Security proposals: increasing the age for full retirement benefits from sixty-five to sixty-eight; further lowering benefits for workers retiring early at age sixty-two; reducing the annual cost of living increase; eliminating the monthly $122 minimum benefit received mainly by poor women; and canceling survivor benefits for children of deceased workers attending college between ages eighteen and twenty-two.[38]

Durkin became the New York Gray Panther delegate to the city chapter of Save Our Security (SOS), a national coalition that had been formed in 1979 by the AFL-CIO to fight Carter's proposed cuts. During 1981 he spoke about Social Security at Gray Panther meetings in Queens, Brooklyn, Greenwich Village, the Bronx, and at other venues. He represented the Panthers at meetings with New York City members of Congress and joined network members in letter writing to public officials and at protest rallies. He was the only older male Gray Panther, moreover, to join eight female members and me for an evening Coalition for the Homeless leafleting effort at Macy's department store in December 1981. I was fond of Jim Durkin and still recall the dim sum lunch we shared in Chinatown after a demonstration against the Reagan cuts. His passing in 1982 was the first death of an older Gray Panther friend I experienced.

During 1981 New York Gray Panthers traveled to Washington, D.C., to march against U.S. intervention in El Salvador and joined a rally at the New York Public Library to mark the twelve months remaining for ratification of the Equal Rights Amendment, a goal not reached. In September more than twenty New York Panthers returned to Washington for the AFL-CIO–led "Solidarity Day" protest of Reagan's Social Security and budget cuts, his military buildup, and his firing of 11,000 air traffic controllers. I captained a Solidarity Day bus provided by the Machinists Union carrying forty Panthers and friends. We departed at six in the morning and returned at midnight but heard none of the speakers because the public address system designed for 100,000 was insufficient to reach the 400,000 who arrived. The racially diverse crowd included more white male union members than any 1960s or 1970s demonstration I recalled. Among the political messages of the day was one Caribbean contingent's chant that has remained stuck in my head ever since: "Reagan you mess up America. Reagan you mess up America. Everywhere you go, everybody say, Reagan you mess up America."

On the New York City front during 1981, Gray Panthers participated in a speakout on transit issues organized by NYPIRG's Straphangers Campaign, as well as demonstrations for affordable housing and against tax giveaways to developers at Donald Trump's Hyatt Regency Hotel, Harry Helmsley's Palace Hotel, and Mayor Edward Koch's rent-controlled apartment. I advanced "the case against Koch," who faced reelection, in *Network Report*. During his first term the city's one million elderly residents, a quarter of whom lived on $4,000 or less a year, experienced sharply increasing rents, even with rent control or stabilization. Despite the city's budget surplus, police numbers fell by a third and muggings and robberies of elderly victims rose. Ambulance response times lengthened by ten minutes after twenty-five hospitals throughout New York were closed. "Planned shrinkage" of services to low-income residents—designed to make them leave the city—was complemented by "wealthfare"—hundreds of millions in unnecessary property tax abatements awarded to the rich.[39] Successfully fending off a primary challenge from state assemblymember Frank Barbaro, whom several Gray Panthers worked for as volunteers, Koch was reelected,

During the summer of 1981 Mildred Sklar and other health committee members manned a table with national health service brochures at a busy West Side commercial intersection on Friday afternoons, and Lillian Sarno and Sudie George recorded editorials on Reagan's budget and Social Security cuts for municipal radio station WNYC's "Senior Edition." In the fall new housing and peace task forces were started and the network mailing list, mostly financial supporters, stood at 320. At the end of 1981 Sarno was reelected convener and shifted meetings to the Jewish Association for Services for the Aged building on West 68th Street, near the network office. A dozen New York Panthers attended the national Gray Panther convention in December and joined Maggie in front of the White House to protest the stifling of dissent at the ongoing White House Conference on Aging. I was elected to the National Steering Committee and my Gray Panther activities now extended to the six other Panther groups meeting in New York City.

More New York Networks

After hearing Maggie Kuhn in 1973, Brooklyn Heights residents Anne Cohen and Ruth Rafael found their way to a New York Gray Panthers meeting and soon were speaking on issues in their borough as the Brooklyn Division of the Gray Panthers. In 1974 they cosponsored a health care forum with borough-wide groups and began a successful campaign to prevent a health center used by Brooklyn Heights residents from moving. They fought the loss of their neighborhood's residential hotels, which provided affordable housing to many low-income elderly renters. Both in their sixties, Cohen and Rafael testified at public hearings, distributed leaflets and fact sheets, spoke on radio programs, badgered elected officials, and showed films and circulated petitions at Brooklyn colleges, libraries, and Democratic clubs. Their advocacy on health care, housing, and transportation garnered attention in the Brooklyn press, and Cohen received an award from the borough's National Organization for Women chapter.

The pair participated in the Manhattan network's activities and at Gray Panther conventions and regional meetings. In 1979 their efforts were augmented for a year by Shel Horowitz, a young VISTA volunteer assigned to the Brooklyn Gray Panthers under a grant to NYPIRG administered by Glen Gersmehl. A newsletter was launched before Horowitz departed and weekly meetings begun at Generations, a Downtown Brooklyn senior center. Cohen and Rafael were joined by a handful of active compatriots, including retired social worker Maggie Bennett, convener of the Brooklyn network during the early 1980s. The Brooklyn Panthers remained primarily roving advocates who brought Gray Panther voices and petitions to borough events and to their circuit of six Brooklyn senior centers. Meetings at Generations ended in 1983 but Cohen and Rafael continued Panther activities on their own.

A third New York City network, the Gray Panthers of Queens, was organized in 1977 by Evelyn Neleson, a first-grade teacher retired after thirty-five years in the city school system. "I was not looking to be put on the shelf . . . I felt that I had to join the struggle to make this a better world."[40] With help from New York Gray Panthers—Gersmehl was an early speaker—the new network began nighttime meetings at the Free Synagogue of Flushing, a site convenient to nearby apartment dwellers as well as drivers from Fresh Meadows where Neleson lived, Bayside, and other Queens neighborhoods. The members were mainly middle-class New Yorkers who had moved to Queens after World War II. Several had participated in housing and school struggles in the 1950s and 1960s[41] or in professional and peace organizations. Neleson kept members busy with letter or postcard writing at each meeting and visits with Queens' four members of Congress to press for the Dellums National Health Service bill and to protest Social Security cuts.

I attended my first Queens Gray Panther meeting in November 1980. Neleson spoke to my Queens College "Patterns of Aging" class a few weeks later. Our friendship grew as we worked on arrangements for Maggie's visit to the college. In 1981 I spoke to the Queens Panthers on housing issues and returned in 1982 to report on national Gray Panther matters and in 1984 as panelist at a Medicare forum. Neleson's other Queens College link was Samona Sheppard, a professor of health and physical education in her sixties[42] who in 1981 launched a lecture program for senior citizens utilizing Queens College professors. Queens Gray Panthers attended and served on its advisory panel. Neleson recruited network meeting speakers from the college faculty and NYPIRG chapter and helped bring hundreds of borough elders to forums at Queens College preceding the 1981 White House Conference on Aging and to celebrate Social Security's fiftieth anniversary in 1985.

The Queens Panthers began as a group of eight women, but by the early 1980s only Neleson was left. While the network's membership remained primarily female, she relied upon a core of older male active members (known as "the minyan"). They included Neleson's co-convener for six years, Arthur Cohn, a retired CIO union organizer and Lower East Side settlement house director, who joined her on visits to elected officials and speaking engagements. Bill Lievow, a founder of HIP, a health maintenance organization serving New York City public employees, was health committee chair; Al Eisenberg, a former mechanical engineer, Social Security chair; and Sheldon Dressler, retired from the printing business, peace committee chair. Jesse Stechel and his wife Thelma edited the monthly newsletter. There were few young Queens Panthers, and on a visit to California the Stechels were surprised by the "large number of young people aged 35 or less" in the San Francisco Panther network.[43] Andy Koski, another of Gersmehl's VISTA cohort, worked with Neleson during 1979. In the early 1980s two younger active members joined. Harvey Baylis, thirty-nine, a musician, testified for the Panthers and wrote letters on energy and environmental issues. Susan Meswick, thirty, an applied medical anthropologist at St. John's University in Queens, became steering committee secretary. When she had her first child, her committee compatriots sent a card reading, "Welcome to the Generation Gap—It's in your lap." To their delight she brought her baby to committee meetings. Meswick also joined Maggie on a panel at an International Association of Gerontology meeting in 1985.

As the Queens network grew, Panther activism and media exposure expanded. In 1981–82 Dressler and seven female peace committee members collected hundreds of signatures in Queens supermarkets and parks supporting a nuclear weapons freeze by the United States and the USSR. With other borough groups they presented five thousand petition signatures to Republican representative John LeBoutillier, who agreed to cosponsor the freeze resolution.[44] In 1983 several dozen Queens Gray Panthers, NYPIRG students, and allies picketed the Flushing Social Security office to protest the Reagan administration's increased out-of-pocket Medicare costs. Coordinated by Eisenberg and Meswick, the action was featured in the national Gray Panther newspaper *Network*.[45] In 1984 the Panthers and the Queens Interagency Council on Aging sponsored a Medicare forum attended by five hundred. Sitting on the dais next to borough president Donald Manes, I (at Neleson's request) presented the Gray Panther case for a national health service.

An indefatigable letter writer, Neleson contributed fact-filled arguments about elderly poverty and rising health care costs to the letter sections of the *New York Times* and *Newsday*.[46] She and Eisenberg articulated Gray Panther views on Channel 9 television's *Straight Talk* and on the CBS morning news program Neleson criticized Colorado governor Richard Lamm's contention that old people had a "duty to die" in order to reduce entitlement outlays. In 1985 the Queens Panthers filed complaints with the state attorney general and city Human Rights Commission about "ghoulish" full-page newspaper ads promoting sales of occupied cooperative apartments by listing their elderly tenants' ages. After a press conference and television and newspaper coverage featuring Neleson, the ads were dropped.[47]

Loss of active members during the 1980s became a problem, and Neleson increasingly carried the burden of network management tasks. Heart attacks sidelined two committee chairs and some Panthers working on housing or peace moved to other Queens groups focused on those issues. Attendance at network meetings stood at about three dozen in 1982 (slightly more than New York Gray Panther meetings) and paid membership at 105, with another ninety newsletters mailed to Queens organizations and allies. Meetings were switched to afternoons in 1983 in hopes of building participation.

Six more networks started in New York City during 1980–82, three with assistance from the New York Gray Panthers. In 1980 Heidi Vardeman-Hilf, a young minister at the Jan Hus Presbyterian Church on East 74th Street in Manhattan, organized the "Gray Panthers, East Side" to involve older persons in the Nuclear Freeze campaign. (The New York Gray Panthers now added "West Side" to their name.) In 1983 Marie Maher, sixty-three, became convener. Resourceful and energetic—she had just returned from a six-month backpack trip around the world—Maher focused on housing, alerting her members and other Panther networks to tenant legislation and demonstrations. In 1984 she and four East Side Panthers worked with Hunter College NYPIRG students to compile a booklet listing East Side physicians who accepted "Medicare Assignment"—those willing to take Medicare reimbursement for 80 percent of federally determined "reasonable charges" and bill patients for no more than the remaining 20 percent. East Side Panthers also joined Hunter students in registering voters and lobbying in Albany on transportation issues. In 1985 convener Glenn Miller switched meetings to afternoons and moved to the Community Church on East 35th Street, with membership then at two dozen.

In 1981 New York Gray Panther Lucy Robins, a retired school secretary, started a Bronx network meeting at a Riverdale church. Robins and other Bronx Panthers lobbied their members of Congress on Social Security and health care issues, but membership remained small and Robins disbanded in 1983. She returned to the West Side network where she served as treasurer through the 1990s. More successfully, several New York Panthers living in lower Manhattan, including veteran Peggy Coffey, helped launch the Gray Panthers of Greenwich Village at the Jefferson Market Library on West 10th Street. Nan Pendrell, seventy-six, a politically outspoken forty-year Village resident, was the group's convener. The 1981 meeting where I was guest speaker and a dozen members signed a national "Network Affiliation" form was also a reunion for Pendrell and me. We had met in 1965 in a Columbia University Portuguese class preceding her year-long study of a squatter settlement and my summer fieldwork in Bahia, Brazil. After a career in advertising, she enrolled at Columbia at age fifty, graduated Phi Beta Kappa, and completed an anthropology Ph.D. in 1967. In the 1980s she spent several months each year at the University of Michigan campus in Flint where she had taught and she continued an oral history project with automobile workers. With an older membership that quickly grew to fifty, the Village Panthers held monthly afternoon meetings with a speaker or film, wrote letters, participated in demonstrations with other New York City networks, and vented antagonism to Reagan administration policies. Local Village area health care facilities and transportation service were also their concern. Pendrell died in 1985; with anthropologist Eleanor Leacock I spoke at a gathering in her memory at the Village Vanguard jazz club.

Three more networks began in the borough of Queens. Mollie Katz, a frail but determined Maggie Kuhn admirer, initiated afternoon meetings at the Forest Hills Library in 1981. (Neleson's network renamed itself the Gray Panthers of Central Queens.) Katz recruited speakers and her elderly members wrote letters at meetings. Though membership rose to fifty by 1984 few participated in other actions. In September 1982 a group of Queens College students interested in advocacy on aging issues asked me to be faculty advisor. I suggested they form a Gray Panther network, explaining that the Panthers were intergenerational. The network lasted three semesters under conveners Kenn Wishnick and Debbie Hague, both in their early twenties, and involved a score of young and middle-aged students and college employees. Their activities included a clothing drive for a homeless shelter, voter registration, screenings of *Maggie Kuhn: Wrinkled Radical* and films on health care and nuclear disarmament, and forums with Central Queens Social Security chair Al Eisenberg and pollster Doug Schoen (years later a consultant to Bill Clinton). The fourth Queens network, the Gray Panthers of Broad Channel, an island community in Jamaica Bay, lasted only a year. Organized in 1982 to assist older working-class bungalow owners purchase their plots from the city, the eleven members held only a few meetings on other topics before folding.

The Gray Panthers of New York City

As newly elected NSC member representing New York, I convened a gathering of the city's network leaders in February 1982 at the City University of New York Graduate Center on 42nd Street near Fifth Avenue. I had close ties to the West Side and Central Queens networks, the largest groups, and had met members of the other networks as a guest speaker on housing issues during 1981. In April twenty-three Panther leaders from seven networks agreed to create a citywide umbrella group, the Gray Panthers of New York City. I was elected convener, Evelyn Neleson of Central Queens co-convener, and West Side member Sudie George secretary. The group decided to meet four times a year, create stationery listing all city networks, adopt bylaws, and publish a joint newsletter, *The City Panther*, under George's editorship. Later the new Queens College and Broad Channel groups joined, bringing the network total to nine. Over the next five years I chaired twenty-eight citywide meetings with an average of seventeen Panthers attending, including occasional guests from Westchester and Long Island networks and the Philadelphia national office. More than sixty Gray Panthers participated in the meetings, and eighteen issues of *The City Panther* were mailed to combined membership lists of more than five hundred.

A citywide Gray Panther peace task force began meeting monthly at the Jan Hus Presbyterian Church. Led by West Side member Raya Glinert, a warm and welcoming person able to charm anyone, it enlisted upward of two dozen Panthers from Manhattan, Bronx, Brooklyn, and Queens groups. Sheldon Dressler of Central Queens supplied a steady stream of clippings, brochures, and fact sheets on the Reagan military buildup and nuclear disarmament issues while Glinert kept the focus on action: street tabling and leafleting to publicize the United Nations Special Session on Disarmament beginning on June 12, 1982, and the march and rally in Central Park that day planned by a coalition of hundreds of organizations including Physicians for Social Responsibility, the Riverside Church Disarmament Program, SANE, Women's International League for Peace and Freedom, the United Automobile Workers, and Friends of the Earth.

In April 1982 the Gray Panthers of New York City took its first collective action: an endorsement of city councilmember Miriam Friedlander's resolution proclaiming June 12 "Peace Day in New York City" and calling on the United States and the Soviet Union to negotiate a mutual freeze on the testing, production, and deployment of nuclear weapons. Evelyn Neleson testified for the Panther networks at a council hearing and I sent letters from the citywide alliance to all forty-one councilmembers urging support. (The resolution passed thirty-one to ten.) Glinert's task force presented Nuclear Freeze petitions to New York's senators, Daniel Patrick Moynihan and Alfonse D'Amato; joined a Children's March for Peace in May; and sold Gray Panther and June 12 rally buttons, posters, and T-shirts. On the day of the march scores of New York Panthers assembled at the CUNY Graduate Center to enter the march to the United Nations and Central Park together. We were joined by Panthers from a dozen states and Washington, D.C., many of whom were housed by New York peace task force members. In all, more than two hundred Gray Panthers marched, probably the movement's largest-ever collective public action (Maggie did not attend). Overall the June 12 rally drew between five hundred thousand and one million people, surpassing huge disarmament demonstrations in Bonn, Amsterdam, and Rome that followed the 1979 NATO decision to deploy ground-based nuclear missiles in Europe.[48]

During October 1982 the citywide Panther peace task force worked with a coalition of one hundred groups to distribute blue lapel ribbons, signifying "Stop the Arms Race," to be worn through the November national election. On October 24, the day of the New York Marathon, Gray Panthers distributed blue ribbons among spectators at the 59th Street Bridge exit where runners, many wearing the ribbons, ended the race in Manhattan. In March 1983 New York peace task force members traveled to Washington, D.C., to join a national day of citizen lobbying for the freeze resolution, now endorsed by two hundred members of the House of Representatives.

Although Social Security cuts proposed by the Reagan administration had been defeated in Congress during 1981, concern among Gray Panthers in New York, most of whom depended upon Social Security, continued in 1982. A looming gap between lower-than-projected payroll tax receipts (attributable to high unemployment and stagnant wages), and higher-than-projected COLA (cost of living adjustment) increases due to double-digit inflation meant a temporary shortfall would arrive by mid-decade. (With the full baby boom generation in the workforce, by 1990 surpluses were projected to begin accumulating again for a period of twenty-five years.) To fill the late-1980s gap and maintain full benefits, Democrats and the national Save Our Security (SOS) coalition advocated borrowing from the Medicare and Social Security disability trust fund surpluses, expediting implementation of already-approved payroll tax increases and, if needed, allocating general revenues. Republicans favored benefit cuts, including raising the retirement age from sixty-five to sixty-eight. Late in 1981 President Reagan appointed the National Commission on Social Security Reform, chaired by economist Alan Greenspan, to report at the end of 1982.

In March 1982 fifteen New York Gray Panthers joined a write-in to protest future benefit cuts sponsored by Seniors for Adequate Social Security (SASS). In October I attended a SASS workshop at which Bill Arnone of SOS outlined the likely recommendations of the Greenspan Commission, due to report in two months. I circulated notes from the meeting to all network conveners and invited them to send representatives to the November SOS meeting. Ten Panthers from seven networks attended, and Al Eisenberg of Central Queens agreed to chair a citywide Gray Panther Social Security task force to work with SASS and SOS.

In January 1983 the Greenspan Commission submitted a menu of revenue infusions and benefit cuts to close the shortfall: accelerate the scheduled payroll tax increases, raise Social Security taxes on the self-employed, bring new federal and nonprofit employees into the system, delay COLA increases, and tax half the benefits received by middle- and high-income earners. It suggested modest benefit enhancements for widows and divorced women and for workers who postponed retirement for up to five years after age sixty-five. House Democrats, including Thomas "Tip" O'Neill and Claude Pepper, and President Reagan endorsed the agreement. Days later Eisenberg and Brooklyn Panther Sylvia Kahn traveled to a hastily called national Gray Panther Executive Committee meeting in Philadelphia to register New York City Panther opposition to the commission's report, in particular the COLA delay and taxation of benefits. Before the recommendations came to a congressional vote, however, two items were added: an annual increase in the wage amount subject to the payroll tax (in 1983 it was $35,700, with earnings above this cap untaxed), and a rise in the retirement age to sixty-seven by 2027. SOS, which supported the Greenspan compromise package, objected to the age increase and urged opposition. In March 1983 the legislation passed with Democratic and Republican majorities in both the Senate and the House and was signed by President Reagan.

During 1982 the New York Gray Panthers' health task force chaired by Mildred Sklar and Lani Sanjek campaigned for the Dellums bill with teams of three Panthers presenting a Coalition for a National Health Service slide show with follow-up discussion to sixty union retiree, senior center, and community groups in three boroughs. In the fall the new citywide health task force and SASS cosponsored "The War on Medicare and Medicaid," a forum with letter writing by an audience of eighty to protest Reagan administration health care cuts. Under co-chairs Bill Lievow of Central Queens and Eleanor Smith of Greenwich Village, a retired librarian, the health task force added Medicare Assignment to its agenda, invited Ann Wyatt of the Village Nursing Home to speak about long-term care, and joined the Nursing Home Community Coalition of New York State, an affiliate of Elma Griesel's national advocacy group.

A Celebration

In April 1983 more than two hundred Panthers and friends celebrated the tenth anniversary of the New York Gray Panthers at the CUNY Graduate Center auditorium. Maggie, hospitalized with pneumonia for two weeks in March and unable to attend, sent a message congratulating the network for "a great decade of advocacy." A video about Maggie prepared for her 1981 Gimbel award in Philadelphia was shown, and guests signed a big "Get Well, Maggie" card. Shubert Frye added reminiscences of the Consultation days. Reverend Reuben Gums, who suggested the name "Gray Panthers" during a taxi ride with Maggie, retold the story adding the precise location, Sixth Avenue and 54th Street.[49] New York City councilmembers Miriam Friedlander and Ruth Messinger greeted the audience, and congressional representatives Ted Weiss of Manhattan and Joseph Addabo of Queens sent telegrams. As convener of the Gray Panthers of New York City and emcee, I introduced Gray Panther executive director Edith Giese and network coordinator Sherry Clearwater from Philadelphia, UN representative Sylvia Kleinman of New Jersey, and national Health Task Force chair Frances Klafter of Washington, D.C. I recognized the city's nine network conveners, the citywide task force chairs, and a few veteran New York Panthers who joined in 1972 or 1973, including Lydia Bragger. (Hope Bagger did not attend.)

The four guest speakers were from organizations that Panther peace, health, housing, and Social Security task forces worked with in coalitions. Reverend Robert Davidson of West Park Presbyterian Church, leader of the city's Nuclear Freeze campaign, recalled meeting Maggie in 1954 at a congressional lobbying effort where a House Un-American Activities Committee staffer inadvertently mentioned their secret file on her. He recounted a recent "office visit" by one thousand New Yorkers, including Gray Panthers, to freeze opponent Senator Alphonse D'Amato, during which they handed him 280,000 freeze petition signatures. Tony DiMarco of the Coalition for a National Health Service thanked the Panthers for their Dellums bill advocacy, noting they were "the most active organization on a national scale supporting a national health service." Jane Benedict, chair of the Metropolitan Council on Housing, a citywide tenant group, emphasized the importance of older people being "a bridge to young people" and remembering, "We're not nuts—the Reagans are, and the Kochs are. We are on the right side [in demanding affordable housing for] the poor and middle class." Max Manes of Seniors for Adequate Social Security, a retired hatters' union member, fired up the audience: "The most serious attack on Social Security is right now— to divide the young from the old, to discredit it with propaganda that it is going bankrupt, to frighten the people so they can cut benefits." The program closed with singer Robbie Wedeen's "Social Security Rag":

> With Social Security, I'm independent and free
> You know it's money I paid in when I was a maiden
> So when I grow old I could live unafraid.
> In this Reagan economy, don't balance the budget on me
> You know I paid as I went, now I need it for rent
> My Social Security.[50]

National Public Radio's *Morning Edition* covered the event and aired comments from Maggie and Mannes and from me: "The intergenerational relationships really hold us together. . . . And especially for us younger members—I'm thirty-eight—it gives us a sense . . . that you can continue your political and social feelings into your seventies, eighties. We don't really get that picture of old age from most of the rest of American culture."[51]

Housing Issues in New York

In 1980 New York Gray Panther convener Lillian Sarno asked me to chair a network task force—"Take housing," she suggested. During 1981 I underwent a grassroots education in housing issues by attending demonstrations, hearings, and conferences, reading activist and policy materials,[52] and following housing stories in the press. I consolidated what I was learning for articles in *Network Report* and talks at Panther network meetings, Representative Ted Weiss's annual senior citizen forum, the 1981 Gray Panther convention, and a National Tenants Union conference where I heard housing guru Cushing Dolbeare of the National Low-Income Housing Coalition and immediately subscribed to her newsletter. By the end of 1981 I represented the Gray Panthers in five city coalitions focused on tenant, tax and budget, displacement, disability, and homelessness issues.[53]

Two-thirds of New York's elderly population were residents of the city's 300,000 rent-controlled and 900,000 rent-stabilized apartments. Given an official "housing emergency" vacancy rate of less than 1 percent, older New Yorkers had stakes in these statutory limitations on arbitrary rent increases, as well as in protection from landlord surcharges for appliances and fuel cost spikes added to their rent bills in perpetuity. Since 1975 New York Gray Panthers had traveled to Albany each spring with the Metropolitan Council on Housing to lobby for pro-renter legislation. And they participated in fall Tenant Unity Day rallies—eighteen Panthers attended in 1981—sponsored by the Coalition against Rent-Increase Pass-Alongs (CARIP) comprising Met Council and other tenant groups. During 1981 I attended monthly CARIP meetings (where I met Jane Benedict) and with other Panthers joined Met Council demonstrations protesting Mayor Koch's pro-landlord policies and Senator D'Amato's bill to ban federal housing funds to localities with rent control.

In 1981 I was invited to Save Our City Campaign (SOCC) meetings where city councilmember Ruth Messinger briefed a dozen grassroots activists about New York's alphabet soup of real estate and commercial tax break programs—J-51, ICIB, 421(a)—which annually returned more than $100 million in public resources to the wealthy.[54] To dramatize this, SOCC organized a "Who are the Real Welfare Cheats?" forum followed by a picket line at Donald Trump's Grand Hyatt Hotel, which enjoyed an exemption from sales tax on construction materials and a twenty-year property tax reduction worth $165 million. At a meeting concerning tenanted buildings abandoned by landlords and now owned by the city, I was recruited to Mobilization against Displacement (MAD), a coterie of activists who organized a demonstration against tax breaks for landlord Harry Helmsley's upscale Palace Hotel, and a citywide conference titled "Urban Revitalization: Is It Possible Without Displacement?" MAD connected me to the New York State Tenants and Neighbors Coalition code enforcement committee, and Gray Panthers joined its wintertime demonstration at City Hall protesting landlord noncompliance with heat and hot water laws.

At one Met Council demonstration I met Anne Emerman, forty-four, chair of the New York City Coalition on Housing for People with Disabilities and a motorized wheelchair user.[55] At her coalition meetings I was educated about "accessibility" and "adaptability": sufficient door and hallway widths to accommodate wheelchairs, adequate turnaround space in kitchens and bathrooms, reinforced bathroom walls to install grab bars, and height-adjustable electricity outlets, sinks, and kitchen appliances.[56] She enlisted me to fight for an adaptability requirement in the New York State Building Construction Code, and as convener of the Gray Panthers of New York City I testified at a State Housing Division hearing:

We believe these changes are important for everyone when we consider development through the life cycle. . . . Disability may be lifelong, occur by accident at any age, result from slow or sudden workplace or environmental hazards, or arise with chronic health problems—arthritis, diabetes, stroke—in old age. . . . 36% of Americans age 65 to 74 have chronic health problems leading to physical limitations in carrying out the activities of daily life. For Americans age 75 and older, 53% have such physical incapacities. . . . Too many older people are now forced to leave their homes, their neighbors, their possessions, their community, and move to nursing homes or other long-term care facilities. The savings in vast Medicaid payments to nursing homes by helping to keep people in their own homes would benefit all.[57]

As a result of the coalition's efforts, in 1983 adaptability standards for new multi-unit residential buildings—costing only $440 per apartment—were added to the state code, and in 1987 to New York City's building code.

In 1981 the growing crisis of homeless Americans on city streets registered in numerous press accounts. New York Gray Panthers attended panels and forums, and convener Sarno spoke about solitary older women at risk of becoming homeless before the City Council Committee on the Status of Women. I testified in support of a assessment center for homeless adults at a West Side Community Board hearing where I cited city and state estimates of 36,000 homeless New Yorkers reported in *Private Lives/Public Spaces*, an ethnographic study of homeless persons then receiving considerable attention.[58] Its authors, Ellen Baxter and Kim Hopper, with attorney Robert Hayes and a network of shelter outreach workers, had organized the Coalition for the Homeless in 1980, and I began attending its monthly meetings. In 1981 New York Panthers joined the coalition in distributing leaflets and "Shelter the Homeless" buttons to holiday shoppers, and I traveled with coalition activists to plant 450 wooden crosses in Lafayette Park opposite the White House in commemoration of that number of outdoor deaths of homeless persons since 1980.

In 1982 I began monthly meetings of a citywide Gray Panther housing task force with ten members from four networks and occasional guests including Anne Emerman and Gray Panther national office staffer Rosalie Riechman. We focused on supporting activities of Met Council, the City Project (successor to SOCC), MAD, the Coalition on Housing for People with Disabilities, and the Coalition for the Homeless, as well as legislation endorsed by the National Low-Income Housing Coalition. Panthers continued to travel to Albany with Met Council during May to lobby for pro-tenant measures, and in 1983 we prepared a Gray Panther New York State Housing Agenda flyer to use in legislative office visits.

Homelessness and the Elderly Poor

In 1982 the Coalition for the Homeless invited me to participate in a briefing for Department of Heath and Human Services New York–area administrative staff. I reviewed national housing programs, pointing out that the largest was the entitlement to deduct property taxes and mortgage interest from federal income taxes. Providing homeowners an average subsidy of $5,500 in 1981 and claimed by 92 percent of taxpayers with incomes over $100,000, it totaled $30 billion—four times more than all federal housing programs for the poor (public housing, Section 8 rent subsidies, and Section 202 housing for the elderly and disabled). No federal funds were available for sheltering homeless persons, and the one bill providing a start died in Congress. In essence, most government housing assistance went to those needing it least, and none to those needing it most. My presentation was published by the coalition,[59] and I later joined its board of directors, serving through 1985.

When attendance at Gray Panther housing task force meetings fell in fall 1983, I shifted effort to writing *Crowded Out: Homelessness and the Elderly Poor in New York City*, a sixty-page report published by the Coalition for the Homeless and the Gray Panthers of New York City in 1984.[60] It began with the story of Dorothy Lykes, seventy-eight, who contacted the Gray Panther office in 1981. When I returned her call I learned her terminally ill husband was in the hospital, and she, also terminally ill with cancer, was home-bound, suffering from chronic diarrhea, and weighed only sixty-eight pounds. Unable to afford both hospital bills and property taxes on her husband's Social Security benefit and her Supplemental Security Income, she forfeited the home they owned and had lived in for thirty years, with the city then demanding $300 a month in rent. "Is the next step for me to move to Penn Station?" she asked. I connected her to Bronx Legal Services, and her story continued to haunt me.

Not homeless, but afraid she might become so, her case was emblematic of what faced New York City's quarter-million elderly poor, half with no adult children, who survived on annual incomes of $4,900 or less by scrimping on food, health care, and winter clothing. Those most "at risk" of becoming homeless were the physically frail over age seventy-five, usually with multiple chronic health problems and sometimes forgetful or confused. If homeowners, they confronted rising fuel, repair, and property tax expenses on limited incomes. If apartment dwellers, they faced relentless rent increases and feared landlord harassment and eviction to make room for more remunerative tenants. If residents of abandoned buildings, they faced hazardous surroundings and cold winters, even after the city became their landlord. If living in single room occupancy (SRO) hotels, they had watched the availability of such residences diminish by 90 percent since 1970 as tax breaks induced investors to convert them to luxury housing. If in city shelters, older persons feared theft and victimization by younger homeless adults and increasingly preferred the relative safety of public transportation concourses or the streets.

A majority of the elderly poor had lived in New York for thirty years or more and were "familiar with and know how to negotiate their way around their neighborhoods. As they . . . grow older and frailer and incomes are more limited, they . . . satisfy the bulk of their personal shopping and service needs within the ten block radius of their self-contained neighborhoods."[61] *Crowded Out* recommended more publicly funded housing for the elderly, greater utilization of senior citizen renter and homeowner financial safeguards, and expanded in-home services (meals, personal care, transportation, escorts, financial and legal counseling, repairs, accessibility renovations, family caregiver tax credits) for frail elders. Ideally, mobile geriatric teams in each of the city's fifty-nine community districts should coordinate outreach and case management to help older New Yorkers "age in place" and prevent unneeded nursing home institutionalization or homelessness.[62] *Crowded Out* also recommended experimental relocation services: "After children have left, or when they become widowed, many older persons find themselves with more housing space than they can use or afford. With few alternatives, the elderly find such 'overhousing' is a burden in terms of cost and maintenance. Community-based clearinghouse programs should be tested to see if they can effectively register such 'overhoused' elderly persons, develop local alternatives at lower monthly rent or maintenance costs, and promote home-sharing. Programs of this sort must guarantee registrants that they will not be forced to relocate, that alternative housing will be located within the same community, and that less space will not be more expensive."[63]

The day the report was released I was interviewed on Channel 4's *Live at Five with Gabe Pressman* and Channel 5's *10 O'Clock News*. Radio appearances followed on WNYC's *Senior Edition* and Lydia Bragger's WBAI program, and the report was included in the House Select Committee on Aging's volume *Homeless Older Americans*. I was invited to speak to the staffs of social service programs in Manhattan and Queens, students at City College's Sophie Davis medical school, and the New York City chapter of the National Association of Social Workers. In 1984 and 1985 the Gray Panthers of New York City sent letters to state elected officials supporting SSI and welfare grant increases, elderly eviction protection, and a moratorium on SRO conversions.

Panther Activism Peaks

During 1983–85 Gray Panther activity in New York reached its high water mark. In their largest public action ever, fifty New York Panthers picketed the state Democratic Party headquarters in Manhattan on the opening day of the 1984 Democratic National Convention held in San Francisco. Representing three generations and joined by West Side Peace Action and NYPIRG students, the noontime demonstrators proclaimed their election year priorities: "Freeze All Nuclear Weapons," "No Star Wars System," "No Military Involvement in Central America." Throughout 1984 a dozen Gray Panthers participated at sidewalk tables, government agency offices, Hunter College, and other sites in a New York voter registration campaign organized by academic activists Frances Fox Piven and Richard Cloward.[64] And also in 1984 the grievance that led Maggie Kuhn to meet Hope Bagger in 1972 was rectified when Governor Mario Cuomo signed legislation ending mandatory retirement for most New York State public- and private-sector workers.[65]

In 1983 thirty Panthers gathered in Dag Hammarskjold Plaza, opposite the United Nations, for a vigil against basing U.S. nuclear missiles in Europe, and several returned to join a hastily assembled crowd of ten thousand, including many Caribbean New Yorkers, to protest President Reagan's invasion of Grenada.[66] Panther contingents traveled to Washington, D.C., for marches against intervention in Central America in 1983 and for "Peace, Jobs and Justice" in 1985 where they met Gray Panthers from nine states at a pre-rally breakfast hosted by the Metropolitan Washington network. In 1983 the peace task force began tabling on the West Side with voter pledge cards supporting the Nuclear Freeze and petitions opposing a Cruise missile submarine base in New York harbor. In 1984 chairperson Raya Glinert testified against this nuclear "homeport" before the city council, and members leafleted on peace issues at Lincoln Center and the Metropolitan Museum of Art. During 1985 two dozen Panthers joined a candlelight vigil at the United Nations to mark the opening of arms reduction talks between the United States and the USSR; thirty-five Panthers arrived at the South African embassy to join daily protests against apartheid; and task force members participated in monthly "Freeze Friday" human chains extending for several blocks along Broadway.

At 1983 state hearings health task force cochairs Bill Lievow, Eleanor Smith, and Mildred Sklar supported a moratorium on publicly financed hospital construction in New York State in order to highlight insufficient funding for primary care, especially in poor neighborhoods. Using leaflets prepared by Lani Sanjek and national Health Task Force chair Frances Klafter, the health and Social Security task forces organized simultaneous demonstrations in Queens and Manhattan to protest increased hospital, home health, and doctor visit costs to Medicare beneficiaries. In 1984 New York Panthers participated in large election-year demonstrations in Manhattan, Brooklyn, and Queens protesting Medicare cuts and joined a coalition led by New York StateWide Senior Action Council to press for a prescription drug program for low-income elders, a victory achieved with passage of Elderly Pharmaceutical Insurance Coverage (EPIC) legislation two years later.[67] The health task force hosted speakers on hospice and home health care, and member Lani Sanjek coordinated a fund-raising effort by sixty Panthers to send a $650 emergency medical kit to Nicaragua, then under attack by U.S.-backed contras.

In 1983 Representative Ron Dellums reintroduced his National Health Service bill with sixteen cosponsors, mainly fellow Congressional Black Caucus members but including four white New York City representatives whom Queens and Brooklyn Gray Panthers lobbied to sign on. In 1984 Brooklyn Panther Mary Solomon secured another cosponsor when she presented Representative Charles Schumer a petition with one thousand in support of the Dellums bill. That fall I spoke in favor of a national health service at a Queens Interagency Council on the Aging forum attended by 500. Unlike health *insurance,* I emphasized, a national health *service* would provide health education and preventive screening, reduce paperwork and advertising costs, and redirect health industry profits toward improving health outcomes—in which the United States ranked twelfth internationally in infant mortality and fifteenth in life expectancy.[68] In December 1984 the citywide Gray Panther health task force held a public forum at Fordham University, "Finding Your Way through the Medical Jungle," endorsed by twenty-five health and senior citizen organizations and attended by 350. To dramatize that "the law of the jungle applies to health care in America," Gray Panther ushers wore attention-grabbing pith helmets, later turning them over to receive donations.[69] Keynote speaker Dr. Victor Sidel, president of the American Public Health Association and a Dellums bill supporter, described health care as "a human right" in England and Sweden and contrasted the United States, where thirty-four million Americans had no health coverage. Speakers on Medicare, Medicaid, long-term care, HMOs, and the Canadian universal health system followed. A similar forum in 1985 organized by Gray Panther Solomon and the Brooklyn-wide Interagency Council on the Aging drew one thousand.

When Reagan proposed eliminating the following year's Social Security COLAs in 1985, the New York City networks mailed national Gray Panther "Don't Cut the COLA" postcards to all sixteen members of the city's congressional delegation. Meanwhile, Greenwich Village Panther Isabella Shapiro testified at a congressional hearing on the "notch penalty," a provision in 1977 legislation that reduced Social Security retirement benefits for persons, like her, born between 1917 and 1921. The COLA proposal was killed but "notch baby" legislation failed to pass. Also during 1985, Village network members Jim and Peggy Coffey represented the citywide Panthers in Concerned Citizens for Subway and Commuter Safety, a coalition of advocates for the visually impaired calling for safety gates between subway cars.[70] Finally, Gray Panthers worked that year in a campaign by the Joint Public Affairs Committee for Older Adults (JPAC) to create a City Council Committee on Aging, and several attended a City Hall reception to celebrate success.

In November 1985 seventy New York City and Westchester Gray Panthers gathered at Red Oak, a senior residence in Manhattan, to celebrate Maggie Kuhn's eightieth birthday, Social Security's fiftieth anniversary, and Medicare and Medicaid's twentieth. Two visiting Boston Panthers described their campaign to place a national health service referendum on the Massachusetts state ballot, and after everyone lit birthday cake candles, I spoke about Maggie's activist career preceding her first Consultation meeting in 1970.

Maggie Kuhn on the road in the 1970s. Photo: Temple University Libraries, Urban Archives, Philadelphia, Pa.

Gray Panther demonstration at the American Medical Association convention, Chicago, 1974. Photo: Temple University Libraries, Urban Archives, Philadelphia, Pa.

Maggie Kuhn at first national Gray Panther convention in Chicago, 1975. Photo: Temple University Libraries, Urban Archives, Philadelphia, Pa.

Gray Panther staff members Stanley Earley and Leslie Sussan, ca. 1972.
Photo: Temple University Libraries, Urban Archives, Philadelphia, Pa.

Studs Terkel interviewing Elma Griesel, Linda Horn, and Maggie Kuhn
for the 1975 documentary *Maggie Kuhn: Wrinkled Radical.* Photo: Temple
University Libraries, Urban Archives, Philadelphia, Pa.

Gray Panther executive director Karen Talbot and Maggie Kuhn, 1987.
Photo: Temple University Libraries, Urban Archives, Philadelphia, Pa.

National Steering Committee member Irv Riskin (left) and Washington, D.C., office director Frances Humphreys at Gray Panther Mid-America Conference, 1987. Photo: Temple University Libraries, Urban Archives, Philadelphia, Pa.

Austin, Texas, Gray Panther Charlotte Flynn and National Citizens Coalition for Nursing Home Reform executive director Elma Griesel Holder at Gray Panther convention in Chicago, 1988. Photo: Temple University Libraries, Urban Archives, Philadelphia, Pa.

Lillian Rabinowitz and Maggie Kuhn, Berkeley, California, 1979. Photo by Joe Guyon; Temple University Libraries, Urban Archives, Philadelphia, Pa.

Over 60 Health Clinic, 1978. Photo by Diane Morioka Owyang, author's collection.

Lillian Rabinowitz at her eightieth birthday celebration, Berkeley, California, 1991. Photo by Margot Smith.

Maggie Kuhn at Lillian Rabinowitz's eightieth birthday celebration, Berkeley, California, 1991. Photo by Margot Smith.

Convener Gerda Miller (third from left) with Berkeley Gray Panthers, 1995. Photo by Margot Smith.

Berkeley Gray Panther convener Margot Smith, 2004. Photo provided by Margot Smith.

Berkeley Gray Panther meeting, February 2007. At desk, members Charles Robinson and Henry Clarence (standing) and speaker Barbara Morita. Photo by Lani Sanjek, author's collection.

Roger and Lani Sanjek at Over 60 Health Center, February 2007. Photo by Marty Lynch, author's collection.

New York Gray Panther convener Sylvia Wexler (right) with network members and Bronx Borough President Robert Abrams, 1979. Photo from New York Gray Panther archives in author's custody.

New York Gray Panther (and later convener) Lillian Sarno (right) protesting Jimmy Carter's military policies, 1980. Photo from New York Gray Panther archives in author's custody.

New York Gray Panthers Charlotte Weinstein, Sudie George, Anne Cohen, Sallie Rattien, Fannie Krasnow, Estelle Rib, Mildred Sklar, Stella Murphy, and Bergen County, New Jersey, Panther Sylvia Kleinman at Democratic Party National Convention, 1980. Photo from New York Gray Panther archives in author's custody.

Healthcare advocate Judy Wessler, Central Queens Gray Panther convener Evelyn Neleson, Coalition for a National Health Service member Tony DiMarco, and Gray Panther national Health Task Force chairperson Frances Klafter, New York Gray Panthers tenth anniversary celebration, 1983. Photo by Lani Sanjek, author's collection.

Lillian Sarno, Roger Sanjek, and Stella Murphy at New York Gray Panther's thirtieth anniversary, 2004. Photo by Lani Sanjek, author's collection.

Convener Judy Lear (right of PEACE banner) with New York Gray Panthers Mike Texeira (second from left), Joan Davis (to the right of Lear), Shi-uho Lin (holding the Gray Panthers banner), Jim Collins, and Roger Sanjek and Granny Peace Brigade supporters, 2006. Photo from Judy Lear's collection.

Chapter 6
The Road to Washington (1976–85)

Two weeks before the 1985 New York gathering at Red Oak to celebrate Maggie's eightieth birthday, I attended a wine and cheese reception to mark the opening of the "Washington, D.C. branch of the [Gray Panther] national office."[1] Held in the Dirksen Senate Office Building through arrangement by Steve McConnell, staff director of the Senate Special Committee on Aging and a former Los Angeles Gray Panther, the event attracted an audience of two hundred and fifty. Maggie opened the brief formalities. "This is not the happy hour. This is a joyous hour, where all of us celebrate an event we have been anticipating for many years." She introduced the new Gray Panthers executive director Marcia Abrams, forty-seven, who arrived in Philadelphia with fifteen years of advocacy experience with health and hunger issues in Louisiana and New Jersey. Next she recognized Frances Humphreys, fifty-four, the Panthers' Washington representative based in the new office on 15th Street NW. Neither woman spoke beyond short greetings. Maggie ended her remarks by thanking the nine "Congressional Co-Sponsors" of the event, including Senator John Heinz of Pennsylvania (McConnell's boss and the only one present) and Representatives Ron Dellums, Claude Pepper, and Ron Wyden. "You may not know it, but we have a Gray Panther in Congress," she said referring to Wyden, a former Oregon Panther elected to Congress in 1980.[2] Later Ethel Weisser, convener of the Metropolitan Washington Gray Panthers, introduced her network's still-active founder, Janet Neuman, ninety-four, who spoke about the group's early days.

The audience contained many Washington Panthers as well as members of the three suburban Maryland networks. Several past and current National Steering Committee members were present: Consultation founding member Al Wilson from New Jersey; Glen Gersmehl, now in California; Jean Hopper from Philadelphia; Doris Berk of the New York Gray Panthers; Grace Warfield from Minneapolis; Naomi Harward from Phoenix, Arizona; and Louis Webb of California's Mendocino Coast Gray Panthers. Congressional aides attended, as did staffers from the Older

Women's League, the American Public Health Association, the National Low-Income Housing Coalition, and the National Citizens Coalition for Nursing Home Reform, including its director Elma Griesel Holder. Network coordinator Sherry Clearwater and *Network* editor Christina Long accompanied Maggie from Philadelphia.

During the reception Grace Jacobs, a Los Angeles NSC member, told me, "Maggie's not really for it [the D.C. office]." Irv Riskin of Montgomery County, Maryland, who coordinated the 1985 Gray Panther "Don't Cut the COLA" postcard campaign, remarked, "We couldn't have done it [open the D.C. office] with what's her name," referring to Gray Panther executive director Edith Giese, who had resigned nine months earlier. "We've been pushing for three years."

The decade between the 1975 Chicago convention and the opening of the Washington office was a period of increasing prominence and impact during the later 1970s and growth and internal conflict in the early 1980s. The advent of Ronald Reagan's presidency in 1981 refocused local network attention on national issues, with Panthers mobilizing against threats to Social Security and Medicare, and by the mid-1980s on peace and disarmament. But Gray Panther responses to domestic budget cutting and growing militarism had begun earlier, during the Jimmy Carter years.

Jimmy Carter

The Gray Panthers could not endorse a political candidate and retain their tax-exempt status, yet in 1976 Maggie and the National Steering Committee came close to joining the Carter election camp. The Carter affair began when Maggie and the Democratic nomination seeker were both scheduled to speak to the Sarasota Council on Aging. Unable to attend, Carter sent a note to Maggie: "Too often productive citizens are cast aside at age 65. . . . The Federal government must adopt an active and aggressive policy to eradicate employment discrimination against older people. . . . My mother, Lillian, who is now 77, is still an inspiration to me. . . . In 1966, at age 68, she joined the Peace Corps. She served two years in a small hospital in a remote village in India. It saddens me to know that . . . my mother's service . . . would have been almost impossible in her own country."[3]

Carter's staff approached the Panthers for an endorsement, as did four other Democratic presidential candidates. "We will listen closely to what each candidate says about the issues that are important to us," Maggie announced, "and support them individually, regardless of party."[4] The Panthers let both Democrats and Republicans know which issues they cared about. The task forces formed to implement the Chicago convention resolutions produced an eight-page "Testimony on the Economy and Human Needs," with sections on "Full Employment" by Shubert Frye, "Housing" by Joe Davis of the Metropolitan Washington network, and "National Health Care" by Elma Griesel, Washington Panther Frances Klafter, and Len Rodberg of the Institute for Policy Studies, who was drafting the national health service bill that Representative Ron Dellums would introduce in 1977. Washington Panthers Davis, Janet Neuman, and Ethel Morris presented the document to the Democratic and Republican platform committees. Maggie and NSC chairperson Alice Adler sent President Ford and his challenger Ronald Reagan mailgrams requesting their views "regarding the 22.4 million older Americans in this country and . . . your . . . policies affecting . . . their lives." Their message to Carter was more pointed and personal: "We appreciate your support for flexible retirement since this is a Gray Panther national priority [and] we strongly advocate the creation of an advisory council to the President composed of older people. . . . We look forward to meeting with you at the Convention."[5]

As it turned out, their way to the candidate was through his mother. During the Democratic convention Maggie, Adler, Lydia Bragger, and Philadelphia office volunteer Jean Hopper hosted a Gray Panther breakfast for Lillian Carter, to whom Maggie later wrote, "We were all very pleased to meet you and discover the many areas of common concern[. We] are very happy with Jimmy Carter's nomination."[6] In September Maggie agreed to serve on the campaign's Seniors for Carter/Mondale committee. After Carter was elected she wrote his transition team reiterating the Panthers' call for a White House advisory group on aging as well as a cabinet-level Department on Aging. Maggie was invited to the inauguration and spoke at the Seniors for Carter/Mondale conclave. The Panthers joined the National Council of Senior Citizens, the National Council on Aging, and AARP in hosting a reception for Carter's new cabinet.

After Carter took office in 1977 Maggie was invited to a White House Round Table on Aging, where she blasted existing policy: "The Federal . . . programs provided to help the elderly are themselves ageist. . . . The Older Americans Act is age-segregated. . . . In its implementation by the States and Area Agencies on Aging, old people are treated as a special class, isolated in special age-segregated facilities that reinforce separation, powerlessness and anomie."[7] She continued to convey Panther views to Carter, writing in June, "We will stand strongly behind a decision to stop the B-1 [bomber]."[8] On this the president agreed and in 1978 he rescinded President Ford's B-1 funding.[9] Later in 1977 Maggie returned to the White House for a meeting of the President's Commission on Mental Health and briefings on Social Security, energy policy, and the

Panama Canal treaty. When Carter unveiled plans to cut Aid to Families with Dependent Children and Supplemental Security Income for the elderly and disabled poor, Gray Panther–White House amity began to sour. His proposals were excoriated at the 1977 Gray Panther convention, and Maggie told the House Welfare Reform subcommittee, "The bill fails to provide benefit levels that come close to affording a minimally decent standard of living."[10] Her testimony was mailed to Panther networks with the request that they write members of Congress and local newspapers in protest. Members of Carter's own party also opposed his welfare reform package, and it was defeated in 1978.

A broad Gray Panther attack on Carter policies followed in 1979. In a *Network* editorial Maggie and Los Angeles Panther Steve McConnell objected to proposed cuts in housing, Comprehensive Employment and Training Act (CETA) employment, health career training, school lunches, and summer jobs, and they were particularly averse to a 10 percent increase in military spending. "We believe the defense budget should be cut because it is inflationary and it wastes money, sorely needed for social programs. . . . Carter's budget also ties directly into a 'Proposition 13 hysteria' sweeping the country, an emotional reaction to government spending which carries racist, ageist and anti-poor overtones."[11]

The Panthers stood firmly against Carter's plans for Social Security. Two years earlier they had welcomed his proposal to use general revenues to supplement any Social Security payroll tax shortfall and avoid benefit cuts. Congress had not agreed and the Social Security Amendments of 1977 instead mandated a payroll tax increase and rise in the taxable earnings cap, both to be phased in through the 1980s. But with large Social Security COLA raises resulting from high inflation, and with worker and employer resistance to further payroll tax increases and the door to general revenues closed, Carter's 1979 budget included the first Social Security benefit cuts ever. Payments to deceased workers' children between ages eighteen and twenty-two attending college were targeted, as were support to widowed mothers once children reached age sixteen rather than eighteen, the $225 lump sum burial benefit, and the minimum benefit for retired workers with very low lifetime earnings. The Panthers joined the AFL-CIO, United Auto Workers, National Caucus on the Black Aged, and National Organization for Women in a Save Our Security (SOS) coalition to organize demonstrations, letter writing, and lobbying in Washington. Congress shelved Carter's Social Security proposals but they would be dusted off by the next administration.

Late in 1979 Carter named Maggie to the National Advisory Committee for the third White House Conference on Aging scheduled for December 1981. But as 1980 began the Panthers focused on the president's call to reinstate draft registration in response to the arrival of Soviet troops into Afghanistan. Their newspaper *Network* proclaimed: "We oppose Carter's new military doctrine which eclipses all other goals."[12] The NSC voted to join the Coalition against Registration and the Draft and to endorse actions in Washington and Los Angeles led by Mobilization against the Draft. When Carter signed a draft registration order in July the Panther national office urged local networks to join protests at post offices on the first day of registration: "Hold up those 'Age and Youth in Action' posters . . . and show the young men of this country that registration is the concern of people of all ages!"[13] Dorel Shannon, a Philadelphia office volunteer in her early twenties, coordinated the campaign, and Gray Panthers participated in antiregistration actions in Boston, New York, Philadelphia, Chicago, Madison, Minneapolis, Kansas City, Albuquerque, Tucson, Santa Barbara, and Sonoma. In Berkeley Lillian Rabinowitz led a contingent of thirty Panthers and addressed one hundred and fifty demonstrators. That fall Chuck Preston's front page *Network* editorial read, "The Gray Panthers stand together in saying to the people that war has become so dangerous it is unthinkable; in saying to the Government, hands off our grandsons."[14]

The Gray Panthers Get a Lawyer

While teaching at the University of Southern California in 1976 Maggie met Paul Nathanson, a lawyer in his thirties who founded the National Senior Citizens Law Center (NSCLC) in 1972. A few months later Nathanson attended an NSC meeting to propose the NSCLC become the Panthers' legal advisor and represent them in class action court cases. With forty local networks the Panthers provided Nathanson's staff a client group that did "not have sufficient funds to hire private counsel" and included elderly "low income persons," thus meeting criteria for funding by the federal Legal Services Corporation and Administration on Aging.[15] The offer was accepted and Edith Giese of the Philadelphia office became Panther liaison to NSCLC offices in Los Angeles and Washington, D.C., transmitting proposed court actions for NSC approval.

In the first NSCLC case the Panthers joined Disabled in Action of Pennsylvania in suing the U.S. Department of Transportation to comply with Section 504 of the 1973 Rehabilitation Act by restricting bus purchase funds to low-floored "transbuses" in which all riders, including wheelchair users, used the same ramped entrance. (I remember riding a transbus prototype in Berkeley about this time and being impressed with the ease it afforded a wheelchair user to board and exit.) The suit ended when Carter's transportation secretary agreed with the plaintiffs and ruled that after 1979 mass transit funds be used only for the transbus. Congress reversed this decision under pressure from General Motors, which preferred to fit its existing model with backdoor lifts. (In the 1980s struggles by disabled activists arose nationwide to force drivers to operate the lifts.[16] A transbus driver did not have to do anything other than stop and start his or her vehicle.)

The NSCLC–Gray Panther alliance went to court numerous times on behalf of nursing home residents and their families, including a three-year struggle against federal regulations that permitted states to reduce their Medicaid costs by "deeming" a portion of the income of a noninstitutionalized spouse available to pay nursing home expenses of their husband or wife. If the funds "deemed" available were not paid, a nursing home could evict the resident spouse. This often left a noninstitutionalized partner with inadequate funds for living expenses or precipitated a divorce to legally avoid "deeming." Christina Long of the Philadelphia office and Mississippi Panther Eddie Sandifer documented the case of Ethel Moore, a diabetic amputee who was evicted from a Jackson nursing home because her retired husband could not pay $59 per month. Panthers in other states provided similar affidavits to NSCLC lawyers and in 1979 the U.S. Court of Appeals in Washington, D.C., voided the "deeming" regulation. The Reagan administration appealed and was upheld in *Gray Panthers v. Schweiker* (Reagan's Health, Education and Welfare secretary) in 1981 when the Supreme Court ruled that "deeming" was permissible.

Another group of suits concerned pensions and age discrimination. The Panthers and NSCLC lost a case in which a trucker was denied his Teamsters Union pension because of a three-month involuntary layoff during his twenty-two-year work history. Joined by Ralph Nader's Pension Rights Center and the Securities and Exchange Commission, the Panthers argued that the trucker had not been informed of a provision requiring *uninterrupted* service to qualify. The Supreme Court decided for the Teamsters that "full disclosure" requirements applicable to securities did not apply to pensions. The Panthers and NSCLC also lost a 1983 suit against the Reagan administration for its failure to issue regulations implementing protections against age discrimination in federally funded programs. A victory arrived in 1985 when the Supreme Court sustained a Panther-NSCLC argument that Western Airlines could not force flight engineers to retire at age sixty without determination of their ability to do the job. The unanimous decision was written by Justice John Paul Stevens, sixty, who stated, "Many older American workers perform at levels equal or superior to their younger colleagues."[17]

In *Gray Panthers v. Califano* (Carter's Secretary of Health, Education and Welfare) the NSCLC sued in 1977 to require in-person hearings for all Medicare beneficiary billing disputes, including those under $100. After extended negotiation the Health Care Financing Administration, which administered Medicare, agreed in 1984 to provide all beneficiaries "due process" regardless of claim amount and also to make written notices of doctor visit claim determinations reader-friendly. In concert with the Panthers and NSCLC, in 1985 Representative Ron Wyden introduced legislation further expanding Medicare beneficiary rights to appeal claim decisions.

Thwarted in its attempt to defund the Legal Services Corporation, from which the NSCLC drew most of its financial support, in 1984 the Reagan administration tightened regulations allowing membership organizations to be class action plaintiffs, stipulating that such groups must be composed solely of low-income persons. The Panthers did not qualify, and the NSCLC–Gray Panther legal alliance ended. At the Panthers' convention that year executive director Giese presented an award to the National Senior Citizen Law Center, with special thanks to Nathanson and the ten staff attorneys she had worked with for eight years.[18]

Mandatory Retirement, Coalitions, the United Nations

Maggie's stamp on Gray Panther causes and alliances through the 1970s and early 1980s was evident. In 1976 the issue that spurred her to begin the Consultation, mandatory retirement, reemerged when Philadelphia Gray Panthers persuaded their member of Congress to introduce legislation eliminating the upper age limit of sixty-five to which federal age discrimination protection applied. Maggie testified against mandatory retirement before a Pennsylvania commission, drawing on a background paper by Rosalie Schofield, a Brandeis University social work graduate student who interned at the Gray Panther national office (and later joined the NSC). Schofield argued that older workers were hired and retained when demand for labor was high but became economic scapegoats in "a less than full employment economy." She advocated "the right to work at any age" and attacked "the practice by which the criterion of chronological age overrides considerations of competence, skill, productivity, and health."[19] In 1977 Chicago Panther Eddie Marcus, who confronted age discrimination when seeking employment at age sixty, testified for the Panthers before the House Select Committee on Aging, reminding the legislators that elected officials, unlike other workers, faced no age bar to continued service. He emphasized that mandatory retirement deprived pension funds and Social Security of older workers' contributions and reinforced "stereotypes of older persons as declining, worn out, expendable, and parasitical."[20]

President Carter was on record opposing mandatory retirement, and Commissioner of Aging Arthur Flemming, seventy-two, a longtime friend of Maggie, launched a "crusade" against it. Things then moved quickly. Congressional proposals were consolidated in a bill by Representative Claude Pepper, seventy-seven, to eliminate mandatory retirement for most federal workers and raise the private sector retirement age to seventy. The Gray Panther national office mailed an Action Alert calling this "our best shot thus far," but the networks objected to any compromise and Philadelphia issued an "update" opposing the bill.[21] When it passed and was signed by Carter in 1978, Maggie declared, "Our struggle is hardly over," and called for full abolition of mandatory retirement.[22]

Maggie's housemate and national office mainstay Elma Griesel left Philadelphia after the 1975 Gray Panther convention to work for the National Paralegal Institute in Washington, D.C., teaching older people advocacy skills. In 1977 Beacon Press released *Nursing Homes: A Citizens' Guide*, a revised version of Griesel and Linda Horn's earlier Gray Panther report.[23] Their book tour culminated in a meeting of fifty-eight nursing home advocates, including Ann Wyatt of New York and Gray Panthers from Kansas City and Portland, who elected a steering committee for the dormant National Citizens Coalition for Nursing Home Reform (NCCNHR, pronounced "nic-ner") founded in 1975. In 1978 NCCNHR incorporated and opened a Washington office; Griesel became executive director and with a grant from VISTA began training volunteers from member organizations, including four Gray Panther networks, to staff state nursing home ombudsman programs. She remained a Gray Panther, serving on the NSC from 1975 to 1981. Horn continued to live with Maggie and authored portions of the 1978 Gray Panther *Organizing Manual*.[24]

After the Reagan administration assumed offfice in 1981 NCCNHR lost federal funding and turned to private foundations and support from member groups, which by 1985 numbered 280. In 1982 Griesel led opposition to the new administration's proposed easing of nursing home regulations and appeared on the *McNeil/Lehrer News Hour* and was quoted in the *New York Times*. In 1985 a *Network* interview included her assessment of nursing home monitoring and protest: "In most homes, *minimal* care standards are being met. . . . Overall attention to health care has improved . . . although medical services have not. Administrators of homes are now better trained to understand their responsibilities under the law . . . And, most significant, about 49 percent of nursing homes have some sort of resident council. . . . [But] there is tremendous growth in corporate ownership of nursing homes. It decreases . . . the opportunity for a local group of people to have any control over what's happening in that facility. [And] the workers are so abused in nursing homes, so underpaid, undertrained, undersupervised, underrecognized."[25]

As with Nathanson and NSCLC, and Griesel and NCCNHR, it was Maggie who linked the Panthers to Hobart Jackson of the National Caucus and Center on the Black Aged and to Tish Sommers, chair of NOW's Task Force on Older Women and founder of the Older Women's League, both of whom also wrote for *Network*. Beginning in 1976, Jackson's "Black and Gray" columns dealt with the impact of racism on African Americans' retirement income and access to services, including nursing homes. They ceased with his unexpected death at sixty-one in 1978. Sommers's lively writings focused on the "parallel bars" of sexism and ageism in work, Social Security benefits, and health issues and provided provocative maxims for activists: "Use the system against itself, it has used you," "Have you bugged your Representative today?" "Organize, don't agonize."[26] Sommers attended the 1977 and 1979 Gray Panther conventions and served on the NSC during 1978–81. In 1980 she invited four hundred middle-age and older activist women to the inaugural meeting of the Older Women's League (OWL). Maggie was the event's keynote speaker, and many female Gray Panthers also became OWL members.[27] Sommers's death at seventy-one in 1985 was mourned by many Panthers who worked with her, among them Lillian Rabinowitz, who with Sommers was a member of a cancer support group begun in 1979.

Although the national Gray Panthers joined other national coalitions, including Hospice Action, the Citizens Conference on Pension Policy, the National Coalition for a New Foreign and Military Policy, and the Progressive Alliance, these linkages did not arise via a personal friendship with Maggie. One other involvement that did, however, was the Panthers' non-governmental organization (NGO) observer status at the United Nations. Maggie welcomed the birth of the UN in 1945 and attended seminars there for the Presbyterian Church. Her UN-based friendship with Cameron Hall, who after retirement represented the International Senior Citizens Association at the UN, continued from 1970 to 1981 at Gray Panther steering committee meetings. Hall kept Maggie apprised of UN interest in the elderly worldwide, and at his suggestion the Panthers obtained "non-governmental observer" status with the UN Office of Public Information in 1977 and "consultative status" with the Economic and Social Council in 1981. Hall was instrumental in organizing a UN World Assembly on Aging in 1982 in Vienna, Austria. Maggie attended with Sylvia Kleinman, the Panthers' UN representative beginning in 1978 and with a handful of Panthers organized a disarmament seminar and an international press conference. Kleinman, a Bergen County, New Jersey, Gray Panther, participated in the UN Committee on Aging comprising more than forty religious, professional, and advocacy NGOs and was its chair from 1982 to 1985.

Maggie's Changing Role

During the decade following the first Gray Panther convention Maggie traveled widely and spoke to thousands of Americans in person and to millions via television. Caring at home for her mentally ill brother, Sam, preoccupied her, but his death in 1975 freed her to devote full effort to the burgeoning Gray Panther movement and escalating requests for speaking engagements, press interviews, and television appearances.[28] Her honorarium earnings were important to the Panthers' livelihood. In 1977 she contributed $6,900 to the organization. The following year she approved a new arrangement whereby all honoraria went to the Gray Panthers Project Fund and she was paid $20,000 in salary, and her secretary $8,000. This placed pressure on Maggie to maintain a heavy schedule, which she did, clocking 100,000 air travel miles and speaking publicly 200 times during 1978.[29]

Charging a minimum of $750 per day and represented by three booking agencies, Maggie traveled to thirty-nine states over the next five years. She appeared at more than one hundred colleges and seminaries, ranging from Harvard to Hendrix College, Arkansas, and was a featured speaker at more than fifty meetings or conventions of gerontologists and aging services professionals, including governor's conferences and statewide assemblies in Iowa, Kansas, Illinois, New York, Massachusetts, Maryland, and Wyoming. She addressed some forty-eight congregations and religious groups, more than a third of them Presbyterian but also Unitarians, Lutherans, Catholics, Jews, and the Light of Yoga Society of Cleveland. She lectured a dozen times at medical schools and hospital staff seminars and participated in meetings of the National Senior Citizen Law Center, NOW, OWL, the American Public Health Association, and California's Legislative Council of Older Americans. She spoke to audiences of high school students, women, retirees, librarians, accountants, bankers, funeral directors, fundraisers, grant makers, and peace activists.[30]

Maggie accepted some invitations that offered no speaking fee, particularly when she could piggyback them on an already remunerative trip. She often spoke twice or more on the same day, as in 1981 at Queens College to an afternoon student group and an evening public lecture audience. She added still more events while on the road: on a 1982 visit with New Haven Gray Panthers she toured low-income and senior citizen housing, spent the night at a retirement home, and gave interviews to the *New Haven Advocate* and Connecticut Public Radio.[31] To economize she often stayed with Gray Panthers.

Maggie budgeted time for national Gray Panther tasks. Her calendar included Panther conventions in 1977, 1979, 1981, and 1984; annual rounds of a half dozen or more National Steering Committee, Executive Committee, regional, and state Gray Panther meetings, most lasting two or three days; and speaking invitations from eight or more networks each year. Local conveners made the most of Maggie's visits. During a 1981 trip to Florida she traveled with Eddie Marcus, now transplanted from the Chicago network, on a weeklong organizing tour of six cities. In 1984 the Gray Panthers of Montgomery County arranged for their county executive to designate her visit "Maggie Kuhn Day." Forty guest legislators, clergy, and organization leaders were among 225 in attendance, and sixty-four new members, including Maryland's attorney general, joined the Montgomery County network.[32]

Maggie was highly conscious of her image and demeanor and their impact on others. Observers first noted her appearance: "She stands five feet three inches tall, weighs 105 pounds, and has brown eyes and bright gray hair"; she wore " 'sensible' brown shoes" and "dresses in soft colors, often adding a bright scarf to her neckline and a silver bracelet or two to her wrists. Her half-rimmed glasses slip down her nose when she laughs and listens." She was quick, however, to define her physical persona herself: "I'm 73 years old, and I haven't dyed my hair and I can't afford a face lift. I enjoy my wrinkles and regard them as badges of distinction."[33] Any discrepancy between her perceived image and her message was turned to Maggie's advantage. "She manages to look grandmotherly, innocent, wise, and elfish simultaneously while admonishing her audience to 'get off their asses.' "[34] And she communicated with a voice at once clear and high-pitched, yet soft and with a slight lilt. " 'Maggie has the gift,' says one admirer, 'of knowing how to shout at someone in a whisper.' "[35] She was magnetic in person and remarkably photogenic, as pictures attest; it was impossible not to look at Maggie, and equally impossible not to listen to her.

Her words were intended to rouse, inspire, and include. Frequently she began, "This is the new age of liberation and self-determination," following with the observation that human life is a continuum, "from erection to resurrection."[36] She made bold, unexpected comparisons: "The young and the old in this society are equally discriminated against. Both groups have identity crises. . . . Both groups are in the drug scene, although there are different drugs and different pushers." She told audiences she favored "nationalization of energy sources, health care, transportation, and utilities as essential structural changes for the nation, particularly to the elderly."[37] When asked if the health system she advocated was "socialized medicine," she responded: "If it's so great for the armed forces, and Congress, and the President and his family, we would like to have it for everybody."[38] Her talks drew on a four-page topical outline with sections adapted to fit various audiences. And usually she ended with the yogic "Gray Panther growl," urging everyone to stand, "raise both arms . . . reaching toward a peaceful world," "open our eyes as wide as we can, envisioning . . . suffering and need," "open our mouths . . . to cry out against injustice," "stick out your tongue," and "growl three times . . . from the depth of your belly."[39] Whether enthusiastic or embarrassed, those joining Maggie in her "growl" would smile, experience solidarity with her and each other, and be energized.

Maggie delighted in turning her shock and inspire tactics on academic gerontologists. At the 1977 meeting of the Gerontological Society, Maggie and young and older Panthers leafleted conventioneers with a questionnaire asking: "Is the profession of gerontology a parasite feeding on the expanding population of older people?" Before an audience of one thousand Maggie faced off with the society's president, George Maddox, and proclaimed, "From the advocates' viewpoint we are still pressing for research that places the process of aging into the proper societal context. Aging itself is not a problem, but the structural, political, economic forces of our . . . society are grave problems."[40] She presented Maddox a Gray Panther T-shirt, which he immediately donned. During the 1978 Western Gerontological Society meeting Maggie continued her dialogue with Maddox as Elma Griesel, Paul Nathanson, Tish Sommers, Steve Mc-Connell, and older Panthers Ruth Haefner of Portland and Bernie Winter of San Diego led panels on nursing homes, advocacy, older women, and health care "needs vs. profits."

Maggie conducted many weeklong seminars before her forced retirement and did so again at the University of Southern California (co-teaching with Steve McConnell) and at the San Francisco Theological Seminary[41] in 1976, Cornell University and the University of Hawaii in 1977, the Pacific School of Religion in Berkeley, Whitman College in Spokane, and Chaminade University in Honolulu in 1979, the University of New Mexico in 1981, and the University of California, San Francisco, in 1983. Maggie's trips abroad were quasi-seminars. In 1976, just weeks after Mao Zedong's death, she spent an exhilarating month in China with twenty Americans, including several Gray Panthers, and was impressed by "the priority given to health and preventive care."[42] She went again in 1978 with eight Panthers, including Tish Sommers, this time focusing on the life of older people. Among their stops was one of China's "Homes of Respect for the Aged," a facility for seventy retired miners without families, some physically or mentally disabled, staffed by twenty attendants.[43]

At the Australian government's invitation she attended an international conference in 1979 and while there visited local councils on aging, spoke to the press, and met with an elderly activist group inspired by the Gray Panthers. Six years later she made a similar trip to Britain. In 1983 she and five Gray Panthers were delegates to a World Peace Council "Assembly for Peace and Life, against Nuclear War" in Prague, an event that, she said, "stirred me . . . profoundly" and "cannot be shrugged off as 'more communist propaganda.' "[44] In 1985 she returned to Canada, where she had spoken a dozen times, to study the health and social services system with nine Gray Panthers including Lillian Rabinowitz and Health Task Force chair Frances Humphreys. After seeing "the difference between a profit-oriented [U.S.] system . . . and a consumer-oriented [Canadian] system that bases decisions on the health-care needs of the people," Maggie and the other Panthers renewed their commitment to bring about universal health care in their own country.[45]

Maggie's profile as a national spokesperson and celebrity soared after 1975. She testified before congressional committees on "disease care" versus a neighborhood-based "healthy block" approach in 1976; on fragmented and uncoordinated social services for older persons and on negative television stereotypes in 1977; and for enhanced National Institute on Aging funding in 1978. Once the Gray Panther flirtation with the Carter White House was over, Maggie voiced her political views more often in the streets. Her speech at an antinuclear rally in New York in 1979 was included as a brief cameo scene in *No Nukes*, a concert film with musicians James Taylor, Carly Simon, Bruce Springsteen, and Gil Scott-Heron. Maggie returned as a congressional witness only once during the Reagan years, on behalf of the Legal Services Corporation in 1981. In 1983 she spoke in Lafayette Park, opposite the White House, to the 250,000 assembled to commemorate Martin Luther King Jr.'s 1963 March on Washington. And that year the American Civil Liberties Union presented her its Roger N. Baldwin Bill of Rights Award.

The *New York Times*, which started "the pounce of the media" after her 1972 Denver news conference, continued to feature Maggie, with reports on Gray Panther conventions, a "Style" story on her home and housemates, and her 1983 op-ed piece opposing increases in out-of-pocket Medicare costs.[46] Stories about her appeared in numerous newspapers and magazines including the *Christian Science Monitor, San Francisco Examiner, Honolulu Advertiser, USA Today, Parade, Ladies' Home Journal, Ms., New Internationalist, In These Times*, south Florida's *Sun-Sentinel*, and Long Island's *Port Washington News*. Following her first appearance on the Johnny Carson *Tonight Show* in 1974, television exposure expanded. She was a *Tonight* guest four more times. (After one appearance Lillian Rabinowitz wrote complimenting the "Chairman Mao jacket" she wore when presenting Carson a Gray Panther T-shirt.)[47] Maggie was also a guest on ABC's *Good Morning America* and PBS's *Black Perspectives on the News* and *Over Easy*. She was interviewed during the 1981 White House Conference on Aging on NBC's *Today Show* and PBS's *McNeil/Lehrer News Hour*. In

1983 she was the first guest on the new *Larry King Live* show on CNN, and in 1985 she celebrated her eightieth birthday with a live call-in program on C-SPAN cable television.

Maggie's fame propelled her into the company of other celebrities. At demonstrations she was greeted warmly by such political figures as Senator Ted Kennedy, Representative Bella Abzug, Gloria Steinem, Jesse Jackson, and Ralph Nader. A mutual friend introduced her to Margaret Mead, four years older than Maggie, and they met several times before the anthropologist's death in 1978. In 1975 she met Dr. Robert Butler, forty-eight, who coined the term "ageism" in 1968 and was author of *Why Survive? Being Old in America*, which Maggie used in seminars.[48] That year Butler's book won the Pulitzer Prize and he was appointed the first director of the National Institute of Aging, part of the federal National Institutes of Health. They remained friends, appeared in panels together, and in 1980 joined Representative Claude Pepper, another friend of Maggie's, on a National Public Radio Town Meeting on "The Dilemma of Aging in America." Maggie befriended actor Ed Asner, entertainers Harry Belafonte and Pete Seeger, pediatrician and peace activist Dr. Benjamin Spock, and astronomer Carl Sagan. They and others composed a Gray Panther advisory board listed on direct-mail funding appeals. She enjoyed and marveled at her celebrity. "I feel more alive than I ever did," she admitted in 1979. "I really can't believe that it's all happening. All of my life I was primarily involved in groups and group activities, and so never was one for . . . personal acclaim. . . . Often it's quite frightening . . . more than ever I need support, friendship, love, criticism, and assistance."[49]

Her movement's love for Maggie was evident when Panther networks nationwide celebrated her eightieth birthday in 1985. Criticism from fellow Panthers also came that year after Maggie consented to producer Lili Zanuck's request to endorse *Cocoon*, a science-fiction film about Florida retirees rejuvenated by mysterious waters from outer space. A beaming Maggie was feted at a Lincoln Center gala in New York where she presented the film's stars Hume Cronyn and Jack Gilford a "Gray Panthers' Award for Outstanding Achievement in Challenging Ageism." In return the $100 per ticket receipts went to the Gray Panthers Project Fund. While Panther Executive Committee members and Philadelphia office staff applauded, Boston and San Francisco Panther media watchers panned "Cocoon" in an issue of *Network* as a "perpetuation of this society's worship of youth and downgrading of senior citizens." They termed its portrayal of nursing home residents "dismal" and deemed the Panther award "inappropriate."[50]

The "support, friendship, and assistance" Maggie requested came from three concentric circles around her: her housemates, the national office staff, and the Gray Panther Executive Committee. Living upstairs in Maggie's three-story stone and stucco house, each in a suite of four rooms with kitchen and bath, Elma Griesel and Linda Horn provided welcomed assistance and consolation to Maggie during her brother Sam's last year.[51] When Griesel left, Philadelphia Gray Panther Bobbi Granger, thirty-three, and Bob Jaffe, twenty-four, both students, moved in, married, and remained for the next ten years. Maggie renovated the adjoining house, and in 1980 seminary student Ann Egan, thirty, arrived, joined in subsequent years by others in their twenties and thirties who stayed for varying periods. Egan and Maggie, who were the same size, shopped for clothes together and it was Egan who convinced Maggie to stop driving after she sideswiped another car. All the housemates paid rent, though at a submarket rate. Like Maggie, who entertained men friends, they lived their own lives but gathered for dinner once a week, watched *Saturday Night Live* together, and celebrated holidays as "a family of choice."[52]

None of the national office staff who succeeded Griesel lived with Maggie, but they were the Gray Panthers she saw and spoke with most often. Next came the Executive Committee members with whom Maggie spent up to two weeks each year at meetings and conferences. In 1985 the three circles merged when Executive Committee chairperson Grace Warfield, seventy-five, a retired professor of special education, filled in as executive director for six months and moved into Maggie's house.

Maggie's dedication to shared housing was unshakeable: "I love the vitality of these young people; having them around re-energizes me." She relished other examples of intergenerational living with young people "not just as boarders but as *friends*," including Tish Sommers's living arrangements, and lamented that "in most areas of our country, the housing and zoning laws make it illegal for living arrangements like mine to exist." Gray Panthers in some networks, including Berkeley, Brooklyn, and Denver, expressed similar interest, and the Boston Panthers secured a grant to open a "Shared Living Project" residence. But Joe Davis, Gray Panther Housing Task Force chair from 1976 to 1981 and active in Washington, D.C., tenant struggles, was unsupportive. He warned that "alternatives such as congregate housing and intergenerational housing are only stop-gap measures; they will not provide housing for the millions of elderly who need it now." He feared that Panther advocacy of shared housing, and he meant Maggie, would encourage the federal government to fund "scattered projects of alternative housing and neglect to provide for an enlightened program" like the Scandinavian-style public housing with green space and accessible dwellings for all generations that he advocated.[53]

Maggie struck back. In 1981 she created a Shared Housing Resource

Center in her second house and recruited a director, Dennis Day-Lower, a Presbyterian minister who worked on the Boston shared housing project. She raised $4,000 from the Presbyterian Church and created an advisory committee including three members of Congress, architects, and friends Steve McConnell and University of California sociologist Carroll Estes. The Gray Panther office staff were disturbed that Maggie's energy and fund-raising effort were flowing to this separate organization, as she well understood: "I've sometimes infuriated my co-workers at the Gray Panthers by taking on new causes."[54] In 1982 Maggie and the center held a two-day conference at Princeton University attended by 150 and funded by the federal Department of Housing and Urban Development. In 1985 the center, still in Maggie's house, estimated there were 300 nonprofit shared housing residences and 150 matching programs nationwide and claimed annual individual savings for older house sharers of up to $2,400.[55]

Sex, a long-standing cause for Maggie, was one more area in which she steered her own course. It was a staple in her public talks. "Another wrong and cruel myth is that old age is sexless—that in one's old age human sexuality withers and declines. . . . I can tell you that it's not that way." Drawing on clinical research she declared, "Age is no barrier to female sexuality, . . . and male capacity extends beyond age 80." She validated her views with writings of Dr. William Masters and friend Dr. Robert Butler,[56] but the most controversial part of her message was pure Maggie. She insisted it was unreasonable that "an older man partnered with a younger woman is tacitly approved by the community, while the reverse . . . is frowned upon," adding, "A growing number of us old women are involved sexually . . . with men who are younger than us." Maggie spoke openly about her past affairs, including one lasting fifteen years with a married man, but not until her 1991 book did she write about her relationship with a twenty-one-year-old male Gray Panther that began in 1976.[57] There were rumors about it at the time, and perhaps revelations to friends and Gray Panther inner circles. Still, few Panthers I encountered spoke personally about sex as Maggie did, even as many understood its importance to her.

Maggie maintained her intense speaking schedule despite cancer, worsening arthritis treated with painful medication, and back problems beginning in 1982. Her first encounter with cancer came at age forty-one, resulting in a mastectomy. In 1976 she was diagnosed with cervical cancer, underwent a hysterectomy, and six weeks later attended Jimmy Carter's inauguration. A third cancer in 1977 involved risky surgery that housemates Horn and the Granger-Jaffes urged her to undergo against her initial disinclination.[58] In 1983 she was hospitalized for two weeks with pneumonia. During the following months she missed a California

Gray Panthers convention and the New York Gray Panthers tenth anniversary celebration.

Ever the consciousness-raiser, just before her eightieth birthday, in 1985, she gave *Network* editor Christina Long an accounting of her disabilities. "The thing that is hardest is my diminishing vision. . . . I have deterioration of the retina, and at the present time they don't know what to do about it. I have very thick reading glasses now. . . . My arthritis is getting worse. My right hand is a nuisance. I have difficulty cleaning my teeth. Isn't that ridiculous? I have to clean my teeth with my left hand, which is hard to get used to. . . . My legs are stiff and my knees bother me, but the best thing to do is to keep moving. . . . I have trouble eating. I have to swallow very carefully and take tiny little bites. I take forever to get through a meal." Was this slowing down her traveling, Long asked. "Yes, but not too much. . . . Marilyn [Vowels], my secretary, says to me, 'Do you *have* to do this?' And I say, 'I must!' "[59]

Ideology: A Radical Organization?

The Gray Panthers maintained an ideological roominess or expansiveness due in part to Maggie's desire to "try ideas on for size" but also to the diverse motivations and experience of those who joined the movement. Still, two persisting components of Panther ideology were noteworthy: an intergenerationalism rooted in practice as well as Maggie's thinking, and a "radical" versus "reformist" straddle with the same dual wellsprings. In 1978 both were called into question, and both affirmed.

In May two dozen Panthers gathered at the National Steering Committee meeting in Philadelphia. Objecting to "media portrayals of the Gray Panthers as . . . another 'interest group for the elderly' [and use of] 'Gray Panthers' as a generic term [for] 'senior power activists,' " Billie Heller, fifty-eight, and Rosalie Schofield, thirty-one, proposed a disclaimer:

1. We are NOT a vested interest group for the elderly.
2. We are NOT out to win points for older people at the expense of other groups.
3. We ARE a movement comprised of ALL ages dedicated to changing people's attitudes about aging.
4. We ARE a movement dedicated to improving the quality of life for ALL people.

Everyone concurred, and the NSC, two-thirds over age sixty and one-third under, approved the statement for publication in *Network* and circulation to local conveners. They also directed that "Age and Youth in Action" be used with "Gray Panthers" whenever possible, in press releases as well as on buttons, T-shirts, posters, newsletters, and in public statements and speeches.[60]

A more far-reaching debate followed concerning the Gray Panther Articles of Agreement. As amended at the 1977 convention, Point Five of the "Purposes and Goals" section read: "To act independently and in coalition with other movements to build a new power base to achieve short-term social change and ultimately a new and just economic system which will transcend the profit motive, eliminate the concentration of corporate power, and serve human needs through democratic means." Before the meeting the Beach Area Gray Panthers in Los Angeles telegrammed to express "severe opposition from many active members" to the phrase "transcend the profit motive." Shubert Frye, chair of the Panthers' Economy Task Force, responded, "We Gray Panthers want a system which will rise above or surpass the dominant motivation of profit as opposed to the motive of concern for human needs." After some discussion the NSC agreed to seek "continuing dialogue" with the Beach Area network over the wording.[61]

At the October NSC meeting held in Los Angeles the group of thirty heard from Steve McConnell, thirty, a Beach Area Panther who helped organize several Los Angeles area networks. Addressing "Some Nagging Contradictions in Gray Panthers," he pointed to the changing LA member profile: fewer young members, most of whom, like him, were gerontology professionals (McConnell had recently completed a Ph.D. in sociology at the University of Southern California Andrus Gerontology Center); and new cohorts of older members, not recruited by Maggie, who saw the Panthers less as the "radical" group McConnell had joined in 1974 and mainly "interested in reform kinds of issues." Some current LA Gray Panthers, he added, did not even support rent control. Perhaps Point Five helped "screen out" such members, he conceded, but it also worked against enhancing Panther numbers. Could it "be worded in such a way . . . that it does not offend the sensibilities of any major constituency and still provide a progressive position?"[62]

McConnell's remarks were summarized in *Network* and letters from the grassroots poured in. One West Los Angeles member urged the Panthers to abandon critiques of "military hardware" and "corporate profit" and support for the Dellums national health service bill and concentrate on improving private health insurance coverage. This went too far for most. A Philadelphia Panther warned against becoming "another 'Senior Citizen' group." Five Long Beach, California, Gray Panthers asserted, "Our system *should* put people before profits." A Santa Cruz network member insisted, "To transform [Point Five] is to make the Gray Panthers another wing of the Democratic Party."[63]

Following an NSC recommendation, Point Five was amended at the

1979 Gray Panther convention. The old language, "a new and just economic system which will transcend the profit motive," now read, "a society which will put the needs of people above profits"—perhaps less
stark to some, perhaps more bold to others. The change provoked no
controversy or resignations. In practice, local network members like
those in Berkeley and New York saw no contradiction between advocating radical positions on nuclear disarmament or health care and joining
"bread and butter" struggles to prevent Social Security cuts or preserve
rent control.

Network Growth and Regional Development

The number of Gray Panther local networks quadrupled in the late
1970s, from twenty-eight at the time of the Chicago convention to a peak
of 122 in 1980. Maggie's visits and help were the key factor, although, as
in the Bay Area and New York, several new networks were midwifed by
nearby existing ones. Some groups, however, proved to be "one-person
networks" or "paper networks" headed by conveners making little attempt to recruit members or organize action on Panther issues. In 1982
the NSC imposed stricter affiliation requirements: networks must have a
minimum of ten members, report annually, create a steering committee
and bylaws, hold at least six meetings per year, charge dues, and work
on one priority issue established at the biannual convention. The network total then dropped, and by 1985 stood at ninety-three. Of these,
sixteen had existed for a decade or more: Boston, Rhode Island, New
York, Buffalo, South Jersey, Metropolitan Washington, Chicago, Madison
(Wisconsin), Kansas City, Denver, San Diego, Greater Los Angeles, Long
Beach, Berkeley, San Francisco, and Seattle. The national impact was
even wider. Between 1972 and 1985 some 257 networks in forty-three
states affiliated with the Gray Panther national office.[64] Some failed to
thrive (like the Bronx and Broad Channel groups in New York) but half
the networks that were closed or defunct by 1985 had lasted two years or
longer (like Queens College and Brooklyn).

In 1981 total network membership was some six to seven thousand. Groups varied in size from seven members to the more than five
hundred–strong San Francisco Gray Panthers. About a third were small
networks averaging fourteen members; a third medium-sized groups averaging forty-six; and a third large networks averaging two hundred, with
these bigger Panther groups accounting for two-thirds of the national
movement's network membership. "Active members"—those who did
more than attend meetings or pay dues—were probably about twelve
hundred nationwide, with active member contingents of up to forty in
the largest groups. In 1981 most networks were adding new members,

growing by about 25 percent that year. A majority of network members were over sixty, and less than 10 percent under thirty; members between thirty and sixty amounted to perhaps 25 or 30 percent, with great variation from one group to another. In a few networks, including college-based groups, half or more of members were under sixty, but in the Rhode Island Gray Panthers "99 percent" were over sixty. Most networks met monthly, a third of them at night, typically for two-hour sessions at libraries, churches, senior centers, other public buildings, or in a few instances in homes. A dozen large networks, including Berkeley and New York, had offices and were incorporated as tax-exempt organizations. Network activities minimally included demonstrations, letter writing, public speaking, and participation in coalitions, most often with senior citizen and peace groups. During 1981 a third of the networks had direct contact with Maggie, either on her visits, at state and regional meetings, or at the Gray Panther national convention.[65]

Cooperative activity between neighboring networks began in 1976. That year Panthers from the Philadelphia and two suburban New Jersey networks picketed a John Wanamaker department store after learning four hundred company workers would be terminated the day before Christmas because they had reached sixty-five that year. The Panthers distributed "Scrooge Reincarnated" flyers and the TV cameras rolled. Also in 1976 the Southern California Coordinating Council was formed, which in two years grew to encompass ten networks. It included the Greater Los Angeles Gray Panthers, an umbrella group of networks that comprised a peak membership of seven hundred by the end of the decade. Greater LA held an organizing workshop attended by forty Panthers in 1978, and through its Andrus Gray Panthers network at the University of Southern California sponsored a "National Health Service Versus National Health Insurance" forum in 1979. Its seminars with geriatric medical professionals and community members in 1980 were funded by the California Council for the Humanities.

The formation of statewide network ties in California began at the Western Regional Gray Panther Conference in Berkeley in 1977. Both energizing and exhausting, the four-day meeting was hosted by the Berkeley, Western Contra Costa, and Oakland/Emeryville networks and was planned by Lillian Rabinowitz and Mollyann Freeman of Berkeley. Some two hundred Gray Panthers from Texas, Oregon, Washington, Montana, and California attended and Maggie gave the keynote address.[66] Following reports from each network, workshops focused on Medicare reform, mandatory retirement, grassroots advocacy, and alternatives to nursing homes. Several network founders and leading activists were in attendance, including Ruth Haefner of Portland, Cookie Smith of Austin, Bernie Winter of San Diego, and Abe Boxerman, Grace Jacobs, and Steve McConnell of Los Angeles.

Soon after this gathering Lillian wrote to the national office, "In California, in my opinion, the empowerment we felt by a mixing of northern and southern groups was significant. But how we will translate this into action remains to be seen. There are some important bills in the upcoming Legislative session hopper that we should move on jointly and I hope that we can make it happen."[67] As a first step, Bay Area Panther health activists met with Southern Californians Winter and Boxerman in Berkeley to form a statewide health task force, and met again during 1978 in Los Angeles. The following year the Bay Area Council of Gray Panther Networks was started to pool local efforts and help organize new groups. This six-network council also hosted a meeting of northern California networks extending to Sonoma and Sacramento. The Bay Area groups continued to work cooperatively, particularly on nursing home issues, and to demonstrate jointly, including a 1983 march opposing U.S. intervention in Central America.

With both southern and northern regional groups now organized, California Panthers met during the 1979 Gray Panther convention in Washington, D.C., to plan a statewide convention. Held the following year in San Jose with Karl Grossenbacher of the Western Contra Costa network presiding, it elected Tom Moore of Sacramento president of the new California Gray Panthers, and he immediately became their spokesperson in the state capital. Nearly two hundred Gray Panthers attended a second convention in Santa Monica in 1981 and created statewide task forces on housing and utilities and Social Security. The largest networks, Berkeley, San Francisco, and Santa Barbara, provided the biggest shares of one-dollar-per-member annual dues but voted as equals with the other twenty-one member networks. In 1982, with 235 Panthers in attendance, Frieda Wolff of Western Contra Costa was elected president, with vice presidents for northern and southern California and Moore as continuing legislative representative in Sacramento.[68] Wolff had remarkable enthusiasm for Gray Panther projects, and the state organization matured under her leadership. She also edited the much-appreciated *California Panther* newsletter, a guide to pending state legislation and symbol of the state organization. She succumbed to cancer in 1984, and Grossenbacher became president of what were then twenty-eight networks plus Los Angeles and Bay Area umbrella groups. Attendance at the sixth California convention in 1985 fell to sixty-one, perhaps due to its remote setting in the Santa Cruz mountains, but delegates represented twenty-five networks and more than two thousand members.

Attempts to create state Gray Panther groups in Florida during 1979–

81 and New York and Oregon in 1981–82 were unsuccessful. Other than in California, the only lasting multinetwork organization was the Gray Panthers of New York City formed in 1982. Earlier multistate meetings brought together up to fifty Panthers from northeastern networks between 1978 and 1980, and beginning in 1980 annual "Mid-America" conventions were attended by up to one hundred Panthers from networks in Illinois, Indiana, Iowa, Kansas, Kentucky, Michigan, Minnesota, Missouri, Nebraska, Ohio, and Wisconsin. These regional events were devoted to exchanging information about local activities, socializing, and preparing resolutions for the biennial national Gray Panther conventions.

Conventions

By 1985 four national conventions had followed the first in Chicago. The 1977, 1979, and 1981 four-day gatherings were held near Washington, D.C., at the suburban Chevy Chase, Maryland, 4-H Center, which offered modest accommodations to the several hundred Panthers attending. This location also facilitated an "action" at each convention. In 1977 Billie Heller led a Gray Panther picket at the U.S. Chamber of Commerce building to protest its opposition to the Office of Consumer Affairs that President Carter had pledged to create (and later did). "Older people are critically affected by Federal decisions involving drug safety, product prices, air pollution, [and] pension rights," Maggie declared. "Business has advocates in and out of government . . . so why shouldn't consumers also have advocates representing them?"[69] In 1979 the Panthers joined a demonstration of five hundred religious leaders and Mobilization for Survival activists against nuclear weapons and power plants at the Department of Energy. The 1981 action bussed scores of Panthers to the front gates of the White House to object to Reagan administration proposals to cut Social Security benefits and maneuvers to blunt recommendations from the ongoing White House Conference on Aging. The following day's *New York Times* coverage of the conference featured a picture of Maggie in front of the White House surrounded by old and young Gray Panthers.[70]

The 1977 convention keynote speaker was Representative Ron Dellums, who recounted his decision to introduce a national health service bill after reading the Medical Committee for Human Rights' 1971 position paper. The 1981 keynote address, "Social Security and Our Future," was by William Winpisinger, president of the International Association of Machinists and Aerospace Workers and a leading organizer of the massive Solidarity Day protest three months earlier. Other Gray Panther convention guest speakers included writer Gloria Steinem, journalist Studs Terkel, Representatives Claude Pepper and Parran Mitchell (advocate of the military budget guns-to-butter "transfer amendment"), Democratic Socialist Organizing Committee leader Michael Harrington, Karen Ferguson of the Pension Rights Center, and economists David Gordon and Robert Lekachman. The business of the conventions centered on panels and workshops led by Panthers including Cameron Hall, Shubert Frye, Elma Griesel, Lillian Rabinowitz, Hope Bagger, Glen Gersmehl, Sylvia Wexler, Paul Nathanson, Tish Sommers, Rosalie Schofield, Steve McConnell, and in 1981 Dennis Day-Lower on shared housing and Roger Sanjek on "abandonment, displacement and shelter security." Oregon Panther Ron Wyden co-chaired the resolutions session in 1977, participated in a Medicare reform panel in 1979, and as a freshman member of Congress introduced Maggie's evening speech in 1981.

Little of note was added to the Chicago convention's lengthy resolutions agenda beyond a 1979 plank affirming "no discrimination whatsoever against homosexual men and lesbian women, including in . . . employment, housing and education." Still, at each convention the resolutions grew more numerous, and debate more vociferous. At the 1977 convention Maggie observed, "We need to tighten up the process," but in 1979 a "snarl over procedure" wasted an hour before debate even began. In 1981 resolutions chair Lillian Rabinowitz mailed five edited pages of submitted items in advance and debate was limited to two hours. Some objected to this move while others appreciated it. "More time needed, conference should be a day longer" was one response; "a few men displayed severe testosterone poisoning" was another, a critique of excessive windbaggery.[71]

More than 330 attended the 1977 convention, and nearly 400 in 1979. Metropolitan Washington Panther Frances Klafter handled logistics for the first of these and chaired the organizing committee for the second. Grants from the Administration on Aging subsidized these conventions' expenses as well as publication of *The Gray Panther Manual: Vol. II Programs for Action*, a thick sourcebook Klafter edited with contributions by Griesel on nursing homes, Gersmehl and Sommers on organizing and lobbying, and sections on housing, income, nuclear power, solar energy, conservation, and health care.[72] Registration fell to 240 at the 1981 convention organized by national office staffer Rosalie Riechman. The half-dozen New York Gray Panthers who attended enjoyed participating in the White House demonstration, meeting other Panthers, and hearing Maggie, in particular her closing comments about a possible Gray Panther "D.C. presence." Fewer than 170 registered at the 1984 convention in San Jose, California.[73] California Gray Panthers had held their own convention a month earlier in Los Angeles and attendance there surpassed that in San Jose.

"National"

As the number of networks mushroomed during the later 1970s most members had only a vague understanding of "National," symbolized to them by Gray Panther headquarters in Philadelphia. To most, National was where conveners ordered T-shirts and buttons or purchased copies of the Gray Panther newspaper *Network*, which was not mailed to local network members until 1982. Before then it was sent only to individual subscribers or "national members" who contributed financially to Philadelphia; network conveners were encouraged to purchase bulk copies for their members, most of whom never saw or read it. Compounding the National-local gap, between 1975 and 1985 none of the office staff had prior Gray Panther experience, including office coordinator (and from 1978 executive director) Edith Giese, thirty-six when hired in 1975, and network coordinator Sherry Clearwater, who joined at twenty-nine in 1977. Moreover, the closest network, the Philadelphia Gray Panthers, had few active members. By the later 1970s it was mainly a "paper network," or occasionally a "one-person network" represented in local coalitions by a vocal member, and was closed in 1984.

The office sent new conveners the Gray Panther "Purposes and Goals" and copies of previous convention resolutions, and all networks received occasional issue updates (on mandatory retirement, the B-1 bomber, draft registration, and so on.) Only a third of networks returned surveys mailed by the national staff in 1977 and 1979, and just three submitted nominations for the 1979 National Steering Committee election. Yet for network activists attending the 1977 and 1979 conventions, perceptions of National sharpened. In 1980 nearly two-thirds returned the network survey, and three-quarters sent the thirty-five-dollar annual affiliation fee instituted that year. Through telephone calls, visits to network and regional meetings, and office mailings Clearwater became known to many local Panthers, but Giese, who focused on national administrative matters and fund-raising, did not.

At the 1975 convention the NSC was reconstituted with a mix of veteran Consultation members, newer friends of Maggie (Elma Griesel, Rosalie Schofield, Tish Sommers), and network members from New York, Washington, D.C., Chicago, Kansas City, and Los Angeles. The thirty-member NSC, however, failed to develop effective ties to the expanding number of networks and their emergent regional and state organizations. Reports from NSC members about their own networks ended in 1977, decisions to link each network with an NSC member never materialized, and monitoring of local network activities was delegated to the Philadelphia staff. A rough numerical balance between National friends of Maggie and network-based members persisted for nearly a decade. At the 1981 convention an amendment to the Articles of Agreement was approved requiring that in the next election, not held until 1984, two-thirds of NSC seats be reserved for network members. In 1985 a network member majority took office.

Composed of NSC officers, appointed committee chairpersons, and Maggie, the seven-to-ten-person Executive Committee, plus staff members Giese and Clearwater, formed a "National" faction within the Gray Panther movement. Headed by chairpersons Alice Adler of Chicago from 1975 to 1979 and Leslie Kwass of Berkeley from 1979 to 1983, it was increasingly at odds with the movement's network-based leaders. The twice-yearly Executive Committee meetings were devoted to setting organizational priorities and fund-raising for the Philadelphia office.

After the 1975 Chicago convention the national Gray Panthers faced serious economic problems. None of the foundation proposals submitted during 1976–77 was funded. At the 1977 convention Maggie announced that National would end the year in deficit. Berkeley Panthers Ann Squires and Lillian Rabinowitz immediately organized a collection that raised $1,500. That year Anacapa, a liberal-leaning direct mail firm, sent out one hundred thousand "prospect" letters signed by Maggie soliciting support for the Gray Panthers, and over the next two years this produced twenty thousand new donors. By 1980 direct mail returns provided three-quarters of the Gray Panther Project Fund's half-million-dollar budget. A third of this was ploughed back into funding appeal letters, but Anacapa proceeds also financed additional office space and more staff. Three Philadelphia office employees worked on the mail campaign, and Rosalie Riechman, thirty-six, also without prior Gray Panther experience, was hired in 1981 to coordinate national projects. Other staffers included a secretary working at Maggie's home office and the editor of *Network*, which grew in circulation from three thousand in 1978 to sixty thousand, including all direct mail donors. Chuck Preston edited *Network* from his home until 1979 when health problems led him to pass the reins to Christina Long, twenty-three, and he continued to write for *Network* until his death in 1982. Long worked at a nursing home while a college student, saw the *Wrinkled Radical* film, and after graduation from McGill University arrived in Philadelphia to volunteer. Under her editorship the paper expanded to six issues a year and grew from twelve to twenty pages by 1983.

In 1980 the Executive Committee switched the direct mail contract to a new fund-raising consultant. Costs rose and net returns began to fall, declining precipitously by 1983. There was little financial cushion. Maggie's honorarium earnings, now contributed by her on top of travel and living expenses, provided only minor support, as did sales of Panther publications and paraphernalia. After the Administration on Aging

1977 and 1979 convention grants (obtained by Metropolitan Washington Panthers Lou Teitlebaum and Frances Klafter) and another for a 1981 New York Media Watch conference, only one substantial grant was received—$70,000 over three years from the Levi-Strauss Foundation. The consequences were severe: six issues of *Network* were canceled during 1983 and 1984 and Riechman left for another job. Giese maintained that foundations were "opting for 'safe' organizations to fund" over groups like the Gray Panthers,[74] yet Maggie was able to obtain grants for the Shared Housing Resource Center, and networks in Berkeley, Boston, Kansas City, Los Angeles, and San Francisco received foundation funding. In 1984 the Villers Foundation (later Families USA), which gave the Panthers $10,000 in 1981, gave another $60,000, half for the national office and half for ageism seminars with local networks.

Local-National Conflict

Several things bothered grassroots Panthers about their Philadelphia office. Santa Barbara and Denver Panthers felt slighted when it chartered new networks near them without prior notification. Several networks rankled that National refused to share addresses of direct mail donors who lived in their area. (On the few occasions networks were permitted to use the national donor list, responses were meager. Philadelphia had little to lose from donors shifting contributions to local networks, or networks many new members to gain, but control of addresses by National engendered grassroots mistrust.) Networks long complained about not receiving issues of *Network*—even in 1984 the national office admitted "delay[s] in getting *Network* to new and not-so-new members." The "convener mailings" and *Local Links* newsletter that Philadelphia staffer Clearwater sent to each network were also problematic. Some New York conveners found them voluminous and unhelpful. In a 1984 survey another convener declared, "There is practically no communication of value that comes from the national office."[75]

By 1981 the staff adopted their fund-raising consultants' labeling of network members as "volunteers" and financial donors as "members-at-large." They and the Executive Committee envisaged the Gray Panther " 'movement' . . . becoming an organization" with networks its "lower operational levels." Over the next two years they discussed "closing" most networks, retaining "25 to 35 stable" groups that would be pressed to raise annual budgets of $10,000 or more, and transforming the Gray Panthers into "a Rapid Response Network and invit[ing] interested people to join."[76] Many network-based NSC members recoiled from the staff–Executive Committee agenda. A skit by two consultants on how NSC members would "make [fund-raising] telephone calls to . . . corporations and foundations" was "not well received [and] many board members were opposed to most of their ideas."[77] The Executive Committee's distance from network-based sentiment was also evident in its decision that "disarmament cannot be of direct concern to our program," approved just four months before two hundred Gray Panthers marched in the 1982 mass disarmament demonstration in New York.[78]

Maggie supported the National faction's all-consuming focus on fundraising. By the early 1980s, then in her later seventies and in declining health, she worried about the future of the Gray Panthers after she was gone. Hoping that a "Maggie Kuhn Endowment Fund" would provide permanent support for the national office, she made telephone calls to potential wealthy donors and attended dinners with major contributors.[79] Yet aside from Alida Rockefeller Dayton's $10,000 gift in 1981, individual donations remained small. The office staff and Executive Committee, who enjoyed more face time with Maggie than any other Panthers, supported this plan and doubted that the future of the movement resided in the networks. Some network-based views of National were correspondingly dim. As the Metropolitan Washington network saw it: "The [Executive Committee] consists of individual members of the Gray Panthers who are not in the leadership of local networks and they are not aware of the specifics of grass roots concerns."[80]

In March 1982 I attended my first NSC meeting, held in San Francisco. The thirty new and reelected members reflected the current Panther movement: two-thirds were women; eight were "young," in their thirties or forties (I was thirty-seven); ten northeastern members were complemented by nine Californians; and the last Consultation veterans were gone, as were NCCNHR and OWL leaders Elma Griesel and Tish Sommers. Half the NSC were active network members and half were "National" Gray Panthers, including NSC chairperson Leslie Kwass, who was no longer active in the Berkeley network.

During the meeting local-National tension bubbled to the surface. Karl Grossenbacher of Western Contra Costa County objected that the Philadelphia office refused to acknowledge the now two-year-old California State Gray Panthers, referring to them only as "a meeting of networks in California." Frieda Wolff, head of the California group, which composed a third of the entire movement, was present through the three-day meeting but permitted to speak only once. A month earlier the Executive Committee turned down California's request for a seat on the NSC. (In fact, the 1979 management study that the staff and Executive Committee cited as charter for their plans recommended apportioning a majority of NSC seats to local and state network leaders.)[81] Official recognition of the California Panthers came in 1983. The Gray Panthers of New York City, founded in 1982, was not recognized until 1984, and the Bay Area

Council of Gray Panther Networks dating to 1979 was never formally recognized.

Soon local-National conflict arrived in New York. In September 1982 the national office informed me that New York governor Hugh Carey had joined the new Gray Panther Advisory Board, a group of celebrities, policy consultants, and wealthy donors to be listed on Gray Panther direct mail funding appeals. Panthers in New York had fought Carey policies for years. I wrote to executive director Giese, "Carey has just vetoed part of a package of bills we had been working for to extend [eviction] protections to age 62+ tenants statewide. . . . His wife [Evangeline Gouletas-Carey] is partner with her two brothers in a national firm, Invsco, that specializes in converting buildings to condos and coops. They are notorious in Chicago and Washington DC for their ruthless methods in forcing tenants out of buildings they buy to convert." His Advisory Board nomination would "compromise us in relation to groups we work with in coalition."[82]

A month later the NSC met and was presented a list of thirty-five acceptances to Advisory Board invitations, which had been extended by Executive Committee members, executive director Giese, and the fundraising consultant. While Ed Asner, Pete Seeger, Benjamin Spock, Robert Lekachman, Elma Griesel, and Tish Sommers seemed appropriate, Lillian Rabinowitz objected to San Francisco mayor Diane Feinstein "because she owns much land in the Tenderloin district . . . an area of increasing gentrification where many old people are being evicted."[83] Both Carey and Feinstein were dropped. Later that fall New York City councilmember Carol Grietzer accepted an Advisory Board invitation. The Greenwich Village Panthers objected: "On a recent visits she appeared with photographers for a local newspaper; had her picture taken with Gray Panthers; and then left, not staying for the meeting she had been asked to address."[84] At the January 1983 NSC meeting Grietzer was dropped. National was now furious with New York and blamed the messenger, me, for the message.

The Social Security battles of 1981–83 also widened the local-National rift. Gray Panthers had mobilized in 1979 against Carter's proposed cuts with letters, pressure on elected representatives, and participation in SOS coalition actions. In 1981 New York Panther Jim Durkin gave his first "Social Security under Fire" talk a week after Ronald Reagan's January inauguration. At the March 1981 NSC meeting, Joe Davis of Metropolitan Washington raised an alarm over Reagan's budget proposals and was echoed by Lillian Rabinowitz, Tish Sommers, Karl Grossenbacher, and Alice Adler. The NSC voted to move that year's national convention from California to Washington, D.C.

During the first half of 1981 program coordinator Rosalie Riechman worked with Giese, Maggie, and an outside consultant on an ambitious "Social Security Summer" proposal, which was not funded. They solicited no network input; rather, National's view was "We need . . . to educate the networks on Social Security."[85] Later in 1981 Riechman produced a Gray Panther Social Security flyer featuring a cartoon of Reagan speaking from both sides of his mouth, and a Mother's and Father's Day card with a photograph of an infant wearing a Gray Panther button and a message from Maggie reading, "Now is the time to work together to insure a secure social security for the baby on this card, as well as people who are old today."

At the March 1982 NSC meeting, response to Riechman's work was underwhelming. While Grace Warfield of the small Minnesota Twin Cities Gray Panthers loved it, members from several large networks criticized the card for lacking political thrust or urgency and objected to the flyer's return coupon as "using the Social Security issue to raise money for the Gray Panthers."[86] The Philadelphia office encouraged networks to reproduce the flyer and purchase packs of the card, which thirty networks did, and for the next four months this constituted the Gray Panther Social Security campaign. Meanwhile Riechman initiated contact with local Panther Social Security activists, and her mailings included an Arizona Panther Social Security fact sheet and reports on Gray Panther demonstrations in Washington, D.C., and Sarasota. Not until July 1982 did any Philadelphia office mailing mention the Greenspan Social Security Commission appointed in 1981 and scheduled to report at the end of the year. The Philadelphia office's Gray Panther Social Security Organizing Packet did not arrive until September 1982.

By the end of 1982 the office had a list of Social Security activists in sixty Panther networks. Rather than "educating the networks," staffer Riechman was tutored by the likes of Metropolitan Washington's Social Security Task Force chair Ethel Weisser, a retired economist who conducted actuarial research for the original Social Security Act. In November 1982 the Greenspan Commission met in Virginia where the Metropolitan Washington and Montgomery County networks organized a demonstration that received coverage in *U.S. News & World Report* and *Business Week.*[87] In December Maggie joined Panthers from these two networks at the commission's Capitol Hill meeting. There, after attempting to speak, she was ejected from the meeting room and conducted an impromptu press conference that upstaged the commission.[88]

When the commission announced its recommendations in January 1983 Weisser was disturbed to learn that National supported the "compromise," and Maggie pronounced it "a victory." She alerted other networks, and Irv Riskin of Montgomery County called Philadelphia to insist on grassroots input before Gray Panther support was announced.

After messages "showing signs of rebellion and dissatisfaction" poured into the national office, seventeen Panthers representing nine networks from Washington to Long Island were invited to the January Executive Committee meeting. They implored the National leadership not to support the recommended benefit cuts. Maggie was reluctant to oppose her friend commission member Claude Pepper but understood that her movement felt otherwise.[89] In February 1983, sitting with Metropolitan Washington Panther Arjun Makhijani, thirty-seven, Greenwich Village Panther Isabella Shapiro, and Max Manes of SASS, Maggie testified before the House Ways and Means Committee: "Some of the elements of the Commission's report are meritorious, but the 'package' as a whole is unacceptable to us."[90]

In April 1983 newly elected NSC chairperson Grace Warfield commended "the National Office staff [for] the effectiveness of the major program efforts on Social Security."[91] Many network-based Panthers did not concur. "After all, we lost," I wrote to Executive Committee members. "The hooplah about our wonderful Social Security campaign in the last [Philadelphia staff's] *Local Links* [newsletter] made the office look silly to our members. Our Bronx convener . . . was embarrassed for her members to see it. . . . NSC member [Naomi Harward of the Arizona Valley of the Sun network] told me in March that the office materials were not as good or as timely as what SOS was sending."[92]

Rise of the Task Force System

Following the 1975 Chicago convention the NSC created three task forces to implement resolutions. The Economy Task Force, chaired by Shubert Frye and including Cameron Hall and Glen Gersmehl, was charged to formulate Gray Panther "national . . . economic priorities." Over the next two years they studied works by progressive economists and sent an annotated reading list to ninety task force members nationwide. Their position paper supporting defense budget cuts and the Humphrey-Hawkins Full Employment Bill was presented to the 1976 Democratic and Republican platform committees. In 1977 Frye testified against the B-1 bomber before the Senate Appropriations Committee. At the Panther's second convention the group's manifesto, titled *Economic Rights—Economic Democracy,* received wide support, including Maggie's, but also opposition from some newer members. It was approved "as a working document for study in the Gray Panther movement" and issued by the national office in pamphlet form.[93] It stated:

The failure of our economic system is sharply evident in the conditions in which society has placed older and younger people. . . . One-quarter [of older persons] are below the poverty line. . . . In our urban centers . . . youth today are being scarred by the injustices [of a society] cruelly deficient in job-training opportunities. . . . Our economic system need not or should not . . . continue the co-existence . . . of poverty with national affluence. . . . Our position on Social Security . . . is informed by our long-term goal . . . of an adequate income . . . for all Americans.

In the United States . . . corporations make the basic decisions . . . concerning employment, working conditions, inflation, the type of goods we can buy, and which sectors of the economy will get the necessary investment to grow and which will wither. Our economic system determines priorities by the criterion of profitability and not that of satisfaction of human needs. . . . The food industry is largely free to impose upon the public a mass of junk products. . . . Transportation has been distorted away from urgently needed mass transit toward excessive focus on the automobile. . . . The corporate structure penetrates deeply into our cultural life . . . through corporate ownership of the major mass media. . . . Corporations exercise their decisive influence in the determination of government economic policy through . . . lobbying, campaign contributions, control of key Congressional committees, and [circulation of personnel] between business and government agencies.

Planning in an economic democracy must be under the control of elected representatives of the people while utilizing the expertise of scientists, technicians, economists, workers, [and] consumers. . . . Some [planning should be] on the federal level, but much can be by regional and community bodies [with] as much local control as possible. . . . Public ownership is . . . essential [for] services which are basic to our needs, such as energy resources, transportation, and public utilities. . . . Private enterprise . . . must be subject to effective regulation [to] protect the health and safety of consumers by banning harmful additives in food[, to] subject drug manufacturers to the strictest measure of socially responsible control[, and to] provide safeguards for workers' health [and] safety. . . . We must develop systems of recycling useable waste materials. . . . and move decisively to the development of new sources of energy, with special attention to solar and geothermal sources.

The right of each individual to access to food, health services, adequate housing, and legal services . . . should be included within the concept of human rights. . . . In today's world of global interdependence our . . . food and other aid programs and our arms sales are designed for our own corporate profits. . . . We call for a foreign economic policy that . . . give[s] priority to meeting human needs.

During 1979 more than two dozen Gray Panther networks formed *Economic Rights—Economic Democracy* study groups. In 1980 the Panthers joined a national Big Business Day coalition with environmental groups, labor unions, and allies Ralph Nader, Representative Ron Dellums, and economist Robert Lekachman. On April 17, the day income tax returns were due, Panther actions in New York, Austin, California, Michigan, and Minneapolis spotlighted economic and energy issues, and Maggie proclaimed, "Big Business Day affirms the goals of our Gray Panther [Economy] Task Force . . . and makes public our outrage at the unbridled economic power of the multinationals."[94] The task force waned when Frye's NSC term ended in 1981, and Gray Panther activism on economic issues shifted to Reagan's Social Security cuts.

Joe Davis, a retired engineer, chaired the Panthers' Housing Task Force. After joining the Metropolitan Washington network he organized the City Wide Housing Coalition that brought rent control to the District of Columbia in 1974. His next campaign targeted condominium conversions, which were forcing older tenants out of their apartments. He also joined a losing struggle to save the home of older Gray Panther Martha Brown, whom the District refused to pay fair compensation after condemning her house to make room for a supermarket. *A Call for Decent Housing,* Davis's task force newsletter published between 1975 and 1981, spotlighted housing concerns of Panthers nationwide as well as information about public housing, energy conservation, federal rent assistance programs, tenant-managed cooperatives, homeowner issues, mobile homes, and shared housing. The *Call* was mailed to one hundred national Housing Task Force members, many of whom Davis corresponded with, and his updates on housing issues also appeared in *Network.* In 1980, following formal testimony, Davis conducted a far-reaching dialogue on urban housing issues with the House District of Columbia Committee chair Ron Dellums. And "with financial help from Maggie" he visited three California Panther networks.[95] In 1981 Davis died at age seventy-two.

The mainstay of the Health Task Force between 1976 and 1983 was Frances Klafter, a Metropolitan Washington Panther since 1974. Though new to health care issues, in 1975 she organized a coalition that prevented loss of Medicaid benefits to forty thousand D.C. residents. In 1976 she and Elma Griesel became co-chairs of the Gray Panther Health Task Force, and at a Department of Health, Education, and Welfare panel Klafter gave her first testimony for the national movement: "This is a rich country and we can afford to provide quality health care not just for the elderly, but for people of all ages. . . . We must continue to try to patch up and improve the present health care delivery system; but we must simultaneously press for a national, community-based health service that will free health care delivery from the dollar sign."[96] Klafter embraced the national health service bill introduced by Representative Dellums in 1977 and in 1979 helped bring Dellums bill advocates under one Coalition for a National Health Service banner.

Klafter paid close attention to health care activism in the growing number of local networks. When she learned that the Brooklyn Gray Panthers convinced a local member of Congress to endorse the Dellums bill, she urged in *Network* that other Panthers ask their representatives for copies of the bill and then request co-sponsorship, which several networks did. In 1978 she produced a statement of "Gray Panther Goals in

Health Care" for the first statewide meeting of California Panther health activists; she refined it at a Northeast Regional Panther meeting later that year. It included advocacy for the "long-term" goal of a national health service but also "immediate" action to defend Medicaid and other safety-net programs, expand Medicare to cover all health needs of the elderly and disabled, and press for a "continuum" of community-based long-term care alternatives.[97] She mailed the "Goals" statement to all local networks and included contact information on national advocacy groups she worked with in D.C.–based coalitions.

Klafter testified on home health care before a Senate committee in 1979 but spent most of the year organizing the third Gray Panther convention and editing *The Gray Panther Manual: Vol. II Programs for Action.* This included analyses of the Carter, Kennedy, and Dellums health care proposals; materials on Medicare from the National Senior Citizens Law Center and the San Francisco Gray Panthers; fact sheets on long-term care from the National Citizens Coalition for Nursing Home Reform; and a summary of the Greater Boston Gray Panthers' national health service referendum campaign in Cambridge, Massachusetts.

In 1981 Public Citizen's Health Research Group issued *Your Money or Your Health*, a report revealing that nearly half of all U.S. doctors refused to accept Medicare Assignment (Medicare's payment of 80 percent of "reasonable changes" with patients billed for the remaining 20 percent) and were charging substantially higher fees. With a foreword by Maggie, it included information on excessive billing practices, obtained through a Freedom of Information Act request, for a sample of physicians in the Washington, D.C., area.[98] Klafter proposed that Gray Panther networks use the same method and compile local directories of doctors who accepted Medicare Assignment. This would assist beneficiaries searching for affordable physicians as well as pressure doctors not accepting Medicare Assignment to do so. Earlier the San Francisco Panthers wrote to individual doctors requesting that they accept Medicare Assignment, and Portland Gray Panthers worked with their county medical society to publish a list of doctors who accepted it. In 1982, on Capitol Hill, the Metropolitan Washington, Montgomery County, and Prince George's County Gray Panthers unveiled their directory of six thousand D.C. area physicians' Medicare Assignment practices. Maggie, Klafter, and Representative Ron Wyden spoke and the *Washington Post* covered the event. Over the next two years Panther networks in Florida, California, Texas, Michigan, Boston, and New York undertook Medicare Assignment projects.

At the 1981 Gray Panther Convention Klafter organized a congressional staff briefing on Reagan administration Medicare and Medicaid cuts. She was reelected chair of the Health Task Force by its members, who included Lillian Rabinowitz and Dellums bill activists Abe Boxerman and

Karl Grossenbacher from California, Cookie Smith from Austin, Eddie Sandifer from Mississippi, Gladys Elson from Westchester, and Mildred Sklar, Lani Sanjek, and Bill Lievow from New York. Klafter communicated with task force members by conference call, updating them on Washington developments as she did Maggie and local network conveners, and urged calls and telegrams to members of Congress at key points during the legislative calendar. In 1982 she wrote several articles for *Network*, produced new Gray Panther health care brochures, and mailed all networks the first two issues of her *Health Watch* newsletter, which included legislative updates and reports of local Panther activities. She continued to testify for the Gray Panthers in Washington, met with Health Task Force members at the 1983 California Gray Panther convention and the New York Gray Panthers tenth anniversary celebration, and was invited to speak at the Mid-America Panther gathering.

Fall of the Task Force System

Gray Panther activists appreciated the task forces. Their written materials and updates enhanced grassroots network activities, and they facilitated cross-network ties at regional meetings and national conventions.[99] "National" saw things differently. The Philadelphia office viewed the task forces as generators of additional work for them and beyond their control. In 1980 executive director Edith Giese requested that the Executive Committee "pare down our multiplicity of issues" and hire a staff "coordinator" to direct Panther projects and develop proposals for outside funding. "This salary would replace any substantial budget allocations for . . . task forces," which would become "consultants. . . . honchod by [the] staff project coordinator."[100] The Executive Committee approved, and Rosalie Riechman was hired in 1981. No one, however, discussed this new arrangement with the task force chairs or members.

The Economy Task Force expired at the end of 1981 and Housing Task Force chair Joe Davis died that year. I met Davis earlier in 1981 at a National Tenants Union conference, and we discussed housing issues and the groups I worked with in New York. After joining the National Steering Committee in 1982 I agreed to become Housing Task Force chair, taking Davis and Frances Klafter as my role models. From reviewing network newsletters and letters sent to the Philadelphia office, I learned that various Panther networks were working on rent control, property tax fairness, condominium conversion, shared housing, senior citizen congregate residences, and reverse annuity mortgages (which transferred ownership to a bank but allowed elderly homeowners to remain in their homes). I met with Metropolitan Washington members of Davis's task force, including Steve McConnell, then a staffer for the

House Select Committee on Aging, and learned about their efforts on "repair and deduct" legislation for tenants, public housing, and cooperatives. I also met with Berkeley Gray Panther housing activists while in California. I sent all network housing contacts and conveners a packet including a National Low-Income Housing Coalition sign-on letter urging Congress to restore housing funds to Carter-era levels, and a list of housing questions for congressional candidates prepared by Mobilization against Displacement in New York. I also began a *Network* column that over the next four issues addressed tenant organizing, affordable housing, tax subsidies to developers and wealthy homeowners, and the growing homelessness crisis.[101]

In Philadelphia I met with Maggie and the office staff about sponsoring a Gray Panther "shelter security" forum that would include tenant, homelessness, shared housing, accessibility, and long-term care advocates. Just as Gray Panther health conferences stimulated interest in a national health service and the Dellums bill, I believed a forum on "housing needs through the life cycle" might spur Panther networks to sponsor similar forums and be a step toward model legislation.[102] Before plans moved further, however, New York governor Hugh Carey was nominated to the Gray Panther Advisory Board. This placed things on hold for months. During this time it became clear that the Philadelphia staff saw the housing forum as a means to obtain grants and not to encourage network activism or organizing. Frustrated, I resigned as Housing Task Force chair at the March 1983 NSC meeting.

National's purge of Frances Klafter from the Health Task Force chair a month later shocked its members and proved disruptive to the entire Gray Panther movement. During 1982 Klafter managed her task force travel, testimony, contacts with members and local conveners, reports in *Network*, and production of *Health Watch* on a budget of $3,500;[103] she received little Philadelphia staff support, which she noted at the March 1983 NSC meeting.[104] The possibility of substantial external Health Task Force funding, however, became likely after Klafter attended a 1982 Villers Foundation health seminar and submitted materials about task force activities. Villers, with a forty million dollar endowment, was interested in Medicare Assignment, which Klafter now advocated should be mandatory for doctors accepting Medicare patients.

At the March 1983 meeting the NSC voted unanimously "that work on national health issues take the same place as the [1981–82] work . . . on Social Security and that the Health Task Force and the staff begin to work out specific organizational proposals."[105] After the meeting, and without conferring with Klafter or Health Task Force members, Philadelphia staffer Riechman wrote to her Social Security network contacts asking if they wanted to work on health, an area in which she had no previous experience. The same day she wrote to Klafter, suggesting that she continue "the fine work which you have been doing on the Hill . . . participating in coalitions and testifying" and "do[ing] the first draft of Gray Panther health position papers," but removing her from contact with local networks and Health Task Force members.[106] National's staff "honcho" was now in place.

Alarmed that "Rosalie plans to take over my Task Force [although] she is going to permit me to ghost write!," Klafter wrote to Health Task Force members that "serious friction between me and the National Office staff" threatened Gray Panther "health work." She asked their approval for Gladys Elson of the Westchester Gray Panthers to join her as Health Task Force co-chair until a new chairperson from "among our own ranks" could be found.[107] Before task force members could respond, NSC chairperson Grace Warfield sent Klafter a special delivery letter "accepting" her "resignation" as chair. Letters were also sent to organizations in Washington and congressional staffers stating that Frances Klafter no longer represented the Gray Panthers. Maggie backed up Reichman and Warfield and declared herself interim co-chair of the Health Task Force with Jim Davis, a young Panther who had been a member of Klafter's task force.[108]

A four-month storm began. Letters protesting Klafter's dismissal and pointing out she had not submitted any resignation were sent to Warfield, Maggie, and all NSC members and Gray Panther networks by a group of Health Task Force members, ten Washington, D.C., area Panthers, and twenty New York Panther conveners and active members.[109] Maggie's response to the D.C. Panthers poured oil on the fire by extolling the national staff's Social Security campaign and by alluding to "Frances' disruptive behavior through the years," an innuendo mystifying those who worked with her.[110] Next, a mailing to network conveners about Philadelphia's application to Villers for "possible funding . . . for our health and field work" heightened suspicions about National's motive for displacing Klafter.[111] In June I wrote to Maggie:

There are two contending views of what the GPs will be in the 1980s. One [is] of a national alliance of local activist groups—better organized, and better connected through the NSC, national task forces, *Network*, and staff. . . . The second view is one the staff projects [and] may be held by other members of the NSC. . . . In this view, the Gray Panthers are to become a fund-raising, publicity-seeking organization in which networks are a subsidiary, troublesome, even unnecessary part. . . . There is no recognition of the networks' local issues and struggles, of their immense contribution in members' time and energy, or even of the funds we raise and spend locally on our work. Rather we are seen as contributing only one percent of the national staff's budget, and eight percent of the membership. . . . In this view, the important Gray Panthers are the "member-at-large" donors on whom the staff depend. . . . The fact that donors contribute because there *are* local activists out there is missed. . . . It is only you, Maggie, and national publicity that the staff sees as Gray Panther activity. . . . Many of us in the networks are dispirited, dismayed and disheartened by what has happened in the last few months. . . . Will we be squeezed out? Should we just ignore the national and do our own local work?[112]

Klafter made clear to her Panther supporters, "I certainly have no intention of fighting Maggie."[113] Hoping to preserve the esteem and effectiveness Klafter enjoyed in Washington and among Gray Panthers nationally, in July New York Panthers Evelyn Neleson, Lillian Sarno, Mildred Sklar, and Roger and Lani Sanjek went to Philadelphia to request the Executive Committee to reinstate Klafter.[114] (Lillian Rabinowitz had written us that she agreed with the New York position and had said so to Executive Committee member Leslie Kwass.)[115] There Maggie told us that she was attempting to conduct a "beautiful symphony" and we were "trombones." After we left, the Executive Committee ratified Klafter's dismissal. In protest I then resigned from the NSC. Unrest among Panthers nationwide continued. NSC chairperson Warfield and the Philadelphia staff even feared that networks might secede from the national Gray Panthers.[116] Maggie requested an August meeting in New York where eighteen city and Westchester Panthers affirmed the importance of network participation in the task forces and called for greater NSC supervision of the national staff. By the end of the summer local-National relations were at their nadir.

In fall 1983 the Gray Panthers received a Mandatory Medicare Assignment Project grant from the Villers Foundation. But rather than the Philadelphia office staff, it was members of Klafter's task force who carried forward Gray Panther work on health care. Frances Humphreys, a Prince George's County Panther who during 1982 and early 1983 had worked one day a week with Klafter, became Health Task Force chair in 1984. She revived *Health Watch*, reestablished Gray Panther ties with D.C. advocacy organizations and congressional staff, and alerted local networks to Republican plans to cut Medicare and Medicaid. She continued Klafter's Medicare Assignment campaign, which had scored a victory in fall 1983 when the Reagan administration consented to nationwide release of information on physician Assignment practices. At the 1984 convention Abe Boxerman of Los Angeles created a National Health Service Task Force. Like Klafter, he urged Gray Panthers to request copies of the Dellums bill from their congressmember, and in 1985 he organized a Chicago meeting of forty-two Coalition for a National Health Service and Gray Panther activists, including Maggie. A new Housing Task Force also was formed in 1984. Its chairperson's first action was to ask local networks to endorse the current National Low-Income Housing Coalition sign-on letter.

The national Peace Task Force chaired by veteran Panther Glen Gersmehl also was started in 1984 and flourished for the next two years. Based in Oakland, California, Gersmehl avoided the Philadelphia office and contacted networks directly, many of which, like New York and Berkeley, already had committees or task forces working on the Nuclear Freeze campaign and U.S. intervention in Central America. Gersmehl organized peace workshops at the 1984 California and National Gray Panther conventions, mailed his fact-filled *Peace Report* newsletter to each network, produced a sixty-page guide to peace organizations and publications, and visited several Midwest and East Coast Panther groups. He orchestrated a 1984 Gray Panther National Peace Day on which West Coast networks, joined by Maggie, protested on the opening day of the Democratic Party convention in San Francisco and Panther groups elsewhere staged local actions. In 1985 the task force joined a coalition of fifty groups sponsoring an April "Peace, Jobs and Justice" march in Washington to demand military budget cuts and protest nuclear weapon deployment and South African apartheid. Gersmehl sent networks information about the marketing of war toys, like Hasbro's "G. I. Joe," which "inculcate in the minds of succeeding generations the notion that war is noble, patriotic, manly, [and] a necessary foreign policy option."[117] Several Panther groups added this cause to their peace agendas.

A D.C. Presence

Maggie was no stranger to the nation's capital. Yet she and the national office were in Philadelphia, and a Gray Panther voice on the spot in Washington was needed. In 1976 the NSC appointed Ethel Morris as D.C. lobbyist to facilitate presentation of Gray Panther testimony to the Democratic and Republican platform committees. In 1978 retired professor Bernard Forman, already a volunteer with the National Senior Citizens Law Center, became the Panthers' D.C. representative, lobbying that year against mandatory retirement and testifying at congressional hearings on the Older Americans Act. Metropolitan Washington Panthers also lobbied and testified in Congress, and in 1979 their NSC member Thelma Rutherford implored the Executive Committee: "We must show our faces up on Capitol Hill."[118]

With Reagan's election in 1980, Gray Panthers nationwide sharpened their sights on Washington and the several "new coalitions" formed to fight the Reaganite thrust. Early in 1981 Metropolitan Washington Panther Joe Davis told the NSC, "Meetings of all these [groups] are held in Washington D.C.! We [D.C. Panthers] cannot attend them all. . . . It is recommended that we have a liaison person from the National Office to help us with this battle."[119] In July the Executive Committee assigned Rosalie Riechman to draft a "D.C. Presence" funding proposal for an office to link Philadelphia headquarters and Panther networks with Washington-based activities. At the Panthers' 1981 convention Maggie announced plans to open a Washington, D.C., office in cooperation with OWL and NCCNHR, and network members enthusiastically applauded the news. The D.C. office proposal was not funded, however, and in 1982 the Executive Committee decided to drop the idea. Meanwhile, Health Task Force chair Frances Klafter was the Gray Panther whom national advocacy groups in Washington invited to their "social program defense team" meetings."[120] Panther representation ended with her dismissal in 1983.

By 1984 the national office had weathered the direct mail financial crunch, mainly by canceling publications and losing Riechman. Gray Panthers nationwide were focused on the presidential election. For four years Maggie had told audiences, "I look forward to the day that Ronnie . . . rides out into the sunset in a scene from one of his B movies."[121] In fall 1984 the National Conservative Political Action Committee complained to the Federal Elections Commission that the Gray Panthers violated federal election law "by sending out mailings which 'made partisan points.' " Executive director Edith Giese filed a response and the complaint was dismissed after Reagan was reelected.[122] As 1985 began Maggie and her Panther movement looked forward uneasily to another four years before "Ronnie's" White House departure.

As a result of the 1984 NSC election, active network members now comprised nearly two-thirds of the membership. They included eight Californians, New York Gray Panther Doris Berk, and Frances Humphreys and Abe Bloom from suburban Maryland networks working closely with the Metropolitan Washington Panthers. As Gray Panther representatives, Humphreys, fifty-three, and Bloom, seventy-one, a retired National Bureau of Standards scientist long active in antiwar groups, pressed for mandatory Medicare Assignment in meetings with Medicare officials in 1984. In 1985 they and Irv Riskin, another suburban Maryland Panther, sent all network conveners Action Alerts on threats to Social Security COLAs and health programs. Humphreys appeared on the *NBC Evening News*, where she urged that Social Security be removed from the unified federal budget, and Bloom testified before the House Select Committee on Aging that Social Security's payroll tax earnings cap should be eliminated.

During the Executive Committee meeting held one day before the February 1985 NSC gathering, chairperson Grace Warfield recommended that executive director Giese be given a three-to-five year contract, and Giese requested that the vacant program coordinator position be refilled using anticipated Villers Foundation funding. At the next day's NSC meeting, when the question of replacing the vacant position arose, Bloom countered that the Villers grant should be used to staff a Washington office. Lillian Rabinowitz seconded the motion. The National faction, now a minority, objected but the motion carried, with some NSC members suggesting "perhaps the entire Philadelphia office should be moved to Washington." Before the meeting ended Giese resigned, joined by two staff members.[123] The organization's balance of power had shifted to the new network-based NSC majority.

Events moved rapidly. Warfield arrived in Philadelphia as interim executive director and oversaw the national office's move to less costly Philadelphia quarters. By September a new executive director was on board and in October the Washington office opened, at last providing the Gray Panthers their D.C. presence.

Chapter 7
Loss and Continuity (1986–95)

On a Sunday in April 1995 a front-page headline keyed *New York Times* readers to a story inside: "Gray Panther Founder Dies," an obituary of eighty-nine-year-old Maggie Kuhn, who "died yesterday at the home she shared in Philadelphia with a like-minded coterie. . . . She spent the last 25 years leading people young and old in the fight against age discrimination and other forms of what she saw as social injustice and stereotypical thinking."[1] Maggie died in her sleep at 8:30 a.m. on April 22, with her home attendant, Bertha Monroe, sixty-three, beside her. Later that day her personal assistant Sue Leary and former *Network* editor Christina Long fielded press inquiries and called Gray Panther Board chairperson Charlotte Flynn, who relayed the news to other members. The next week an "extra" issue of *Network* was mailed containing tributes to Maggie and details about memorial services at the First Presbyterian Church in Philadelphia and the Presbyterian Church of the Pilgrims in the nation's capital. In lieu of flowers it requested that donations to the Maggie Kuhn Endowment be forwarded to Gray Panther headquarters in Washington, D.C.

Five months later Maggie was inducted posthumously into the Women's Hall of Fame in Seneca Falls, New York. Other testaments followed, among them dedication of the Maggie Kuhn Gardens at the State Correctional Institution at Graterford, Pennsylvania, where Maggie helped start a Gray Panther network in 1989. Her elderly incarcerated followers erected a plaque on the prison grounds reading, "These gardens are dedicated to the memory of the great lady, Ms. Maggie Kuhn, pioneer and organizer of the world wide Gray Panthers movement. Ms. Kuhn lived and stood for what was right and dignified, especially on behalf of senior citizens. According to Ms. Kuhn, even a scoundrel has the right to maintain dignity and self respect. *R.I.P. Gracious Lady.*"[2]

Stronger Center, Weaker Base

During the later 1980s conflict between the networks and National dissipated. By 1986 network conveners and activists constituted almost the entire National Steering Committee, renamed the Gray Panther Board of Directors, and included Lillian Rabinowitz, Abe Bloom and Irv Riskin of the Montgomery County Panthers, Karl Grossenbacher, president of the California state organization, and Charlotte Flynn, convener of the Austin, Texas, network. National Panthers and friends of Maggie unconnected to networks were now gone. The Board's chairperson from 1986 to 1990 was Doris Dawson. She had been a Kansas City Gray Panther since 1974 and the network's newsletter editor, legislative chair, and convener, and a participant in nursing home and shared housing projects. In 1986 Dawson, seventy-one, moved to Torrance, California, where she joined the South Bay Gray Panthers and became active in statewide and southern California Panther groups. Though a soft-voiced Midwesterner trained in sociology, she was politically outspoken, urging fellow Panthers to organize demonstrations, write letters, and meet with members of Congress to protest the Reagan administration's "cuts in Medicaid, in Medicare, in education, in food stamp eligibility," its "military aid to El Salvador, to guerrillas in Angola and Afghanistan and to Contras in Nicaragua," and "the discredited Star Wars program."[3] Under Dawson the Board shrank to a more manageable twenty members, including Life Member Maggie Kuhn.

As 1986 began the new Washington, D.C., office was staffed by Frances Humphreys, who had returned to college after raising her children and then became a Prince George's County Panther. Humphreys spoke for the Panthers on Capitol Hill and mobilized a stream of young interns to produce network mailings on Social Security, the federal budget, and handgun control, plus two newsletters, *Health Watch* and *Washington Watch*, containing information on legislation, hearings, demonstrations, and Washington-based allied organizations. In 1987 she added a weekly recorded "Hotline" telephone message that provided Panther callers a three-minute update on D.C. events. She coordinated Gray Panther actions in the capital with Metropolitan Washington and Maryland network members. As an economy measure in 1988 she moved the D.C. office to space in Elma Griesel Holder's office, reactivating the Gray Panther–NCCNHR link.

In Philadelphia the executive director hired to replace Edith Giese resigned after four months, and staff member Sherry Clearwater oversaw the Philadelphia office for the next year and a half. In 1987 *Network* editor Christina Long resigned to teach in Philadelphia public schools, and Abby Lederman, a former VISTA volunteer and newspaper reporter in her thirties, replaced her and for the next five years maintained the standard set by Chuck Preston and Long, though with more advertisements. Later that year a new executive director, Karen Talbot, fifty-three, arrived, and in 1988 Clearwater departed. A longtime peace activist and daughter-in-law of an Oregon Gray Panther, Talbot had met Maggie in 1983 in Prague during a conference she had organized while working for the World Peace Council in Helsinki. Bringing an activist orientation to the position, Talbot immediately began visiting networks in several states and attended Northeast Regional and California Gray Panther gatherings. She also authored *Network* editorials on arms control and the Iran-Contra hearings. During 1988 Talbot testified on health care issues before the Federal Trade Commission, prepared Gray Panther position statements for the Democratic and Republican platform committees, and attended the Democrats' convention in Atlanta where she conferred with Representative Ron Dellums. In Washington she worked closely with Humphreys, Bloom, and D.C.-area networks and represented the Panthers on the forty-member Leadership Council of Aging Organizations and in other coalitions.

Increasingly frail, Maggie had confidence in Dawson, Humphreys, and Talbot, but between Board meetings she saw less of these or other Panther leaders, and spent little time in the Philadelphia or D.C. offices. With Maggie less visible in public, the funding base she stimulated stagnated and revenue fell from $615,000 in 1986 to $533,000 in 1990. Villers Foundation support ended after 1987,[4] and *Network*'s circulation dropped by half to thirty thousand by 1990. In 1989 the financial outlook demanded personnel cuts, and while Maggie and Dawson appealed to supporters for "survival" donations, Talbot and other Philadelphia staff departed.[5] In Washington, Humphreys became executive director. To Maggie's dismay, in 1990 the Philadelphia office closed, leaving her new personal assistant Sue Leary the only staff member close at hand. One bright spot was a bequest of $750,000 for "scholarly work [on Gray Panther issues by] persons aged 70 and over" in the will of child psychiatrist Margaret Mahler, an acquaintance of Maggie, who died at eighty-eight. Between 1988 and 1995 the Gray Panthers Mahler Institute awarded grants of up to $10,000 to more than two dozen elderly academics, writers, activists, and artists.[6]

During the later 1980s the number of local networks remained static, at eighty-one in 1986 and eighty in 1990. However, thirty-six networks folded during these years, and only twenty-four new networks were begun, including a few that revived after periods of dormancy. More seriously, most remaining younger Gray Panthers from the 1970s and early 1980s were exiting due to career demands, and few young or middle-aged replacements were arriving. In 1985 Maggie noted, "Some of our local networks have difficulty establishing contacts and relationships with young people," and at the 1990 convention she asked pointedly, "Where are the young?" Afterward she reflected, "The crowd [this year] was noticeably older than in years past. The organization has aged with me, and many of our members are in their late seventies and eighties."[7] The Board epitomized this change. By 1986 there was only one younger member, Jim Davis, forty, of the Portland Gray Panthers. This worried movement leaders, and in 1990 three members were elected to the Board from networks continuing to practice "age and youth in action": Austin Gray Panther Paula Mixson, forty-three, a Texas Department of Public Health social worker; and young Berkeley Gray Panthers Terri Thomas Hamstra and Varya Simpson.

Additional problems were affecting the networks. Some still were, or had become, "paper networks" or "one-person networks." Others found themselves unable to grow or to transfer leadership beyond the founding convener. The 1985 network survey revealed "pressing" worries about a lack of "new members—we have stagnant membership" and about "recruiting members to accept responsibilities in leadership positions." The burden on many local leaders was increasing. "We must invigorate our leadership on [the] network level . . . a lot of us oldies are burnt out," a San Pedro, California, convener insisted.[8] The regional and state groups, too, were losing vitality and by 1990 were inactive. Where ten networks were represented at the 1980 Mid-America conference, only five attended in 1987. One hundred and fifteen Panthers from seventeen networks registered at the 1986 Northeast Regional meeting, but substantially fewer came in 1987 or 1989. When the California Gray Panthers met in 1986, no candidate to succeed its president, Karl Grossenbacher, could be found among the eighty Panthers from thirty networks present. The state organization met again in 1988, but thereafter only northern or southern California meetings occurred.

Saving the Gray Panthers

Following the 1990 Gray Panther convention Frances Humphreys resigned as executive director to accompany her terminally ill husband to their home city of Knoxville, Tennessee, where he died in 1991. No full-time executive director replaced her until 1994, and during these years the leader of the Gray Panther movement was Charlotte Flynn, seventy, the national Board's chairperson and convener of the Austin network. Flynn joined the Panthers in 1977, attended her first convention in 1979, and became network convener in 1980, succeeding founder Cookie Smith, a retired League of Women Voters executive. Trained as a nurse, Flynn had vivid memories of the Depression years and the rise of

Hitler. She worked for the Girl Scouts of America from the 1940s until retirement and then dedicated herself to Gray Panther activism—from lobbying in the Texas legislature to organizing a guerrilla theater protest at the 1984 Republican Party convention in Dallas. Her network, with half of its 270 members under forty-five, was "always intergenerational. That was Maggie. That was the vision, and she had it right." Flynn joined the Panther National Board in 1986 and became chairperson four years later.[9]

In 1991 a former congressional staffer replaced Humphreys at the D.C. office. With direct mail contributions continuing to fall, he quickly resigned, telling Flynn she should close down the Gray Panthers. At the next Board meeting some members agreed, and Maggie initiated contact with the National Council of Senior Citizens about an organizational merger or takeover of the Panthers. Flynn was determined to save the organization "I've invested 14 years in." She visited Maggie in Philadelphia—"she was very frail then"—and they co-wrote an "Open Letter" in *Network* appealing for donations to prevent "the real possibility of closing our national office."[10] By September four thousand supporters, including thirty-two local networks, responded with nearly $70,000, enough to keep a D.C. staff of three and *Network*, *Health Watch*, and *Washington Watch* afloat. Later that fall Flynn obtained a $5,000 grant from the Unitarian Universalist Church for consultant Jule Sugarman, a former director of Head Start and the Special Olympics, to assess the future of the organization.

After interviewing Panthers throughout the movement, Sugarman reported to the Board, "If it was any other organization, you should close your doors. But it is the Gray Panthers, the potential is there." His reorganization plan, approved at the 1992 convention, included a smaller fifteen-person Board (plus Life Member Maggie), revised Articles of Agreement recognizing the networks as "the core of the Gray Panthers," and acknowledgment of all contributors of twenty dollars or more as "members" of the Gray Panthers. Six "nationwide priority areas" were listed: health care, reduced military spending, affordable housing, preservation of the environment, economic and social justice, and antidiscrimination, including elimination of ageism.[11] As part-time overseer of the D.C. office, Sugarman instituted economy measures—*Health Watch* and *Washington Watch* were eliminated, *Network* reduced in frequency and to newsletter size, the staff relocated to less expensive quarters, and computerization initiated. Humphreys had brought direct mail operations in-house, which dramatically lowered costs, yet donor numbers continued to fall, reaching 21,000 in 1993. That year's budget was under $300,000.

The next year donor numbers fell to fifteen thousand. On Sugarman's advice the Board dipped into the $111,000 Maggie Kuhn Endowment to hire a full-time executive director, Dixie Horning, forty-five, a former city government official in Arkansas and Louisiana without previous Gray Panther experience. She reestablished Panther ties with Washington organizations, testified before congressional committees, and represented the Panthers to the public and the press. Horning fully computerized the D.C. headquarters and Leary's office in Maggie's home and began the movement's transition to e-mail. She also met personally with members of forty networks.

Thirty-two networks folded or were terminated between 1991 and 1995, with a handful absorbed by nearby Panther groups. Only five new networks were recognized, and grassroots network membership declined to 3,500. Internal network problems were aired at Board meetings: "lack of focus," "inability to find leaders to replace those lost by illness or death," "decline in total membership," "inability to attract younger members." The Board again was primarily older, with only two or three members in their forties and fifties after the 1992 reorganization. By 1995 the number of networks dipped to fifty-four, with a third in California.[12] Thirty of the remaining networks had been founded in the 1970s. These Panther groups, now the movement's core, had developed their own cultures and traditions and had weathered one or more leadership transitions.

Conventions and Issues

Attendance at Gray Panther conventions, which peaked at four hundred in 1979, averaged half that number in the later 1980s and early 1990s. The 1986, 1988, and 1990 conventions followed earlier patterns: Maggie gave opening and closing remarks, and Gray Panther allies and friends of Maggie were featured speakers, including Ralph Nader, Benjamin Spock, Robert Butler, Victor Sidel of Physicians for Social Responsibility, and Sidney Wolfe of Public Citizen. Conventions in Washington (1988 was in Chicago) included demonstrations—at the White House for "Health Care, Not Warfare" in 1986, and in 1990 a four-block march to the Capitol, where a handful of congressmembers, including Ron Wyden, joined the call for "a national health-care system" and a hundred Panthers visited legislators' offices. Resolutions continued to consume convention time until 1990, when they were edited and distributed in advance by Paula Mixson.

The 1992 convention was devoted to approval of Sugarman's reorganization plan and to Board members' position papers on health care, housing, the military budget, economic justice, and the environment. At the 1995 convention Board member task forces drafted the resolutions, and keynote speaker Ann McBride, president of Common Cause, urged the Panthers to add campaign finance reform to their agenda. To open this gathering, Board chairperson Charlotte Flynn held a press conference with Handgun Control and other groups to support the Brady Law and a ban on assault weapons. At the convention's close fifty Panthers, including Maggie, rallied with striking Philadelphia transit workers at a union picket line.

Victory on the Panthers' founding issue came in 1986 when Congress banned mandatory retirement in nearly all private-sector employment.[13] Championed in the Senate by John Heinz and in the House by Claude Pepper, then eighty-six and its oldest member, the legislation was signed by President Ronald Reagan, seventy-five, who had proclaimed, "When it comes to retirement, the criterion should be fitness for work, not year of birth."[14] The following year Heinz appended a Gray Panther amendment to the renewed Older Americans Act that funded children's tutorial and after-school programs utilizing elderly volunteers. These two Panther congressional allies were soon missed: Pepper died in 1989, and Heinz, fifty-two, in a 1991 airplane accident.

On other fronts, the Panthers continued to emphasize the intergenerational importance of Social Security and advocated separating its trust fund from the unified federal budget where it masked large deficits during the Reagan years. They objected that President George H. W. Bush failed to convene a decennial White House Conference on Aging for 1991 and applauded when President Bill Clinton scheduled a White House conference for 1995 to coincide with the thirtieth anniversaries of Medicare and the Older Americans Act and the sixtieth anniversary of Social Security. Clinton's WHCoA executive director Robert Blancato briefed the Panther Board in 1994 and spoke at their 1995 convention. Five Panthers were WHCoA delegates, including Charlotte Flynn, an appointee of Texas governor Ann Richards, and the event was less contentious than the 1971 or 1981 conferences.

A Gray Panther Disability Task Force operated from 1984 to 1990. Its organizer, Naomi Harward, a retired social work professor and convener of the Arizona Valley of the Sun network, recruited two co-chairs, Louis Webb of the Mendocino Coast Gray Panthers and Mary Jane Owen, a wheelchair user and former social work professor who became a disability activist after losing her sight in 1972. The task force did not develop a broad network-based following but did act on principles affirmed in Gray Panther convention resolutions: "Physical, mental and emotional limitations should be treated as normal aspects of living . . . rather than personal tragedies. . . . All public transportation [should] be made accessible [and] available in a timely and convenient form. . . . Facilities that provide care for persons with disabilities [should] allow them maximum independence and control over their personal care. . . . The disabled and elderly [should] be encouraged to work jointly to meet their common needs."[15]

A task force newsletter sent to each network included updates on Reagan administration attempts to restrict eligibility for Social Security disability benefits, reports on meetings of disability activist organizations, and news about disability issues pursued by Panther networks in Arizona, Westchester, Montgomery County, and Texas. In 1988 the Disability Task Force summarized the positions of the two presidential contenders: while Democrat Michael Dukakis had an admirable record on access issues as Massachusetts governor, Bush declared at the Republican convention, "I'm going to do whatever it takes to make sure the disabled are included in the mainstream," a vow which a Harris poll indicated swayed enough disabled voters to provide half his victory margin.[16] Bush made good by signing the 1990 Americans with Disabilities Act, prohibiting discrimination against persons with disabilities in employment, housing, public accommodations, and provision of government services. Panther Owen lobbied Congress for passage and attended the White House signing ceremony, representing the Gray Panthers.

Soon after Bill Clinton took office in 1993, his executive order permitting gay and lesbian military personnel to serve openly was overturned, and the "Don't Ask, Don't Tell" policy instituted.[17] In response, a March on Washington for gay and lesbian rights was organized and endorsed by the national Gray Panthers. At the event a group of fifty Panthers led by the D.C.-area networks stationed themselves on the Mall to cheer participants, chanting, "Gray Panthers support your civil rights."

On peace issues, the Panthers' focus remained constant. In 1986 dozens of networks demonstrated and wrote letters opposing U.S. military support for Contra guerrillas seeking to overthrow Nicaragua's elected government. Gray Panther D.C. staff hand-delivered an "Open Letter to Members of the House of Representatives" urging defeat of Contra aid, later revealed at the Iran-Contra hearings to have been illegally transmitted anyway via Reagan's National Security Council and Central Intelligence Agency.[18] To mark the 1986 UN International Year of Peace, Maggie provided the first U.S. signature on an international "People's Appeal for Peace" urging President Reagan and USSR secretary general Mikhail Gorbachev to negotiate "a verifiable comprehensive nuclear test ban; a freeze, phased reduction, and eventual elimination of all nuclear, chemical, and biological weapons; [and] a transfer of resources from military to human needs."[19] Joining a coalition of religious and peace groups, Gray Panthers at sidewalk tables nationwide collected forty thousand Peace Appeal signatures by Hiroshima-Nagasaki Day in August 1987. The following year a Panther delegation of fifty traveled to the Soviet Union for a meeting and Dnieper River cruise with the Ukrainian

Peace Committee, sponsor of the Peace Appeal petition in the Soviet Union.

In 1987 the UN Secretary General's office presented the Gray Panthers its "Peace Messenger" award, and the Panther NGO delegation, joined by executive director Karen Talbot, participated in a UN "disarmament and development" conference that Board chairperson Doris Dawson chided the Reagan administration for boycotting.[20] Later that year Talbot welcomed the Reagan-Gorbachev summit agreement curtailing intermediate-range nuclear missiles. She noted, "It resulted from the persistent work of the global peace movement," but with long-range missiles and Reagan's Star Wars missile defense still looming, "our task is far from over."[21] In 1988 several Washington, Oregon, and Berkeley Panthers boarded a three-hundred-passenger "Citizens' Train" traveling east to demand Congress "shift budget priorities from weapons to people." Gray Panthers welcomed the riders in Oakland, Denver, and Chicago; at Union Station in Washington, D.C., Talbot and local Panthers joined peace advocates and Oregon and Washington congressmembers to greet the train's arrival.[22] "Panthers on the Prowl" signs were visible throughout a mass march welcoming the Third UN Special Session on Disarmament in 1988. That year Panthers in Boston, Detroit, and Austin appeared on streets to protest holiday season war toy sales, now topping one billion dollars a year. In 1990 they returned, joined by Panthers in San Francisco and Washington, D.C.

After Iraq invaded Kuwait in 1990 Maggie telegrammed President Bush: "Using war to solve conflict in the nuclear age is totally unacceptable. . . . Under the auspices of the United Nations, the United States should support a negotiated settlement." California, Boston, D.C. area, and New York networks followed with protest actions, and after the United States invaded Iraq in 1991, Gray Panthers condemned "the escalation of American military presence in the Middle East and the approval by the U.N. and the U.S. Congress of the use of force. . . . The best support we can offer our troops is to stop the war and bring them home alive."[23] Throughout the first Clinton term Gray Panthers at the UN and in local networks continued to advocate for peace and disarmament and to denounce U.S. arms sales to third world nations.

From National Health Service to Single-Payer

Maggie's Gray Panther study group that visited Canada in 1985 found a national health system administered separately in each of the ten provinces. People chose their own doctors who worked privately, not on government salary as in Great Britain, and who billed the provincial government for each patient they saw. No one was denied care, and no one was charged for doctor visits or hospital stays. Health care was financed by employer-employee payroll taxes supplemented by central government funds. Without the administrative burden of multiple private insurance plans, the Canadian system was cheaper than in the United States, yet it provided the same or better health outcomes. The Panthers noted problems and room for improvement but urged that individual U.S. states consider adopting similar plans.[24]

With Reagan's reelection, the likelihood of enacting the Dellums National Health Service Act, similar to the British model, seemed remote. Though the Panthers had championed a national health service for a dozen years, they decided to broaden their approach. Without abandoning the Dellums bill, the 1986 Gray Panther convention endorsed work at the local and state level to increase public support for a universal health "program." Networks in Seattle, Berkeley, and Tompkins County, New York, sponsored forums on the Canadian health system. A Greater Boston Gray Panther–led coalition of three dozen organizations placed an initiative on the 1986 Massachusetts state ballot urging Congress to create a "national health program" that would be "universal in coverage" and "equitably financed, with no out-of-pocket changes."[25] Voters approved it two to one. In Philadelphia Karen Talbot coordinated a 1988 Gray Panther campaign resulting in nineteen local hearings on health care proposals. She produced a new national health system brochure that praised both Canadian and British approaches for delivering universal coverage with lower costs. The Gray Panther Board issued a statement of principles applicable to both the Dellums bill and a Canadian-style approach: "We urge adoption of a national health system that provides . . . comprehensive . . . preventive, curative and occupational health services; is universal in coverage, with no charge at the point of delivery; . . . and is equitably financed, with public accountability for public funds."[26]

Polls indicated that two-thirds of Americans favored a "tax-funded national health insurance program,"[27] and lawmakers felt pressure to do something. During 1987 Congress enacted the Medicare Catastrophic Coverage Act, signed by President Reagan in 1988. Gray Panthers objected that the legislation did not protect older persons from the real "catastrophe" they and family members dreaded: the expense of long-term nursing home or in-home care for chronic illness. Instead it raised monthly Medicare premiums and added an income-tax surcharge to pay for lengthy acute-care hospital stays, which affected only 3 percent of older persons.[28] While the Panthers supported its provision that increased the asset total the spouse of a Medicaid-eligible nursing home resident could retain, they opposed the rest of the bill. Maggie, Frances Humphreys, and Representative Claude Pepper spoke against it at a Capitol rally organized by the Washington office and D.C.-area networks.

Letters from Gray Panthers poured into congressional mailboxes, and Talbot objected to it on radio and television. Once passed, it attracted more ire from supposed beneficiaries, and Congress soon repealed it.

In 1989 national debate was reheated by a Canadian-type proposal unveiled in the *New England Journal of Medicine*. Endorsed by more than four hundred doctors, its authors included physicians David Himmelstein and Steffie Woolhandler, Boston Gray Panthers Dave Danielson and Art Mazer, Dellums bill drafter Len Rodberg, and physicians Vicente Navarro and Howard Waitzkin, both longtime critics of the U.S. health care regime.[29] Their proposed "national health program" would be administered by the states, cover everyone, preserve the "pluralistic" U.S. mix of individual fee-for-service and institutional health care providers, and eliminate private health insurance through "single-source payment" by the federal government. In 1990 a PBS documentary on the Canadian health system narrated by Walter Cronkite further stirred the pot.

At their 1990 convention the Gray Panthers noted that some forty-seven million Americans were unable to afford the "co-payments, deductibles, out-of-pocket costs, and balance billing" their insurance plans required and "call[ed] upon Congress to follow the example of Canadian and European health systems in designing an American national health program."[30] To increase pressure the Panthers launched a postcard campaign to remind the Bush administration, which rejected the Canadian model, about the thirty-nine million Americans who were uninsured. They endorsed Minnesota senator Paul Wellstone's Canadian-style universal health care bill, backed as well by the American Public Health Association, Consumers Union, the National Council of Senior Citizens, and a dozen unions. During 1992 they collected 100,000 petition signatures nationwide urging all political parties to support a single-payer health care system. Charlotte Flynn presented the petitions to the Clinton/Gore campaign and informed the Bush and Perot campaigns of the Panther stance.

Candidate Bill Clinton rejected single-payer and favored a "play-or-pay" approach requiring employers to either provide health insurance or contribute to a public fund that would cover uninsured workers. Gray Panther Health Task Force chair Abe Bloom testified against "play-or-pay" before the Senate during 1992, criticizing its continued reliance on private insurance companies and the problems it would create for marginal businesses and for workers changing or losing jobs. With nearly forty bills in Congress and health care a key issue to voters, President-elect Clinton vowed to give it top priority and appointed his wife, Hillary, to design a comprehensive health care proposal during his first hundred days in office.

As 1993 began the Panthers stepped up local network actions and lobbying in Washington for a plan that would "cover everyone; allow choice among providers; cover all necessary services including long term care; control costs by eliminating unnecessary paperwork . . .; and have a single payer, the United States, with revenues based on progressive tax policies."[31] Selma Bonham of the Montgomery County network and national Board represented the Panthers at a meeting with Vice President Al Gore where Citizen Action and other groups delivered one million postcards demanding a single-payer system. Bloom, Flynn, Bonham, and other Panthers lobbied in Congress for the single-payer bill sponsored by Wellstone in the Senate and by Jim McDermott of Washington and John Conyers of Michigan in the House. At a meeting with Hillary Clinton, Bonham reiterated the Panthers' preference for single-payer, and during an Older Americans Month White House ceremony, she told Bill Clinton: "Go for a single payer system, Mr. President!"[32]

In September 1993 the Clinton "managed competition" plan was unveiled. The Panther Board met to consider it and afterward Flynn sent the Clintons a letter, also hand delivered to all congressional offices, stating: "Gray Panthers commend you for proclaiming health security for everyone [but] our country can do better. In the Clinton plan, people will not have equal access to health care. Another layer of bureaucracy, health alliances, will be added and insurance companies, not consumers, will remain in charge."[33] The Panthers continued to lobby, petition, and speak out for a single-payer alternative, but with fewer than one hundred congressional backers it died in 1994. So did the Clinton plan and its Democratic successor bills, all defeated by intense opposition from Republicans, the independent business lobby, and, as Abe Bloom put it, "the medical industrial complex, representing one seventh of our total economy[:] the insurance and pharmaceutical companies plus the AMA, appliance manufacturers, and hospitals."[34]

Maggie's Last Years

Maggie attended the 1986 Gray Panther convention walking with a cane. Her worsening vision and mobility impairments limited her travel, but during the next two years she met with the Greater Boston, Bergen County, and Harlem networks, and in Philadelphia she stirred Northeast Regional conferees: "We have shared our apprehensions about the times we live in [and] we have, collectively, a great enormous reservoir of power."[35] Her own reservoir was dealt an unexpected blow on a rainy November night in 1987 when two boys grabbed her young housemate's purse and pushed Maggie to the ground "with my teeth hitting first." Her bruises and broken shoulder required five days in the hospital, yet Maggie's message to the public conveyed no anger. "I pity those boys. . . .

What is ahead for them except a life of assault and criminality? . . . The root causes of the problem are visible all around us: the failing schools, the lack of federal monies for city programs, the unemployment rate."[36] Nonetheless, her lengthy recovery left Maggie despondent. She postponed a Gray Panther–Shared Housing Resource Center conference she had helped to plan and told a hushed 1988 Gray Panther convention, "I realize my days are numbered."[37] But this was not the last hurrah her audience feared, and she returned for three more Panther conventions.

In 1989 Maggie responded to the inauguration of President George H. W. Bush with a Valentine's Day greeting—"None of us voted for you, but we wish you the best"—and sent several "gifts" including a "gold-plated toilet seat" symbolizing Pentagon waste, sparklers for his "thousand points of light," and a cardboard box to house the homeless.[38] In April she joined D.C.-area Panthers at a massive march for reproductive rights where her presence attracted numerous well-wishers who noted Gray Panther placards supporting legal abortion, the Equal Rights Amendment, and a national health system. Closer to home, at the suggestion of Julia Hall, a professor of sociology at Drexel University in Philadelphia, she visited twice with a group of inmates age fifty and older at the state prison at Graterford, Pennsylvania. There Maggie and Jean Hopper, eighty-three and eighty, reiterated Panther demands to cut military spending and provide universal health care and encouraged their audience, who constituted themselves a new Gray Panther network, to convey their perspectives on penal reform to "us, the outsiders." Maggie also introduced them to the Gray Panther growl.[39]

While these activities buoyed Maggie, she suffered another blow to her mobility when "my eleventh vertebra collapsed, eliminating my waistline and depositing my ribcage on my pelvis."[40] Now more home-based than ever, she delighted in her garden's spring azaleas, summer tiger lilies, and fall chrysanthemums, and in her black-and-white cats Charlotte and Emily Bronte, companions since 1975 and stationed at her head and feet while she slept. In her Germantown house she worked with Christina Long and Laura Quinn on her 1991 autobiography, *No Stone Unturned: The Life and Times of Maggie Kuhn,* and with her assistant Marilyn Vowels, replaced in 1990 by Sue Leary, thirty-six. She relied upon nurse's aide Bertha Munroe, who visited daily to help bathe and dress her. From time to time she visited with her three young upstairs housemates and attended symphonic performances at the Philadelphia Academy of Music, where she could "forget about everything else."[41] While recovering from her back problem, Maggie underwent grueling physical therapy as well as healing touch treatments to alleviate pain. To overcome depression she threw herself into recruiting friends Carroll Estes, Robert Butler, and Ralph Nader to speak at the 1990 Gray Panther convention.

Maggie's public appearances in the early 1990s were more limited and selective. In Los Angeles and New York she spoke before the International Senior Citizens Association, the Columbia School of Social Work, and the American Society on Aging, where she received the Administration on Aging's "Outstanding Role Model for Successful Aging" award. At the Omega Institute for Holistic Studies in 1992 she told her audience, "I am not exactly a New Age person," and then addressed "the demographic revolution where people are living longer today than any time in human history," the need for "repentance, restitution, and reconciliation . . . in the light of the great ethnic [and] racial diversity in our world today," and the "environment [that] is threatened in this country and around the world [by] fossil fuels and nuclear power."[42]

While Maggie was candid about becoming "old old" and "frail" during these years, she also emphasized her "passion for the world, for people, for a better way. . . . I am more interested than ever in the larger story." On her eighty-fifth birthday she told *Network* editor Abby Lederman, "I'm hoping that before I call it a day, or a night, that there can be much more support for democratic socialism. . . . We must narrow, not widen, the gap between the rich and poor." With Leary's assistance she continued to follow "the alternate press" and alert others to articles in the *Nation* and *In These Times* about, for instance, attacks on the United Nations by the conservative Heritage Foundation. In one of her last messages in *Network* she urged individuals as well as society to embrace "interdependence, not independence; cooperation, not competition; intergenerational involvement, not age segregation; working for the public interest, not self interest."[43]

In her final decade Maggie was an iconic figure in American public life. She joined Jesse Jackson's Rainbow Coalition board in 1987, was interviewed by *The Progressive* magazine in 1988, saluted in a *Nation* editorial in 1990, and honored as a "leading thinker and visionary" by the *Utne Reader* in 1994. For her criticism of President Bush's policies she was treated to a Ben & Jerry's "1000 Pints of Light" award—one thousand pints of their ice cream delivered to her home (and shared by Maggie with her neighbors). Her Gray Panther activism brought recognition from her alma mater and the religious denominations she worked for— a Distinguished Alumni Award from Case Western Reserve University, a Ministry to Women Award from the Unitarian Universalist Women's Federation, the first Award for Justice and Human Development by the Witherspoon Society, a progressive Presbyterian group, and a Peace-seeker Award from the United Presbyterian Peace Fellowship. In Philadelphia there were honorary doctorates from the Medical College of Pennsylvania, the University of Pennsylvania, and Drexel University, a proclamation of "Maggie Kuhn Day" by Mayor Ed Rendell, and a "Maggie Tree" planted in a city park near her home. She received honorary college and university degrees from Antioch, Albright, Grinnell, Marycrest, Moravian, Northern Illinois, Simmons, the State University of New York at Fredonia, and Swarthmore, and ceremonial keys to sixteen U.S. cities. Especially meaningful to Maggie was a United Nations "First Intergenerational Citizen of the World Award" in 1994, though she was unable to accept it in person.

Maggie did not attend the Gray Panther Board meeting in October 1993 and resigned the following June. Now herself failing, she witnessed the passing of several Gray Panther friends and leaders—Dellums bill stalwart Abe Boxerman in 1986, Cameron Hall in 1987, Austin convener Cookie Smith in 1989, Kansas City leader Angie Aker and California Gray Panther founder Tom Moore in 1990, former NSC chairperson Grace Warfield in 1991, Margaret Hummel of the Philadelphia Committee of 65 in 1993, Arizonan Naomi Harward in early 1995. And she mourned the deaths of her beloved cats Charlotte in 1993 and Emily, at age nineteen, in January 1995. In February Maggie issued her last Gray Panther public statement, a denouncement of Republican proposals to trim the budget of National Public Radio: "I have been a devoted listener and supporter . . . for years. Because of failing eyesight I depend on public radio. . . . Do not deny us our right to know."[44]

During the Panthers April 1995 convention three hundred Gray Panthers and friends attended an evening gala to honor Maggie and the movement's twenty-fifth anniversary. Seated in a wheelchair, Maggie enjoyed tributes from emcee Carroll Estes, Charlotte Flynn, Dieter Hessel (editor of the 1977 book *Maggie Kuhn on Aging*), Steve McConnell, folk singer Peter Yarrow (of Peter, Paul, and Mary), Robert Blancato, Robert Butler, and many others. (Among the guests was Maggie's young Gray Panther lover from the 1970s.) A week earlier President Bill Clinton had written to "commend you and the Gray Panthers for your deep concern about our future and for your exemplary commitment to improving our world."[45] After the event Maggie wrote to her admirers: "Our 25th Anniversary Gala was the happiest moment of my life. I was deeply moved by the presence of so many friends and colleagues. It was a great opportunity to express my gratitude to all those who have enriched my life and helped me to carry forward Gray Panther goals."[46]

In 1991 Maggie signed a living will stipulating no external means be used to extend her life. And she wrote in *No Stone Unturned*, "I approach death willingly. . . . I know my body would not hold up well, and so I would prefer not to live into my nineties."[47] Maggie Kuhn died three weeks after the gala, and less than four months before her ninetieth birthday.

Continuity in Berkeley

In the later 1980s and early 1990s Berkeley Gray Panthers founder Lillian Rabinowitz initiated several projects that added to the "continuum of care" achievements of her network's first decade. In 1986 the Berkeley network organized the forum "Moral and Legal Issues Confronting Terminally Ill Adults," attended by two hundred nurses, lawyers, professionals in aging issues, and health care advocates. Panelists identified gaps in California's "Right to Die" law, by then replicated in thirty states, and recommended further action. The event gave birth to a Berkeley Gray Panther "Death with Dignity" committee that lobbied in Sacramento to update the decade-old law and harmonize it with state "Durable Power of Attorney for Health Care" legislation.[48] A year later Lillian and Terri Thomas Hamstra, an epidemiology student at the University of California School of Public Health, coplanned an "Options for a National Health Program" forum, with speakers on the Canadian and Swedish systems and on the Dellums and national health insurance bills before Congress. Funded by the Villers and Henry J. Kaiser foundations and attended by three hundred and fifty, the program was videotaped by Berkeley Panthers who later produced several documentaries about universal health care.

Another of Lillian's projects arose from complaints by Gray Panthers about inattention to older patients at the Kaiser Permanente HMO clinic in Oakland. After picket-line demonstrations and negotiations with Kaiser officials, the Berkeley network's health committee won a new geriatric services clinic at Kaiser, a health educator assigned to older patients, and a Senior Advisory Committee that included Gray Panther Kaiser members. Two forums in 1990 and 1994, again on the University of California campus, concerned "board and care" homes that housed isolated or frail older persons not medically eligible for nursing home placement.[49] Concurrently, Lillian led the Coalition for Quality Assurance in Residential Care Facilities for the Elderly, which issued a study of board and care facilities statewide and pressed for government oversight. Meanwhile, a guest speaker in 1991 alerted the Berkeley Panthers to the growing number of older Californians raising grandchildren but who, unlike foster parents, were ineligible for public financial assistance. Lillian and Meredith Minkler, a UC Berkeley public health professor, then created "Grandparents Parenting Grandchildren" to remedy the situation.

Lillian completed her last Berkeley Gray Panther convener term in 1986 but remained a health committee and board member. The network honored her that year with a seventy-fifth birthday gala attended by eighty Panthers and friends, and again in 1991 with an eightieth birthday party for which Maggie traveled to Berkeley. Lillian received testimonials from guests, including Berkeley mayor Loni Hancock, at the network's fifteenth anniversary celebration in 1989, and at its twentieth anniversary party in 1994, where entertainment was provided by Ronnie Gilbert of the 1950s folk music group the Weavers and 1970s folk-rock musician Country Joe MacDonald, a Berkeley resident. Other acknowledgments of Lillian's accomplishments included a Senior Advocacy award from the American Society on Aging, an Award for Community Service from the San Francisco Foundation, and public recognition at the Oakland Athletics baseball team's 1988 Senior Day.

During these years Lillian and other Berkeley Panthers continued to serve as board members and volunteers at the Over 60 Clinic. Its director Marty Lynch in turn co-chaired the network's health committee for two years and was a frequent speaker at Gray Panther events. In 1988 the clinic, now collecting Medicare and Medicaid reimbursements or billing clients on a sliding fee scale,[50] began an outreach program to homeless older persons. By 1991 it operated "outclinics" at fourteen sites in Alameda County. The Panthers continued to be proud of "their" clinic, and in addition to individual financial contributions they donated $1,800 from their 1993 raffle proceeds to Over 60's fund to construct a larger facility. Throughout Berkeley and beyond, moreover, the Panthers could point to results of past network projects: the Center for Elders' Independence, successor to the adult day health care center they helped create; Bay Area Advocates for Nursing Home Reform (later California Advocates for Nursing Home Reform); the Community Hospice of the East Bay; ECHO/Project Share, their shared housing match service later funded by the cities of Berkeley and Oakland; and Redwood Gardens, the apartment complex for elderly and disabled renters located on site of the former School for the Deaf and Blind.[51]

Like its health committee, the Berkeley network's housing and peace committees remained active. The Panthers worked in Sacramento and Berkeley to uphold Berkeley's rent control ordinance. They shuddered in 1991 when the rent board of their gentrifying city approved a 28 percent rent hike, and they then campaigned for a protenant slate elected in 1994. They joined other groups mobilizing to aid the homeless and supplied volunteers and food to a drop-in center for homeless women and children. With peace organizations and other Bay Area Panther networks they joined marches, vigils, and tabling at the Oakland airport to protest Reagan's military budgets and overseas interventions. Berkeley Panther Harry Sheer, seventy-four, was among the twenty-nine arrested at a San Francisco demonstration against aid to Nicaraguan contras. Network members picketed nursing homes with Bay Area Advocates for Nursing Home Reform (BANHR) and tabled with petitions, postcards, and flyers for a 1994 single-payer initiative, which California's "medical industrial complex" mobilized to defeat. They testified at meetings of the Berkeley and Alameda County Commissions on Aging and each May joined other groups on Senior Rally Day in Sacramento.

The Berkeley Gray Panthers remained the largest network on the West Coast, with three hundred and fifty members in the late 1980s and a mailing list of five hundred, including Oakland Gray Panthers, legislators, and allied organizations. New recruits, often older people moving to Berkeley after retirement, replaced members from the network's early days, some of whom remained active nearly to their passing—like Rose Dellamonica, who died in 1986, Lorna Brangwin in 1987, Joe Guyon in 1989, Helene London in 1992, and Eugenia Hickman and Gregory Bergman in 1994. Housing activist Gerda Miller became convener in 1987 and served again from 1990 to 1995 while entering her eighties. Retired teacher and Nixon "enemies list" member Ellen Butler, a newcomer to Berkeley, oversaw the vital work of membership recruitment and renewals.[52] And Virginia Morgan, long active in the African American community, managed calls and visitors at the Panther office.

Former staffer and housing committee activist Carla Woodworth, thirty-six, was elected to the Berkeley City Council in 1990 and reelected in 1992 and 1994. Several younger Panthers continued their nursing home advocacy work with BANHR. A few new young members appeared. Terri Thomas Hamstra, twenty-four, joined the health committee in 1986, was elected convener in 1988, and remained an active member until leaving Berkeley in 1991. Varya Simpson, in her thirties, was executive director for three years before beginning law school in 1988, and then she joined the network board. With member dues, bake sales, the annual raffle, and gifts and bequests the Panthers continued to employ a full-time staff member, usually a younger person. And like the student interns attached to network committees, they developed close ties with active older Panthers. In the 1990s the number of young members and interns diminished, and veteran members, many in their eighties, acknowledged the network needed to "attract younger members."[53]

The Berkeley network continued to innovate. In 1986 a young staffer shifted office operations from typewriter to computer. New members Robert Purdy and Margot Smith, a longtime activist couple, took up video production in retirement and joined young Panthers Terri and Scott Hamstra in filming *Canada's Single Payer Health System* in Vancouver in 1989, a documentary later aired on public television stations with an introduction by Senator Paul Wellstone. In 1994 a Berkeley public access cable television channel was started, and still more Panthers joined in producing short videos. The network created education and transportation committees in 1993 reflecting interests of new members. Transportation activism focused on bus service. Education committee members volunteered in classes and after-school programs at Martin Luther King Jr. Middle School, located next to the Panther office.

Ties to the wider Gray Panther movement, rooted in Maggie's and Lillian's friendship, remained firm. Lillian concluded her eight-year tenure on the NSC and Board in 1988, and was succeeded in 1990 by Hamstra and by Simpson, who later became national vice-chair, and in 1992 by Irv Rautenberg, network housing committee chair. Hamstra worked with Gray Panthers executive director Karen Talbot on health care hearings in Alameda County and San Francisco in 1988. After leaving Philadelphia Talbot became a member of the San Francisco network in the 1990s and participated in northern California meetings drawing up to forty Gray Panthers and hosted in turn by the Berkeley, Oakland, Western and Central Contra Costa, Marin, San Francisco, and Sacramento networks. Five Berkeley Panthers traveled to Chicago for the 1988 Gray Panther convention, and Miller and Simpson attended the Philadelphia convention and gala for Maggie in 1995.

Contraction in New York

During 1985 East Side Gray Panther Muriel Clark, seventy-nine, joined an investigative sting organized by New York State's Special Prosecutor for Nursing Homes. She posed as a prospective resident accompanied by her "son," an undercover detective who wore a hidden taping device to record illegal requests for cash "contributions" in return for expedited nursing home placement. With stooped back and weighing 108 pounds, Clark feigned frailty when in fact she frequently participated in political demonstrations in New York and Washington, D.C., and had not visited a doctor in forty years. As a result of her work, two nursing homes were prosecuted for soliciting $55,000 in bribes.

A retired social worker, Clark had joined the Gray Panthers in the 1970s. She was active in the health and peace task forces and volunteered at a homeless shelter. In 1987 her picture and a story about her undercover work appeared on the front page of the *New York Times*; in the story she explained that she was "passionately angry about . . . the powerful in New York who take advantage of the poor . . . and the dispossessed." Other Panthers had been unaware of her clandestine adventure, and we congratulated her. Characteristically, she responded that the publicity "has bothered me a great deal because it is all so exaggerated. . . . It did not take the slightest courage on my part."[54]

By the later 1980s most active Gray Panthers in New York were, like Clark, in their late seventies or eighties. Although a total of one hundred and fifty attended the various networks' monthly meetings, ranks were diminishing through disability, moves to other states, or death. Few new members of any age were joining, and network leaders voiced frustration over "apathy" and a reluctance of members to do more than attend meetings. The last citywide conveners meeting was held in 1988, and by then only the citywide peace and health task forces were functioning, one working on the People's Appeal for Peace, the other on understanding the new Medicare Diagnostic Related Group (DRG) payment system that attached a fixed reimbursement to each medical condition, thus making it profitable for hospitals to discharge patients "quicker and sicker."

In the Forest Hills group attendance fell from forty to twenty by 1987. Due to illness, founder Mollie Katz no longer attended, and when the network folded in 1988 its three active members affiliated with the Central Queens and New York Gray Panthers. The Greenwich Village Panthers experienced leadership losses in 1987 when health task force co-chair Eleanor Smith moved to San Francisco, and Social Security activist Isabella Shapiro died. Naomi Schott, a retired medical social worker and nurse, served as convener for three years, but the Village network disbanded after she moved to Santa Rosa, California, in 1988. (Like several Panther relocatees, she joined another network, the Gray Panthers of Sonoma County, participating until her death in 1990.) The Brooklyn Gray Panthers revived in 1986 when convener Mary Solomon inaugurated the new group with a Social Security forum featuring Representative Charles Schumer. Though Solomon remained an outspoken advocate at Brooklyn events, the network failed to grow and was closed in 1990. The Central Queens network lost its founding convener in 1987 when, facing serious health problems, Evelyn Neleson, seventy-five, sold her house and moved to Brooklyn. Though numbers fell sharply, a core of Central Queens Panthers continued to meet and publish a newsletter into the 1990s.

The New York Gray Panthers, still meeting on Manhattan's West Side, were the largest of the three remaining city networks. In 1985 Los Angeles transplant Dave Brown, seventy, a retired pharmacist, became convener. He joined the New York Panthers in 1979, often voicing contrarian views at meetings, but after becoming friendly with Maggie during the 1983 Prague peace conference, he directed his energy to the Gray Panther movement. Elected to the national board in 1986, Brown was a prime mover of the People's Peace Appeal campaign. He organized Northeast Regional meetings in 1986 and 1989 and proposed numerous convention resolutions on peace, full employment, and procedural matters. In the 1990s he fanned opposition to Charlotte Flynn's efforts to reorganize to avoid shutdown. Brown described himself as "curmudgeon, pest, troublemaker," and few disagreed.[55]

In New York Brown helped start a Harlem network in 1987 when Henrietta Phillips, seventy-nine, a retired telephone company employee and president of the A. Philip Randolph Senior Center on 146th Street, affiliated her forty-member Social Action Committee with the Panthers' Philadelphia office. Maggie attended the network's debut, and members were active in housing and issues championed by other New York senior citizen organizations. In 1992 the New York Gray Panthers absorbed the Harlem group, now just ten members, and the East Side network. Monthly meetings then rotated between the West Side, the Randolph Center, and the Community Church on East 35th Street.

Lillian Sarno, eighty in 1989, continued to serve intermittently as convener or co-convener of the New York Gray Panthers. She remained the network's key strategist, joining if not planning nearly every tabling, leafleting, elected official visit, march, rally, or vigil Gray Panthers participated in between 1986 and 1995. She fulfilled requests for a Gray Panther speaker from New York University, Fordham University, the State University of New York at New Paltz, and Belleview Hospital's Geriatric Nursing Program. She produced a flow of New York Gray Panther correspondence to Mayors David Dinkins and Rudolph Giuliani, Governor Mario Cuomo, Senators Daniel Patrick Moynihan and Alfonse D'Amato, President and First Lady Bill and Hillary Clinton, and other officials. In 1986 Sarno restarted the housing task force and for four years represented the Panthers in the Housing Justice Campaign, a coalition of fifty groups demanding rehabilitation of city-owned properties for low-income housing. She also spoke on housing issues before the city council and on WBAI radio. Sarno remained active in West Side causes and served on her neighborhood's Community Board 7 senior issues committee.

The New York Panthers addressed other issues as well. In 1986 they produced a Social Security brochure opposing privatization and means testing and supporting separation of the trust fund from the unified budget and elimination of the payroll tax earnings cap. They protested high fares charged disabled riders of para-transit vans and opposed bus and subway fare increases. They cosponsored a speakout on hospital discharge practices in 1987 and brought Frances Humphreys and Boston Panther Dave Danielson to New York for a national health care forum in 1988. They joined demonstrations and generated petitions and letters for single-payer universal health care in the early 1990s; and after screening a Berkeley Gray Panther video on national health care they sent that network $100 for the 1994 California single-payer campaign. On peace issues, Lenore Fine, a new member and later convener, led fellow Panthers in protests against war toys at New York's annual toy industry show. Contingents of New York Panthers participated in demonstrations in Washington, D.C., and New York to oppose South African apartheid in

1986, U.S. intervention in Central America in 1987, housing program reductions in 1989, and federal budget cuts in 1992.

The New York Gray Panthers celebrated their twentieth anniversary in 1992 at Rutgers Presbyterian Church, next door to the site of their first meeting in 1972. The honorees were Fannie Krasnow, an eighteen-year veteran member who helped maintain the network's financial records, and Lydia Bragger, the first convener. (Hope Bagger's death in 1988 went unnoted.) During the 1980s Bragger continued to monitor television programming, was interviewed on news programs, and consulted on older characters in television series (*All in the Family, One Day at a Time*). Her national Gray Panther Media Watch funding ended in 1986, but her biweekly WBAI *Gray Panther Report* radio program continued, with Dave Brown and Lillian Sarno among her guests.

When Maggie spoke in New York City during the later 1980s and early 1990s, New York Panthers were alerted and several attended. She also participated in two Northeast Regional conferences held in New York. Doris Berk of the New York Gray Panthers served on the national board from 1984 to 1988, and Dave Brown to 1992 when Henrietta Phillips of the Harlem group was elected. Sizeable contingents traveled to Gray Panther conventions—the largest, twenty-two, in 1990—and Brown, Sarno, Stella Murphy, and five others were at Maggie's 1995 gala in Philadelphia. Members of the Panther UN delegation maintained the closest links to Maggie. Headed by Sylvia Kleinman from New Jersey, it included Mildred Blechman, recruited by Maggie and later a convener of the East Side Panthers, Myrna Lewis, wife of Dr. Robert Butler, and Lenore Fine, representative to the NGO Committee on Disarmament.

The New York Panthers financed office and newsletter expenses through dues and donations, which declined from $4,700 in 1986 to $2,800 in 1995. Supplementing these funds, North Star Foundation grants of $2,900 paid for flyers, signs, and tabling paraphernalia used on West Side sidewalks near Lincoln Center, Zabar's food emporium, and other locations where petition and postcard signatures were solicited for the People's Peace Appeal, Housing Justice Campaign, and single-payer health care. In 1992 this annual summer-to-fall weekly operation moved indoors to a rented booth at the Democratic Party convention. The New York Gray Panther office did not computerize, and the newsletter, appearing eight and later four times a year, remained a type and paste production. Even with the absorption of three other networks, total membership fell, from about 200 dues-paying members in 1986 to 120 by 1995. Monthly meetings continued to draw from twenty to thirty, including many Panthers I knew from the early 1980s, but members were frustrated that their network was not growing. "[We] need . . . additional membership to staff our projects," "The big issue is membership. What are we going to do?," co-conveners Edna Graig and Mildred Blechman worried in 1994.[56]

Thirty-eight New York Gray Panthers attended the 1995 holiday party at the Community Church. They watched a videotape of a recent *Phil Donahue Show* on which some of them appeared. In between refreshments, music, and conversation, many stopped at the "Action Table" to sign letters to President Clinton and Senators D'Amato and Moynihan, protesting Medicaid cuts. After the party seventy-four letters were mailed.

Chapter 8
Reorganizing for a New Century (1996–2007)

For two years after Maggie Kuhn's death the national Gray Panthers drifted. In Washington executive director Dixie Horning endorsed a spectrum of causes from reducing air pollution to pension reform, adding a Gray Panther signature to 118 organizational sign-on letters.[1] In Philadelphia Sue Leary was appointed "grassroots coordinator" for the fifty-four networks but left within a year to become executrix of Maggie's estate and organizer of her archive deposited at Temple University. A 1996 Gray Panther "Age and Youth in Action Summit" cohosted with the United States Students Association honored Marian Wright Edelman, president of the Children's Defense Fund. The keynote speaker was Betty Friedan, whose 1993 book *The Fountain of Age* contained an appreciative portrait of Maggie. Three hundred were expected but only "scores" arrived, mainly Panthers and students plus Washington, D.C., organization staffers.[2] A new funding shortfall descended later that year, "the worst . . . since 1991," again portending "closing our doors," Board chairperson Charlotte Flynn warned.[3] Staff salaries were cut 20 percent and a Board meeting was canceled to conserve resources. At the end of 1996 Horning resigned.

After Maggie

In 1997 the Gray Panther Board appointed Tim Fuller, fifty-four, as its new executive director. A friend of Charlotte Flynn, Fuller was head of the Live Oak Fund for Change, a private philanthropy in Austin, Texas. Flynn met him early in the 1990s when seeking funding for the Panthers, and he attended the 1995 gala for Maggie, whom he knew from boards both served on. Fuller began his political career on the Boulder, Colorado, city council in the early 1970s. He later became executive director of the Missouri Democratic Party and the National Campaign to End

Hunger and Homelessness. His first Gray Panther task was organizing the 1997 national convention in San Francisco. At that event one hundred and fifty Panthers honored Lillian Rabinowitz and were addressed via video by Senator Paul Wellstone. Resolutions reaffirmed support for a single-payer health plan and opposed "fast track authority" to extend the North American Free Trade Agreement without "provisions for rights of labor, for protection of the environment, and for the protection of national sovereignty and democracy."[4] Following their gathering the Panthers joined a demonstration of five hundred protesting the launch of the plutonium-bearing Cassini Space Probe and any extension of the arms race into outer space. This assembly was stirred by Metropolitan Washington Panther Louise Franklin Ramirez, ninety-two, whose mapping of twenty-two thousand nuclear radiation sites in the United States was a Gray Panthers Mahler Institute project unveiled at Washington's National Press Club and later published in *Network*.[5]

Fuller began his tenure with direct mail donations rising, and he increased the national staff to five. In Washington, D.C., he represented the Gray Panthers in coalitions and at press conferences on nursing homes, welfare reform, and the Congressional Progressive Caucus's "Fairness Agenda" of living wages, defense budget reductions, and campaign finance reform. Fuller met with network leaders in California, New York, and Michigan, and staff members visited still others. He kept in touch with D.C.-area Panthers, who also joined staffers at meetings and rallies or volunteered at the office.

Early in 1997 the Long Beach, California, Panthers alerted the national office to Wall Street proposals for using Social Security payroll taxes to create individual private investment accounts. Then the Montgomery County network picketed the Cato Institute, a Washington, D.C., libertarian think tank, during a Social Security privatization seminar covered by the ABC *20/20* television news magazine, which also interviewed the Panthers.[6] When Clinton White House Summit on Social Security events followed, Fuller responded with Action Alerts and *Network* salvos proclaiming "Let the rich pay their fair share" by extending the payroll tax to all earned income. Eliminating the earnings cap would fill most of any projected benefits shortfall, Fuller maintained, and federal revenues, then anticipated to produce annual surpluses, could fill the rest. Networks in Rhode Island, New Mexico, California, Texas, Michigan, Washington, D.C., and Florida held Social Security forums advocating the Panther position.[7]

In the federal budget battles of the later 1990s, Medicare also faced privatization threats.[8] Republican plans for a balanced budget by 2002 were coupled with large tax reductions paid for by deep cuts in health programs. In response, Clinton proposed saving $100 billion over five years by cutting payments to Medicare providers. The Balanced Budget Act compromise passed in 1997 mandated Medicare provider savings of $116 billion and a doubling of beneficiary premiums. It also allocated increased funds for private "Medicare Plus Choice" managed-care plans, which received monthly payments from Medicare for each enrollee. Further, it created a Bipartisan Commission on the Future of Medicare to propose additional "savings" and report in 1999.

Carrying "No More Cuts" and "Field Hearings Now" placards, Montgomery County and Metropolitan Washington Panthers led by Abe Bloom joined the National Council of Senior Citizens at Bipartisan Commission meetings. With publicity including *New York Times* coverage, they won additional public hearings during 1998. Taking a cue from the San Francisco network, in 1999 Fuller encouraged Gray Panthers nationwide to "Ring in the New Year for the Future of Medicare" by calling the White House each Tuesday until the commission reported, demanding an expansion of benefits to include prescription drugs and long-term care. With several Democratic commission members unwilling to support higher beneficiary costs or raise Medicare's eligibility age from sixty-five to sixty-seven, the commission report was tabled. The Panthers did back Clinton's suggestions to devote part of the projected budget surpluses to Medicare and Social Security and to allow uninsured individuals between fifty-five and sixty-four to buy into Medicare. Like the surpluses themselves, consideration of these proposals vanished under Clinton's successor.[9]

In 1999 Fuller and the Gray Panther Board met with leaders of the Universal Health Care Action Network (UHCAN) formed in 1992 to build support for the single-payer approach. The Panthers were a UHCAN charter member—Flynn and Bloom attended its first national meeting—and decided to hold their twelfth biennial convention in Washington, D.C., on the same weekend as UHCAN's annual conference, allowing members to participate in both events. The meetings' focus would be a "Universal Health Care 2000," or "U2K," drive to make single-payer an issue in the upcoming presidential election.

The weekend began with a modest Friday noon UHCAN rally at the Capitol steps addressed by three Democratic members of Congress. Amid Gray Panthers and UHCAN supporters, Lani Sanjek and I stood with members of the New York Network for Action on Medicare (NYNAM), an alliance of senior citizen, health, and disability advocacy groups she helped form in 1998 to fight Republican Speaker of the House Newt Gingrich's privatization push. (He pledged to let Medicare "wither on the vine" by transforming it into a private insurance voucher program.) Our NYNAM group later visited the offices of Representative Charles Rangel and Senator Charles Schumer, both of New York, to lobby against

HMO inroads into Medicare and for prescription drug coverage. Lani and I stayed for the Gray Panther convention.

The principal convention speakers were Representative Eleanor Holmes Norton of Washington, D.C., and Ted Marmor, a Yale University public policy scholar who met with Fuller to plan the U2K campaign.[10] An evening session featured young Gray Panther alumni who reminisced about the 1970s: Ron Wyden (since 1996 a U.S. senator), Steve McConnell, Elma Griesel Holder, and Stanley Earley and Leslie Sussan, the first Philadelphia office staff members and still best friends. In an open mike plenary, former executive director Karen Talbot spoke passionately about international peace and opposing World Trade Organization policies. Ninety Gray Panthers attended.

Fuller's Campaigns

When introducing himself to the Panther movement, Fuller stated his "strongest suit . . . is building and directing campaigns, whether an issue campaign, or candidate or fundraising campaign."[11] In 2000 this became his primary Gray Panther mode of operation as he co-chaired the U2K campaign for "Universal . . . Comprehensive . . . Affordable [and] Publically accountable" health care.[12] *Network* ceased publication, replaced by Action Alerts, Gray Panther funding appeals, and U2K information kits and e-mails to supporters, who held forums, lobbied candidates, and secured organizational endorsements. Five hundred groups signed on, including twenty-three Gray Panther networks. Health care did not become a decisive election issue, however, and even before the Supreme Court declared George W. Bush president in December 2000, Fuller wrote to Gray Panther donors of his fear of "regressive legislation" and congressional "reapportionment by Republican legislatures."[13] During 2001 Gray Panther direct mail contributions fell, and following the September 11 attacks three foundation grants were withdrawn or reduced. That year's Gray Panther convention was canceled and the national office staff cut to two.

In 1998 Fuller editorialized in *Network* about growing prescription drug profits while "most drug research and development is financed by taxpayer's money . . . without accountability or public oversight."[14] Early in 2001 he initiated a Gray Panther "RePhorma" campaign aimed at leading brand-name drug companies, all of which were members of PhRMA (the Pharmaceutical Research and Manufacturers of America), the industry's lobbying arm. He enlisted more than one hundred organizations to join a Panther-led Stop Patient Abuse Now (SPAN) Coalition. SPAN sued successfully to cancel Bristol-Myers Squibb's patent extension for BuSpar, a widely used anti-anxiety medication whose original twenty-year patent expired, thus opening the market to less-costly generic equivalents. SPAN's second target was Abbott Laboratories' thyroid drug Synthroid, used by eight million, which the Food and Drug Administration determined was not "safe and effective." Fuller invited Abbott to a Gray Panther–sponsored debate with generic manufacturers of equivalent medications at an annual meeting of the Endocrine Society. Under this public pressure Abbott stopped marketing the drug.[15] Fuller prepared a video on the RePhorma campaign, and sent it to Gray Panther networks.

His third battle focused on AstraZeneca's heartburn, or "acid reflux," drug Prilosec. The patent expired in October 2001, jeopardizing $4.5 billion in annual sales. AstraZeneca invested copiously in advertising and free samples to convince doctors and patients to switch to its new patented drug Nexium, which differed only slightly from Prilosec, rather than adopt cheaper versions of Prilosec available from generic manufacturers. As AstraZeneca's litigation to keep generic Prilosec off the market moved through federal court, a SPAN organizer from the Gray Panther D.C. office worked with Lani Sanjek and a dozen members of NYNAMSS (the renamed New York Network for Action on Medicare and Social Security) to stage a picket in front of the Manhattan court house. By this time eighteen governors, whose state Medicaid programs would benefit from a ruling against AstraZeneca, were also opposing Prilosec/Nexium's manufacturer.[16]

The fourth sally in the RePhorma campaign was Gray Panther testimony to the Senate Commerce Committee in 2002 urging elimination of the loophole permiting pharmaceutical companies to extend their patents for up to thirty months by filing meritless legal actions, which automatically placed a hold on generic equivalents.[17] A month later the San Francisco Gray Panthers, the California Nurses Association, and other SPAN supporters filled the two hundred–seat Zeum Theater to view *The High Price of Heartburn,* Fuller's video on Prilosec, and applaud his recitation of Panther RePhorma battles. Picketing of a medical conference sponsored by AstraZeneca at the Moscone Convention Center next door followed.[18]

Meanwhile, Gray Panthers nationwide opposed President Bush's 2001 tax cuts rewarding high-income earners, and Fuller's donor mailings generated more than one hundred letters to Congress against them. When administration plans to invade Iraq were advanced during 2002, Board chairperson Barbara Aldave, a Texas Gray Panther and law school professor, wrote to Bush, "A preemptive, unilateral action is unconscionable and illegal under international law and will only serve to destabilize an already fragile situation within the region." The Panthers' D.C. office urged networks to join antiwar actions and to counter Bush's invasion rationale by insisting there was "no evidence of links between Saddam Hussein and the terror attacks of September 11, 2001" or that "Iraq currently has useable weapons of mass destruction"; that "any attack on Iraq will further alienate US allies and . . . increase anti-American sentiment throughout the world"; and that "war risks the lives of thousands of US soldiers and tens of thousands of Iraqi civilians." Once the March 2003 invasion occurred Fuller labeled it "unnecessary," and Panther networks continued their opposition.[19]

To follow the U2K and RePhorma campaigns, in 2002 Fuller began a Corporate Accountability Project "to make corporations more publicly accountable and socially responsible [and] to increase [Gray Panther] visibility and funder credibility." Its target was MCI WorldCom, which that year "committed the largest corporate fraud in history" by overstating its profits by billions, after which it fell sharply in value and declared Chapter 11 bankruptcy. In April 2003 ads reading "paid for by the Gray Panthers" appeared in the *Washington Post, The Hill, Roll Call,* and newspapers in Florida, Michigan, Iowa, and Nevada. They stated, "Thousands upon thousands of seniors have had their retirements jeopardized" because of WorldCom "investment losses by individual shareholders and pension funds." The ads charged, "The U.S. Government has actually *rewarded* MCI WorldCom with new contracts, including a multi-million dollar contract for a wireless phone network—in Iraq." The ads generated press coverage about this Panther campaign and spurred a World-Com investigation by the Senate Governmental Affairs Committee and later its suspension from new contracts with the federal General Services Administration.[20]

In June 2003 the *Corporate Crime Reporter* revealed that Issue Dynamics Inc. (IDI) provided Fuller with $200,000 to pay for the newspaper ads. "One of Issue Dynamics major clients is Verizon Communications, which has launched a campaign to make sure that [its competitor] MCI WorldCom doesn't emerge from bankruptcy." The story added, quoting the Center for Media and Democracy, "Issue Dynamics is one of the leading players helping corporations find public interest groups that will accept industry money and front for industry causes. . . . The Gray Panthers should publicly disclose where the money came from for the ads." Fuller responded, "I don't know the source of IDI's budget. But I have no objection to using the enemy to bring down the enemy. Verizon may get some benefit from this, but it also might change their behavior." Two weeks later, after the Gray Panthers testified in federal court that World-Com's $500 million fine "was not severe enough," the *Washington Post* confirmed the Verizon-IDI-Gray Panther conduit and quoted Fulller: "I was happy to find a donor."[21]

Reseeding the Grass Roots?

When Fuller became executive director there were forty-six networks, including seventeen in California. His young field director found "a mostly senior active membership" and reported that five networks needed "new leadership" and fewer than half issued newsletters. During the later 1990s nine networks disbanded and only one formed—the Gray Panthers of Greater Albuquerque, created following a Social Security forum. With just one staff member to assist Fuller after 2000 and no national newsletter, only one new network was chartered, and it folded in 2005. Overall, during the first seven years of the new century twenty-four Panther networks went out of existence, and the total fell to twenty-three in 2007.[22]

At the end of 2003 Fuller resigned the executive directorship and was succeeded by Susan Murany, forty-nine, a Gray Panther staff member since 2000. "Not a child of the 1960s," Ohioan Murany traced her activist awakening to the 1970 National Guard shootings of four anti–Vietnam War protesters at Kent State University, when she was a high school student: "my whole political outlook changed." Following college she worked in Cleveland for faith-based organizations concerned with homelessness, child sexual abuse, and antiracism and directed a disability rights group for five years before moving to Washington. After joining the Panther staff she befriended veteran D.C.-area Panthers Ethel Weisser and Abe Bloom, both in their late eighties, and visited them frequently until their deaths in 2004. A one-person office from 2004 to 2006, Murany initiated no new Gray Panther campaigns but rather worked closely with network conveners defending Medicare and Social Security and opposing the Iraq war. She acknowledged, "The national office could not exist if it weren't for the work and support of the networks."[23] She represented the Panthers in the Leadership Council of Aging Organizations and other coalitions, and after the John Kerry campaign contacted her in 2004, she briefed it about Gray Panther positions on Medicare and other issues. (Her offer to advise the Bush campaign was turned down.)

In 2004 Murany organized the first Gray Panther convention in five years. Held in Seattle on a November weekend after George W. Bush's reelection, it featured plenary speakers Barbara Aldave, former Gray Panther Board chairperson; Luis Navarro, forty-one, of the Service Employees International Union (the SEIU helped fund the convention); and Emily Cunningham, twenty-six, of the League of Pissed-Off Voters, a national youth coalition. Each addressed lessons from the presidential campaign, in which Kerry won more votes than any Democrat ever but still lost to Bush. Lani Sanjek and I were among fifty Gray Panthers attending, nearly half of them Californians and representing fifteen networks. Awards were presented to Charlotte Flynn, who was buoyed by the

gathering—"It's exciting to think that we might just rebound, finally"—
and to Judy Lear, leader of the Gray Panther UN delegation since 2002.
Resolutions consumed only one hour. National priorities until the 2008
convention were determined by delegates placing stickers next to items
listed on a poster. On Sunday morning the winning choices were announced: health care, Social Security, and peace.

To kick off the convention Murany scheduled a "Think Health Care"
noon-hour rally in a downtown Seattle shopping plaza, intended as well
as to raise spirits and numbers in the troubled Seattle network. Formed
in 1975, its eighty members were led during the late 1990s by Marge Lueders, a spirited convener who popularized the "Prevent Truth Decay"
Gray Panther slogan. After her move to Denver in 1999 the network's
aging ranks diminished. Some forty-five Panthers, mostly convention attendees, turned out for the rally, with a half-dozen engaging passersby
about health care issues and recording names the Seattle network might
contact. Seattle's "Raging Grannies" sang antiwar lyrics to the melodies
of well-known songs. Murany was a whirlwind—talking to people, selling
Gray Panther buttons, introducing speakers. The day was very cold, and
demonstrators nearly outnumbered Seattleites who stopped to listen.

Within a year the Seattle Panthers disbanded. Between 1996 and 2007
so did fifteen other networks founded in the 1970s (including Boston,
Bergen County, Montgomery County, Chicago, Denver, and five in California). But fifteen Panther groups active in 2007 were 1970s survivors,
most with histories of three decades or more. Here messages of resil-
ience and renewal could be read. Eight networks at the Seattle convention had more than one hundred members (Berkeley, San Francisco,
Sacramento, Austin, Detroit and Huron Valley in Michigan, Metro D.C.,
North Dade and South Dade Counties in Florida), and a few counted
more than two hundred. Houston had faded and then reorganized,
and so had New York. Under convener Joan Lee, a retired senior citizen
health program director, Sacramento grew in the late 1990s to eighty-
five members—"not only in the 80s bracket but also in their 40s." In
2002 it helped restart the California Gray Panthers, with Lee as capitol
lobbyist for Panther-backed health, housing, and energy bills. In 2004
the California Panthers, with eight member networks, worked successfully with the SEIU to increase wages for nursing home and home care
workers. In 2005 they received a $32,000 grant for a postcard campaign
protesting the "donut hole" in the Republican-sponsored Medicare Part
D prescription drug benefit beginning that year. Part D coverage ended
when enrollee drug expenses reached $2,250 and resumed after costs
topped $5,100. The amount in between, paid by Medicare beneficiaries
themselves, was termed "the donut hole." Designed by the Panther national Board's "action issues" committee, the postcard featured a picture

of a donut and read, "PhRMA got the donut, we got the hole," a barb at the enormous profits pharmaceutical corporations would make from a law they had lobbied to shape and pass.[24] Murany helped distribute cards and sample messages to Panther networks and other groups. In all, eleven thousand postcards were mailed to senators, members of the House, and the White House.

In the years after Maggie, the Panther movement grappled with new technologies reshaping communications and grassroots activism. In 1997 only a third of Board members and just eight network conveners used e-mail; even in 2004 half the conveners communicated by U.S. mail. By 2006 all Board members and conveners used e-mail, although many older network members did not. Fuller started a Gray Panther website in 1998, and by 2006 the San Francisco, Sacramento, California state, Twin Cities, Detroit, Washington, D.C., and New York Gray Panthers had websites announcing events and meetings and posting newsletters. After the 2004 convention San Francisco convener Michael Lyon began a Yahoo e-mail listserv connecting forty-one Gray Panthers nationwide. It was used to exchange plans and information as Panthers in eleven networks participated in demonstrations, forums, and radio and television programs to combat President Bush's Social Security privatization campaign. It was later used to share information on Medicare, Hurricane Katrina relief, and U.S. policy toward Iran and Haiti.

In 2003 the Gray Panthers received a boost when *Maggie Growls!*, a documentary about Maggie Kuhn by Barbara Attie and Janet Goldwater, was aired on 125 PBS stations. The film used historical footage, photographs, animation, clips from Johnny Carson's *Tonight Show*, and interviews with Maggie to trace her life before and after founding the Gray Panthers. It included a lively sequence from her 1982 protest at the Greenspan Social Security commission and details about her love affairs beyond those in her 1991 autobiography. Christina Long, Steve McConnell, and Studs Terkel were the on-camera narrators, with commentary from Ralph Nader, Edith Giese, Abe Bloom, Sue Leary, and Graterford State Correctional Institution Gray Panthers. Fuller used the film's debut to launch the Maggie Kuhn Action Fund for Social Justice and Peace, which grew by $52,000 over the next two years. Murany and Board co-chair Tim Allison, forty, a lawyer and Democratic Party activist who joined the Santa Barbara network in 1996, also employed *Maggie Growls!* in fund-raising. They screened it at the 2005 meeting of the National Council on Aging and American Society on Aging, with follow-up remarks by Long, Leary, sociologist Carroll Estes, and Dave Taylor of New York's Presbyterian Senior Services, which helped pay Maggie's living expenses during her last five years.

In 2007 the Gray Panthers maintained a national staff of two by fund-raising mailings, member dues, donor gifts, bequests, and grants. Whether they would "rebound, finally" or continue to lose network members, numbering less than one thousand in 2007, rested in the hands of local leaders and the national Board. The fifteen-person board included several veteran Panthers: Sue Leary; Californian Joan Lee, seventy-nine; Clint Smith, seventy-one, of Austin; Randy Block, sixty, a Vietnam War conscientious objector and community organizer who joined the Detroit Gray Panthers in 1978; and co-chair Sally Brown, sixty, a Peace Corps alumna and human services foundation administrator and a Twin Cities Panther since 1983. Five members were in their seventies or eighties, and three in their twenties or thiries. Like Murany, five were baby boomers born between 1946 and 1964, and two others were a year or two outside this cohort poised to begin crossing the age sixty-five threshold in 2011.

Berkeley Perseveres

In 1996 local cable Channel 25 aired *The Berkeley Gray Panthers: Working for a Better World*, a ten-minute documentary produced by network member Bob Purdy. It began with a frail Lillian Rabinowitz recounting the founding and growth of the Over 60 Clinic and voicing support for single-payer health care. Peace and justice committee chair Rose Borgersen spoke about voter registration and Panther tabling on city, state, and national issues. Transportation chair Charlie Betcher described efforts to prevent cuts in Alameda County Transit bus service, used mainly by low-income, elderly, and disabled residents. Betcher would later organize a Panther-led "Bus Riders Union." At the 1999 inauguration of Oakland mayor (and former California governor) Jerry Brown its members protested elimination of bus shelters and reductions in weekend and nighttime service. Betcher also chaired the Berkeley Commission on Aging, whose purview included affordable housing, telephone and utility rates, the city's three senior centers, and the scrip issued to older Berkeleyites to pay taxi drivers, who then redeemed it with the city.

The centerpiece of the 1996 documentary was the "edible schoolyard" at Martin Luther King Jr. Middle School, located next to the Panthers' 1325 Grant Street office in North Berkeley. There "children are taught about ethnic diversity through being introduced to the cooking from various cultures, healthy eating through being introduced to fresh vegetables, respect [for] honest labor through growing, harvesting, preparing, cooking and serving of food, [a]nd respect for the environment."[25] The idea originated with restaurateur Alice Waters, owner of the renowned Chez Panisse in Berkeley and a regular donor of dinner-for-two gift certificates to Gray Panther raffles.[26] Ground was broken in 1995 and vegetables and fruits planted for use in cooking classes and school lunches. Gray Panther Gerda Miller's education committee embraced the "edible schoolyard," helping to design garden trellises and edit a student volume documenting it and containing interviews with older Gray Panthers. When the network's office moved in 1997 their ten-year involvement in "King school" programs ended. Other education committee projects continued, including campaigning against ballot measures to end affirmative action at the University of California and bilingual education in California public schools, both of which voters approved.

In the later 1990s a Gray Panther card table appeared once a month in the heart of Berkeley's Shattuck Avenue "gourmet ghetto" and at the City of Berkeley Fourth of July celebration and the annual Solano Avenue "Stroll," a street fair attracting thousands. There Panthers registered voters, distributed flyers on pending referendum items, and collected petition signatures to end the U.S. blockade of Cuba, raise California's minimum wage, and add prescription drug and long-term care coverage to Medicare, as well as extend it to people under sixty-five. They also picketed and demonstrated—against the Republican "Contract with America," "wealth-fare" tax cuts for the rich, and staff downsizing at nursing homes and Kaiser clinics and hospitals. Co-convener Miller and health committee chair Margot Smith testified at hearings in opposition to a merger of Berkeley hospitals, and two vanloads of Panthers lobbied successfully for a state Department of Managed Care to monitor HMOs. In 1998 Panthers joined members of other Bay Area networks at a forum on "The Future of Medicare" organized by Berkeley's Representative Barbara Lee and San Francisco's Nancy Pelosi, who assured her audience she would "fight off privatization."[27]

The life of the network continued to revolve around monthly meetings at the North Berkeley Senior Center and festive events like the 1997 opening of the 1403 Addison Street office attended by seventy-five Panthers and friends, the summer picnic sometime cohosted with nearby Panther networks, and the annual holiday season party at Redwood Gardens, with Ron Dellums the guest of honor in 2003. Student interns continued to arrive, but there were few active younger members beyond Varya Simpson and Carla Woodworth, who after leaving the Berkeley City Council became executive director of the California Physicians' Alliance, the state's chapter of Physicians for a National Health Program, which advocated single-payer health care. Older, frailer Panthers who no longer attended meetings relied on the monthly newsletter for background information about issues for letter writing or telephone calls, as well as synopses of local and state ballot items. Though numbers declined, new members continued to join, often aroused by a particular issue. In 2006 the network roll stood at two hundred.[28]

The local causes Berkeley Gray Panthers espoused often had immediate impact on members. Efforts to preserve and expand housing for low-income tenants were underscored when two Panthers were evicted after their landlords quit the federal Section 8 rent subsidy program.[29] More positively, it was through ECHO/Project Share that Panther Charlotte Knight, eighty-three and widowed, found a young housemate who provided companionship, transportation to shopping and medical visits, and help with home repairs and care of Knight's pet. Knight "kept in touch with 'her Panthers' by telephone" until her death in 1999, the year Panther Leatha Phillips, like Knight a long-time Over 60 Clinic board member, also died.[30] Several Berkeley Panthers I knew in the 1970s, and others from later years, were eulogized in the network newsletter by veteran member Dan Trupin, whose death at ninety-six also came in 1999.

In 2001 Margot Smith, seventy-one, and a doctor of public health, became co-convener; after 2004 she was convener. ("Margot IS the Berkeley Gray Panthers," an admiring member told me in 2007.) During the late 1990s at forums and meetings she and other Panthers educated themselves about World Bank, International Monetary Fund (IMF), and World Trade Organization (WTO) policies. They rued the austerity budgets, land privatization, and accommodation to foreign investment imposed on Third World countries. They deplored neglect of worker rights and environmental protection in WTO rulings and U.S. trade agreements, and erosion of local and national sovereignty in favor of multinational corporations and "the market." In 2000 Smith joined a Washington, D.C., gathering of 20,000 peace, environmental, labor, and student activists to protest World Bank and IMF actions. Smith was arrested—"my first time"— and spent a week in jail with 160 demonstrators. There she "was adopted as grandmother to a group of [young] women" and heartened by a "whole new generation of activists coming up." She returned home "much more sensitive to the corporate takeover of the basics in our society and across the planet. . . . Media mergers, corporate farming, mining and forestry, . . . and arms sales are just parts of the total picture."[31]

Smith combined her Panther activism with the video making she and Bob Purdy began in the 1980s. Her portfolio included documentaries about the 1995 UN World Conference on Women she attended in Beijing; *Democracy in the Workplace*, produced with Purdy, on three Berkeley worker-owned businesses; a video of Iraq war protester Cindy Sheehan's 2004 talk in Berkeley; and another on the World Social Forum in Venezuela she and Berkeley Panther Bea Howard attended with a U.S. delegation in 2005. Like the earlier universal health care videos, these were shown on local cable television and distributed nationwide by Off Center Video, a project of the network's media committee.

With three Panther committees leaderless in 2000, the network merged its education, housing, health, peace, and transportation work into one "social action committee" meeting monthly. In 2001 the last paid staff member departed, and the office was kept open three or four days a week by volunteers. The final network raffle was in 2002, and thereafter member dues plus bequests and memorial gifts covered rent and other expenses. In 2004 the network added a monthly "Panthers at Night" supper meeting, and in 2006 a Saturday book discussion group. In addition, after 2000 the office was used for monthly meetings by allied groups with overlapping Gray Panther membership: the United Nations Association East Bay Chapter, Women's International League for Peace and Freedom, the Fair Election Campaign, and the East Bay Raging Grannies.

In the years following the election of George W. Bush in 2000, new issues appeared on the Berkeley Gray Panther agenda: electoral reform, the war in Iraq, civil liberties, prescription drug prices, global warming, and immigration. When the second Bush term began in 2005 the Panthers continued "working for a better world." They protested budget cuts in federal housing programs and promoted California assemblymember (and former Berkeley mayor) Loni Hancock's bill for public financing of state elections, similar to systems already in operation in Maine and Arizona. In 2004 and 2005 Panthers participated in demonstrations to mark the first and second anniversaries of the Iraq invasion, and on Valentine's Day 2006 they joined three hundred and fifty "Grandmothers against the War" at the Oakland military recruiting station to demand an end to U.S. occupation. At a Hiroshima Day forum in August that year convener Smith addressed the continuing threat of atomic weapons: "The effects of testing and using nuclear bombs and weapons are still with us—the cancers and birth abnormalities of the people of Hiroshima and Nagasaki, . . . Russia's Chernoble, . . . [and] the Downwind people in Nevada and the islands of the South Pacific."[32]

In these post-Maggie years national Panther figures Charlotte Flynn and Dixie Horning were guests at the 1996 Berkeley summer picnic; Tim Fuller visited in 1999 and 2000; and Susan Murany in 2006. Several Berkeley Panthers attended the 1997 convention in San Francisco; three traveled to Washington, D.C., in 1999; and four arrived at the 2004 Seattle gathering sporting snazzy "You Can Make a Difference! Age and Youth in Action" black-and-gray T-shirts the network designed and sold. Varya Simpson served on the national Board through 1999 and was succeeded by Joan Lee of Sacramento representing the California Panthers. In 2005 the Berkeley network showed *Maggie Growls!* and celebrated founder Kuhn's one-hundredth birthday with reminiscences of Maggie by sociologist Carroll Estes.

Three passings marked the beginning years of the Berkeley Panthers' fourth decade. In 2003 past convener Gerda Miller, disabled by a stroke and broken hip in 2000, died, and members celebrated her life at Brennan's, a West Berkeley bar Miller had selected for her memorial. In 2005 Bob Purdy, husband of Margot Smith, died, and memorial gifts from well-wishers added $1,600 to the network treasury. Later that year Lillian Rabinowitz died at ninety-four. She had been reelected to the network's board in 1997 but soon experienced advancing cognitive deficits of Alzheimer's disease. Nonetheless she joined fund-raising efforts for the Over 60 Clinic's new building and was honored at its opening in 2000. By then the clinic was renamed LifeLong Medical Care and had expanded to cover low-income children and families. Lillian later moved to a nursing home. At her memorial in 2006 speakers included LifeLong executive director Marty Lynch, Carroll Estes, Varya Simpson, and other Panther friends and family members.

Revisiting Berkeley

In February 2007 Lani Sanjek and I spent five days in Berkeley, our first visit since the 1980s. Our initial stop was a Saturday-night "Crab Feed" fundraiser for LifeLong Medical Care, held at the North Berkeley Senior Center. We sat with Marty Lynch, beginning his twenty-fifth year as Over 60 Health Clinic and LifeLong executive director. We enjoyed reunions with Jacque Ensign, daughter of our 1970s Gray Panther friend Helene London and now herself aging in place in Berkeley, and Joel Garcia, since 1992 chief executive officer of Tiburcio Vasquez Health Center in south Alameda County, and like Lynch still an Alameda Health Consortium board member. State assemblymember Loni Hancock spoke about universal health care legislation in Sacramento, and Mayor Tom Bates and two city councilmembers greeted the racially diverse and intergenerational roomful of two hundred. During the next two days we reconnected with the Over 60 nurses Lani had hired: Nancy Makowsky, now an ESL teacher, and Janet Peoples, a film screenwriter. We reminisced about Berkeley Gray Panther history and conveners Lillian Rabinowitz and Gerda Miller with Carla Woodworth, now an organizer for the California Federation of Teachers, Varya Simpson, senior counsel at a San Francisco law firm, and Charlene Harrington, a professor and associate director of the geriatric nursing program at the University of California, San Francisco.

On Monday we met Lynch at the Over 60 Health Center at 3260 Sacramento Street in South Berkeley. Over 60 shared its impressive two-story, 17,000-square-foot quarters with the Center for Elders' Independence day health care program for disabled older persons. And above, occupying the third and fourth storys, were forty units of federally financed housing for low-income elders. The total complex had cost $10 million.[33] Lynch gave us a tour, introducing some of the dozens of doctors, nurses, therapists, social workers, and administrative staff and pointing out a plaque listing the founding Gray Panther board members. He filled us in on Alamada Health Consortium developments, as well as the growth since 1995 of LifeLong, now employing three hundred full and part-time staff who worked at seven facilities in Berkeley and Oakland, a headquarters site, and outreach programs at eight residences for formerly homeless adults. In all, LifeLong provided health, dental, podiatry, mental health, and social services to more than sixteen thousand patients, of whom 42 percent were black, 27 percent white, 22 percent Latino, and 10 percent Asian, with three-quarters at or below twice the federal poverty level. Two-thirds were covered by Medicare, Medicaid, or private insurance, including several HMOs contracting with LifeLong, and one-third were uninsured. Patients "over 60" in age were now a third of the total, with younger families predominating at newer sites like the West Berkeley Family Practice clinic where Lynch completed our tour.[34]

On Tuesday morning we visited Redwood Gardens at 2951 Derby Street near the University of California campus. University student dorms occupied most of the former School for the Deaf and Blind site, renamed the Clark Kerr Campus, but the Panthers and other advocates had saved three acres for low-income housing. We walked around Redwood Gardens' five interconnected three-story residences opened in 1986 and built in the Spanish colonial style of its one original building. The complex housed two hundred elderly and disabled tenants in 170 federally subsidized rental units, each with its own kitchen. In 2006 the Department of Housing and Urban Development renewed Redwood Gardens' twenty-year contract, assuring residents, including Gray Panther Charlie Betcher, eighty-six, they could remain.[35]

Next we arrived at the Gray Panther office located in a row of stores facing a parking lot, supermarket, and Mexican restaurant. We met Chris Caldwell, sixty-two, a retired City of Berkeley employee who volunteered three hours each Tuesday and informed us that network membership stood at 150. Two long tables and a dozen chairs occupied the center of the room, with file cabinets, folded card tables, a computer desk, copier, VCR, photographs, posters, and shelves of books, videos, T-shirts, brochures, and newsletters lining the walls. The glass front windows were covered with posters and flyers facing outward, their messages conveying Panther concerns: "We Need Single Payer Health Care—It Covers Everyone!," "U.S. Out of Iraq Now," "Register to Vote Here," "Use Berkeley Scrip for All Berkeley Taxis."

On Wednesday afternoon we returned to the North Berkeley Senior Center for the monthly network meeting. A table contained petitions, flyers on current issues, network literature, and Gray Panther buttons. About twenty attended, mainly in their seventies or older and all but three women, including two in wheelchairs. Avis Worthington, social action committee chair and editor of the monthly newsletter (and a 1960s *Berkeley Barb* reporter), told us attendance averaged thirty, although sixty came the previous month when 1960s Black Panther leader Bobby Seale, a Berkeley resident, spoke about his life, including meeting Maggie Kuhn. Charles Robinson, a retired jazz photographer and Gray Panther representative to Kaiser Permanente's Senior Advisory Committee, chaired the meeting. (His wife, Sarah Robinson, was a former Over 60 board member whom Lynch mentioned during our visit.) Lani introduced herself as the Over 60 Clinic director and nurse practitioner during 1976–78, and I recalled that my first Berkeley Gray Panther meeting was exactly thirty years before, in February 1977.

Member Henry Clarence reported on a meeting with Representative Barbara Lee about impeachment of President George Bush. The City of Berkeley had passed an impeachment resolution, and Panthers were circulating impeachment petitions. Leona Wilson recounted that four Berkeley Panthers were among the six hundred who rallied in Sacramento two days earlier to support reintroduction of state senator Sheila Keuhl's bill to create a payroll-tax-funded health insurance plan covering all California residents and replacing private insurance. California's Senate and House passed the bill in 2006 but Governor Arnold Schwarzenegger vetoed it. Eva Bluestone announced the weekly anti–Iraq war vigil at the Federal Building in Oakland and an "anti-torture village" demonstration near the University of California law school building where John Yoo, the former Justice Department author of memos endorsing Bush interrogation policies, was a faculty member. She urged calls to the White House supporting legislation to facilitate labor union organizing and to Governor Schwarzenegger opposing cuts to public transportation.

The guest speaker was Barbara Morita, a physician assistant and member of a disaster assistance team that conducted medical triage in New Orleans following Hurricane Katrina. Using slides, Morita described the Superdome's 110-degree heat, 98 percent humidity, lack of water and electricity, and "horrible stench" of trash and human waste that thirty thousand people endured for five days. Her team treated medical emergencies, including stranded disabled persons, women in labor, and nursing home residents, with a new patient arriving every three minutes. Eight thousand patients were airlifted from New Orleans, and three thousand city residents died during this "predicted disaster."

Following the Panther meeting Lani and I walked to King Middle School to see the one-acre "edible schoolyard," where organic squash, lettuces, leeks, potatoes, eggplant, basil, mint, plums, kiwis and other vegetables and fruits, as well as eggs from free-ranging chickens, are produced. In the kitchen building where classes are held and school lunches prepared, two teachers explained that by the time students graduate they have participated in garden and kitchen classes during all seasons of the year. The project receives funds from Alice Waters's Chez Panisse Foundation, and visitors have included Bay Area students and teachers, educational and government officials, and mayors from Russia, China, Taiwan, Peru, and Mexico.[36]

During our trip we missed Berkeley convener Margot Smith. She had left for Iran with a delegation of two dozen "civilian diplomats" organized by the Fellowship of Reconciliation. There they met students, university faculty, religious leaders, and ordinary citizens, including survivors of chemical warfare during the eight-year conflict with Iraq. Smith hoped the trip would "show that not all Americans agree with cowboy diplomacy" and that "the idea of attacking Iran is abhorrent" to many. She found Tehran "like San Francisco, a developed, urban city," and was impressed that many Iranians spoke "not only English, but American English." After returning she spoke to Berkeley and Sacramento Gray Panthers and a score of other audiences. She also showed her video about the trip, *Listen to Iran's People: A Call for Peace*, at film festivals.[37]

A Network Winding Down

Despite absorbing the ten remaining Central Queens Panthers in 1997, New York Gray Panther membership continued to decline—to seventy-seven in 1999, and fifty-six in 2000. The twenty or fewer who came to meetings were mainly in their eighties. Several formerly active Panthers were home-based or in nursing homes, and others had moved, often to live near adult children. Still others died and were commemorated at meetings and in the newsletter: Mildred Sklar in 1997, Henrietta Phillips in 1998, Muriel Clark and Sudie George in 1999. Meetings still rotated between the West Side, Harlem, and the East Side and usually ended with members signing letters or postcards mailed to elected officials. The holiday season party continued through 1999, with fourteen attending that year. In 1996 and 1997 two Saturday-morning meetings featuring Representative Jerrold Nadler and state senator Catherine Abbate failed to boost attendance. In 1998 the board concluded the network "needs a new lease on life. Looking at our situation, aside from what each of us does personally, we are going nowhere."[38] The remaining active member were aware that other Panther groups faced similar situations, as did several New York senior citizen and peace organizations.

The handful of active New York Panthers attended demonstrations for numerous causes, including support of the United Nations, handgun control, and opposition to President Clinton's 1998 bombing of Iraq. They participated in voter registration campaigns and leafleted on the

West Side during summers and at the Labor Day Parade. In 1999 five members joined daily protests at One Police Plaza demanding indictments of four police officers who shot and killed African immigrant Amadou Diallo in front of his home. As struggles over Social Security and Medicare raged, New York Panthers circulated petitions, wrote letters, and telephoned their representatives to oppose privatization and subsidies for HMOs. In 1999 they made office visits to Representatives Nadler and Carolyn Maloney to reiterate their concerns and joined the national Gray Panther weekly call-in to the White House. Two New York Panthers attended the 1997 convention in San Francisco, and Tim Fuller came New York in 1998, but none went to the 1999 Gray Panther convention. In 2000 communication with the national office ceased.

In 1996 Lillian Sarno, then in her mid-eighties and with failing eyesight, consented to again become convener, and in 1998 co-convener. Despite her disability, Sarno remained active. She spoke about the Gray Panthers to groups of nurses and high school students and to audiences at St. John's and New York University, and she attended a 1997 City Hall rally to protect rent control. As network convener she wrote scores of letters to city, state, and national officials. The topics included welfare reform, assault weapons, land mine and chemical weapon treaties, Medicare, Social Security, housing, nursing home staffing policies, global warming, single-payer health care, the Donald Trump "towers" on Manhattan's West Side, and campaign finance reform. She dictated the letters to Martha Frankel, who had joined the Panthers in 1992 after retiring and twice a week visited the Panther office after its 1998 move to West Park Presbyterian Church on West 86th Street. The network did not make a transition to computer or e-mail; financial and membership records were kept in handwritten ledgers, and newsletter copy was typed and pasted.

The last membership meeting, with a speaker from the Metropolitan Council on Housing, was in April 2000, and the last newsletter was published in May. In June 2001 eight members gathered to consider the "crisis facing our organization. . . . We have only four active members to do all the work. . . . The practicality of our continuing is in question."[39] Three months later two jet airplanes destroyed the World Trade Center towers, and a follow-up meeting postponed to 2002 never occurred. Convener Edna Graig, seventy-seven, insisted on keeping the Panther office open, and Sarno continued to dictate Gray Panther letters during 2002, including correspondence concerning estate gifts totaling $14,000, plus smaller donations in memory of Lydia Bragger, who had died in 2001.

New York Regroups

In the mid-1990s the Gray Panther UN delegation of six was headed by Mildred Blechman, a retired interior designer who with her husband, Ralph, an accountant, led a Gray Panther group on Long Island before moving to New York City in 1984. The Blechmans joined the East Side network and participated in New York Panther meetings through 2001. The link between UN Panthers and the New York network was reinforced when Joan Davis, sixty-three, a former nursing home activities leader and case manager, joined both in 1995. As network secretary, Davis recorded meeting minutes and edited the newsletter, in which she listed UN forums on peace and disarmament issues. She arranged for passes to UN events, including a 1998 briefing attended by five New York Panthers and Gerda Miller of Berkeley. In 1998 Blechman, blind since 1995, resigned as Gray Panther delegation head. Her successor, a New Jersey Panther, died in 2001.[40]

That year Tim Fuller named Judy Lear, fifty-eight, to the Panthers' UN delegation.[41] A Minnesotan long active in the National Council of Jewish Women and former member of her state's advisory commission on aging, Lear returned to school in 1992 for a master's in public administration at Harvard's Kennedy School of Government. She then lived in Santa Fe, New Mexico, until she moved to New York in 2001 with the aim of participating in United Nations NGO work. After learning of an opening in the Panther delegation, she traveled to Washington, D.C., to meet Fuller, who in 2002 elevated her to delegation head. "When I get involved in something I tend to jump into the swimming pool at the deep end," Lear told the Gray Panther convention in Seattle in 2004. She joined NGO committees on aging and women and represented the Panthers at the Second World Assembly on Aging in Madrid in 2002 and conferences in India, Japan, and China during 2003 and 2004.

In 2003 Lear decided to help reactivate the Gray Panthers in New York City. She met with Lillian Sarno and Panthers Martha Frankel and Edna Graig, who continued to visit the network office. She held "planning meetings," including one where Lani Sanjek spoke about the Medicare Part D prescription drug bill about to be passed by Congress. Mary Springer, forty-four, of the senior citizen program staff at Penn South, a large apartment complex in Manhattan's Chelsea neighborhood, learned that the Gray Panthers were active again and invited Lear to hold a January 2004 meeting there. Forty attended, including me and a handful of veteran Panthers, among them Sarno, Joan Davis, and two I knew from the 1980s—Marie Maher, a former East Side convener, and former Westchester Gray Panther Estelle Katz, now living in Penn South. A guest speaker discussed the single-payer health care bill cosponsored by seventy-five congressional Democrats, and there was much griping about AARP helping to pass Bush's Medicare Part D drug plan.

A month later I joined Lear and five others at a meeting to form a network board. Lear agreed to serve as convener, and I volunteered to be secretary, taking minutes at meetings and later reviving *Network Report*, the New York Gray Panther newsletter. I called Lillian Sarno before the next meeting, and she confided that the office cohort was apprehensive at first but agreed, "Judy is doing a good job in organizing." The New York Gray Panther bank account and office were entrusted to the new board. In August 2004 four Panthers participated in a demonstration against Bush policies at the Republican National Convention in New York, and Lear was interviewed on the NBC evening news. She was seen by friends nationwide as well as Gray Panther executive director Susan Murany, who called to congratulate her. Lear's Panthers, numbering fifty paid members, were also featured in a Manhattan neighborhood newspaper.[42]

In October 2004 thirty-two Gray Panthers and friends attended a Sunday lunch honoring veteran members. The idea was Lear's; she was assisted in organizing the event by Sarno, Davis, and Shiuho Lin, a recently retired lab scientist who learned about the Gray Panthers from fellow Taiwanese friend Weishan Huang, a member of the UN Panther delegation. Nine Gray Panthers of twenty or more years' standing, including five in their nineties, received certificates and pins, among them Lillian Sarno, Stella Murphy, now living in a Brooklyn nursing home, the Blechmans, and Lani and me. Recognition was given to Davis, Frankel, and Graig for keeping the network from closing after 2001. I spoke about the network's history, Mildred Blechman reminisced about UN activities, and Sarno, ninety-five, addressed the future:

Every empire has the seeds of destruction within it . . . and we have them too. The seed of our destruction is greed; greed is what has brought down this country today. . . . That is where the Gray Panthers fit in perfectly because we believe in social justice. . . . Social justice means . . . that you don't have a country where people can work a regular job and not make enough to live. We don't have a country where people work and still have to go to a food bank to finish out the month. . . . *We* don't want that kind of country . . . and we've got to make sure that everybody doesn't. . . . We have to keep fighting . . . by supporting Social Security . . . by supporting affordable housing. . . . We're for peace and disarmament, of course. We're for . . . Medicare, of course. And . . . we do try to help the poor; we don't do a good job of it but we do try. The rich don't need our help. . . . They get all sorts of extra goodies, like tax deductions. . . . My running around days are over, and believe me I miss them. But you have to live with what you've got [and] with what I've got I still can think, thank God, and I still can influence . . . people I meet [and] know. I'm continuing to do that and I hope we all will.[43]

New York Panthers on the Prowl

New York Gray Panther programs and actions from 2004 onward were in accord with Sarno's social justice agenda, but with new turns reflecting changing times. At one meeting Nora O'Brien summarized her International Longevity Center report on the absence of planning for transportation, health care, or delivered meals that affected lower Manhattan elderly and disabled home-based residents for days following the September 11, 2001, attack.[44] At another meeting four city school psychologists and social workers spoke about the impact of media violence on youth, emphasizing that the video games "Grand Theft Auto" and "Mortal Combat"—which "nearly every school-age boy has at home"— are replete with blood, punching, dismembering, and killing. Exposure to TV violence, whether entertainment or news, correlates "like smoking to lung cancer" with increased levels of conflict and weapon confiscation in schools.[45] Speakers at a "politics of food" meeting explained that food pantries and soup kitchens serve one million New Yorkers a year, but the absence of nutritious, affordable food in low-income neighborhoods contributes to rising levels of obesity and diabetes. Expanding the city's eighty community and farmers' markets and making fresh produce more available to food stamp users and in senior centers could stem chronic health problems as well as benefit New York State's thirty-six thousand family farms.

Other network activities fit into the familiar grooves of health care, Social Security, peace, housing, and accessibility. Jim Collins of the New York Citizens Committee on Aging and Lani Sanjek of New York State-Wide Senior Action Council briefed Panthers on Part D's roll-out as a confusing menu of private insurance plans rather than a "one card, one plan, one price" Medicare-administered benefit, and about bills to allow Medicare to negotiate drug prices "like the Veterans Administration already does."[46] Four Panthers joined a "Health Care for All" march over the Brooklyn Bridge organized by the largely immigrant SEIU-32BJ building maintenance workers union, cheered on by Senator Charles Schumer.[47] An evening Gray Panther forum attended by ninety surveyed prospects for universal health care as speakers addressed single-payer, expansion of Medicare and Medicaid, state initiatives, and presidential candidate proposals.

During the first half of 2005 President Bush barnstormed the country touting his proposal to allow workers under fifty-five to invest a portion of Social Security payroll taxes in private stock and bond accounts. As I updated myself about Social Security I discovered many excellent reports and fact sheets, plus ongoing newspaper coverage of Bush's campaign, on Internet think tank and political group websites.[48] Remembering the

outspoken Social Security advocacy of New York Gray Panther Jim Durkin and Max Manes of SASS in the 1980s, I led a February 2005 Gray
Panther Social Security workshop, which thirty-five attended. I prepared
a four-page handout addressing "What Social Security Is & Isn't," "What
Happens after 2042?" (the year payroll taxes were projected to be insufficient to pay full benefits), "What Are the Bush Benefit Cut/Privatiza-
tion Proposals?," and "Why People in Their 20s, 30s & 40s Should be
Worried!"[49] I stressed that Social Security provides inflation-protected
benefits to wage-earners and their families after retirement, in the
event of disability, and after the death of a working spouse or parent. If
a mid-twenty-first-century shortfall ever arrived, and there were reasons
to doubt this, it could be filled by raising the payroll-tax earnings cap,
bringing state and local government workers into Social Security, and
other measures that would not reduce benefits.[50] Bush's "personal accounts" were predicated on benefit cuts that would escalate in future decades, hitting most severely those currently in their forties and younger.[51]
Moreover, a beneficiary could outlive a "personal account," but Social
Security would continue for the rest of his or her life.

Over the next four months I repeated my presentation to aging services professionals at the Queens Interagency Council on Aging, to a
student audience at a Queens College NYPIRG forum, on a Manhattan
public access cable television show, and at two senior centers. Susan Murany circulated my Social Security handout to other Panther networks,
and New York Teamster retirees reprinted it in their newsletter. I joined
a NYNAMSS-NYSARA (New York State Alliance for Retired Americans)
working group with Lani, union staff and retirees, and other advocates,[52]
part of a nationwide pushback to Bush's privatization plan by union,
Democratic Party, and community activists. By June support for Bush's
handling of Social Security plummeted to 25 percent, and he abandoned
his campaign.[53]

More than any issue it was the war in Iraq that mobilized the reconstituted New York network. In 2004 and 2005 the gray-on-yellow Panther
banner returned to city streets when five members joined protests mark-
ing the first and second anniversaries of the U.S. invasion. Convener
Lear was invited to a 2005 meeting where members of Grandmothers
against the War, who conducted a weekly vigil at Rockefeller Center,
and Code Pink Women for Peace, Elders for Peace and Justice for the
Next 7 Generations, Grandmothers for Peace International, New York
City Raging Grannies, Peace Action, and Women's International League
for Peace and Freedom planned a demonstration at the Times Square
Armed Forces Recruiting Station. There on October 17 this "Granny
Peace Brigade" coalition declared, "We are grandmothers heartbroken
over the huge loss of life and limb in Iraq. We feel it is our patriotic

duty to enlist in the United States military today in order to replace our grandchildren who have been deployed there far too long and are anxious to come home now while they are still alive and whole. . . . They were sent there on a web of lies and deceit resulting in untold harm to them and countless innocent Iraqi people." Finding the door locked, eighteen brigade members between fifty-nine and ninety-one, including Gray Panther Lear, sat down in front of the recruiting station. They were arrested for disorderly conduct, handcuffed, and jailed for five hours.

New York Times, Newsday, News Channel One, and Associated Press coverage followed. With scores of supporters and continuing media attention they returned for court appearances. Following a six-day trial in April 2006, all were acquitted. Three days after the verdict the Granny Peace Brigade was the lead contingent in a 350,000-strong march commemorating the third anniversary of the Iraq invasion.[54] In June they embarked on a ten-day road trip of protest events in Staten Island, New Jersey, Pennsylvania, Delaware, Maryland, and Washington, D.C. In September they and two hundred supporters marched across the Brooklyn Bridge carrying three-foot "Troops Home Now" black balloons and rallied at the World Trade Center ground zero site. On January 1, 2007, they staged a midtown Manhattan vigil and march to recognize the three-thousandth U.S. military death in Iraq. Later that month they returned to the Capitol to lobby against the war at each of the one hundred Senate offices. In March they revisited the Times Square Recruitment Station for a five-day recitation of names of American and Iraqi war dead. In all, twenty-one Gray Panthers joined Lear at Granny Peace Brigade events.

Ten Panthers attended demonstrations of 5,000 New Yorkers at City Hall in 2005, and 7,000 at Stuyvesant Town in Manhattan in 2007, to demand preservation of the city's affordable rental housing stock.[55] Both actions were organized by Housing Here and Now, a coalition of ninety housing and grassroots community organizations including the Coalition for the Homeless, Metropolitan Council on Housing, Disabled in Action, unions, and clergy. At a 2006 Gray Panther forum a Housing Here and Now organizer warned the city was likely to lose 300,000 rent-stabilized apartments by 2011, and its public housing units were endangered by federal, state, and city funding cuts. A second forum panelist, Presbyterian Senior Services executive director Dave Taylor, described the new PSS GrandParent Family Apartments in the Bronx housing fifty residents over sixty-two and their eighty-seven grandchildren. Taylor estimated there were 87,000 grandparents raising 200,00 grandchildren in the city overall. The third panelist, Anne Emerman, outlined past and current struggles to incorporate accessibility standards in the city's building code. A psychiatric social worker, Emerman, sixty-nine, was director of Mayor David Dinkins's Office for People with Disabilities from 1990 to 1993 and senior policy advisor to the City Council mental health and disability committee from 2002 to 2005. Upon retiring she became an active Gray Panther.

Disability issues were a Gray Panther concern at the United Nations, where delegation member Gloria Korecki participated in the Disability Conference. In 2005 Korecki and Mildred Blechman testified before the city council for installation of "audible traffic signals," common in many countries, which used sound and recorded messages to assist the visually impaired and wheelchair users at street crossings. Testifying for both Disabled in Action (DIA) and the Gray Panthers at a 2006 council hearing, Ann Emerman insisted that Mayor Michael Bloomberg's plan to build 165,000 units of housing conform to federal law by ensuring that 5 percent of units were accessible to New Yorkers with mobility impairments, and 2 percent to blind or deaf city residents.[56]

In 2007 Emerman organized a briefing for DIA and Gray Panther members with two attorneys from the Multiple Sclerosis Society and New York Lawyers for the Public Interest who had participated in the city's four-year rewriting of its building code. In addition to laudable energy conservation and post–9/11 safety provisions, the new code would supersede and weaken accessibility and adaptability provisions passed in 1987. Two months later Emerman, five disability activists, Lear, and I met with the city council housing committee staff. Emerman stated that the new code contained numerous accessibility exemptions and loopholes and had no requirement in new one- and two-family homes for "visitability"—for "one entrance without steps, an accessible bath/toilet room on the ground level, and accessible routes throughout the dwelling unit negotiable by walker or wheelchair." Lear and I emphasized that these features were critical for older New Yorkers to age in place as well as for people with disabilities of all ages to visit relatives or friends.

In June 2007 Emerman testified before the city council housing committee:

The 1980s [New York State and City] Codes required all new (and renovated) buildings . . . to have . . . adaptable or useable spaces . . . and signage for safe use by all persons, with limited exceptions. . . . That . . . drove the manufacturers to develop and standardize equipment, such as 32-inch wide doors [and] frames, and utilities (dishwashers) to fit under lowered kitchen counters. . . . [The current] code process was . . . stacked with real estate interests. . . . I sat in on two meetings and was astounded to witness individuals representing BOMA [the Building Owners and Managers Association], REBNY [the Real Estate Board of New York], and Condo/Coop Associations admit that as individuals they would like to vote with the advocates for accessibility, but they had their marching orders.

She urged council members to hold further consultations to "analyze the cost/benefit to your constituents, the families and communities in your district."[57] My testimony followed.

More New Yorkers will be living into their 80s and 90s [and] families will be smaller, with . . . fewer available adult children to help elderly parents. And the experience of caring for an older parent will be nearly universal for New Yorkers in their 50s, 60s, or even 70s. . . . We know that after age 75 the likelihood of disability increases. . . . Arthritis, rheumatoid conditions, diabetes, obesity, stroke, hip fractures will be more prevalent in an 80+ and 90+ population. . . . Younger family members do not want to isolate and institutionalize their parents. They want them to be able to remain in their homes. . . . They want to be able to visit, and have their parents visit them. . . . Accessibility and adaptability standards . . . do add costs to new construction. But those costs are small . . . compared to costs that are displaced onto families and to government. . . . Someone will pay later, either individual families, or government—which means all of us—in renovations, or transportation, relocation, or health and home services, or even building additional residential facilities.[58]

We lost, and the council passed the new building code two weeks later.[59] Before the vote council staff told us that a "clean-up" bill would be forthcoming in 2008, or perhaps separate "visitability" legislation. We responded that we would be back.

In 2007 the New York Gray Panthers had fifty-seven paid members. Most received meeting notices and the newsletter by e-mail. A year earlier the West Park Presbyterian office was closed and a "virtual office" established with a rented mailbox and telephone calls forwarded to convener Lear's home. A GrayPanthersNYC.org website was managed by board member Michael Texeira, fifty-nine, a Hunter College School of Social Work faculty member who worked on intergenerational and foster housing programs. Also a national Board member, Texeira authored Gray Panther position statements on U.S. policy in Haiti and FEMA's response to Hurricane Katrina.

The nine members of the New York Panther board ranged in age from forty-eight to seventy-six. Three were baby boomers and three in their early sixties. Four were retired and five still worked, including Lear, who taught English as a second language. They had arrived through Lear's UN network, old Gray Panther connections, and recent network activities. They reflected a network rebuilding.

Chapter 9
The Gray Panther Legacy

Leaders shape and galvanize social and political movements, but followers empower leaders.[1] A movement leader who inspires followers must possess the ability to "translate personal troubles into public issues" and draw attention to "their human meaning for . . . individuals."[2] Forced to retire against her will at sixty-five, Maggie Kuhn proclaimed the injustice of mandatory retirement and struck a responsive chord for others in her situation, who were legion. Among the thirteen million retirees over age sixty-five in the early 1970s, four million "did not retire by choice but rather were forced to retire." More broadly, 86 percent of Americans of all ages agreed "nobody should be forced to retire because of age if he [or she] wants to continue working and is still able to do a good job."[3]

The Gray Panthers, however, did not become a single-issue, anti–mandatory retirement organization. The older members who responded to Maggie included forced retirees, voluntary retirees, early retirees, and persons still employed. They all understood what the labeling of themselves and others as "senior citizens" or "elderly" entailed. Although "at no point in one's life does a person stop being himself [or herself] and suddenly turn into an 'old person,' " they realized that "the public image of most older people is far more negative than the view [those] 65 and older hold of themselves."[4] Negative characterizations and treatment of the old became more common with the transition from nineteenth-century preindustrial republic to twentieth-century corporate state.[5] In 1968 Robert Butler coined the term "ageism" to describe them.

Ageism is the systematic stereotyping of and discrimination against people because they are old. . . . Old people are categorized as senile, rigid in thought and manner, old-fashioned in morality and skills. . . . Ageism allows the younger generation to see older people as different from themselves; thus they subtly cease to identify with their elders as human beings. . . . Ageism is manifested in . . . outright disdain and dislike, or simply subtle avoidance of contact; discriminatory practices in housing, employment and services of all kinds; epithets, cartoons and jokes. At times ageism becomes an expedient method by which society promotes viewpoints about the aged in order to relieve itself of responsibility toward them.[6]

Maggie and the Gray Panthers offered something different.

Aging begins with the moment of birth, and it ends only when life itself has ended. Life is a continuum; only we—in our stupidity and blindness—have chopped it up into little pieces and kept all those little pieces separate. . . . Old age is nothing to be ashamed about. Rather, it is a triumph over great odds, something to be proud of. To be old and gray is beautiful. . . . Don't deny your history. . . . Review what you've done and be strengthened by it. . . . Old age should be esteemed as a flowering not a fading of life. . . . We're the elders of the tribe and the elders are charged with the tribe's survival and well being! . . . Our [Gray Panther] movement has three characteristics that distinguish it from other groups of elders. . . . We are . . . an age-integrated action-coalition working for *change*—not just adjustment or accommodation to the exiting order. . . . We are very much concerned about all forms of injustice and oppression, including unjust treatment of citizens because of their age. . . . We are experimenting with new, flexible structures and with multiple leadership.[7]

Maggie's message resonated with many in their sixties or seventies whom she targeted as recruits—the former union organizers, peace activists, left-wing political party supporters, women's rights advocates, and retired social workers who first became politically active in the 1930s, a time when, as Tish Sommers put it, "Radicals were much more common then than they are now. They were equivalent to liberals today in terms of numbers and influence."[8] In addition, many were attracted by the Panthers' active opposition to the war in Vietnam, which distinguished this movement from self-identified "senior citizen" organizations.

The antiwar stance was also the initial link to young recruits, beginning with the 1970 Consultation meeting with Philadelphia college students. While peace and opposition to U.S. foreign intervention remained central Gray Panther causes, additional young members were attracted by the movement's nursing home activism—first in Philadelphia, then with Griesel and Horn's project, and in local network activities like those in Berkeley and New York. These young Gray Panthers of the 1970s had been molded by the decade of the 1960s, in the same way their older compatriots were by the 1930s. In addition to the Vietnam War, which did not end until 1975, they had lived through African American civil rights struggles and the assassinations of President John Kennedy in 1963, Malcolm X in 1965, and Martin Luther King Jr. and Senator Robert Kennedy in 1968. They had participated in or been exposed to "the student movements of the 1960s [that] represented a backlash on the part of middle-class youth against the . . . failure of America to live up to its moral claims."[9]

It was the union of these two generations that made the Gray Panthers the unique organization it was. For both generations the political was already personal, and each brought their experiences and values with them. Both the young, not yet encumbered with the demands of careers, and the old, now freed from theirs, had time to devote to activism. The Panther intergenerational milieu was new to each cohort, as were the friendships rooted in shared political commitments and activities that crossed three, four, even five decades. Not based on kinship or neighboring, such bonds were unusual in American society. I treasure the close ties I had during the 1970s and 1980s with several older Gray Panthers. In 2007 Berkeley Panther Carla Woodworth reflected, "All my close Gray Panther buddies have passed on . . . the trouble of having friends in their 90s! But I learned so much from all plus had the time of my life raising hell with Dan & Sophie Trupin, Gerda Miller, Hilda Judelson, Hilda Cowan, and of course, Lillian [Rabinowitz] . . . what a crowd."[10]

The movement had a multi-issue focus from the start given Maggie's pre-Panther involvements in union work, women's equity, racial justice, health care, housing, and peace. And the focus widened rather than narrowed. Members brought their favored issues with them, and from speakers at meetings and fellow Panthers they learned about and embraced new ones. In local networks and nationally the Gray Panthers participated in coalitions with a multitude of movements and organizations: disarmament, Nuclear Freeze, and anti-apartheid groups; national health care, women's, nursing home advocacy, senior citizen, and disability rights organizations; and coalitions to defend rent protections, reduce bus and subway fares, and preserve Social Security and Medicare.

Maggie possessed leadership skills that were "effective with large groups of people and in a variety of changing situations." And like other movement founders she "strengthen[ed] those [she] influence[d], inspiring them to work on their own initiative." She thus empowered a "large number of individuals at national, regional, or local levels" who expanded Gray Panther accomplishments and influence.[11] Hundreds of women and men undertook to "convene" a Gray Panther network; some failed, others had lasting success. In many groups there was no succeeding convener, or none with sufficient energy and dedication to sustain a network. In Berkeley, however, Lillian Rabinowitz was followed by Gerda Miller and then Margot Smith, with others serving briefer periods as convener or co-convener. In New York the Bagger-Bragger standoff gave way to more generative leadership: Sylvia Wexler, Lillian Sarno, and Judy Lear, again with others contributing to continuity. Similar histories occurred in the dozen other networks active from the 1970s through 2008.

The movement empowered countless individual Panthers, directly by Maggie at the national level, and in the local networks. With Maggie's blessing, Elma Griesel undertook hearing aid and nursing home projects, and Chuck Preston created the newspaper *Network*, each making substantial contributions to the overall movement as well as entering new, fulfilling periods in their lives. Maggie's green light opened opportunities for Lillian Rabinowitz and other Panthers to build a "continuum of care" for older Berkeley residents, and for Glen Gersmehl in New York to articulate a Panther vision of a national health service. At their best the networks were "free spaces" of "participatory character," with "a mix of people and perspectives . . . exchange, debate, dissent, and openness." In the networks members could "analyze problems and their sources, write leaflets . . . debate alternatives," and hone "essential political skills: writing constitutions, electing officers, running meetings, raising money, recruiting members, voting, planning and coordinating campaigns."[12] Like Maggie, the conveners encouraged people to participate in Panther activities, serve as officers and network spokespersons, and join or chair committees. People did things they had never done before, in some cases changing the direction of their lives. Lillian Rabinowitz's request that Lani Sanjek become director of the Over 60 Clinic opened pathways she has followed since. Lillian Sarno's suggestion that I begin a housing committee led to new, enriching activities and experiences in my life.

In the Consultation period most organizing and recruitment was done by Maggie. After the 1972 Denver press conference she became the main national organizer of Gray Panther networks, and this role continued into the 1980s. In the new local groups Maggie's appearances were at first the principal means of member recruitment, but by the mid-1970s increasingly it was conveners and active committees that were adding members to network rosters. From this point onward some of the stronger Panther groups began helping fledging conveners start new networks: Los Angeles Panthers organized several Southern California networks; Berkeley midwifed Bay Area groups; New York members did the same in Manhattan, the Bronx, and Queens; and the Washington, D.C., Panthers helped start the suburban Maryland networks.[13]

The numerical growth of Gray Panther networks in the later 1970s and early 1980s presented a challenge common to social movements—coordinating dispersed units. "Absent such coordination, not only is regional or national action hampered; so too is local action. Connections among units provide mechanisms for comparing results and trading information."[14] National conventions were the chief means of maintaining coordination, but they peaked in attendance in 1979.[15] Other means were neglected. From the 1970s through the 1990s the National Steering Committee or Board periodically resolved to designate its members "liaisons" to a number of individual networks, but such linkages never materialized. *Network*, the movement's standard, was sent to donors but was largely unread by network members before 1982, when they were added to its mailing list.[16] The national task forces and the umbrella organizations in California and New York were resented by the Philadelphia staff and Executive Committee. Their cross-network capacities "for comparing results and trading information" were beyond the control of "National," which ignored a 1979 management consultant's recommendation that state organizations be encouraged and given voting power on the national board.

The local-National conflict that erupted in 1982, the networks' Social Security revolt and the purge of Health Task Force chair Francis Klafter in 1983, the election of a network-member NSC majority in 1984, and the resignation of executive director Edith Giese in 1985 were acts in a drama that began earlier. By 1980 the direct mail funding stream swelled the national office budget and financed a larger staff. An Executive Committee decision to switch to a new fund-raising consultant that year led to reduced returns, and by 1983, financial crisis.[17] At the same time the Executive Committee and national office staff, encouraged by the new consultant, proposed to turn the Gray Panthers into a top-down advocacy group, with a "rapid response" base of individual donors to make calls and write letters, and with fewer local networks each contributing larger amounts to Philadelphia.[18]

The turmoil that beclouded the Gray Panthers between 1982 and 1985 should be seen in a larger context.[19] From the 1820s to the 1960s America's national civic life operated through organizations composed of local chapters and state federations. Members joined a local unit, participated in meetings and elections, and attended conventions. In the 1960s, "a great civic reorganization from membership federations to professionally managed groups" began to occur. Few social movements of the 1960s or 1970s produced lasting membership organizations composed of local groups, but the Gray Panthers did, no doubt capitalizing on the experiences of the older members. Activists like the Gray Panthers, however, increasingly were marginalized by professionally managed, issue-based organizations with "mailing list memberships" that spanned the political spectrum (like the National Right to Life Committee, the Concord Coalition, Mothers against Drunk Driving, or the Children's Defense Fund). Less democratic and less participatory, these groups would "forgo or deemphasize individual membership and local chapters" and instead operate through targeted direct mail appeals, foundation and corporate grants, and Washington-based staff who lobbied elected officials and federal bureaucrats. "Associations rooted in individual membership—especially those with large networks of local chapters—lost visibility and clout."[20]

At the time of the Philadelphia staff's and Executive Committee's aborted overture to this larger trend, movement founder Maggie Kuhn was entering a period of diminished vigor and frailty. In the spring of 1983 she was hospitalized and missed large Panther events sponsored by the California and New York City umbrella groups. Soon afterward the conflict between national office staff and Frances Klafter (who attended both gatherings) ensued. Maggie sided with the staff and Executive Committee, but like the direct mail flow of cash, her charisma within the movement was waning.[21] Her success as a leader, however, should be gauged not by alignment with a threatened national staff and loyal Executive Committee but rather by her creation of a movement that provided its "multiple leadership" (Lillian Rabinowitz, Sylvia Wexler, Lillian Sarno, Tom Moore, Frieda Wolff, Elma Griesel, Tish Sommers, Joe Davis, Frances Klafter, and many others) with opportunities to develop their own followings, and even their own charisma.[22] While the center grew rigid, focused more on process than content, criticism of the movement's direction was forthcoming from the grassroots. When the move to Washington occurred in 1985 it reflected the wishes of the networks, if not those of the national convener.

For the next dozen years leadership of the Gray Panthers rested in the hands of Frances Humphreys, who provided a task force–like model of network coordination from the D.C. office, and Charlotte Flynn, who appreciated the movement's grassroots foundation. But the membership was aging as the 1930s activist cohort was moving into its eighties. Few of the next generation, who entered their sixties with political outlooks shaped in the later 1940s or 1950s, became Gray Panthers. Moreover, to the question posed by an observer of the 1977 convention—"Will the young Panthers stay committed as they acquire middle-aged responsibilities?"—the answer in most cases was no.[23] And neither did new troops of young Panthers arrive to replace them. For the generation of young persons acquiring their political orientations in the Reagan-era 1980s, it was entrepreneurial, private versus public, and politically conservative rather than socially activist values that predominated.[24] As the 1990s began, the Gray Panthers, now two decades old, were primarily older senior citizens.

In 1995 Maggie died. A decade and a half later the Gray Panthers survive. Flynn's executive director choice, Tim Fuller, was unable to replenish the network ranks and in 2000 chose an issue-based, advocacy group model. His campaigns for universal health care and against the pharmaceutical industry resonated with network sentiments, but coordination and nourishment of the dispersed Panther units lapsed as *Network*, now a newsletter, was abandoned, and no convention was held for a period of five years. Fuller's successor Susan Murany refocused on the networks, organizing a convention in 2004 and planning another for 2008. The 2007 board, with a majority in their sixties or younger, was an indication that the Gray Panther intergenerational vision might continue.

A Summing Up

Among America's past and present activist groups, the Gray Panthers have had a good run. Between 1800 and 1945 there were five to six hundred multichapter, multistate labor, antislavery, nativist, women's suffrage, socialist, peace, and reform organizations, most of them single-issue groups. Half were active for eight years or less, and only a tenth as long as the Gray Panthers, who marked their thirty-eighth year in 2008. The groups varied in size from less than one thousand members to several million, with only half claiming ten thousand or more members at their peaks.[25]

The meaning, or the reality, of claimed and estimated membership in activist organizations is difficult to assess. In the Gray Panthers, local network rolls include both "active" members, who attend meetings and may participate in committees and in actions, and dues-paying members, some of whom do no more than write an annual check while others carefully read newsletters and may write letters, make phone calls, or send e-mails about issues that concern them. There have also been nationally based "active" Panthers, unconnected to any network, engaged in projects at the Philadelphia or Washington offices, or participating in task forces and Board committees. In addition, there are national financial donors, ranging from "checkbook members" to substantial givers, and there were friends of Maggie (most also donors) who had no formal tie to the national organization or a network (like Ralph Nader and Robert Butler). Among active network and national members a few were "full-time" Panthers, including both rank-and-file members and paid staff. For most Gray Panthers, however, their activities were an occasional involvement, perhaps a few hours per week or month.[26] I have been a Gray Panther donor to Berkeley, New York, and national groups for thirty years, and an active Berkeley member for two years (1977–78) and active New York Panther for a dozen years (1980–87 and since 2004). I was a "full-time" Gray Panther during the Proposition 13 summer in 1978 and a 1981–82 sabbatical year, but otherwise my Gray Panther commitments amounted at most to several days per month. Many Gray Panthers were also members and participants in other progressive and activist groups, some maintaining primary affiliation elsewhere or dividing loyalties between two or more organizations.

With this in mind, at the peak in the early 1980s there were 6,000 to 7,000 Gray Panther network members and 60,000 donors. To put this in perspective we can compare Panther numbers with a few other activist organizations. At its peak at the end of World War II, the Communist Party USA had 80,000 members; Cold War fervor beginning in the later 1940s reduced this to 10,000 by 1957.[27] Membership in the NAACP, never exceeding 2 percent of the African American population, numbered in the hundreds of thousands in the 1950s and 1960s.[28] Students for a Democratic Society (SDS), organized in 1962, grew to 4,000 members and 124 chapters by 1966 and claimed 100,000 members in 1968.[29] The National Organization for Women (NOW) had 1,100 members in 14 chapters within a year of its 1966 founding, and 60,000 members by 1975; membership peaked at 280,000, and 800 chapters, in 1993.[30] The mainly African American National Welfare Rights Organization (NWRO), founded in 1967, had 22,000 dues-paying members within two years, and its total following approached 100,000.[31] The Older Women's League (OWL), launched in 1980, had more than 15,000 members and nearly 100 chapters by 1985.[32] Today SDS and NWRO are long defunct, and the other groups have shrunk in numbers.

Smaller than some of these, comparable in size to SDS and OWL, the Gray Panthers were conscious of their vanguard role. "We've had enormous success, all out of proportion to our numbers. . . . We've been very outspoken . . . and we've caught the attention of the media," Maggie reflected in 1988.[33] In relation to mainline aging groups, the Panthers were "gadflies to keep older, more established . . . organizations moving toward ever more radical goals."[34] They could hardly compete with AARP, which claimed twenty-five hundred locals and seven million members in 1974, and thirty-three million by 2003. Yet with a Washington, D.C., legislative and policy unit of 165, and more than twelve hundred staff members nationwide, less than 10 percent of AARP "members" were affiliated with local units.[35] Gray Panthers sometimes worked with, or belonged to, local AARP chapters. They also allied with AARP and other groups as members of the Washington-based Leadership Council of Aging Organizations.

Activist organizations with any "enduring power and depth always find their strength in community-based" grassroots units that, like Panther networks, are marked by "informality, decentralization, and cooperative ethos" and "generate innovative tactics by encouraging group input."[36] Since 1972, 288 Gray Panther networks have been recognized by the national movement. The peak number at any one time was 122 networks in 1980. Twenty-three networks, including several dating from the 1970s, remained in operation in 2007. A majority of Gray Panther network conveners and members have been women, and most have been white, both middle class and working class.[37] African American Gray Panthers have contributed to the movement's story, among them the first office staffer

Stanley Earley; Berkeley Over 60 Clinic founder Eugenia Hickman; leaders in the handful of networks with substantial black memberships—Angie Aker in Kansas City, Thelma Rutherford in Washington, D.C., Henrietta Phillips in Harlem—Louis Webb of the Mendocino Coast Gray Panthers; and in 2008 Charles Robinson, co-convener of the Berkeley network, and national Board members Mike Texeira of New York and Clint Smith of Austin. Still, the Panthers have long been concerned that they were less multiracial than their ideals warrant.

The reach of the Gray Panther movement was wide. Maggie's national television appearances, perhaps especially those on Johnny Carson's show, made "Gray Panthers" a household word. Her extensive press exposure reinforced her prominence, and her public speaking brought her to at least thirty-nine states. Gray Panther networks formed in all but seven of the fifty states, and talks by local Panthers before varied audiences, as well as Panther actions and media coverage, added to the movement's impact. Gray Panther groups also arose in Germany (Graue Panther), Belgium (De Grijze Panters), France (Les Pantheres Grises), Canada (Grey Panthers), Switzerland, Japan, Ireland, and Russia. This delighted Maggie, who in 1992 endorsed renaming the movement "Gray Panthers International," but no formal ties with the overseas groups were established.

The reach of the Panthers was also more extensive than a six to seven thousand network membership peak might suggest. Countless more people than that participated as members of Gray Panther networks over the thirty-six years between 1972 and 2008. This registered with me in 2005 when I was walking to an anti–Iraq war demonstration in New York. Noticing my Gray Panther pin, a man in his thirties told me that he had been a member of the Huron Valley network while a law student at the University of Michigan. And in 2007 a speaker from the Medicare Rights Center told New York network members that she had been a Boston Gray Panther in the late 1970s.

Actions undertaken by individual Gray Panthers, whether network or national members, even if briefly or loosely affiliated, must be added to the movement's record of accomplishments. Elvin Adams, "Staten Island's only Gray Panther," was a Greenwich Village network member during 1985. A veteran of World War II and the Korean conflict, and a former Veterans Administration rehabilitation counselor and high school teacher, he traveled once a month by public transportation to network meetings, a six-hour journey. He participated in several Staten Island AARP chapters but sought out the Panthers "to belong to a more liberal, more civically involved organization." An early riser, he kept himself informed on many issues and spent "a lot of time writing letters" to public officials to support a national health service ("That might be called socialized medicine by some. . . . And it's not only [for] old people"), Nuclear Freeze ("Peace is . . . one of our priorities"), and Social Security ("a paramount concern") and to oppose a Staten Island naval missile base.[38]

What are the Gray Panther movement's most important successes? First, the Panthers played a catalytic role in ending mandatory retirement. And as part of "the larger progressive movement"[39] they helped to end the Vietnam War in 1975 and later to oppose recalcitrant White House support for intervention in Central America, maintenance of South African apartheid, and "victory" in Iraq. Elma Griesel's Gray Panther reports on hearing aids and on nursing homes (with Linda Horn) raised public awareness, as did Media Watch critiques of how old people were portrayed on television, and they spurred consumer-oriented regulation.[40] The Panthers helped create the National Citizens Coalition for Nursing Home Reform, which used a task force–like approach in coordinating local long-term care activists, including some Gray Panthers (Eddie Sandifer, Leslie Kwass, Ann Wyatt). They influenced Tish Sommers' launching of the Older Women's League, which adopted a local membership model like the Panthers rather than a direct mail, advocacy organization alternative.[41] Oregon Panther Ron Wyden was elected to Congress, and Panther Carla Woodworth to the Berkeley City Council. Gray Panthers in New York brought kneeling busses to city streets, and Berkeley Panthers helped place the Over 60 Health Center, Redwood Gardens, and the "edible schoolyard" on their city's landscape. The Gray Panthers championed a national health service from the early 1970s and single-payer health coverage from the mid 1980s, neither yet achieved. On Social Security, Medicare, and housing, like others, they played defense.

More broadly, the Gray Panthers offered a vision of old age counter to prevailing stereotype: active, zesty (Maggie's word), connected to others, politically engaged, savoring life, leaving "no stone unturned" in the struggle for social justice. Indeed, the affirmative, expansive visions of old age in Betty Friedan's *The Fountain of Age* (1993), Theodore Roszak's *Longevity Revolution* (2001), or William Thomas's *What Are Old People For?* (2004) are difficult to imagine without Maggie's pronouncements and example two or three decades earlier.[42] And at a time when Maggie pointed to a rising "ghettoization of age" in housing, health care, advertising, and media representations, the Panthers proclaimed and practiced an intergenerationalism that three-quarters of Americans of all ages agreed was preferable.[43] It was epitomized by New York Panther Hope Bagger in a letter to the National Council of Senior Citizens: "We envy your vast union membership and we hope eventually to make inroads upon them. On the other hand, you may be envying us our active, dedicated, *young*

Gray Panthers, who give us reassurance that we are on the right track for succeeding generations . . . and often give us real leadership. No other group of elders . . . is coalescing with the young people who see the need for social action for social change. . . . When youngsters and oldsters combine their idealism and their realism, their new ideas and their old wisdom, the results can be good for the entire society."[44]

Last, the Gray Panthers leave us an ideology and tactics still relevant and usable, hundreds of young Panther alumni now approaching their own elderhood, and a social justice agenda not yet completed.

The Gray Panther Concept of the Person

"Every movement has its ideology—a few basic tenets [that] provide a foundation of conceptual unity [and] a vision or master concept of future states of society." More than ideas on paper or words before an audience, a movement's ideology gives members a "framework by which . . . events may be interpreted, . . . provides rationale for envisioned changes, defines the opposition," and "encourage[s] individual and group persistence . . . for the cause."[45] Underlying various Gray Panther statements and motivating their actions was a vision of every person traversing the life cycle in "equal dignity," with "basic human needs" met and with "collective empowerment of all people, including the dependent."[46] This contrasted with the "traditional liberal view of people as essentially independent, self-interested, and utilitarian" and motivated, as Maggie put it, by "individualism, greed and competition."[47] Hardly celebratory of unfettered capitalism, the Gray Panther concept of the person reflected Maggie and her age peers' formative socialist and humanistic Christian values. And it brought into central focus segments of the population marginalized or excluded as producers and consumers—racialized groups, women, the elderly, the disabled.[48]

Racism, sexism, and ageism in the Panther view were "rampant social pathologies . . . which need to be eradicated." For Maggie, "Racism is the root of contemporary violence, a seed from the imperial aggression that brought Columbus to America 500 years ago, and which destroyed indigenous people and . . . provided the base for a thriving slave trade." In the Panther vision for the world, racism had no place in determining a persons' worth or status. And the diminished life chances justified by sexism were something Maggie and many female Panthers had experienced. "To get along in a man's world, you had to dress like a lady, look like a schoolgirl, think like a man, and work like a horse. . . . Sexism is still widespread with covert sex discrimination in the corporate world. . . . Women are established in jobs once considered 'men's work,' but without equal salaries or opportunities for career advancement."[49]

Persons of color and women were born with physical characteristics that a white and male-dominated society deemed deserving of second-class treatment. Age, however, was different from race or gender in that "old" was a status all persons, if they lived long enough, would achieve. Maggie thought of old age as "a great universalizing force. It's the one thing that we all have in common." Except for "rich old people who do have power," and perhaps even some of them, all old persons would confront the second-class treatment ageism entailed. "We victimize people over 65 until we become victims," Charlotte Flynn asserted. "And it's the one discrimination that no one misses. When you get to that age you will feel it . . . the stereotypes that old people are cranky, senile, toothless, sexless, or they are sweet and loving and baking cookies." The Gray Panthers targeted mandatory retirement at sixty-five as "ageist," but they accepted bodily signals of old age as part of the human condition. Enjoy sex, Maggie prescribed, but embrace gray hair and wrinkles as badges of experience.[50]

For a person to attain and fully experience the final stages of the human life span, he or she requires adequate health care, economic security, housing, an accessible environment, and peaceful, safe surroundings. The Gray Panther conception of health care—"comprehensive, including preventive care, dental and eye care, pre-natal and long-term care"—was embodied in their national health service proposal dating to the movement's early years. Their later, second-best alternative, Canadian-style single-payer, Maggie explained, was still "like socialized medicine." The Panther rationale for both approaches focused more on political and economic objections than the importance of health care for individual persons: "We have a 'socialized' military service; . . . 'socialized' police and fire departments; . . .'socialized' highways, water departments, and sidewalks. Why should we balk at the idea of 'socialized' medicine?," Austin Panther Paula Mixson contended. "The money to provide universal, comprehensive medical care is already circulating in our nation's economy—we're just not spending it wisely."

In terms of individual health outcomes, Maggie's friend Robert Butler predicts improvments in health across the life span if the United States institutes "universal health coverage encompassing all age groups. . . . Babies with low birth weight are at increased risk of developing type-2 diabetes and coronary health disease in adulthood. . . . Programs that prevent, from earliest life, some of the diseases of old age, through comprehensive prenatal, pediatric, and adolescent programs . . . should reduce disease in old age." His recommended "continuum of services" for older persons resembles the "continuum of care" that Berkeley Gray Panthers worked to create and monitor: "health promotion and disease prevention; outpatient diagnosis and treatment of acute [and] chronic . . .

illnesses; . . . [adult] day-care centers . . .; long-term care, end-of-life, and hospice care."[51]

The Gray Panthers doubted that private enterprise and free markets could provide all persons the resources needed for lifelong economic security. They defended Social Security—"one of the most remarkable and well-managed social programs this country has ever seen," Maggie called it—but they also supported their Economy Task Force's *Economic Rights—Economic Democracy* platform. In 1977 Maggie endorsed "nationalization of energy sources, . . . transportation and utilities" as "essential structural changes" for a society "in trouble" and unable to rectify "unequal opportunities." In the Reagan years the Panthers objected to an "increasing concentration of corporate and individual wealth which is resulting in greater poverty and the erosion of large segments of the middle class" and called for "more regulation" and "corporate and government . . . actions to remedy dislocations." In one of her last messages Maggie warned, "Millions of Americans have lost their jobs by corporate mergers, bankruptcies and exportation of jobs to areas where labor is cheap. . . . There is . . . depletion of the ozone layer, large scale pollution of air, water and farmland, destruction of wetlands and forest." Rather than personal responsibility and entrepreneurship, the Panther movement declared in 1995 that worldwide political action was needed to make "governments . . . the agencies of the people for attaining social justice."[52]

As with health care, Gray Panthers believed that people needed "a continuum of housing choices" across the life cycle, and particularly in old age—"from larger homes . . . while raising children, to smaller, more manageable apartments, to congregate living with on-site social services, to accessible adult day health care and day hospitals, to nursing homes. And [these] choices [are needed] within the same neighborhood where people live, have friends and acquaintances, shop, and know their way around." Berkeley Panthers wanted all older persons to "have a choice of intergenerational housing or seniors-only housing," including "persons who cannot live independently but [can] with in-home services or other assistance." Many Panthers participated in struggles to preserve and expand affordable housing for people of all ages and to provide shelter for homeless persons. And many heeded Elma Griesel Holder's call for more public involvement in long-term care. "The ideal situation in any community is where people take the nursing home facilities as seriously as they do the schools. . . . In a community that really cares about everybody that's there, they'd [help make decisions about] long term care [and] want to have control and continual monitoring over what happens."[53]

Older Gray Panthers were candid about their own disabilities. "You have to compensate for things you start to lose as you get older," Charlotte Flynn, then seventy-two, explained. "Your vision changes. Your mobility changes." In her mid-eighties, Maggie reflected, "Those of us who are very old and frail are a reminder to the world of the delicate interdependence of us all. We are more human than ever before because we see so clearly how finite life is. Unfortunately, those of us who are dependent . . . are often deemed a separate species. . . . You are going to be talked right past like a child. . . . The same thing happens to people in wheelchairs." Rather than countenancing marginalization, the Gray Panthers resolved in 1986 that physical disabilities "should be treated as normal aspects of living." The political course a handful of Panthers followed, often with guidance from disability activists, was to press for fully accessible public environments and transportation and for building code standards mandating accessibility, adaptability, and visitability.[54]

"What can we do collectively, cooperatively, for the common good?" Maggie often asked her audiences. In her last years, her commitment to international cooperation and peace was crystallized in heartfelt pleas to "reject all forms of violence, including war," and "slash the military budget; stop Pentagon waste, and eliminate all nuclear weapons and other weapons of mass destruction," objectives her followers understood as critical to "the health and well being of the people of the earth." She also urged Americans "to understand and reach out to those who are different in race and ethnic and religious background. . . . We are part of the human family. We are one human race, [and] that oneness . . . transcends diversity and strife and hatred and war." In 2006 Berkeley Panther Margot Smith posed questions about the relationships between persons of different nations and backgrounds in the twenty-first century. "I hear [people say:] guard our borders against those seeking to sustain their lives, deny people their language, religious and cultural heritages, and profiteer in developing countries [that are] a potential market for arms, pesticides, herbicides, [and] resource for producing cheap goods. . . . Here in the United States we are raising college tuition, creating barriers to high school diplomas, and underfunding and overcrowding schools in poor areas. . . . What are we saying about our country, our values, what are we doing to our planet?"[55]

Age Out of Place

One of Maggie's dictums was, "until rigor mortis sets in . . . do one outrageous thing every week."[56] Many of the tactics Gray Panthers used were not outrageous but were shared with other concerned citizens and activists: letter writing and contacting public officials, circulating petitions, presenting speakers, organizing forums and conferences, issuing position statements and reports, speaking to public audiences, appearing on radio and television talk shows, monitoring government and health care services, testifying at public hearings and before legislative committees, meeting with elected officials and government agency personnel, promoting legislation, establishing model projects, endorsing coalition positions and actions, participating in court suits.

Other Panther tactics were more disruptive of daily routines for participants and onlookers, but hardly "outrageous" in themselves: leafleting on streets and in public buildings, tabling in public locations with flyers and petitions, picketing government offices or health care facilities, demonstrating in vigils, marches, and rallies, and joining mass "crowd lobbying" at elected officials' offices. Actions like these were considered effective if they resulted in media coverage, led to changes in public or service provider policies, affected votes on pending legislation, or marshaled support for candidates who agreed with demonstrator positions. Such public actions, in addition, increased internal solidarity among Gray Panther participants.[57]

But if this was all there was to the Gray Panthers, they would not have registered the "success out of proportion to our numbers" Maggie acknowledged and that motivated members even after her passing. Their dramatic, even "outrageous" tactics included:

Being where older people were not expected to be. Gray Panthers disrupted American Medical Association conventions in the 1970s with street theater and demands to speak. Maggie's guest appearances and provocative statements on the Johnny Carson show reached millions. Her attempt to testify and immediate ejection from a Social Security Commission meeting created news. In 1990 Western Contra Costa County Panther Karl Grossenbacher, eighty, "drove to his local mall, unfolded his ironing board on the walkway in front of McDonald's, and began to distribute literature about a national health system." He was challenging the mall management's requirement of several days' written notice and their selection of where demonstrators should locate. He contended that a California Supreme Court decision permitted him unimpeded access, and after his arrest for "misdemeanor trespassing" a judge agreed and dismissed the case.[58]

Doing what older people were not expected to do. Maggie's spirited retort, "Mr. President, I'm an old woman," to Gerald Ford's sexist query, "Young lady, do you have something to say?," was jarring. Berkeley Gray Panthers' unwelcome picket of a Kaiser Permanente HMO clinic won better treatment for older patients. Washington, D.C.–area Panthers' group cheering was appreciated by gay rights marchers protesting "Don't Ask, Don't Tell." And when Panther Margot Smith joined a Washington demonstration against World Bank and IMF policies, she and three companions "dressed as redwood trees with foam leafy headdresses and a brown foam trunk. Everyone with a camera seemed to click at us."[59]

Including young Gray Panthers in causes affecting the elderly. In Berkeley older and younger Panther teams lobbied for living will and anti–mandatory retirement legislation and participated together at senior citizen rallies in Sacramento. Nursing home advocacy brought young recruits to the New York, Berkeley, and other networks, and young Panthers Elma Griesel and Linda Horn directed the movement's long-term care project. As convener of the Gray Panthers of New York City in my late thirties and early forties, I represented the New York networks in Social Security and housing meetings and presented the Gray Panther case for a national health service before several hundred senior citizens in Queens.

Taking action on issues that affect the young. Older Gray Panthers at demonstrations against the Vietnam War and Central American intervention stood out among mainly young participants. In 1980 older Panthers added generational moral authority to protests against President Carter's draft registration order, and since 2005 New York Gray Panthers have joined Granny Peace Brigade actions against military recruitment of young men and women to fight in Iraq. In 1984 the Metropolitan Washington Gray Panthers organized a coalition of peace groups and churches "to draw attention to the alarming number of war toys." A day after hosting a Christmas party for "over 150 refugee children, mostly Salvadorean and Guatemalan," they "gathered at Panther headquarters and drove to a local Toys R Us store for a spirited picket line to protest war toys. Over one dozen reporters and television crews covered the event [which] was seen on national network television."[60]

Gray Panther Alumni

While President Bush was campaigning for privatization in 2005, Rosalie Schofield, fifty-eight, a professor of social work at Temple University in Philadelphia, organized a Social Security teach-in for students, faculty, and community members, enlisting a local member of Congress as guest speaker. A Gray Panther national office intern and National Steering Committee member in the 1970s, she later worked for the Social Security Administration. In Albuquerque, University of New Mexico law professor Paul Nathanson, sixty-two, a Panther ally at the National Senior Citizen Law Center in the 1970s, published a newspaper op-ed criticizing Bush's intention "to . . . leave it to the private sector to deal with our most vulnerable populations." In 2005 Nathanson served as board chairperson of the National Committee to Preserve Social Security and Medicare, a Washington-based advocacy group representing several million donors. After arriving at UNM in 1980 he taught in its Elderly Law Program, was president of the American Society on Aging, and helped create the American Bar Association Commission on Legal Problems of the Elderly.[61]

Scores if not hundreds of other young Gray Panthers of the 1970s and 1980s pursued careers that built on their experiences with the movement. Three operated in the nation's capitol. Elma Griesel Holder, sixty-seven, was executive director of the National Citizen's Coalition for Nursing Home Reform (NCCNHR) until 1998, when she stepped down after developing cancer but continued her long-term care policy and advocacy work. She helped write the 1987 Nursing Home Reform Act, which endorsed the right of residents "to attain and maintain the highest practicable physical, mental and psychosocial well-being." In 2006 NCCNHR had twelve hundred individual and group members in forty-two states, including citizen advocacy organizations, state and local long-term care ombudsmen, legal services programs, religious organizations, and professional and worker groups.[62] After working for the House and Senate aging committees, Steve McConnell, sixty, headed a campaign on long-term care financing during the 1988 presidential election. In 1989 he moved to the Alzheimer's Association, founded in 1980, where he became vice president for advocacy and public policy and played a leadership role in aging, health, and long-term care issues. Senator Ron Wyden of Oregon, fifty-nine, elected in 1996 after fifteen years in the House of Representatives, focused on health care, technology, and the environment. His positions now often differ from those of the Gray Panthers—he voted for the Medicare Part D prescription drug program and in 2006 unveiled a bipartisan plan to expand access to private health insurance.[63]

Among young Berkeley Gray Panthers of the 1970s and 1980s Carla Woodworth, Tim Orr, Rick Smith, Rick McCracken, and Patricia McGinnis plus several older members created Bay Area Advocates for Nursing Home Reform in 1983 and affiliated with NCCNHR. Renamed "California" Advocates and located in San Francisco, it continues to provide information and legal advice to residents and families statewide and to press for tougher regulation and sanctions against abusive conditions. In 2007 McGinnis, sixty-one, continued to serve as executive director, and board of directors' member McCracken, fifty-five, was treasurer. McCracken also was executive director of Bay Area Outreach and Recreation Program (BORP), begun in Berkeley in 1976 to offer sports, fitness, and recreation programs for adults and children with physical disabilities. Tim Orr, fifty, founded and still coordinates BORP's youth sports program and since 1986 has coached its "Bay Cruisers" wheelchair basketball team.

Other young Berkeley Gray Panthers, like Lani Sanjek and me, left the Bay Area. Maxine Lyons, sixty-four, was a member in the late 1970s while teaching in the gerontology division of Vista Community College. Her classes at senior centers and elderly residences included life review, stress management and relaxation, and yoga and tai chi. After moving to Boston she led discussion groups that she trademarked as "Older and Growing," and in 1986 she began a cable television show featuring exemplars of positive aging, including activists, writers, and retired professors. In 1997 she published *Elder Voices: Insights and Reflections*, a collection of narratives from her classes and interviews, and she still works in the aging field.[64]

New York Gray Panther and national Peace Task Force chair Glen Gersmehl, sixty-two, continued his organizing work on peace issues and earned a master's degree in conflict and international security at Harvard University's Kennedy School of Government. In the later 1980s and 1990s he developed public school curricula and teacher training programs in multicultural and conflict studies, led workshops and consulted for government bodies and public policy groups, and in 1994 became national coordinator of the Lutheran Peace Fellowship located in Seattle. After leaving the Village Nursing Home, social worker Ann Wyatt, sixty-three, became director of care management for Independence Care System, a provider of home care services for people with disabilities. She published articles on long-term care and AIDS and was an adjunct faculty member of the New School University's Milano Graduate School in New York City. She remains a member of NCCNHR. Andy Koski, fifty-two, a VISTA volunteer under Gersmehl who worked with the Central Queens Gray Panthers, pursued an advocacy career in aging, first at Hunter College's Brookdale Center on Aging and later with the New York State Homecare Association, where he is vice-president for public policy.

Middle-aged and older Gray Panthers also moved on to other causes or organizations. Karen Talbot, fifty-five when she left the national office as executive director in 1989, was a co-convener of the San Francisco Gray Panthers in the 1990s and a Communist Party USA national committee member. She was an active speaker and organizer on peace and international issues and published articles on Yugoslavia, Afghanistan, Venezuela, and Iraq between 2001 and her death in 2003.[65] Frances Klafter continued her health care advocacy work in New York, where she moved in the mid-1980s. She joined New York StateWide Senior Action Council and the Joint Public Affairs Committee for Older Adults and played a leading role in a successful campaign to limit doctor overcharges to Medicare patients in New York State.[66] She later moved to Minneapolis near her daughter and granddaughters. In 1998 she testified for the Minnesota Federation of Seniors at a Bipartisan Commission on the Future of Medicare field hearing, and her picture appeared in the St. Paul *Pioneer Press* report of the event. "This Commission should strongly recommend against proposals such as vouchers, medical savings accounts, even mandatory participation in HMOs," she stated. "[Traditional] Medicare . . . is the most efficient health insurance system we have, public or private, keeping administrative costs at a remarkably low level. . . . Eventually . . . a broke health care system can only be fixed by making universal health care a right."[67] In 1999 Klafter organized a party to celebrate her nintieth birthday in Minneapolis, where Lani and I joined many friends and family members from across the country. In 2003 she made a last train trip east and later moved from her senior citizen residence to a nursing home.

A Gray Panther Social Justice Agenda for a New Century

In 1979 Gray Panther hopes for Carter's presidency were crushed by his proposals to cut Social Security benefits and increase the military budget. "What if the present policies and practices continue?" Maggie asked. "There is a danger of establishing a permanent underclass of older Americans—roleless, powerless, living at the edge of poverty, out of the mainstream." She acknowledged that her forecast was "gloomy." In fact, it recalls Mabel Louise Nassau's 1913–14 visit to Blackwells Island, where thousands of impoverished older people lived in cramped and meager "huge dormitories" in the midst of a great city. "There is the further danger," Maggie noted, that "poverty threatens all but the very rich, . . . and over all these dangers and fears hangs the threat of nuclear annihilation." She urged that "we who are old . . . build coalitions, and close ranks between the disadvantaged groups . . . contending for small slivers of power. [We] have the responsibility to transcend our personal needs and [work] for a just and humane society that puts people first."[68]

The rich are vastly richer now than in 1979. Then the top 1 percent of Americans earned 8 percent of all income. Now they earn more than 17 percent, a higher proportion than at any time since the 1920s, and they own 32 percent of all national wealth. By 2030 the number of Americans over sixty-five is expected to double, rising from thirty-five million to seventy million, or from 12 percent of the population to 20 percent. "If America's economy expands robustly in the decades ahead" as, in aggregate, it has since 1979, then "sufficient resources will be available to make the transition to a larger retired population relatively painless."[69]

As the rich become richer, however, an increasing portion of the national bounty is being devoted to luxury. In 2006 one of the nation's richest men, the CEO of the Blackstone Group, a private equity investment firm, earned $400 million. In 2007 he spent $3 million on his sixtieth birthday party. At the same time, Robert Butler despairs, "the two shames of American society are the roughly equivalent poverty rates of 20 percent for both children and older women." The poverty threshold in 2006 was an annual income of $9,699 for a single person age sixty-five or older, and $24,444 for a household of two parents and two children.[70] Whether sufficient resources are available for the economic, health, housing, and accessibility needs of Americans as they age or whether they continue to flow to luxuries for the rich is a political, not an economic, question. Neither new Blackwells Island–type residences nor more extravagant Blackstone Group executive parties need represent an inevitable future.

Since 1979 the economic situation of the old has become increasingly imperiled. Social Security taxes have been raised and benefits reduced, and the entire idea of social insurance attacked repeatedly by Republican presidents indifferent or hostile to government programs. Their watchwords have been "privatization" and "individual responsibility," the very opposite of the social vision and cooperative engagement Maggie and Gray Panther activists embraced. One in five older Americans depends upon Social Security for all his or her income; for two-thirds it supplies half or more of annual resources. Privatization would substantially diminish the value of lifelong Social Security benefits.

The other two legs of today's retirement stool are shaky or missing. Between 1940 and the early 1980s the share of workers covered by private pensions grew from 7 to 40 percent. The figure has since plummeted to 20 percent and will continue to fall, as underfunded and ineptly run plans have failed, corporate managers and buyout specialists have discarded pension obligations in bankruptcy reorganizations, and employers have shifted from "trademark . . . American dream" pensions with lifelong, guaranteed "defined benefits," to limited, "defined contribution" cash retirement accounts that workers may add to and invest on their own. These diminishing worker assets, with savings, amount to less than $13,000 for the average, middle-aged, middle-income worker. Only 27 percent of workers have 401(k) investment accounts, which many withdraw from prior to retirement. Only 6 percent have tax-favored individual retirement accounts (IRAs).[71] To offset the decline in pension coverage the labor union-backed Economic Policy Institute has advocated increasing Social Security benefits, which currently replace on average 43 percent of preretirement income, and phasing out recent tax cuts, which contribute little to most Americans' retirement assets.[72]

The outlook for health care is also troubled. The United States "leads the world in Nobel Prizes for medicine" and offers "world-class high-tech surgery and some space-age medical procedures. But these benefit 2 or 3 percent of the population at most."[73] Life expectancy for American women, eighty years, ranks thirty-second among nations, and male life expectancy, seventy-five years, ranks thirty-third. (The highest figures are eighty-six for women in Japan, and eighty for men in San Marino, a tiny country within Italy; every Western European country, plus Chile, Costa Rica, and Singapore, does better than the United States.) Sixty percent of Americans over sixty-five do not receive preventive health services; only 10 percent are screened for colorectal and prostate cancer; three-quarters are overweight, risking heart disease and diabetes, and one third are obese. Geriatric medicine, which can improve the health and quality of life of the chronically ill and very old, is taught at just one quarter of U.S. medical schools, and the number of certified geriatricians is falling, not increasing. (Plastic surgery, in contrast, is booming.)[74]

The average amount spent on health care for each American rose from $1,000 in 1980 to more than $6,000 in 2006. We now devote 16 percent of gross domestic product to health care, compared to France's 10.5 percent, Canada's 9 percent, and Japan's 8 percent, each with longer life expectancy and lower infant mortality than the United States. Moreover, while other industrial nations cover everyone, forty-seven million Americans have no health insurance, and seventy million lack coverage at some point during each year. Eighteen thousand unnecessary deaths occur annually among the uninsured, as well as numerous bankruptcies to meet medical bills. Workplace-based private health insurance, which covered 80 percent of American families in the early 1980s, now covers 60 percent and continues its decline. Health insurance costs rise faster than wages or inflation, and already exceed a minimum wage worker's total annual earnings.[75]

Advocates of universal health care, whether a national health service or single-payer, stress the savings from eliminating the profits and paperwork of private insurance.[76] Already the U.S. government pays half of all health care expenses through Medicare, Medicaid, military and children's health programs, and health insurance for federal employees. Adding the costs of tax-deductible private health insurance premiums and mandated hospital "charity" care for the poor, plus state and local government worker plans, two-thirds of the system is "socialized," although inefficiently and haphazardly in terms of managing purchasing costs, patient records, and information about treatments and outcomes. The one-third of the system run by private insurers is even less efficient or coordinated. However, even with maximum efficiency we might choose to expend greater resources on the well-being of our populace. An older population uses more health care: annual costs are $8,000 per Medicare beneficiary age sixty-five to seventy-four, and $18,000 for those over eighty-five. Yet society's aging accounts for less than a third of our growing health care costs—new, more expensive procedures and treatments used by people of all ages are the chief contributing factor. The share of gross domestic product devoted to health care, some economists calculate, could comfortably continue to grow, and even double, as U.S. incomes continue to rise and the share devoted to other consumer essentials falls.[77] Whether greater health care expenditures are "unsustainable" or, in fact, desirable is a matter for vigorous public debate.

In the early 1980s one-quarter of older Americans had one or more physical or cognitive disabilities requiring assistance with daily life activities. The proportion today is one-fifth, but with a larger elderly population the actual number is greater. Since that time, federal housing programs designed for the elderly and disabled have been cut. From the Gray Panther perspective, new housing should be age-integrated or offer that option and should be accessible and visitable. A more ambitious goal would be "universal design," a term coined in 1989, that moves beyond fighting for specific entryway, kitchen, and bathroom building code requirements, or set-aside numbers of accessible units, to one standard creating "environments usable by as many people as possible, including people with no disabilities at all."[78]

In the 1970s Gray Panther and NCCNHR advocacy spotlighted abuses in nursing homes and helped bring about improvements. In 2007, however, the federal Government Accountability Office reported that "little seems to have changed at the worst-performing homes. The Bush administration rarely uses its authority to deny payment to homes with a history of compliance problems and typically imposes fines far less than the maximum of $10,000 a day." The industry remains dominated by for-profit nursing home chains that wield their power in state capitals to limit inspections and citations.[79] Nursing home costs average $200 per day, ranging from half to more than twice that amount in different states and cities. One million six hundred thousand older persons live in the nation's sixteen thousand nursing homes, almost half of them over age eighty-five. Another million who require daily personal care reside in assisted living residences. While nursing homes house only 5 percent of older Americans, three times that many with similar disabilities reside in their own or a relative's home and receive care from family members or a home care aide. Overall, a third of persons who reach age sixty-five eventually will spend time in a nursing home.

Total government outlays for long-term care are predicted to double or triple by 2050. This is due in part to the elderly population boom but also reflects projected staff growth in view of fewer adult-child caregivers in America's more "lineal" families. Community-based care by paid workers will likely become more common to conform with the 1999 Supreme Court *Olmstead* decision stipulating that state-funded services to persons with disabilities be provided in "the least restricted environment." Long-term care aides are poorly paid, perform difficult tasks, and have no career ladder. Increasingly they are immigrants, and preventing future labor shortages will require changes in current immigration policy that makes it difficult for potential long-term care workers to obtain U.S. visas.[80]

The military budget increases, mass impoverishment, and threats of nuclear destruction that Maggie warned against remain pressing concerns. Billions have been spent on enormous Pentagon and intelligence establishments, with consequences at home and abroad that Gray Panthers have feared and protested for almost four decades.[81] The United States has less than 5 percent of the world's population but controls a third of global wealth, and the North-South gap, except for upper sectors in China and India, is widening. The bottom 50 percent of the world's population, whose average net worth is less than one-sixtieth that of the average American, possess just 1 percent of global wealth. The abolition of nuclear weapons envisioned by Ronald Reagan and Mikhail Gorbachev in 1985 is stalled. Their breakthrough agreements on missile reduction were not followed with additional steps, and in 2007 Gorbachev lamented, "The ABM Treaty has been abrogated; . . . the treaty on comprehensive cessation of nuclear-weapons tests has not been ratified by all nuclear powers. The military doctrines of major powers, first the U.S. and then . . . Russia, have re-emphasized nuclear weapons as an acceptable means of war fighting, to be used in a first or even a 'preemptive' strike. All this is a blatant violation of the nuclear powers' commitments under the Non-Proliferation Treaty."[82]

"You Can Make a Difference!"

In 2006 Sacramento convener Joan Lee replaced the "Age and Youth in Action" motto on her network's lapel pin with "Raising Our Voices Together," which sounded more appropriate to members and retained the same cadence. The Berkeley Gray Panthers, although also lacking young members, did not go this far. Their T-shirt featured both the original motto and, just above it, their new one: "You Can Make a Difference!" The sentiments in both new mottos are fitting, consistent with Gray Panther activism. But new mottos do not substitute for new blood. At a 2007 Gray Panther Board meeting Michael Texeira warned, "We need to do something dramatic and drastic, because we're not touching base with the people we were historically."

Will the Gray Panthers find new members and grow?

Wrong question.

"Organizations come and go, but the struggle continues," longtime activist Tish Sommers affirmed in 1983.[83] The Gray Panthers' future, like its origins, will be tied to "the larger progressive movement" in the United States. Any one activist group is linked to others within a larger, wider field of interconnected political groups—as the Gray Panthers of the 1970s, 1980s, and 1990s were linked to groups within the peace, progressive health care, senior citizen, women's, housing, nursing home reform, and disability rights movements.[84] Organizations thrive "at moments when large numbers . . . are roused to indignation and defiance and thus when a great deal seems possible. Organizers do not create such moments . . . but they are excited by them" and by the "political energy among the masses, which itself breaths life into the belief that large organizations can be developed and sustained." As goes the liberal, progressive, left spectrum within American political life, so will go the Gray Panthers.[85]

Still, individual organizations as base-camps for activism are important. They provide infrastructures of communications, offices, and meetings and facilitate refinement of ideology and tactics. As face-to-face settings, they "create opportunities for self-definition, for the development of public and leadership skills, for a new confidence of the possibilities of participation, and for the wider mappings of the connections between the movement members and other groups and institutions. . . . [They] create a consciousness that many people can act together."[86] Political activism in the twenty-first century, however, depends on screen-to-screen communication as well as face-to-face interaction. Anti–Iraq war activities, including those of the Granny Peace Brigade, have relied upon e-mail and the Internet to muster supporters. The Panthers have made the transition to these technologies and in 2007 unveiled a new national website. But new communication media are also utilized by the direct-mail, D.C.-based advocacy organizations with which the Gray Panthers and other grassroots groups compete for support and attention. Moreover, both types of group may move in the other's direction, the top-down organizations by cultivating local chapters and activities, groups like the Panthers by becoming more media-savvy and thus attracting additional supporters.[87]

The two potential generations to replace the 1930s and 1960s Gray Panther activists are the baby boomers and Generation Y. The seventy-eight million boomers born between 1946 and 1964 are beginning to enter their sixties. Many have higher incomes than their parents, and half can expect secure retirements. A quarter of boomers, however, have little or no savings, and another quarter could fall into insecurity with a health crisis or economic downturn. Many, in Robert Butler's opinion, are not "a bit prepared for old age. They are often fat, unhealthy, and there aren't enough nursing homes and elder care facilities to accommodate them." Unlike mandatory retirement for the 1930s generation, there is no shared "rite of passage" to old age for the baby boomers. Retirement now arrives at varying ages, sometimes early, sometimes not at all (whether through choice or economic necessity), and is highly personalized.[88] An experience that many boomers do share is the care of aged parents, who live longer and have more contact with government programs and agencies than did parents of earlier generations.[89] Frustration and anger over the inadequacies of health care benefits, long-term care, and Social Security might have a radicalizing impact and present opportunities for turning adult children into activists.

Potentially the boomers could have a major impact on American activism and politics.[90] Overall, the baby boom generation will swell the proportion of the U.S. electorate over sixty-five from 17 percent in 2000 to 24 percent in 2025, and to 41 percent in 2040. Although they have been "politically diverse—even apolitical," one observer contends, "with retirement approaching . . . they are likely to converge again around a common issue—a secure retirement—that will even exceed the one they had back in the [19]60s of opposing the draft and the war." This applies mainly to "early boomers." The "later boomers" who entered their twenties in the Carter and Reagan years do not share these political memories. It is the early group, devotees of Bob Dylan, Motown, and the Rolling Stones, who are more likely to become Gray Panthers.[91]

Generation Y, the seventy million "millennials" who began entering their twenties at the turn of the new century, are the most socially tolerant cohort in American history. Only two-thirds are white, most have friends of other races, and few object to same-sex marriage. Most have working mothers, and they remain close to their parents as they attend college in record numbers and embark on careers where they expect to work hard, be recognized for their accomplishments, and begin repaying college loans and then saving for retirement.[92] They take computers, the Internet, and cell phones for granted. And in their world homelessness and AIDS, new public phenomena in the 1980s, are givens. They have witnessed scandals involving politicians, business figures, and athletes. They saw Republicans impeach a Democratic president in 1998, and the Supreme Court decide the 2000 presidential election. Their lives have been shaped by the Iraq war and its domestic and global impact, although they were not subject to a military draft. How they will become politically active, and to what degree, is not clear.

In 2008 boomers were represented among Gray Panther activists in New York, Detroit, the Twin Cities, Austin, and on the Board. Generation Y has barely appeared. Whether this younger cohort will relate to a Gray Panther social justice agenda focused on intergenerational economic security, universal health care, accessible environments, late-life care, militarism, global poverty, and nuclear threat remains to be seen. Perhaps they will appreciate the experience and wisdom of elders who became politically active in the 1960s and 1970s, as we young Gray Panthers appreciated our mentors and colleagues shaped by the 1930s.

Whether or not the Gray Panthers survive or flourish, the world of the twenty-first century will require something like them. Future political activists, old or young, will not need to reinvent the Gray Panthers' view of the human life cycle, their concept of the person, their array of tactics, or their intergenerationalism. What they will need is a readiness, as Maggie urged, to "get out there and do something about injustice."

Notes

Preface

1. Estes 1979:6–12, 228–29.
2. Piven and Cloward 1979:6. The anthropologist Maurice Bloch (1977) posited that human societies contain both (1) an ideological "cognitive model," encapsulated in ritual, ceremony, and leaderly pronouncement, which enshrines "a system of classification of human beings" that "*institutionalize[s]* hierarchy," and (2) a pragmatic model concerned with production and "flesh and bone" practical concerns. From the first perspective it would be culturally appropriate for the retired and economically unproductive elderly to disengage.
3. Piven and Cloward 1979:7. Viewing contemporary capitalism "as a cultural system," the anthropologist Marshall Sahlins (1976:205–21) proposed that hierarchical "symbolic valuations" may be transformed by either "changes in the structure of production"—the Marxist perspective—or by "superstructural" forces, such as "a new radical movement." See Sahlins 2000:277–351 for his perspective on individual agency.
4. Brecher 1972:144–216; Evans and Boyte 1992:69–94; Fleischer and Zames 2001:49–56; Lofland 1985:265–69, 299–314; Morris 1984:188–215; Shields 1981:49–56.
5. See Sanjek 1977, 1987.
6. Clark 1973; Clark and Anderson 1967. For overviews of the anthropology of aging, see Keith 1982; Cohen 1994; and Shield and Aronson 2003, all of which invoke Maggie Kuhn and the Gray Panthers.
7. Sanjek 1998.
8. Kuhn, Long, and Quinn 1991.
9. This talk, to the City University of New York Anthropology Colloquium in May 1978, was later given before other audiences and published as Sanjek 1987.
10. As the anthropologist Simon Ottenberg explains, written notes are complemented by "the memories of my field research. I call them my headnotes. . . . The published record [thus] is a construction of reality out of my two sets of notes" (1990:144–45).
11. Scratch notes, Ottenberg writes, are "taken in longhand with a pen[:] brief sentences, phrases, words, sometimes quotes—a shorthand that I enlarged upon in typing them up, adding what I remembered" (1990:148).
12. Jacobs 1980; Kuhn 1994.
13. The ethnohistorian William Fenton (1962) uses "upstreaming" to refer to interpretations of earlier written records by persons with direct ethnographic knowledge of a particular community or people; see Sanjek 1998:9–10. A splendid example is Fenton 1987.

14. Sanjek 1990.

15. I agree that anthropological writing "formulates knowledge that is rooted in an author's autobiography" (Fabian 1983:87–88) and that whatever "ethnographic truths" this book contains "are thus inherently *partial*—committed and incomplete" (Clifford 1986:7). But I also agree that "if we insert the ethnographer's self as positioned subject into the text, we are obliged to confront the moral and political responsibility of our action" (Okely 1992:24) and that "the responsibility for ethnography, or the credit, can be placed at no other door" than that of its author (Geertz 1988:140). These thoughts have continuously occupied me in writing this book.

Chapter 1

1. Nassau 1980 [1915]:83–85.

2. This chapter draws on historical treatments of old age in the United States: Achenbaum 1978, 1983; Fischer 1978; Graebner 1980; Haber 1983; Myles 1989; Pratt 1976; Quadagno 1988; Van Tassel and Stearns 1986.

3. Harrington 1962:111–30.

4. See Ball 1988; Leuchtenburg 1963:103–6, 130–33.

5. Estes 1979:1–2. Compare Myles 1989:1–2, 6–7, 122, and more broadly Miliband 1989:4–5, 7, 22–23, 40, 45, 95–98, 110–11; Posner 1990:10–11, 15. Dahrendorf notes: "Retirement has become a *troisieme age*, a third life which for many lasts twenty years and more, and which has generated proper structures, including 'grey panthers' [*sic*] to represent them in the political area" (1988:144).

6. In 1929, as in 1910, only 10 percent of workers were unionized. The winter of 1932–33 saw worker strikes and demonstrations by the unemployed, and speculation on "whether the country faced imminent revolution." The 1933 National Industrial Recovery Act strengthened labor's hand, and more strikes followed in 1934. In 1935 the Wagner National Labor Relations Act "threw the weight of government behind the right of labor to bargain collectively, and compelled employers to accede peacefully to the unionization of their plants." The American Federation of Labor (AFL) then launched a Committee for Industrial Organization to unionize mass production workers, which spurred automobile, steel, and other factory worker strikes and sit-downs in 1936–37; in 1938 it became the independent Congress of Industrial Organizations (CIO). The Fair Labor Standards Act of 1938, championed by Florida Senator Claude Pepper, led to pay increases and improved workplace conditions (Leuchtenburg 1963:24–28, 106–14, 150–51, 239–43, 262–63; 1995:130–34, 250–53). By 1945 the AFL had seven million members and the CIO six million, together representing one third of blue-collar workers. See also Piven and Cloward 1979:41–180.

7. Roosevelt used the phrase "senior citizens" in a 1941 letter to Lyndon B. Johnson (Leuchtenburg 1993:129).

8. There exist a few brief discussions of the Gray Panthers (Butler 1975:340–41; Dychtwald and Flower 1990:105–6; Friedan 1993:632–35; Graebner 1980:249–50, 252; Huckle 1991:186–89; Keith 1982:104–5; Pratt 1976:52; Roszak 2001:36), and two narrowly focused articles by social scientists (Jacobs 1980; Sanjek 1987). Aside from the movement's own publications and numerous newspaper and magazine stories, there are also published writings by founder Maggie Kuhn (1976, 1977–78, 1994; Kuhn, Long, and Quinn 1991; Hessel 1977).

9. See Evans and Boyte 1992; Garner 1977; Polletta 2002. This tradition is also

"successive" (Nicholas 1973:70): "earlier movements . . . become paradigms for later ones."

10. See Huckle's biography (1991) of Tish Sommers, a Communist Party member from 1936 to the mid-1950s who during the 1970s joined the National Organization for Women and the Gray Panthers National Steering Committee (NSC). In 1980 she founded the Older Women's League. In Maggie Kuhn's foreword to this book she acknowledged that other NSC members "had been on the same long political journeys through the ranks of socialism and communism in search of justice and peace in a profit-centered, acquisitive society." See also Andrews's portraits and analysis of fifteen lifelong British political activists of middle- and working-class origins, ranging from Christian socialists to Communists. Interviewed in their seventies and eighties, they believed "through collective action, individuals can contribute to social and political outcomes"; their "political commitment has become the cornerstone of their lives"; and they "identify themselves strongly as members of a group . . . with like-minded others" (Andrews 1991:32, 141, 155).

11. "Panther Profile: Doris V. Mendes," *Network*, August 1976. On the Chicago CIO strikes and sit-downs, see Brecher 1972:208. On Alinsky, also active in Chicago CIO campaigns, see Alinksy 1969; Evans and Boyte 1986:139–40; Polletta 2002:176–81. On the range of "women's liberation" and "women's rights" feminist groups in the 1960s and early 1970s, see Cassell 1989; Polletta 2002:149–75.

12. Chuck Preston, "Panther Profile: Frances Klafter, 'She Couldn't Say No,' " *Network*, May-June 1980. On the Federal Emergency Relief Administration, see Leuchtenburg 1963:120–24. On the CIO and Communist Party in the 1930s, see Bell 1967:141–53; Garner 1977:173–81; Piven and Cloward 1979:161–66. On Spanish civil war activism, see Andrews 1991:108–11; Leutchenburg 1963:222–24. On Senator Joseph McCarthy and his impact, see Goldman 1960:134–45, 212–24, 233, 250–60, 270–79, 289; Jezer 1982:88–91, 98–106.

13. Chuck Preston, "Panther Profile: Angie Aker, Four Strikes and Still Running," *Network*, January-February 1981; Eri Fouts, "Panther Sired by Jack Rabbit," *Network*, August 1976. On Mississippi and the political economy of cotton in the 1930s, see Davis, Gardner, and Gardner 1941; Quadagno 1988:125–51.

14. Chuck Preston, "Panther Profile: The Nine Lives of Tom Moore," *Network*, May-June 1981; Lillian Rabinowitz, "Thomas Garland Moore: October 1912–July 1990," Gray Panthers of Berkeley newsletter, October 1990. On Wallace, Truman, and the 1948 election, see Carroll 2006:111–18, 133; Goldman 1960:38–40, 81–90; Jezer 1982:20–24, 41–42, 79–80, 85–88; Leuchtenburg 1993:14–18, 26–33. On the House Un-American Activities Committee, see Carroll 2006:139–40; Jezer 1982:81–84, 91–98, 284, 308–9; Leuchtenburg 1963:280–82. On local efforts by progressive whites outside the South to combat racial segregation, see Huckle 1991:152–63; Jezer 1982:297; Morris 1984:128–30, 157–58.

15. "Panther Profile—Billie Heller," *Network*, Fall 1978; Jacobs 1980:94.

16. "Panther Profile: Eddie Sandifer, Rebel with a Cause," *Network*, March-April 1979.

17. Chuck Preston, "Panther Profile: Leslie Kwass, Old Hand at Reform," *Network*, January-February 1980. On Students for a Democratic Society and 1960s campus, "underground," and anti–Vietnam War activism, see Carroll 2006:311–14; Miller 1987; Polletta 2002:120–48.

18. "Oregon Panthers Busy as Beavers," *Network*, August 1976; "Panther Profile—Ron Wyden," *Network*, December 1977; "Plot Thickens in Oregon," *Network*, Spring 1978; Chuck Preston, "Panther Profile: Age-Youth Team Takes

Oregon by Storm," *Network*, November-December 1981. On the Tonkin Gulf Resolution, see Weiner 2007:239–43.

Chapter 2

1. Eleanor Blau, "Gray Panthers Out to Liberate Aged," *New York Times*, May 21, 1972.

2. Maggie Kuhn, audiotaped interview by Lois Boyd, May 23, 1978, unpaginated typed transcript, 36 pages (hereafter Boyd interview); Cobey Black, "The Best Is Yet to Be," *Honolulu Advertiser*, February 22, 1978 (hereafter Black interview).

3. Boyd interview. Also see Kuhn, Long, and Quinn 1991:5, 17–20.

4. Boyd interview; Black interview; "Kuhn, Maggie," *Current Biography*, July 1978, 13–16.

5. Boyd interview; for more on her college years, see Kuhn, Long, and Quinn 1991:33–48.

6. Boyd interview; Pamela Booth, "'We Can Still Yell!' An Interview with Maggie Kuhn of the Gray Panthers," *HealthRight* 1(3):1, 4, 1975 (Booth interview). On Maggie's YWCA years, see Kuhn, Long, and Quinn 1991:48–51, 54–65.

7. Kuhn, Long, and Quinn 1991:51. This no doubt was the Young People's Socialist League, a division of the Socialist Party whose 1924 presidential candidate, Robert La Follette, also the Progressive Party's designee, was nominated in and carried Cleveland, where Maggie, then nineteen, resided. See Bell 1967:104, 120–22; Leuchtenburg 1958:128–39. The league "began a renewed challenge with the onset of the stock market crash and the depression. It attempted to mobilize young workers and students toward the achievement of socialist political and economic goals" (Gamson 1975:152).

8. Boyd interview.

9. Ibid. See also Kuhn, Long, and Quinn 1991:74–91.

10. On Sam's life and illness, see Kuhn, Long, and Quinn 1991:22–23, 52–53, 67–71, 90, 119–25, 162–66.

11. For a fuller account, see Kuhn, Long, and Quinn 1991:97–117, 124–29.

12. Boyd interview.

13. Ibid.

14. Ibid.; see also Kuhn, Long, and Quinn 1991:110–12.

15. Margaret E. Kuhn, "Sex and the Single Woman," Resource Paper #2, "Sexuality and the Human Community," typescript, n.d.

16. Boyd interview. See also TeSelle 2003:1–4.

17. Boyd interview.

18. Ibid.

19. Kuhn 1972:123–25.

20. Judy Klemesrud, "Gray Panther Founder and a Family of Choice," *New York Times*, June 22, 1981.

21. Boyd interview.

22. Born in 1898, Hall pastored a Presbyterian congregation in New York City's Hell's Kitchen neighborhood in the later 1920s and during the Depression. There he hired Italian, Greek, and Armenian staff to serve his diverse congregation and began a youth program and a birth control clinic. In the mid-1930s he joined the National Council of Churches and directed its economic justice program until he retired in 1968. See "Panther Profile: Cameron Hall, Man of the World," *Network*, May-June 1979; Maggie Kuhn, "Remembering Cameron Hall," *Network*, Summer 1987.

23. Boyd interview.

24. Ibid. See also TeSelle 2003:2

25. Boyd interview.

26. "Gray Panther History," mimeographed, n.d. [ca. March 1972].

27. Margaret E. Kuhn, "A Proposal to the Board of Pensions Concerning the Church's Ministries with Older Persons[;] A Program to Utilize the Experience, Wisdom, and Skills of Retired Persons in Community Service and in Extended Ministries to Other Older Persons," typescript, March 25, 1970. Hereafter "Proposal."

28. Margaret Kuhn to Dr. Ron White, March 26, 1970.

29. Margaret E. Kuhn to Helen H. Smith, April 3, 1970.

30. Margaret Kuhn to Participants in Consultation on Church and Retirees, April 13, 1970.

31. Booth interview.

32. Magaret Kuhn to Dear Friends, April 22, 1970.

33. Telephone conversation, July 4, 1984. Cameron Hall also told me that Elma Greenwood "was only involved briefly. She thought it was too much centered on Maggie. Helen Baker felt the same way."

34. Margaret E. Kuhn, proposal, typescript, May 4, 1970.

35. Margaret E. Kuhn, "Summary of Discussion on May 4, 1970, Consultation of Older Persons," mimeographed. While these minutes report "fourteen persons attended," curiously Kuhn, Long, and Quinn (1991:131) state, "The meeting was a smashing success. About one hundred people came."

36. Jaeger and Simmons 1970.

37. "A Program Proposal to Utilize the Experience, Wisdom, and Skills of Retired Persons for Action on Public Issues," mimeographed, June 10, 1970.

38. Telephone interview with Reuben Gums, June 1, 1982.

39. Margaret Kuhn, "Report of Older Adults Consultation," mimeographed, November 11, 1970.

40. Ibid.

41. Maggie Kuhn, "Why Men Ought to Know about the Women's Liberation Movement," handwritten notes, November 17, 1970.

42. Margaret E. Kuhn to the Honorable William Scranton, December 17, 1970.

43. "Gray Panther History," mimeographed, [ca. March 1972].

44. "Notes on Meeting of Older Adults," March 9, 1971.

45. Margaret E. Kuhn, "New Life for the Elderly," reprinted from *Enquiry*, September-November, 1971, mimeographed, 1974.

46. Kuhn 1972.

47. Shubert Frye and Maggie Kuhn, G. R. report, February 14, 1972.

48. Hobart Jackson, "Black and Gray," *Network*, November-December 1976.

49. Margaret E. Kuhn, "Report on the Consultation of Older Persons," mimeographed, December 9, 1971.

50. On the 1971 Black House and WHCoA events and on Arthur Flemming, see Pratt 1976:129–53, 158–59. See also Jackson 1976.

51. "We Are the Gray Panthers," mimeographed, n.d.

52. Minutes, Gray Panthers Consultation, February 21, 1972.

53. Shubert Frye to Maggie Kuhn, February 29, 1972.

54. Shubert Frye to Maggie Kuhn, April 24, 1972.

Chapter 3

1. G. Shubert Frye, "Report of the Steering Committee," typescript, October 10, 1975.

2. "Gray Panther Resolutions Adopted by the National Convention," October 1975, mimeographed.

3. Frye, "Report of the Steering Committee."

4. *Network*, December 1975.

5. Maggie Kuhn to Gray Panthers National Steering Committee, November 3, 1975. On July 4, 1984, Cameron Hall, who chaired the convention resolutions committee, told me in a telephone conversation, "When we left there was far more substance to the Gray Panthers as a result. No one got around as much as Maggie. I had no idea there was something that went beyond the small steering committee group. It was really the doing of Maggie Kuhn. When we went home we had a sense of the living reality of the Gray Panthers that spread from New York to California."

6. Stanley Earley, "The History and Development of the Gray Panthers," typescript, April 1973.

7. Leslie Sussan, minutes of meeting of June 20, 1972, typescript.

8. Ms. Margaret Kuhn and Ms. Janet Neuman, "Statement for National Democratic Platform Committee from Consultation of Older Adults—Gray Panthers," typescript, n.d.

9. Stanley Earley, "Gray Panthers," mimeographed, ca. August 1973.

10. "ABC Television Network Directions Presents 'The Gray Panthers,' " transcript, November 12, 1972.

11. Nader 1965.

12. Townsend 1971.

13. Maggie Kuhn and Leslie Sussan, "The Network," n.d., handlettered and typescript.

14. Chuck Preston, "Panther Profile: Elma Griesel," *Network*, July-August 1981.

15. Griesel 1973.

16. Ibid.

17. Margaret E. Kuhn to Ralph Nader, May 4, 1973.

18. Margaret E. Kuhn to Ralph Nader, January 14, 1976.

19. Ehrenreich and Ehrenreich 1970. A second collection of Health/PAC writings followed; see Kotelchuck 1976.

20. Harding, Bodenheimer, and Cummings 1972:117–22.

21. Gray Panther Health Committee, "Toward a National Health Service," flyer, 1973.

22. Curtin 1972.

23. Gray Panthers Statement on Health Care before Senate Sub-Committee on Health, July 12, 1973.

24. Margaret E. Kuhn to Malcolm Todd, M.D., January 11, 1974.

25. "Gray Panthers Special Report," July 1974.

26. Griesel and Horn 1975:69.

27. Ibid., 1.

28. "Gray Panther National Steering Committee Meeting," typescript, May 29, 1973.

29. *Network Organizing Manual 1973–4*, mimeographed, December 1973.

30. "Report of the Budget and Finance Committee to the Steering Committee of the Gray Panthers," typescript, November 21, 1974.

31. *Network*, October 1975.

32. Leslie Sussan, minutes of the Gray Panthers Steering Committee, July 10, 1973.

33. "Goals of the Gray Panthers," March 9, 1974.

34. Elma Griesel to Steering Committee, "Proposal for agenda consideration for 1974–75," typescript, n.d.

35. Robert McClellan, National Steering Committee of the Gray Panthers minutes, May 23, 1975.

36. Roderic Frohman, "The Gray Panther's National Steering Committee," February 22, 1973.

37. *Network*, August 1973.

38. Anne Sterrett and Maggie Kuhn, minutes National Steering Committee, January 31 to February 2, 1974.

39. Peg Diefenderfer, minutes Gray Panther National Steering Committee Meeting, June 8, 1974.

40. Peg Diefenderfer, "Working Paper, National Steering Committee," November 22–23, 1974.

41. Susan Schacher, "An Analysis of the Gray Panthers in Operation," typescript, May 1973.

42. Christina Long, "Memories of a Mentor," *Network*, March-April 1982.

43. This piece reveals no familiarity with Maggie's 1972 typescript history. A 1974 version "by Stanley Earley and Maggie Kuhn" was a revision of Earley's work, and later editions listed no author.

44. Kuhn 1976, 1977–78, "Grass-roots Gray Power," *Prime Time*, June 1974.

45. Hessel 1977.

46. Kuhn, "Grass-roots Gray Power."

47. Maggie Kuhn, "Death and Dying—The Right to Live—The Right to Die," typescript, June 11, 1974.

48. Maggie Kuhn, "The Radicals of the Seventies," typescript, July 24, 1974.

49. Maggie Kuhn, "Power and Advocacy for the Elderly from Nader to Kuhn," typescript, July 27, 1974. Kuhn 1976 is an edited version of this talk.

50. "The Gray Panther Media Watch and How It Works," mimeographed, n.d.

51. Rita Ciolli, "Gray Panthers Switched Off by TV Image," *Newsday*, January 22, 1976.

52. Margaret Kuhn to President Gerald Ford, August 23, 1974.

53. *Assignment America*, transcript of *Maggie Kuhn: Wrinkled Radical*, Educational Broadcasting Corporation, 1975.

54. Margaret E. Kuhn to John Gardner, September 9, 1974.

55. "Panthers Take Part in White House Summit," *Network*, January 1975.

56. *Network*, July 1975.

Chapter 4

1. Joan McKiney, "Gray Panthers: A New Alliance," *Oakland Tribune*, November 2, 1975.

2. Charles Burress, "Rabinowitz Is Modest, But Still Determined," *Daily Cal* Summer Magazine, July 31, 1981.

3. Sanjek interview, March 1982.

4. Lillian Rabinowitz to Margaret Kuhn, June 12, 1973.

5. Chris Delsol, "Grey Panthers Fight Age Old Myths," *Berkeley News*, April 1975.

6. Sanjek interview with Maggie Kuhn, 1982.

7. Tish Sommers to Maggie [Kuhn], August 3, 1973.

8. Lillian Rabinowitz to Maggie [Kuhn], September 17, 1973.

9. Lillian Rabinowitz to Maggie [Kuhn], December 6, 1973.

10. Sanjek interview, September 11, 1985.

11. Huckle 1991; Shields 1981.

12. Local Area Agencies on Aging were created in the 1973 amendments to the Older Americans Act; see Estes 1979:21–22, 35–36, 38–42, 72–75.

13. [Lillian Rabinowitz], "History of the Geriatric Health Services Program," mimeographed, n.d.

14. Social Planning Department, *Berkeley Census Information*, [City of Berkeley], July 1973.

15. Johanna Cooper, "Inspiring Local Clinic Serves Elderly," *Health Sciences Journal* 5, no. 7, University of California, Berkeley, April 1977.

16. The clinic staff saw more than one hundred older clients during a sample week in January 1977. Those with appointments arrived on Monday afternoon (following the weekly morning staff meeting), Wednesday, and Friday. Tuesday was outclinic day at a senior citizen housing site in downtown Oakland. Thursday morning was devoted to home visits, and Thursday afternoon to a Gray Panther health committee meeting. Fifteen new clients were seen during the week and spent an average of one hour and forty-eight minutes with a screening volunteer and a nurse. Thirty-one returning clients saw only a nurse, with visits averaging fifty-six minutes. Five additional new clients and eight returning ones arrived without appointments and were slotted in for shorter visits. In addition, thirty-five older people stopped by for a blood pressure reading and interpretation of the results; for most this was their first contact with the clinic and they were encouraged to return for a full screening. Five more persons came to make future appointments or obtain information about Over 60, and three who lived in the neighborhood stopped to visit or arrange transportation. Finally a regular clinic user came with her granddaughter who was in acute pain from an ingrown toenail; a nurse saw the girl and arranged a podiatrist appointment that same afternoon.

17. All Over 60 client names are pseudonyms except those of Gray Panther founders, volunteers, and members of the board of directors.

18. Sanjek 1977, 1987.

19. Melissa Lagusis to L. A. White, San Francisco Foundation, June 28, 1978.

20. Berkeley Planning Associates, "A Report on Primary Health Care Clinics Receiving Revenue Sharing Funds," September 1977.

21. Interview, March 1982.

22. Kuhn, "Grass-roots Gray Power," *Prime Time*, June 1974.

23. Roger Sanjek, Gray Panther Clinic Committee minutes, September 29, 1977.

24. For excellent analysis of Proposition 13, see Kuttner 1980.

25. See Sanjek 1987.

26. Five were founding Gray Panthers—Lillian, London, Hickman, Knight, Brangwin. The others were Rose Dellamonica, convener of the Oakland Gray Panthers; clinic volunteers and clients Greene and Muhammad; and clients Daniel Frazier, Harold Rousseau, and Rae Wahrhaftig of Berkeley, James Harrington of Emeryville, and George Pulford and Aquilla Robinson of Oakland.

27. The Black Panther Party for Self-Defense was started by Huey P. Newton and Bobby Seale in Oakland in 1966. It achieved notoriety in 1967 when members

appeared with guns in the state capital in Sacramento. In 1968 Seale was arrested in protests outside the Democratic Party convention in Chicago, and the following year Black Panther leaders were killed by police in gun fights in Los Angeles and Chicago. Newton spent 1967 to 1970 in prison, returned to Oakland, and in 1974 fled to Cuba for three years; he died in 1989. Seale left Oakland in 1974. For Black Panther chronology, see Brown 1992; Pearson 1994.

28. Margaret E. Kuhn to Lillian Rabinowitz, August 11, 1976.

29. Joan Kelley met Elaine Brown and joined the Black Panthers in Los Angeles in 1969, moved to Oakland later that year, and in 1975 was placed in charge of the survival programs by Brown, who became party chairman in 1974; see Brown 1992.

30. Lillian Rabinowitz to Margaret E. Kuhn, August 18, 1976.

31. Lillian Rabinowitz to Margaret E. Kuhn, September 16, 1976.

32. Margaret E. Kuhn to Lillian Rabinowitz, September 29, 1976.

33. Lillian Rabinowitz to Margaret E. Kuhn, September 3, 1976.

34. Margaret E. Kuhn to Lillian Rabinowitz, September 10, 1976.

35. Margaret E. Kuhn to Jenifer Rogers and Gil Clark, January 12, 1977.

36. Gray Panthers of the Berkeley Area newsletter, July 1983.

37. Hessel 1977:109–11.

38. Gray Panthers of the East Bay newsletter, February and April 1977.

39. See Estes 1979:xvi, 17, 57, 121, 226–27; 1993.

40. Fleisher and Zames 2001:29, 37–43, 53–54.

41. On Reagan's Central America policies, see Carroll 2006:398–402; Weiner 2007:379–82.

42. Jean Jernigan, "Gray Panthers Elect New Leaders," *Berkeley Daily Gazette*, March 17, 1976.

43. UNA supported itself through donations solicited by door-to-door canvassers, who retained a percentage of their collections.

44. Robert Pear, "Reagan Proposals to Alter Rules for Nursing Homes Are Assailed," *New York Times*, July 16, 1982.

45. Gray Panthers of the East Bay newsletter, December 1976.

46. Anne Kenin, "Report to Meeting of Commission on Aging of Berkeley on Status of Adult Day Health Care Bills," May 11, 1977.

47. Anne Kenin to the Membership of the Gray Panthers of the East Bay, October 17, 1977.

48. The modern hospice movement began with St. Christopher's in England in 1967; following this model, the first American hospice opened in Connecticut in 1974. See Robin Marantz Henig, "Will We Ever Arrive at the Good Death?," *New York Times Magazine*, August 7, 2005.

49. Gray Panthers of the Berkeley Area newsletter, February 1980.

50. By 1985 there were fifteen hundred hospice programs nationwide caring for one hundred and sixty thousand that year. Under Medicare hospice coverage, by 2005 the number expanded to thirty-three hundred programs and nearly one million people. See Henig, "Good Death."

51. Gray Panthers of the East Bay newsletter, October 1976.

52. Project Share flyer.

53. Alice Adler to Dr. Alexander M. Riskin, January 20, 1977.

54. See Fleischer and Zames 2001:79.

55. Compare Gerlach and Hine 1970:110–37 on "the commitment process" in social movements.

56. Gray Panthers of the Berkeley Area newsletter, April 1978.

57. Gray Panthers of the Berkeley Area newsletter, July 1983.

58. Gray Panthers of the Berkeley Area newsletter, February 1979.

59. Trupin 1984.

60. Charles Burress, "Rabinowitz Is Modest, but Still Determined," *Daily Cal* Summer Magazine, July 31, 1981.

61. Gray Panthers of the Berkeley Area newsletter, October 1984.

62. Fleischer and Zames 2001:41–42.

63. Fleischer and Zames 2001:49, 54, 71–74, 214.

64. Gray Panthers of the Berkeley Area newsletter, March 1985.

Chapter 5

1. Hope Bagger to Regina [Gartner], ca. 1982.

2. Lydia Bragger to Ms. Kuhn, May 23, 1972.

3. Shubert Frye to Lydia Bragger, September 14, 1972.

4. A report by Loretta Wavra, November 21, 1972.

5. Loretta Wavra, New York Gray Panthers' meeting, November 13, 1972.

6. Hope Bagger to Maggie Kuhn, March 2, 1973.

7. Jane Wholey, "Planning a Conference—An Action Example," *Gray Panther Network Organizing Manual 1973–74*, 19–25.

8. The Gray Panther Health Committee, draft Health Policy Statement, June 1973.

9. Hope Bagger to Shubert Frye, Helen Baker, Cameron Hall, August 18, 1973, and subsequent undated letter.

10. Loretta Wavra, Gray Panthers minutes of meeting, September 10, 1973.

11. *The Gray Panthers* (newsletter), November 19, 1973.

12. "Blumenthal, Chisholm Tell Forum to Demand Better Health Care," *The Westsider*, January 17, 1974.

13. Elma Griesel to National Steering Committee, June 8, 1974.

14. Lydia Bragger to Organizing people of N.Y. Gray Panthers, April 26, 1974.

15. Hope Bagger to the National Steering Committee, July 1974.

16. Hope Bagger [untitled four-page memo], October 28, 1974.

17. Hope Bagger to Dear Associates in the New York Gray Panthers, May 18, 1974.

18. Randi Koren, note to the members of the New York Executive Board and G.P. members, June 5, 1974.

19. Randi Koren Schmidt to National Steering Committee of the Gray Panthers, report on status of special project "an organizing conference" in New York City, [June 8, 1974].

20. See Fleischer and Zames 2001:57–63.

21. *Gray Panther NY Network Report*, July 1975.

22. Judy Klemesrud, "March and Rally Celebrate First International Women's Day," *New York Times*, March 9, 1975; *Gray Panther NY Network Report*, April 1975.

23. Sanjek 1998:83–93.

24. *Gray Panther NY Network Report*, May 1975. The network also reprinted in pamphlet form New School for Social Research economist David Gordon's "Recession Is Capitalism as Usual," *New York Times Magazine*, April 27, 1975.

25. See Burgess 2003 on the history of New York StateWide Senior Action Council.

26. "The Gray Panthers Want TV to Stop Portraying Old People as Doddering, Crotchety Has-Beens," *TV Guide*, June 21, 1975.

27. Lydia Bragger to Ms. Stella Murphy, Secretary, New York Gray Panther Network, January 24, 1980.

28. *Gray Panther NY Network Report*, April 1975.

29. See Kotelchuk 1976:122–31.

30. *Gray Panther NY Network Report*, Fall-Winter 1976.

31. *Network Report*, April-May 1980.

32. After presentations at the CUNY Graduate Center, University of Massachusetts at Amherst, University of Connecticut, and the Montefiore Hospital Social Medicine Residency Program in the Bronx, my talk was published as Sanjek 1987.

33. Chris Erikson, "Speaking Out," *Manhattan Spirit*, June 17, 1993.

34. Gray Panther Media Watch Task Force 1983.

35. See Lopata 1973:70, 216, 244–47.

36. Strelnick 1983:20.

37. Huckle 1991:188–89.

38. James H. Durkin, "The Social Security System under Assault," *Network Report*, July-September 1981.

39. Roger Sanjek, "Koch's Campaign against the Elderly (and Others)," *Network Report*, September-October 1981.

40. Joanne Summer, "Gray Panthers on the Prowl," *Moving On: The Newspaper for the Mature Person Living in Flushing, Fresh Meadows, and Bayside*, March 3, 1982.

41. See Murray 2003.

42. Before teaching at Queens College and returning to graduate school for her Ph.D., Sheppard had been active in Queens school protests in the 1950s; see Murray 2003:114.

43. *Gray Panthers of Queens Newsletter*, March 1981.

44. On the Nuclear Freeze campaign, see Carroll 2006:375, 384–95.

45. Jesse Stechel, "Queens GPs Picket SS Office," *Network*, July-August 1983.

46. Evelyn Neleson, "The Problems of the Aged Are Not Myths," *New York Times*, December 2, 1981; "It's No Fault of the Elderly," *Newsday*, April 26, 1986.

47. David Krajicek, "Ads Termed Ghoulish, Gray Panthers Condemn Pitch for Condo Purchases," *Daily News*, October 31, 1985.

48. On the June 12 demonstration, see Carroll 2007:374–75, 386–87, 582; on the wider background of nuclear weapons deployment and protest, see Krasniewicz 1992.

49. Gums remained a religious radio broadcaster in New York City until he retired in 1996; see Charles Bell, "A Microphone Ministry," *Newsday*, December 28, 1996.

50. "A Celebration! Gray Panthers of New York City, 1972–1983," April 9, 1983, audiotape.

51. *Morning Edition*, April 11, 1983, audiotape.

52. Gilderbloom 1980; Hawley 1978; Homefront 1979; Kuttner and Kelston 1979; LeGates and Hartman 1981; Marcuse 1981.

53. Roger Sanjek, "Fighting Age Discrimination in Housing," National Tenants Union, July 11, 1981, typescript; "An Overview of Housing in America Today—Where Do We Go From Here?", National Gray Panther Convention, December 2–4, 1981, typescript.

54. See Messinger and Domurad 1982; Sanjek 1998:94–96, 165–84.

55. On Emerman, see Fleischer and Zames 2001:33, 214–15.

56. Anne Emerman, "Special Housing" (letter), *New York Times*, October 14, 1984; Fleischer and Zames 2001:45, 225.

57. Roger Sanjek, statement at Division of Housing and Community Renewal Hearings, New York State, 2 World Trade Center, October 22, 1982.

58. Baxter and Hopper 1981; see also Hopper 2003.

59. Sanjek 1982, reprinted as Sanjek 1986.

60. Sanjek 1984.

61. Cantor 1975.

62. See Myers 1982.

63. Sanjek 1984:47–48. An anthropologist who studied the elderly in Cleveland and Leeds, United Kingdom, made similar proposals; see Francis 1984:162–71.

64. See "'Millions More' Could Be More Still" (editorial), *New York Times*, October 4, 1984, and David Bird, "Many Tacks Tried in Voter Registration," *New York Times*, October 5, 1984, which mention the Gray Panthers. Piven and Cloward 1982 analyzes the Reagan policies they hoped greater voter participation would overturn; Piven and Cloward 1988 provides historical analysis of voting as well as the national campaign they organized in the 1980s, and mentions Gray Panther efforts in New York and Colorado.

65. Burgess 2003:76–77.

66. On Grenada, see Carroll 2006:444–45; Weiner 2007:392–93.

67. See Burgess 2003:79–101.

68. My talk drew on materials from the Gray Panthers, the Coalition for a National Health Service, Representative Dellums's office, and Starr 1982.

69. Margo Nash, "How to Hack through the Medical Jungle," *The Westsider*, December 13, 1984.

70. See Fleischer and Zames 2001:22–23.

Chapter 6

1. Invitation, November 6, 1985.

2. Author's audiotape of reception for National Gray Panther Washington, D.C., branch office opening, November 6, 1985.

3. Jimmy Carter, mailgram to Maggie Kuhn, February 20, 1976.

4. *Network*, August 1976.

5. Margaret Kuhn and Alice Adler, mailgrams to Gerald Ford, Ronald Reagan, Jimmy Carter, June 24, 1976.

6. Margaret E. Kuhn to Mrs. Lillian Carter, July 17, 1976.

7. Margaret E. Kuhn, "Statement to be Presented at Mrs. Carter's Roundtable," May 10, 1977.

8. Margaret E. Kuhn, "An Open Letter to the President," June 15, 1977.

9. On the B-1, later reauthorized under Ronald Reagan, see Carroll 2006:347, 370–71, 383.

10. "Statement of the Gray Panthers on Welfare Reform," November 1977.

11. *Network*, March-April 1979.

12. *Network*, January-February 1980. On Carter, the USSR, and Afghanistan, see Carroll 2006:371–73; Weiner 2007:365–67.

13. Cheryl Clearwater to Gray Panther Conveners, July 14, 1980.

14. *Network*, September-October 1980.

15. Paul S. Nathanson, Executive Director, National Senior Citizens Law Center, to Ms. Maggie Kuhn, National Convener, Gray Panthers, August 9, 1976.

16. Fleischer and Zames 2001:56–57.

17. *Network*, Summer 1985.

18. The attorneys were Gil Deford, Neal Dudovitz, Toby Edelman, Burton Fretz, Bruce Fried, Peter Komlos-Hrobsky, Paul Lichterman, Trish Nemore, Eileen Sweeney, Sally Wilson. Edith Giese, "Lichterman Honored," *Network*, Spring 1984.

19. Rosalie Schofield, "The Gray Panthers Task Force to End Mandatory Retirement," mimeographed, November 1976.

20. Testimony presented at the March 17, 1977 hearing on retirement age policy before the Select Committee on Aging of the U.S. House of Representatives, Gray Panthers, Philadelphia.

21. "Gray Panthers: Close Ranks on Mandatory Retirement," October 27, 1977.

22. Maggie Kuhn, "The Next Step," *Network*, Winter 1978.

23. Horn and Griesel 1977.

24. Perretz 1978.

25. Esther Jantzen, "Elma Holder: Nursing Homes Back to Health," *Network*, Summer 1985.

26. *Network*, Fall 1978, March-April 1981, March-April 1982.

27. For the OWL story, see Huckle 1991.

28. On the significance of Sam Kuhn's passing to Maggie, see Kuhn, Long, and Quinn 1991:162–66.

29. Robert Bentley to Maggie Kuhn, March 2, 1978; Joanne Kernitz [Maggie's secretary] to National Office, Nancy Nolde, Bob Bentley, February 16, 1978; Maggie Kuhn, "Why Old and Young Should Live Together," *50 Plus*, October 1978.

30. Compiled from "On the Road with Maggie," *Network*, Fall 1978 through July-August 1983. These listings, undoubtedly incomplete, cover most but not all months during these five years.

31. Bruce Shapiro, *In These Times*, August 25, 1982.

32. Irv Riskin to Sherry Clearwater, Maggie Kuhn Meeting, n.d.

33. "What the Gray Panthers Deal With," *Oakland Tribune*, November 16, 1977; "Kuhn, Maggie," *Current Biography*, July 1978; Ken Dychtwald, "Liberating Aging: An Interview with Maggie Kuhn," *New Age*, February 1979; Garson Kanin, "To Rest Is to Rust," *Quest*, June 1979.

34. Jacobs 1980:96.

35. George Michaelson, "Maggie Kuhn: Gray Panther on the Prowl," *Parade*, December 18, 1977.

36. Dieter Hessel, "Tribute to Maggie," *Network*, April 1995.

37. Raymond Fisk, "'The Ghettoization of Age,'" [*Cornell Daily Sun?*], February 24, 1977.

38. "Kuhn, Maggie," *Current Biography*, July 1978.

39. Kuhn 1994:241.

40. Maggie Kuhn, "Relating Research and Advocacy," Thirty-First Annual Meeting of the Gerontological Society, November 19, 1978.

41. Hessel 1977 is a record of this seminar.

42. Maggie Kuhn, "People Assure China's Gains, Maggie Finds," *Network*, November-December 1976.

43. Maggie Kuhn, "Gray Panthers Go to China," *Network*, Winter 1978.

44. Maggie Kuhn, "Behind the Iron Curtain," *Network*, September-October 1983.

45. Maureen Haggerty, "GPs Study Health across the Border," *Network*, Winter 1978.

46. Steven Roberts, "Gray Panthers Fighting Society's Treatment of the Elderly," *New York Times*, October 29, 1977; Judy Klemesrud, "Gray Panther Founder and

a Family of Choice," *New York Times,* June 22, 1981; Margaret Kuhn, "We're Old, Not Senile, Ronald," *New York Times,* July 31, 1983; "Activist, in 70s, Says Age Distinguishes Her," *New York Times,* March 12, 1984.

47. Lillian Rabinowitz to Margaret Kuhn, March 1, 1977.

48. Butler 1969, 1975.

49. Dychtwald, "Liberating Aging."

50. Christina Long, "Maggie's Birthday Celebrations Launched with Screening of *Cocoon,*" *Network,* Summer 1985; "Thumbs Down," "More Youth Worship," Denise Bergman and Caroljean Wisnieski, "*Cocoon*—Ageist or Not?," *Network,* Fall 1985. Betty Friedan in *The Fountain of Age* stated that she "felt uncomfortable" and "repelled" by the older characters "denying age" in *Cocoon* (1993:57).

51. Kuhn, Long, and Quinn 1991:162–66.

52. Klemesrud, "Family of Choice"; Kuhn, "Old and Young"; Kuhn, Long, and Quinn 1991:196–200.

53. "Housing: Exploring New Ways to Live," *Network,* January 1979.

54. Kuhn, Long, and Quinn 1991:222.

55. Day-Lower, Bryant, and Mullaney 1982; "The Shared Housing Research Center," *Aging,* August-September 1984; Michael deCourcy Hinds, "For Older People, Communal Living Has Its Rewards," *New York Times,* January 31, 1985. The Philadelphia Center was succeeded in the 1990s by the National Shared Housing Resource Center in California.

56. Butler and Lewis 1976; Hessel 1977:84–86.

57. Dychtwald, "Liberating Aging"; Kanin, "To Rest"; Chris Sheppard, "Still Prowling, Still Growling," *New Internationalist,* June 1982; Kuhn, Long, and Quinn 1991:184–89.

58. Kuhn, Long, and Quinn 1991:108–9, 177–78; Kuhn, "Old and Young."

59. "Maggie Kuhn: Around the World in Eighty Years," *Network,* Summer 1985.

60. Minutes of the Gray Panther Steering Committee meetings, May 18–20, 1978.

61. *Network,* Winter 1978.

62. Stephen McConnell, "Some Nagging Contradictions in Gray Panthers," Address to National Gray Panthers Steering Committee, October 28, 1978.

63. *Network,* Winter 1978, January 1979, March-April 1979, May-June 1979.

64. South Carolina, Oklahoma, Utah, the Dakotas, Wyoming, and Hawaii registered no Panther activity.

65. Extrapolated from "1981 Grey [*sic*] Panther Network Survey," March 3, 1982, a report to Cheryl Clearwater by Boston Panther Herbert Harrington based on fifty completed network surveys mailed out by the national office late in 1981. The results, which included the older and larger networks, indicated a combined membership of about 4,800. It is unlikely that the fifty-four nonreporting networks, half of which were closed during 1982, contained even half that many members. See also minutes of the Executive Committee, June 19–20, 1982.

66. This was the first time Lani and I met Maggie and heard her speak.

67. Lillian Rabinowitz to Carol Mackenzie, National Office Staff, December 21, 1977.

68. The daughter of a Spanish father and German mother, Wolff (born in 1914) began her political life at twenty-four working to send medical assistance to Spanish antifascist forces and Abraham Lincoln Brigade American volunteers in Spain. During World War II she was an American Red Cross volunteer in Allied forces field hospitals in France, Belgium, and Germany. After the war she worked for the Red Cross with disabled soldiers in Veterans Administration hospitals,

and then as an organizer and fundraiser for the Spanish Refugee Appeal and Joint Anti-Fascist Refugee Committee, which aided displaced persons encamped in France. In 1947–48 she joined the Independent Progressive Party, petitioning for California ballot status and organizing in San Francisco and Philadelphia. She then became a school teacher in the Sacramento Valley, where she worked to improve the lives of her students' migrant worker parents until she was investigated by the FBI and barred from teaching for her refusal to sign a loyalty oath. Wolff then launched a successful business career and continued her activism by exposing U.S. support for the Franco regime in Spain and opposing U.S. intervention in El Salvador's civil war and raising medical funds for its victims. During the late 1970s she was active in the Congress of California Seniors and joined the Western Contra Costa County Gray Panthers founded in 1977. See Lucy Forest and Alice Hamburg, "Frieda Wolff: A Life of Radical Politics," *Network*, Summer 1984; Hon. Ronald V. Dellums, "Frieda Wolff," *Congressional Record*, vol. 129, no. 16, February 17, 1983.

69. Billie Heller, "Gray Panthers Picket U.S. Chamber of Commerce" (press release), October 31, 1977.

70. Warren Weaver, "White House Aging Parley Adopts Agenda for Decade," *New York Times*, December 4, 1981; see also Jack Anderson, "White House Rigged Meeting on Aging in '81," and "White House Tried to Bully Aging Meeting," *Washington Post*, March 8 and 9, 1983; Achenbaum 1983:166–67.

71. Handwritten notes by Maggie Kuhn on "Resolutions adopted by Gray Panther Second National Convention," October 1977; Chuck Preston, "GP's Gear Up for 80s," *Network*, November-December 1979; *Network*, January-February 1980, January-February 1982; Summary of Results of Evaluations from 1981 Biennial Convention.

72. Klafter 1980.

73. "Activist, in 70s, Says Age Distinguishes Her," *New York Times*, March 12, 1984.

74. "Edith Giese, Grace Warfield and Morris Better to National Steering Committee," April 8, 1982.

75. Cheryl Clearwater to Rick Smith, Gray Panthers of the East Bay, September 6, 1978; Timothy Orr, [Berkeley] Office Coordinator, to National Gray Panthers, October 7, 1981; Cheryl Clearwater, "Network Membership Survey Results," January 1985.

76. Edith Giese to Gray Panther Project Fund Executive Committee, Program Planning, July 30, 1980; Cheryl Clearwater to Gray Panther Executive Committee, Attached Gray Panther Organizational Time Line, June 16, 1981; minutes of the Executive Committee, June 30–July 2, 1981; minutes of the Executive Committee Meeting, January 28–29, 1983.

77. Minutes of the National Steering Committee meeting, October 5–7, 1981.

78. Minutes of the Executive Committee meeting, February 6–7, 1982.

79. Working paper prepared for the Fund Raising Committee, June 18, 1982.

80. Executive Committee, Metropolitan Washington Gray Panthers, to Cheryl Clearwater, March 9, 1983.

81. D. F. Beaven Associates, "A Plan for Action for the Future: Gray Panthers," March 1979. Steve McConnell, writing a year before the California Gray Panthers was formed, worried that the Beaven report's recommendations did not give local networks *enough* power on the NSC and advocated "making them the central and driving force of the Gray Panthers"; Stephen McConnell and Leon Kaplan to Alice Adler, May 17, 1979.

82. Roger Sanjek to Edith Giese, September 25, 1982. *Village Voice* reporters Wayne Barrett, Joe Conason, and Jack Newfield spotlighted Gouletas-Carey in their holiday season "Remember the Greediest" column, December 23, 1981; also see Barrett, "Carey's Reaganomics: Let Them Eat Cold Cuts," *Village Voice*, March 30, 1982; Burgess 2003:66–67.

83. National Steering Committee (minutes), October 25–27, 1982.

84. Roger Sanjek to Edith Giese, December 18, 1982.

85. Edith Giese, Maggie Kuhn, Rosalie Riechman, Arthur Waskow, "Proposal for a Gray Panther Organizing Strategy for 1981–1982"; minutes of the National Steering Committee Meeting, October 5–7, 1981.

86. Roger Sanjek, notes on National Steering Committee meeting, March 18–20, 1982.

87. "Social Security: $200 Billion Short," *U.S. News & World Report*, November 22, 1982; "How to Save Social Security," *Business Week*, November 29, 1982.

88. This episode is included in the documentary *Maggie Growls!*

89. Minutes of the Executive Committee meeting, January 28–29, 1983; Executive Committee, Metropolitan Washington Gray Panthers, to Cheryl Clearwater, March 9, 1983.

90. *Local Links*, January-February 1983.

91. Grace Warfield to Gray Panther National Steering Committee and Executive Director, April 13, 1983.

92. Roger Sanjek to Leslie Kwass Zuska, June 26, 1983.

93. Gray Panther Economy Task Force 1978; Jacobs 1980:98–99.

94. "GPs Mix Their Business with Business," *Network*, May-June 1980.

95. *Problems in Urban Centers: Oversight Hearings before the Committee on the District of Columbia*, House of Representatives, serial no. 96–16, pp. 585–99; Joe Davis, Report of the Housing Task Force, October 14, 1980.

96. Frances Klafter, "A Continuum of Conferences?," *Network*, August 1976.

97. Frances Klafter to Members of the National Health Task Force, "Gray Panther Goals in Health Care and Development of a Program around These Goals," July 10, 1978.

98. Sigelman 1981.

99. "Almost every local which returned the 1980 survey requested additional contact with the national TFs in developing of local programs"; [Sherry Clearwater], Local Network Report, June 1980.

100. Edith Giese to Gray Panther Project Fund Executive Committee, Program Planning, July 30, 1980; minutes of the Executive Committee meeting, June 30–July 1, 1980.

101. Roger Sanjek, "A Call for Decent Housing: Passing the Baton," *Network*, September-October 1982; "The Money Is There," *Network*, November-December 1982; "Playing without a Full Deck," *Network*, January-February 1982; "Mean Streets: Two Million Call the Sidewalks Home," *Network*, March-April 1983.

102. Roger Sanjek, An Overview of Housing in America Today—Where Do We Go from Here?, National Gray Panther Convention, December 2–4, 1981; Roger Sanjek to Edith Giese, August 2, 1982.

103. Frances Klafter, co-chair, NHTF, to the National Steering Committee, October 11, 1982.

104. Report of Frances Klafter for the National Health Task Force to the Steering Committee meeting, March 11–12, 1983.

105. Minutes of Gray Panther Project Fund Steering Committee, March 11–12, 1983.

106. Rosalie Riechman to Gray Panther Social Security contacts, March 28, 1983; Rosalie Riechman to Frances Klafer, March 28, 1983.

107. Frances Klafter to Roger Sanjek, April 4, 1983; Frances Klafter to Health Task Force members, April 20, 1983.

108. Grace Warfield to Frances Klafter, April 22, 1983; Grace Warfield to National Health Task Force members, April 22, 1983; Maggie Kuhn to Grace Warfield, April 19, 1983.

109. David Danielson, William Lievow, Arthur Mazer, [and] Lani Sanjek to Grace Warfield, May 6, 1983; Lowell Arye, Samuel Beck, Abe Bloom, Arjun Makhijani, Lee Pikser, David Resnikoff, Irv Riskin, Estelle Rondello, Dr. William J. Vlahov, Ethel Weisser to Grace Warfield, [n.d.]; Members of the Steering Committee and Task Forces, Gray Panthers of New York City to Gray Panther networks, National Steering Committee, National Gray Panther Health Task Force, June 20, 1983; Gladys Elson to Grace Warfield, June 28, 1983.

110. Maggie Kuhn to Gray Panther National Steering Committee, members of Washington Area Gray Panthers, National Health Task Force, May 23, 1983.

111. Cheryl Clearwater to network conveners, May 24, 1983.

112. Roger Sanjek to Maggie Kuhn, June 22, 1983.

113. Frances Klafter to Gladys Elson, Cookie Smith, and Lani Sanjek, April 26, 1983.

114. Shubert Frye later observed, "For my money [Frances Klafter] is one of the most talented and productive of the Gray Panthers. I have always admired her and her work. . . . For several years there seems to have been some sort of canabalistic [sic] appetite among members of the national staff . . . and yes, Maggie, for the hides of those with initiative and imagination." Shubert [Frye] to Roger [Sanjek], March 23, 1984.

115. Lillian R[abinowitz] to Roger and Lani [Sanjek], July 3, 1983.

116. Lee [Pikser] to Roger [Sanjek], August 13, 1983.

117. Glen Gersmehl, "Proposed Gray Panther Post-Election Peace Actions," 1984.

118. Gray Panthers Executive Committee meeting, April 5, 6, 1979. Berkeley NSC member Leslie Kwass, who herself testified for the Panthers on nursing home matters, concluded there needed to be "a [single] person in D.C. to coordinate all [Gray Panther] testimony"; minutes of the Gray Panther Steering Committee meeting, May 18–20, 1978.

119. Joe Davis, "The Reagan Program as It Appears to the G.P. Network in Washington D.C.," March 16, 1981.

120. Frances Klafter to members of the Gray Panther Executive Committee, June 29, 1983.

121. "Maggie Kuhn: A Spirited Fighter," *The Guardian*, Fall 1981; Nancy Connell, "Gray Panthers Pounce on Reagan, Fund Cuts," *Albany Times-Union*, May 12, 1981.

122. Edith Giese, "Year End Report to Gray Panther Conveners," January 1985.

123. Minutes of the Gray Panthers National Steering Committee meeting, February 9–10, 1985.

Chapter 7

1. Robert McG. Thomas Jr., "Maggie Kuhn, 89, the Founder of the Gray Panthers, Is Dead," *New York Times*, April 23, 1995.

2. "Gray Panthers of Graterford Honor Maggie," *Network*, September-October 1995.

3. Doris Dawson to All Conveners, memorandum, March 9, 1987.

4. Gray Panthers 1986 annual report; "The Best Age Is the Age You Are," [1991].

5. Maggie Kuhn and Doris Dawson to Gray Panther Friends, December 4, 1989.

6. "Mahler Fund Announced," *Network*, Fall 1987; Marge Lueders, "Mahler Institute of Gray Panthers: A Selection of Awards Made since Inception," *Network*, May-June 1995.

7. Maggie Kuhn, "Young and Old: More Than Ever We Need Each Other," *Network*, Winter 1985; Richard Griffin, "Where Have All the Young Panthers Gone?," *Network*, September 1990; Kuhn, Long, and Quinn 1991:221.

8. Network Membership survey results, January 1985; Mathew Battinovich, letter to the editor, *California Panther*, Spring 1986.

9. M. B., "The Loss of Compassion," *Texas Observer*, October 26, 1984; "Charlotte Flynn Leads with Optimism and Commitment," *Network*, March 1992; telephone interview with Charlotte Flynn, May 3, 2002.

10. Lawrence Smedley, Executive Director, National Council of Senior Citizens, to Maggie Kuhn, July 10, 1991; Charlotte Flynn and Maggie Kuhn, "Complex Issues in a Complex Time: An Open Letter to Gray Panthers Members and Friends," *Network*, May-August 1991; "Charlotte Flynn Leads with Optimism and Commitment," *Network*, March 1992; Flynn interview.

11. "The Gray Panthers Project Fund Reorganization Decisions," June 3, 1992; Flynn interview.

12. Donald Pelz, "Opinion Surveys Explore Future Gray Panther Directions," *Network*, September 1992; "Highlights of National Board Meeting," October 1–3, 1993.

13. Burton Fretz, "Congress Expands Protection against Age Discrimination," *Network*, Spring 1987.

14. Mark Graven, "Ageism Still at Work," *Network*, Winter 1985.

15. Gray Panther Disability Task Force newsletter, May 1985; "And So Be It Resolved That," *Network*, Fall 1986.

16. Gray Panther Disability Task Force newsletter, February 1989.

17. See Carroll 2006:457–66.

18. On Iran-Contra, see Carroll 2006:402–4; Weiner 2007:398–412.

19. *Network*, Fall 1986.

20. Karen Talbot, "Disarmament and Development are Indivisible," International Conference on the Relationship between Disarmament and Development, August 24, 1987; Doris Dawson to the Honorable Vernon Walters, U.S. Ambassador to the United Nations, August 26, 1987.

21. Karen Talbot, editorial, *Network*, January-February 1988.

22. "All Rails Lead to Washington, D.C.," *Network*, May-June-July-August 1988.

23. Abby Lederman, "The Gulf Crisis: Panthers Rally against War," *Network*, February 1991. On the Gulf War, see Carroll 2006:434–37; Weiner 2007:425–29.

24. Maggie Kuhn and Robert Weiner, "Canada's Program Shows the Way," *San Francisco Chronicle*, July 20, 1985.

25. "First State to Pose Health Question," *Network*, Winter 1986.

26. "Official Position Statement," "National Health Insurance Defined," *Health Watch*, May 1988.

27. Terri Thomas Hamstra, "Public Opinion Polls—National Health Program," Berkeley Gray Panthers, 1988.

28. Gregory Bergman, "New Medicare Act: A Catastrophic Mistake?, *Network*, September-October 1988; Marmor 2000:110–13.

29. David Himmelstein, Steffie Woolhandler, and the Writing Committee of the Working Group on Program Design 1989; Navarro 1976; Waitzkin and Waterman 1974.

30. "Resolutions," *Network*, September 1990.

31. "Gray Panthers 1993 Campaign for a National Health System," January 14, 1993.

32. "Gray Panthers Visit the White House," *Network*, Fall 1993.

33. "Charlotte Flynn to President and Hillary Rodham Clinton, 3 October 1993," *Network*, Fall 1993.

34. Abe Bloom, "Health Care Update," *Network*, August 1994; "Health Reform Update," *Network*, September-October 1994; "New Strategies for National Health Reform," *Network*, November-December 1994; "Health Care Update," *Network*, May-June 1995. For a thorough account of the Clinton health care fiasco, see Johnson and Broder 1996.

35. Karen Talbot to Participants in the Northeast Conference, July 16, 1987.

36. "Activist, Mugged, Urges Understanding," *Newsday*, November 18, 1987; Kuhn, Long, and Quinn 1991:216–18.

37. Bard Lindeman, "Gray Panthers Do Battle," *Network*, November-December 1988.

38. "Join 1989 'Liberals Love America' Campaign," *Network*, January-February-March 1989.

39. Jerry Byrd, "Maggie Goes to Jail," *Network*, September 1989.

40. Kuhn, Long, and Quinn 1991:212.

41. Ibid.

42. Kuhn 1992.

43. Kuhn, Long, and Quinn 1991:214; Kuhn 1992; Abby Lederman, "Past, Present, Future Panther Power: Maggie Kuhn," *Network*, Summer 1990; "*Utne Reader* Honors Maggie Kuhn," *Network*, November-December 1994.

44. "Gray Panthers Making News," ca. April 1995.

45. Bill Clinton to Maggie Kuhn, March 22, 1995.

46. "A Message from Maggie," *Network*, April 1995.

47. Kuhn, Long, and Quinn 1991:231.

48. "The Patient Self-Determination Act of 1991 made advance directives legal documents in all states: it requires that all patients be asked upon admission to any health care institution whether or not they have such documents"; Long 2005:116.

49. Gregory Bergman, "Board and Care Homes for the Old: A Gray Panther Study," *Network*, May-August 1991.

50. Kiefer 2000:161.

51. Jules Yanover, "What Lies Ahead for Berkeley Gray Panthers?," *Berkeley Gray Panthers Newsletter*, January 1989; Berkeley Gray Panthers, *20 Years! 1974–1994*, 1995.

52. Ann Dawson and Virginia Morgan, "Ellen Butler: Membership Chair, Go-Getter, Innovator," *Berkeley Gray Panthers Newsletter*, July 1988; "Here's What's Happening in the Committees, Get Involved!," *Berkeley Gray Panthers Newsletter*, May 1989; Ellen Butler, "Membership Committee," (Berkeley) *Gray Panther Newsletter*, April 1992; "Berkeley Gray Panthers Annual Summer Picnic," (Berkeley) *Gray Panther Newsletter*, September 1992.

53. (Berkeley) *Gray Panther Newsletter*, December 1991; Gerda Miller, "Message

from Berkeley Gray Panther Convener," *Berkeley Gray Panther Newsletter,* September 1994.

54. Peter Kerr, "Undercover Agent, 81, Helps Halt Nursing Home Payoffs," *New York Times,* April 27, 1987; Constance McKenna, "Gray Panther Goes Undercover to Expose Nursing Home Scam, *Network,* Summer 1987; *The City Panther,* Summer 1987.

55. "Spotlight on: Dave Brown," *Network,* December 1991–February 1992.

56. New York Grey [*sic*] Panthers Executive Committee meeting, April 6, 1994.

Chapter 8

1. Karen Harper, Administrative Assistant, to Board of Directors, Task Force Chairs, Network Conveners, Sign on Letters & Actions 1995–96, September 5, 1996.

2. "Age and Youth in Action Summit Rescheduled," *Network,* January-February 1996; Age and Youth in Action Summit Report, July 1996; Friedan 1993:662–35.

3. Charlotte Flynn to Gray Panthers Board of Directors, June 17, 1996; Charlotte Flynn to Friends in the Network, November 21, 1996.

4. *Network,* November-December 1997.

5. *Network,* January-February 1996.

6. On right-wing foundation and think-tank drum beating for Social Security privatization, see Lieberman 2000:34–36, 43–63.

7. Tim Fuller, "Leadership Letter," *Network,* April-May 1998; "Gray Panthers Organizes Progressives in Response to White House Forums," *Network,* September-October 1998; "Gray Panthers' Side by Side Proposals for Social Security," *Network,* vol. 29, no. 2, 1999.

8. See Lieberman 2000:117–48.

9. "Highlights of President Clinton's Healthcare Reform," *Network,* March-April 1997; Abe Bloom, "The Balanced Budget Deal," *Network,* May-June 1997; "Gray Panthers Launches Health Care Campaign to 'Cure Profit Fever,' " *Network,* September-October 1998; "Leadership Letter," *Network,* February-March 1999; "Gray Panthers Leap at Legislation, Devour GOP Agenda," "Gray Panther's Side by Side Proposals for the Future of Medicare," *Network,* vol. 29, no. 2, 1999; Gray Panthers, "Strengthen the Future of Medicare," 1999; Marmor 2000:141–49.

10. See Marmor and Mashaw 1988; Marmor 2000.

11. Tim [Fuller], "Hello to You in the Networks," March 7, 1997.

12. Universal Health Care 2000 Campaign, Frequently Asked Questions.

13. Tim Fuller to Gray Panthers and Friends, [November 2000].

14. *Network,* September-October 1998. For a broader critique of the pharmaceutical industry, see Barlett and Steele 2004:35–45, 63–69, 195–233.

15. Tim Fuller, "NOW, Gray Panthers, SPAN to Take Action against Pharmaceutical Market Abuses," press release, May 14, 2001; Gray Panthers, "Gray Panthers Invites Abbot Laboratories to Public Forum on FDA's Synthroid Safety and Efficacy Concerns," press release, June 15, 2001.

16. Tim Fuller, "Consumers, Seniors Anticipate Substantial Cost Savings from Oct. 5 Prilosec Patent Expiration, According to Stop Patient Abuse Now," press release, October 1, 2001; SPAN Coalition, "Prilosec Costs for New Yorkers," press release, March 8, 2002.

17. Statement of the Gray Panthers regarding pharmaceutical manufacturer's abuse of the Hatch-Waxman Act, presented to the U.S. Senate Commerce Committee, April 23, 2002.

18. San Francisco Gray Panthers newsletter, June 2002.

19. Tim Fuller to All Gray Panthers, An Emergency Appeal for Peace, quoting Barbara Aldave, September 15, 2002 [Fall 2002]; "The Gray Panthers Urges Protests Against the War in Iraq," October 2002; Tim Fuller to Gray Panthers, allies, and friends [April 2003].

20. Tim Fuller to Dear Gray Panther [July 2003]; National office and staff to Gray Panther Leaders, with program summary, briefing book, and sample news reports (after July 26, 2003); Gray Panthers 2004 Program.

21. "Gray Panthers Ads Targeting WorldCom Funded by IDI," *Corporate Crime Reporter*, June 2, 2003; Christopher Stern, "D.C. Firm Helps Organize Protest," *Washington Post*, June 20, 2003. Neither Issue Dynamics nor these articles is mentioned in Fuller's 2003 communications to Gray Panther members cited in note 20.

22. George Neighbors, "Focus on the Field," *Network*, April-May 1998, September-October 1998; Gray Panthers, *Ready for Action to Take on the Future*, 1999; Gray Panthers website (www.graypanthers.org), June 2006.

23. Gray Panthers of Central Contra Costa County newsletter, Winter 2003, April-May-June 2006.

24. Barlett and Steele 2004:69–73.

25. Berkeley Gray Panther *Newsletter*, May 1996.

26. See McNamee 2007 on Waters and Chez Panisse, opened in 1971. On the edible schoolyard, see McNamee 2007:258–61, 266–71, 278–79, 309.

27. Berkeley Gray Panther *Newsletter*, July 1998.

28. Margot Smith to Roger and Lani Sanjek, April 10, 2006.

29. Avis Worthington, "Welfare Reform Worsens Housing Shortage for Seniors, Immigrants," Berkeley Gray Panther *Newsletter*, March 1997.

30. Sandra Decker, "Elders Sharing Housing for Companionship & Safety," Berkeley Gray Panther *Newsletter*, April 1999; Deede Sloan, "Director's Corner," Berkeley Gray Panther *Newsletter*, February 1999.

31. Avis Worthington, "Food First Challenges Dominant Ideas," "Berkeley Gray Panther Busted in DC," Berkeley Gray Panther *Newsletter*, May 2000; Margot Smith, "Margot Freed!," Berkeley Gray Panther *Newsletter*, June 2000 .

32. Margot Smith, "Speech for Hiroshima Day, August 6th 2006," Berkeley Gray Panther *Newsletter*, September 2006.

33. Kiefer 2000:165.

34. See LifeLong Medical Care Annual Report 2005; Kiefer 2000:160–74.

35. Christine Szeto, "Clark Kerr Makes Symbiotic Neighbors of Youth, Elderly," *Daily Californian*, September 7, 2004; Rio Bruce, "HUD Renews Redwood Garden Senior Housing Subsidy," *Berkeley Daily Planet*, July 21, 2006.

36. Chez Panisse Foundation Annual Report 2005–2006.

37. "Activists to Travel on Peace Mission with Fellowship of Reconciliation," Berkeley Gray Panther *Newsletter*, March 2007; Margot Smith, "Hopes for Peace with Iran," Berkeley Gray Panther *Newsletter*, April 2007.

38. New York Gray Panthers Board Meeting (minutes), January 20, 1998.

39. Edna Graig to Dear Gray Panthers, May 16, 2001; New York Gray Panthers' Board Meeting, June 13, 2001; Lillian Sarno to Dear Friends, January 2002.

40. Robert Lipsyte, "Suspicion: The Renters' Story," *New York Times*, June 30, 1996; Leonore Fine and Joan Davis to Miss Helene Hoedl, N.G.O. Section, United Nations, September 23, 1998; Tim Fuller, "Designation of Representatives for 2001," January 5, 2001.

41. Tim Fuller, "Designation of Representatives for 2002," December 18, 2001.

42. Charlotte Eichna, "Still Active after All These Years," *The Westsider*, September 2, 2004.

43. New York Gray Panthers *Network Report*, Winter 2004–5.

44. Nora O'Brien, "Emergency Preparedness for Older People," International Longevity Center, 2003.

45. New York Gray Panthers *Network Report*, Spring 2005.

46. Ruth Kelton, "Seniors Seethe at Medifarce," *The Indypendent*, December 7, 2005; New York Gray Panthers *Network Report*, Winter 2004–5.

47. John Doyle, "A Bridge to Better Health Care," *Newsday*, June 20, 2004.

48. Those most helpful were the Campaign for America's Future, the Center for American Progress, the Center on Budget and Policy Priorities, the Center for Economic and Policy Research, the Century Foundation, the Economic Policy Institute, the Consortium for Citizens with Disabilities, the National Academy of Social Insurance, the National Committee to Preserve Social Security and Medicare, and the National Women's Law Center.

49. Roger Sanjek, "Social Security: No Crisis, but Plenty to Worry About," February 9, 2005.

50. Robert Ball, "Just a Little Maintenance," *Washington Post*, July 18, 2004; Jackie Calmes, "On Social Security, It's Bush vs. AARP," *Wall Street Journal*, January 21, 2005; L. Josh Bivens, "Removing the Social Security Earnings Cap Virtually Eliminates Funding Gap," Economic Policy Institute, February 17, 2005.

51. Bernard Wasow, "The Beginning of Social Security's End?," Century Foundation, January 10, 2005; Dean Baker and David Rosnick, "Basic Facts on Proposed Benefit Cuts," Center for Economic and Policy Research, March 2005; "What You Might *Not* Have Learned about the President's Social Security Plan," Center on Budget and Policy Priorities, April 29, 2005.

52. New York Network for Action on Medicare and Social Security and the New York State Alliance for Retired Americans, *Social Security Works: A Tool Kit for Speakers and Workshops*, May 2005.

53. Richard Morin and Jim VandeHei, "Social Security Plan's Support Dwindling," *Washington Post*, June 9, 2005; Lind Feldman, "Bush Faces Stalled Agenda, as 2006 Races Rev Up," *Christian Science Monitor*, June 20, 2005; Richard Wolf, "Approval of President's Social Security Efforts Dips," *USA Today*, June 29, 2005.

54. Associated Press, "18 Grandmothers Arrested at Iraq War Protest," October 17, 2005; Kristen Lombardi, "Grandmothers of Invention," *Village Voice*, April 18, 2006; Anemona Hartocollis, "With 'Grannies' in Dock, a Sitting Judge Is Bound to Squirm," *New York Times*, April 27, 2006, "Setting Grandmotherhood Aside, Judge Lets 18 Go in Peace," *New York Times*, April 28, 2006.

55. David Chen, "Thousands Rally to Demand Low-Income Housing in City," *New York Times*, February 3, 2005.

56. Anne Emerman, testimony to City Council Housing Committee Fiscal Year 2007 Preliminary Budget, March 8, 2006.

57. Anne Emerman, Committee on Housing and Buildings, June 13, 2007.

58. Roger Sanjek, "A Family-Friendly NYC Construction Code," June 13, 2007.

59. "Editorials: An Overdue Overhaul," *New York Times*, June 24, 2007; Diane Cardwell, "Manhattan: Building Code Changes," *New York Times*, June 28, 2007.

Chapter 9

1. Wallace (1956:365) defines a "revitalization movement" as "a deliberate, organized, conscious effort by members of a society to construct a more satisfying culture." Garner's characterization (1977:1), also applicable to the Gray Panthers, is similar: "A social movement is a set of actions of a group of people . . . self-consciously directed toward changing the social structure and/or ideology of a society, and they either are carried on outside . . . legitimated channels of change or use these channels in innovative ways." Gerlach and Hine (1970:xvi–xvii) add that members are "actively engaged in the face-to-face recruitment of others" to a "segmented, usually polycephalous, cellular . . . network of groups" held together by "various personal, structural, and ideological ties." See also Nicholas 1973.

2. Mills 1959:187, with thanks to Polletta 2002.

3. Harris 1975:vi, 87, 213.

4. Ibid., 52–53, 129.

5. While debate about timing exists, this transition in attitudes is covered in Achenbaum 1978, Fischer 1978, and Haber 1983.

6. Butler 1975:12. See also Shield and Aronson 2003:103–10, 131.

7. Hessel 1977:14; George Michaelson, "Maggie Kuhn: Gray Panther on the Prowl," *Parade*, December 18, 1977; Cobey Black, "The Best Is Yet to Be," *Honolulu Advertiser*, February 22, 1978; Ken Dychtwald, "Liberating Aging: An Interview with Maggie Kuhn," *New Age*, February 1979; Chris Sheppard, "Ageing, Profile of an Activist: Still Prowling, Still Growling," *New Internationalist*, June 1982.

8. Huckle 1991:66.

9. Evans and Boyte 1992:101. See also Garner 1977:196–202; Morris 1984; Miller 1987; Polletta 2002:55–175.

10. Carla Woodworth to Roger Sanjek, February 4, 2007.

11. Gerlach and Hine 1970:39, 90–91.

12. Evans and Boyte 1992:ix, 2, 18, 78, 192.

13. Compare Gerlach and Hine 1970:97: "Recruitment to a movement is largely initiated by lay members of cell groups at the grass roots level rather than by noted leaders, although such leaders may be instrumental in the consummation of the commitment process."

14. Polletta 2002:228.

15. Gerlach and Hine call attention to conferences and demonstrations— Gray Panther conventions conjoined both elements—in strengthening movements. "Various segments of the movement . . . come together temporarily . . . to heighten the commitment of individual participants, attract potential recruits, offer opportunity for cross-fertilization of ideas, and clarify both cleavages and common goals. [They] serve to enhance a sense of common purpose within the segmentary structure of the movement [and] focus public attention on movement goals" (1973:166).

16. Had they been "quickly communicated," *Network*'s reports of local activities might have benefited the Gray Panthers: "Successes on the part of one group heighten the success of the movement as a whole . . . as examples for other groups to follow" (Gerlach and Hine 1973:169).

17. These events conformed to the organizational sequence outlined by Stevens: "Good reputation in the community. Often cash rich. Tend to increase fundraising, rather than cut expenses. Collective arrogance or complacency. . . . Confusion. Quality employees/board members are leaving. Negative cash

flow. . . . Deficit spending. Paranoia paralyzes organization. Internal fighting and back stabbing. Emphasis on *who* caused the problem, not *what* the problem is" (1992:5).

18. "Internal division is a misery that few [social movement organizations] escape completely—it is in the nature of the beast" (Gamson 1975:99). A common pattern is "*oligarchization*, in which an originally democratically structured movement organization separates into a decision-making elite and a disaffected, unheard rank and file. . . . Once entrenched, the movement elite is extraordinarily hard to dislodge and tends to *conservatize* the movement . . . decision making is increasingly confined to organizational maintenance decisions—for example, funding and internal structure" (Garner 1977:14). Moreover, the "internal oligarchy" and "bureaucratic organization" that characterized National in this period "tended to blunt the militancy that was the fundamental source of such influence as the [Gray Panthers] exerted. . . . [It] curbed the disruptive force [the networks] were sometimes able to mobilize. . . . In part, in resulted from the preoccupation with internal leadership prerogatives that organization-building seems to induce [but also from] their search for resources to maintain their organization" (Piven and Cloward 1979:xv–xvi, xxii). This was particularly evident in the 1981–83 Social Security battles.

19. As brilliantly provided in Skocpol 2003.

20. Skocpol 2003:50, 144, 152, 221.

21. For Max Weber "charisma" was a "quality of an individual personality by which he [or she] is set apart from ordinary men [or women] and treated as endowed with . . . superhuman or at least . . . exceptional powers or qualities . . . regarded as . . . exemplary, and on the basis of them the individual concerned is treated as a leader" (Weber 1947:358–59, quoted in Bendix 1962:88). "Neither the 'boss,' with rational-bureaucratic authority, nor the 'lord,' who has inherited traditional authority, . . . the *leader* [is] the formulator and 'speaker' of [a movement's ideological] orientations. . . . A charismatic leader does not gain influence by giving piecemeal advice in particular situations. He [or she] has his impact because he offers an all-embracing definition of the situation" (Fabian 1971:6–7). "The charismatic leader is always a radical who challenges established practice," but she or he "forfeits his authority when he fails to prove himself in the eyes of" his or her followers (Bendix 1962:297, 300). See also Nicholas 1973:80–82.

22. As Evans and Boyte put it, in the dispersed local units of a social movement there is "constant production of new leaders, curbing in some ways the antidemocratic dimensions of charisma" (1992:193).

23. Jacobs 1980:101.

24. Dahrendorf (1988:131–37, 171–73, 181–82) provocatively traces this to a restructured job market, with fewer public service openings and more opportunities in commerce and corporate employment.

25. Gamson 1975.

26. See Lofland 1985:201–18 on members of "social movement locals."

27. Jezer 1982:90.

28. Morris 1984:15.

29. Miller 1987:259; Polletta 2002:138.

30. Cassell 1989:109; Skocpol 2003:161–62

31. Nadasen 2005:xiv, 125; Piven and Cloward 1979:295.

32. Huckle 1991:3, 8.

33. Francesca Lyman, "Maggie Kuhn: A Wrinkled Radical's Crusade," *The Progressive,* January 1988.

34. Gerlach and Hine 1970:26.

35. Cayleff 1991:235; Skocpol 2003:156. See also Lieberman 2000:43–63 on the right-wing think-tank attack on AARP in the 1990s, one championed by Senator Alan Simpson of Wyoming and intended to blunt AARP's defense of Medicare and Social Security from Republican cuts and plans to privatize.

36. Evans and Boyte 1992:187; Polletta 2002:7.

37. Among the elderly British leftists Andrews interviewed, she concluded, "working-class activists appear to be motivated by a desire to help others whom they see as being very similar to themselves, whereas middle-class respondents speak of their work in the more abstract language of conscience, justice and social rights" (1991:115). My Gray Panther experience does not accord with this formula; I can think of Panthers of varying class backgrounds who embraced both these motivations and values, shifting easily from transit fares to nuclear deescalation, for example.

38. Leslie Palma, "Panther Leaps to Action Early When Prowling Asphalt Jungle," *Staten Island Advance*, [ca. 1985]. I found this clipping in the New York Gray Panther files in 2006. I never met Elvin Adams.

39. Nadasen 2005:237.

40. The reforms that *Paying through the Ear* advanced are still in effect, and hearing aids may be sold only by state-licensed specialists or audiologists. Cost is the chief barrier preventing four-fifths of those who could benefit, about twenty-four million mainly older persons, from purchasing them. The average price is $2,200, which Medicare and many private insurers do not cover. See Ann Zimmerman, "The Noisy Debate over Hearing Aids: Why So Expensive?," *Wall Street Journal*, March 24, 2004.

41. Huckle 1991:xi–xii, 186–89.

42. See also Shield and Aronson 2003:1, 18–19, 83, 117–18, 120–25, 171–74, 210–13, 225–32.

43. Raymond Fisk, " 'The Ghettoization of Age,' " [*Cornell Daily Sun*?], February 24, 1977; Maggie Kuhn, "Young and Old: More Than Ever, We Need Each Other," *Network*, Winter 1985; Harris 1975:71.

44. Hope Bagger to William Hutton, September 10, 1973.

45. Gerlach and Hine 1970:xvii; 1973:174–75. See also Nicholas 1973:76.

46. Maggie Kuhn, "The State of the Union," *Network*, March 1992; Gray Panthers 6th Biennial National Convention, "Gray Panther Mission Statement," *Network Report*, October-November 1986.

47. Polletta 2002:152; Kuhn, "State of the Union."

48. In a classic 1938 essay the anthropologist Marcel Mauss contended that cultural conceptions of "the person" vary within most human societies according to their diverse social structures (recognized groupings, status hierarchies, positions of leadership) and the place a particular individual occupies within each such social matrix. With Christianity, he argued, a "moral" equivalence of all persons, regardless of status or position, arose. This was transformed by modern capitalism and the dominance of privately owned property into the "liberal" ideology of personal autonomy and market-based justification of hierarchy. "Hence, by a paradox," J. S. La Fontaine observes, "Western societies conceive of natural man, the individual, as equal in order to disguise the inequalities of achievement." In the contemporary world, morally egalitarian conceptions of the person clash with unequal economic and political power and privilege. See essays by Mauss, La Fontaine, N. J. Allen, Louis Dumont, and Michael Carrithers in Carrithers, Collins, and Lukes 1985.

49. Maggie Kuhn, "Foreword," in Huckle 1991; "State of the Union"; Lyman, "Maggie Kuhn."

50. Julie Bonnin, "Charlotte Flynn Leads with Optimism and Commitment," *Network*, March 1992; Dychtwald, "Liberating Aging"; Kuhn, "State of the Union."

51. Kuhn, "State of the Union"; Lyman, "Maggie Kuhn"; Paula Mixson, "Advocating for National Health," *Network*, September 1991; Marilyn Vowels, "Austin Health Care Hearings Judged a 'Capitol' Success," *Network*, May-June 1988; International Longevity Center-USA 2006c:v, 1–3.

52. Kuhn, Long, and Quinn 1991:207; Fisk, "Ghettoization"; "Gray Panther Mission Statement"; Kuhn, "State of the Union"; Gray Panthers 1994 Annual Report, 1995.

53. Roger Sanjek, "Boxed In/Locked Out: New York City's Elderly Housing Dilemma," keynote address, New York City Chapter, National Association of Social Workers, May 22, 1985; "Berkeley Gray Panther Resolution for Integration and Responsive Management of Senior Housing," *Berkeley Gray Panthers* (newsletter), September 1987; Esther Jantzen, "Elma Holder: Nursing Homes Back to Health," *Network*, Summer 1985.

54. Kuhn, Long, and Quinn 1991:214–15; Bonnin, "Charlotte Flynn."

55. Kuhn, "Foreword," "State of the Union"; Kuhn 1994:239–40; Margot Smith, "Commentary: Immigrant Crisis Is Election Issue," *Berkeley Daily Planet*, May 23, 2006. As indication that Gray Panthers broadly held the "concept of the person" outlined here, a 1991 survey of seventeen hundred network members and donors found "universal national health care" ranked first, "problems of senior citizens" second, "reduce military spending" third, "ageism and age discrimination" fourth, and "affordable and adequate housing" fifth; Donald Pelz, "Opinion Surveys Explore Future Gray Panther Directions," *Network*, September 1992. And upon stepping down after eight years as San Francisco Gray Panther convener in 2000, Aroza Simpson noted, "A large percentage of us want to see our tax dollars spent on funding public education, Universal Health Care, eliminate the growing gap between the rich and the poor, end global warming and environmental destruction, . . . and reduce the exorbitant military budget"; Aroza Simpson, "Outgoing Convener Charts Our Path!," *San Francisco Gray Panthers* (newsletter), December 2000.

56. Sheppard, "Profile." Abe Bloom recalls these words in the film *Maggie Growls*.

57. Compare Alinsky 1969; Lipsky 1968; Lofland 1985:3–10, 20–21, 259–64, 287–98.

58. "Panther Tests Leafleting Limits," *Network*, February 1991.

59. Berkeley Gray Panther *Newsletter*, June 2000.

60. "Washington, D.C. GPs Promote Toys of Peace," *Network*, Winter 1984.

61. Ted Boscia, "Professor to Bring Social Security Debate Home through Teach-In," *Temple Times*, March 24, 2005; Paul Nathanson, "Social Security's Real 'Crisis' One of Morals," *Albuquerque Journal*, January 19, 2005.

62. See National Citizens' Coalition for Nursing Home Reform website.

63. See Ron Wyden and Bob Bennett (Republican-Utah), "Fixing Health Care," *Wall Street Journal*, June 26, 2007.

64. Lyons 1997.

65. Karen Talbot, "Former Yugoslavia: The Name of the Game Is OIL! and the Prize Is Profits," *People's Weekly World*, May 18, 2001; "Afghanistan, Central Asia, Caucasus: Key to Oil Profits," *People's Weekly World*, May 17, 2002; "Coup-Making in Venezuela: The Bush and Oil Factors," *Double Standards*, 2002; "War for World Dominance," International Center for Peace and Justice, February 1, 2003.

66. See Burgess 2003:105–06.

67. Tom Majeski, "Medicare Group Hears Minnesota's Solutions, *Pioneer Press*, July 14, 1998; Frances Klafter, "Statement . . . to the National Medicare Commission," July 13, 1998.

68. Maggie Kuhn, "Advocacy in This New Age," *Aging*, July-August 1979.

69. Century Fund 2006:6, 8; International Longevity Center-USA. 2006a:27.

70. Robert Butler, "Why Survive Revisited," International Longevity Center-USA, 2002; U.S. Census Bureau website; Eduardo Porter, "Study Finds Wealth Inequality Is Widening Worldwide," *New York Times*, December 6, 2006; Daniel Gross, "The Golden Ass," *Slate*, June 16, 2007, and "Thy Neighbor's Stash," *New York Times Book Review*, August 5, 2007; Nelson Schwartz, "Wall Street's Man of the Moment," *Fortune*, February 21, 2007. The cofounders of Blackstone in 1985 were its CEO Steve Schwarzman and former Nixon commerce secretary Pete Peterson, well known for critiques of Social Security and Medicare as unsustainable through his writings and the Concord Coalition, which he backed financially; see Baker and Weisbrot 1999:3–5, 19–20, 33; Freedman 1999:13–15; Rozak 2001:45–46, 51–52.

71. Century Fund 2006:16; Morris 2006:10–11, 19–25. See also Donald Barlett and James Steele, "The Broken Promise," *Time*, October 31, 2005; Roger Lowenstein, "The End of Pensions," *New York Times Magazine*, October 30, 2005.

72. Economic Policy Institute, "EPI Issue Guide: Retirement Security," September 2006; Louis Uchitelle, "Here Come the Economic Populists," *New York Times*, November 26, 2006. See also Saul Friedman, "Emboldening Social Security," *Newsday*, May 12, 2007.

73. Barlett and Steele 2004:12; Bernard Wasow, "U.S. Health Care: World Beaten," Century Foundation, May 3, 2006.

74. Century Foundation 2006:27; International Longevity Center-USA 2006a:8; Associated Press, "Japanese Women Show Longest Life Expectancy," *Washington Post*, May 19, 2007; Butler, "Why Survive Revisited"; Atul Gawande, "The Way We Age Now," *New Yorker*, April 30, 2007; Wasow, "U.S. Health Care."

75. International Longevity Center-USA, 2006c:15; Barlett and Steele 2004:32; Morris 2006:2–3, 10–11, 27; N. C. Aizenman and Christopher Lee, "U.S. Poverty Rate Drops; Ranks of Uninsured Grow," *Washington* Post, August 29, 2007; Robert Bell, "Canadian and U.S. Heath Services—Let's Compare the Two" (letter), *Wall Street Journal*, July 9, 2007; Rafael Gerena-Morales, "U.S. Needs a New Prescription to Slow Health-Care Spending," *Wall Street Journal*, March 6, 2006; Daniel Gross, "National Health Care? We're Halfway There," *New York Times*, December 3, 2006; Justin Lahart, "Rethinking Health Care and the GDP," *Wall Street Journal*, January 25, 2007; David Leonhardt, "A Lesson from Europe on Health Care," *New York Times*, October 18, 2006; Wasow, "U.S. Health Care."

76. On current universal health care proposals, see Robert Frank, "A Health Care Plan So Simple, Even Stephen Colbert Couldn't Simplify It," *New York Times*, February 15, 2007; Saul Friedman, "Medicare for All Would Be a Healthy Move," *Newsday*, March 31, 2007, and "Health Care: The Best Won't Be the Easiest, *Newsday*, April 21, 2007.

77. Barlett and Steele 2004; Century Foundation 2006:25, 28–29; Morris 2006:40–53; Gross, "National Health Care"; H. Gregory Mankiw, "Beyond Those Health Care Numbers," *New York Times*, November 4, 2007.

78. Century Foundation 2006:27; Lisa Chamberlain, "Design for Everyone, Disabled or Not," *New York Times*, January 7, 2007.

79. A newer trend is the purchase of nursing homes and chains by private

equity firms. "As such investors have acquired nursing homes, they have often reduced costs, increased profits and quicky resold facilities for significant gains. . . . Private investment companies have made it very difficult . . . for regulators to levy chainwide fines by creating complex corporate structures that obscure who controls their nursing homes." Charles Duhigg, *New York Times*, September 23, 2007.

80. International Longevity Center-USA, 2006b; Consumer Reports.org, "Nursing Home Guide," September 2006; "Encore: A Guide to Retirement Planning and Living," *Wall Street Journal*, December 11, 2006; Gerena-Morales, "New Prescription"; Beverly Goldberg, "An Absence of Tender Loving Care: The Nursing Home Dilemma," Century Foundation, April 26, 2007; Robert Pear, "Oversight of Nursing Homes Is Criticized," *New York Times*, April 22, 2007; Glenn Ruffenach, "Nursing-Home Costs Jump 6.1%," *Wall Street Journal*, September 28, 2004.

81. For histories of the Defense Department and CIA covering these years, see Carroll 2006 and Weiner 2007.

82. Porter, "Wealth Inequality"; Mikhail Gorbachev, "The Nuclear Threat," *Wall Street Journal*, January 31, 2007. See also Carroll 2006:347, 383, 387, 391, 395–97, 404–17, 421, 436, 454–55, 467–75, 484–85, 500–501.

83. Tish Sommers to Roger and Lani [Sanjek], December 23, 1983.

84. See Cassell 1989; Gerlach and Hine 1970, 1973:154–60, 165–66; Lofland 1985:1–25; Piven and Cloward 1979:5. The biographies in Andrews 1991 reveal individual activists' commitments to the larger progressive left and its causes from the 1930s through 1960s rather than to membership in specific organizations; see also Andrews 1991:115, 156, 171–72.

86. Piven and Cloward 1979:xxi. Miliband contends that the left, and movement groups like the Gray Panthers, win gains only when there is a strong organized labor movement (1989:7, 73, 109). If this is the case historically (see Myles 1989 on "the citizen's wage"), in the early twenty-first century the array of organized political groupings may be unfavorable. In 2006 union membership fell to 12 percent of workers, down from 20 percent in 1983 and 35 percent in the 1950s, and union members comprised only 7 percent of private sector workers. But tellingly, 53 percent of nonunion employees would join a union if they could. See Steven Greenhouse, "Sharp Decline in Union Membership in '06," *New York Times*, January 26, 2007.

86. Evans and Boyte 1992:xix, 192. As Polletta (2002:16) states, "When a group has common interests, consensus-based, face-to-face, and egalitarian deliberations can deliver good decisions."

87. See Skocpol's discussion of organizations "reinventing" themselves via both technology and organizing—despite her pronouncement that "a revival of 'movement activism' in the style of the sixties and seventies . . . will never return" (2003:222, 273–76). See also Huckle 1991:97–98 for Tish Sommers's view of different routes OWL could take in the future.

88. See Savishinsky 2000. See also Eduardo Porter and Mary Williams Walsh, "Retirement Becomes a Rest Stop as Pensions and Benefits Shrink," *New York Times*, February 9, 2005.

89. See Margolies 2004. See also Jane Gross, "Elder-Care Costs Deplete Savings of a Generation," *New York Times*, December 30, 2006; Sue Shellenbarger, "When Elderly Loved Ones Live Far Away: The Challenge of Long-Distance Care," *Wall Street Journal*, July 29, 2004; Kristina Shevory, "Getting Help for an Aging Relative," *New York Times*, June 3, 2006.

90. See Freedman's prediction (1999) of considerable boomer retiree volun-

teer and community service. Roszak's more political view of the boomers fore-
sees "a number of them will choose something rather like Maggie Kuhn's vision,
a reassertion of the ideal of community and the politics of advocacy" (2001:36).

91. Century Foundation 2006:23; Claudia Dreifus, "A Conversation with Rob-
ert N. Butler: Focusing on the Issue of Aging, and Growing into the Job," *New
York Times*, November 14, 2006; John Harwood, "Washington Wire," *Wall Street
Journal*, June 2, 2006; Dave Lindorff, "Senior Partners," *American Prospect Online
Edition*, December 29, 2003.

92. "Generation Y," *Business Week*, February 15, 1999; Eileen Bass, "Generation
Y: They've Arrived at Work with a New Attitude," *USA Today*, November 6, 2005;
"Generation Y: The Millennials," *NAS Insights*, 2006.

Bibliography

Achenbaum, W. Andrew. 1978. *Old Age in the New Land: The American Experience Since 1790.* Baltimore: Johns Hopkins University Press.

———. 1983. *Shades of Gray: Old Age, American Values, and Federal Policies since 1920.* Boston: Little Brown.

Alcaly, Roger and David Mermelstein, eds. 1976. *The Fiscal Crisis of American Cities: Essays on the Political Economy of Urban America with Special Reference to New York.* New York: Vintage.

Alinksky, Saul. 1969 [1946]. *Reveille for Radicals.* New York: Vintage.

Andrews, Molly. 1991. *Lifetimes of Commitment: Aging, Politics, Psychology.* Cambridge: Cambridge University Press.

Baker, Dean and Mark Weisbrot. 1999. *Social Security: The Phony Crisis.* Chicago: University of Chicago Press.

Ball, Robert. 1988. "The Original Understanding on Social Security: Implications for Later Developments." In *Social Security: Beyond the Rhetoric of Crisis,* ed. Theodore Marmor and Jerry Mashaw, 17–39. Princeton, N.J.: Princeton University Press.

Barlett, Donald and James Steele. 2004. *Critical Condition: How Health Care in America Became Big Business and Bad Medicine.* New York: Doubleday.

Baxter, Ellen and Kim Hopper. 1981. *Private Lives/Public Spaces: Homeless Adults on the Streets of New York City.* New York: Community Service Society.

Bell, Daniel. 1967 [1952]. *Marxian Socialism in the United States.* Princeton, N.J.: Princeton University Press.

Bendix, Reinhard. 1962. *Max Weber: An Intellectual Portrait.* New York: Anchor.

Bloch, Maurice. 1977. "The Past and the Present in the Present." *Man* 12: 278–92.

Brecher, Jeremy. 1972. *Strike!* Boston: South End Press.

Brown, Elaine. 1992. *A Taste of Power: A Black Woman's Story.* New York: Pantheon.

Burgess, Michael. 2003. *To the Last Breath: Rose Kryzak and the Senior Action Movement in New York State, 1972–2001.* Albany: New York StateWide Senior Action Council.

Butler, Robert. 1969. "Age-ism: Another Form of Bigotry." *The Gerontologist* 9: 243–46.

———. 1975. *Why Survive? Being Old in America.* New York: Harper and Row.

——— and Myrna Lewis. 1976. *Sex after Sixty.* New York: Harper and Row.

Cantor, Marjorie. 1975. *The Formal and Informal Social Support System of Older New Yorkers.* New York: New York City Office for the Aging.

Carrithers, Michael, Steven Collins, and Steven Lukes, eds. 1985. *The Category of the Person: Anthropology, Philosophy, History*. Cambridge: Cambridge University Press.

Carroll, James. 2006. *House of War: The Pentagon and the Disastrous Rise of American Power.* Boston: Houghton Mifflin.

Cassell, Joan. 1989 [1977]. *A Group Called Women: Sisterhood and Symbolism in the Feminist Movement.* Prospect Heights, Ill.: Waveland Press.

Cayleff, Susan. 1991. "The Silver-Haired Sisterhood: Historical Perspectives on Women and Aging." In *Tish Sommers, Activist, and the Founding of the Older Women's League,* by Patricia Huckle, 225–41. Knoxville: University of Tennessee Press.

Century Foundation. 2006. *Public Policy in an Older America.* New York: Century Foundation Press.

Clark, Margaret. 1973. "Contributions of Cultural Anthropology to the Study of the Aged." In *Cultural Illness and Health,* ed. Laura Nader and Thomas Maretzki, 78–88. Washington, D.C.: American Anthropological Association.

————— and Barbara Gallatin Anderson. 1967. *Culture and Aging: An Anthropological Study of Older Americans.* Springfield, Ill.: Charles C. Thomas.

Clifford, James. 1986. "Introduction: Partial Truths." In *Writing Culture: The Poetics and Politics of Ethnography,* ed. James Clifford and George Marcus, 1–26. Berkeley: University of California Press.

Cohen, Lawrence. 1994. "Old Age: Cultural and Critical Perspectives." *Annual Review of Anthropology* 23: 137–58

Curtin, Sharon. 1972. *Nobody Ever Died of Old Age: In Praise of Old People, in Outrage at Their Loneliness.* Boston: Little, Brown.

Dahrendorf, Ralf. 1988. *The Modern Social Conflict: An Essay on the Politics of Liberty.* New York: Weidenfeld and Nicolson.

Davis, Allison, Burleigh Gardner, and Mary Gardner. 1941. *Deep South: A Social Anthropological Study of Caste and Class.* Chicago: University of Chicago Press.

Day-Lower, Dennis, Drayton Bryant, and Joan Ward Mullaney. 1982. *National Policy Workshop on Shared Housing: Findings and Recommendations.* Philadelphia: Shared Housing Resource Center, Inc.

Dychtwald, Ken and Joe Flower. 1990. *Age Wave: The Challenges and Opportunities of an Aging America.* New York: Bantam.

Ehrenreich, Barbara and John Ehrenreich, eds. 1970. *The American Health Empire: Power, Profits, and Politics.* New York: Random House.

Estes, Carroll. 1979. *The Aging Enterprise: A Critical Examination of Social Policies for the Aged.* San Francisco: Jossey-Bass.

—————. 1993. "The Aging Enterprise Revisited." *The Gerontologist* 33: 292–98.

Evans, Sara and Harry Boyte. 1992 [1986]. *Free Spaces: The Sources of Democratic Change in America.* Chicago: University of Chicago Press.

Fabian, Johannes. 1971. *Jamaa: A Charismatic Movement in Katanga.* Evanston, Ill.: Northwestern University Press.

—————. 1983. *Time and the Other: How Anthropology Makes Its Object.* New York: Columbia University Press.

Fenton, William. 1962. "Ethnohistory and Its Problems." *Ethnohistory* 9: 1–23.

—————. 1987. *The False Faces of the Iroquois.* Norman: University of Oklahoma Press.

Fischer, David Hackett. 1978. *Growing Old in America.* New York: Oxford University Press.

Fleischer, Doris Zames and Frieda Zames. 2001. *The Disability Rights Movement from Charity to Confrontation.* Philadelphia: Temple University Press.

Francis, Doris. 1984. *Will You Still Need Me, Will You Still Feed Me, When I'm 84?* Bloomington: Indiana University Press.

Freedman, Marc. 1999. *Prime Time: How Baby Boomers Will Revolutionize Retirement and Transform America.* New York: Public Affairs.

Friedan, Betty. 1993. *The Fountain of Age.* New York: Simon and Schuster.

Gamson, William. 1975. *The Strategy of Social Protest.* Homewood, Ill.: Dorsey Press.

Garner, Roberta Ash. 1977. *Social Movements in America.* Chicago: Rand McNally.

Geertz, Clifford. 1988. *Works and Lives: The Anthropologist as Author.* Stanford, Calif.: Stanford University Press.

Gerlach, Luther and Virginia Hine. 1970. *People, Power, Change: Movements of Social Transformation.* Indianapolis, Ind.: Bobbs-Merrill.

———. 1973. *Lifeway Leap: The Dynamics of Change in America.* Minneapolis: University of Minnesota Press.

Gilderbloom, John. 1980. *Moderate Rent Control: The Experience of U.S. Cities.* Washington, D.C.: Conference on Alternative State and Local Policies.

Goldman, Eric. 1960. *The Crucial Decade—And After: America, 1945–1960.* New York: Vintage.

Graebner, William. 1980. *A History of Retirement: The Meaning and Function of an American Institution, 1885–1978.* New Haven, Conn.: Yale University Press.

Gray Panther Economy Task Force. 1978. *Economic Rights—Economic Democracy: A Working Paper for Study of the Gray Panther Movement.* Philadelphia: Gray Panthers.

Gray Panther Media Watch Task Force. 1983. *Gray Panther Media Guide: Age and Youth in Action for Advocacy/Programming/Production/Participation.* Philadelphia: Gray Panthers.

Griesel, Elma. 1973. *Paying through the Ear: A Report on Hearing Health Care Problems.* Washington, D.C.: Public Citizen, Inc.

——— and Linda Horn. 1975. *Citizens Action Guide: Nursing Home Reform.* Philadelphia: Gray Panthers.

Haber, Carole. 1983. *Beyond Sixty-Five: The Dilemma of Old Age in America's Past.* New York: Cambridge University Press.

Harding, Elizabeth, Tom Bodenheimer, and Steve Cummings, eds. 1972. *Billions for Band-Aids: An Analysis of the U.S. Health Care System and of Proposals for Its Reform.* San Francisco: Medical Committee for Human Rights.

Harrington, Michael. 1963. *The Other America: Poverty in the United States.* Baltimore, Md.: Penguin.

Harris, Louis and Associates. 1975. *The Myth and Reality of Aging in America.* Washington, D.C.: National Council on the Aging.

Hawley, Peter. 1978. *Housing in the Public Domain: The Only Solution.* New York: Metropolitan Council on Housing.

Hessel, Dieter, ed. 1977. *Maggie Kuhn on Aging: A Dialogue.* Philadelphia: Westminster Press.

Himmelstein, David, Steffie Woolhandler, and the Writing Committee of the Working Group on Program Design. 1989. "A National Health Program for the United States: A Physicians' Proposal." *New England Journal of Medicine* 320: 102–8.

Homefront. 1979. *Housing Abandonment in New York City.* New York: Homefront.

Hopper, Kim. 2003. *Reckoning with Homelessness.* Ithaca, N.Y.: Cornell University Press.

Horn, Linda and Elma Griesel. 1977. *Nursing Homes: A Citizen's Action Guide.* Boston: Beacon Press.

Huckle, Patricia. 1991. *Tish Sommers, Activist, and the Founding of the Older Women's League*. Knoxville: University of Tennessee Press.

International Longevity Center-USA. 2006a. *Ageism in America*. New York: International Longevity Center-USA.

———. 2006b. *Caregiving in America*. New York: International Longevity Center-USA.

———. 2006c. *Redesigning Health Care for an Older America*. New York: International Longevity Center-USA.

Jackson, Hobart. 1976. "Black Advocacy, Techniques and Trials." In *Advocacy and Age: Issues, Experiences, Strategies*, ed. Paul Kerschner, 97–112. Los Angeles: University of Southern California Ethel Percy Andrus Gerontology Center.

Jacobs, Ruth. 1980. "Portrait of a Phenomenon—The Gray Panthers: Do They Have a Long-Run Future?" In *Public Policies for an Aging Population*, ed. Elizabeth Markson and Gretchen Batra, 93–102. Lexington, Mass.: Lexington Books.

Jaeger, Dorothea and Leo Simmons. 1970. *The Aged Ill: Coping with Problems of Geriatric Care*. New York: Appleton Century Crofts.

Jezer, Marty. 1982. *The Dark Ages: Life in the United States, 1945–1960*. Boston: South End Press.

Johnson, Haynes and David Broder. 1996. *The System: The American Way of Politics at the Breaking Point*. Boston: Little, Brown.

Kiefer, Christie. 2000. *Health Work with the Poor: A Practical Guide*. New Brunswick, N.J.: Rutgers University Press.

Keith, Jennie. 1982. *Old People as People: Social and Cultural Influences on Aging and Old Age*. Boston: Little Brown.

Klafter, Frances, ed. 1980. *The Gray Panther Manual: Vol. II Programs for Action*. Philadelphia: Gray Panthers.

Kotelchuck, David, ed. 1976. *Prognosis Negative: Crisis in the Health Care System*. New York: Vintage.

Krasniewicz, Louise. 1992. *Nuclear Summer: The Clash of Communities at the Seneca Women's Peace Encampment*. Ithaca, N.Y.: Cornell University Press.

Kuhn, Maggie. 1972. *Get Out There and Do Something About Injustice*. New York: Friendship Press.

———. 1976. "What Old People Want for Themselves and Others in Society." In *Advocacy and Age: Issues, Experiences, Strategies*, ed. Paul Kerschner, 87–96. Los Angeles: University of Southern California Ethel Percy Andrus Gerontology Center.

———. 1977–78. "Learning by Living." *International Journal of Aging and Human Development* 8: 359–65.

———. 1994. Keynote Address at the Conference on Conscious Aging. In *Women's Voices in Our Time: Statements by American Leaders*, ed. Victoria DeFrancisco and Marvin Jensen, 231–42. Prospect Heights, Ill.: Waveland.

——— with Christina Long and Laura Quinn. 1991. *No Stone Unturned: The Life and Times of Maggie Kuhn*. New York: Ballantine.

Kuttner, Robert. 1980. *Revolt of the Haves: Tax Rebellions and Hard Times*. New York: Simon and Schuster.

Kuttner, Robert and David Kelston. 1979. *The Shifting Property Tax Burden: The Untold Cause of the Tax Revolt*. Washington, D.C.: Conference on Alternative State and Local Policies.

LeGates, Richard and Chester Hartman. 1981. "Displacement." *Clearinghouse Review* 15(3): 207–49.

Leuchtenburg, William. 1958. *The Perils of Prosperity, 1914–32.* Chicago: University of Chicago Press.

———. 1963. *Franklin D. Roosevelt and the New Deal.* New York: Harper and Row.

———. 1993. *In the Shadow of FDR: From Harry Truman to Bill Clinton.* Ithaca, N.Y.: Cornell University Press.

———. 1995. *The FDR Years: On Roosevelt and His Legacy.* New York: Columbia University Press.

Lieberman, Trudy. 2000. *Slanting the Story: The Forces That Shape the News.* New York: New Press.

Lipsky, Michael. 1968. "Protest as a Political Resource." *American Political Science Review* 62: 1144–58.

Lofland, John. 1985. *Protest: Studies of Collective Behavior and Social Movements.* New Brunswick, N.J.: Transaction.

Long, Susan Orpett. 2005. *Final Days: Japanese Culture and Choice at the End of Life.* Honolulu: University of Hawaii Press.

Lopata, Helena Znaniecki. 1973. *Widowhood in an American City.* Cambridge, Mass.: Schenkman.

Lyons, Maxine. 1997. *Elder Voices: Insights and Reflections.* Cambridge, Mass.: Eldercorps.

Marcuse, Peter. 1981. *Housing Abandonment: Does Rent Control Make a Difference?* Washington, D.C.: Conference on Alternative State and Local Policies.

Margolies, Luisa. 2004. *My Mother's Hip: Lessons from the World of Eldercare.* Philadelphia: Temple University Press.

Marmor, Theodore. 2000. *The Politics of Medicare.* 2nd ed. Hawthorne, N.Y.: Aldine de Gruyter.

——— and Jerry Mashaw, eds. 1988. *Social Security: Beyond the Rhetoric of Crisis.* Princeton, N.J.: Princeton University Press.

McNamee, Thomas. 2007. *Alice Waters and Chez Panisse: The Romantic, Impractical, Often Eccentric, Ultimately Brilliant Making of a Food Revolution.* New York: Penguin.

Messinger, Ruth and Frank Domurad. 1982. *The Rich Get Richer: J-51 Tax Breaks in New York City, 1981–1982.* New York: New York Public Interest Research Group.

Miliband, Ralph. 1989. *Divided Societies: Class Struggle in Contemporary Capitalism.* Oxford: Oxford University Press.

Miller, James. 1987. *"Democracy Is in the Streets": From Port Huron to the Siege of Chicago.* New York: Simon and Schuster.

Mills, C. Wright. 1959. *The Sociological Imagination.* New York: Grove Press.

Morris, Aldon. 1984. *The Origins of the Civil Rights Movement: Black Communities Organizing for Change.* New York: Free Press.

Morris, Charles. 2006. *Apart at the Seams: The Collapse of Private Pension and Health Care Protections.* New York: Century Foundation Press.

Murray, Sylvie. 2003. *The Progressive Housewife: Community Activism in Suburban Queens, 1945–1965.* Philadelphia: University of Pennsylvania Press.

Myers, Phyllis. 1982. *Aging in Place: Strategies to Help the Elderly Stay in Revitalizing Neighborhoods.* Washington, D.C.: Conservation Foundation.

Myles, John. 1989. *Old Age in the Welfare State: The Political Economy of Public Pensions.* Lawrence: University of Kansas Press.

Nadasen, Premilla. 2005. *Welfare Warriors: The Welfare Rights Movement in the United States.* New Brunswick, N.J.: Rutgers University Press.

Nader, Ralph. 1965. *Unsafe at Any Speed: The Designed-in Dangers of the American Automobile.* New York: Grossman.

Nassau, Mabel Louise. 1980 [1915]. *Old Age Poverty in Greenwich Village: A Neighborhood Study.* New York: Arno Press.

Navarro, Vicente. 1976. *Medicine under Capitalism.* New York: Prodist.

Nicholas, Ralph. 1973. "Social and Political Movements." *Annual Review of Anthropology* 2: 63–84.

Okely, Judith. 1992. "Anthropology and Autobiography: Participatory Experience and Embodied Knowledge." In *Anthropology and Autobiography*, ed. Judith Okely and Helen Callaway, 1–28. London: Routledge.

Ottenberg, Simon. 1990. "Thirty Years of Fieldnotes: Changing Relationships to the Text." In *Fieldnotes: The Makings of Anthropology*, ed. Roger Sanjek, 139–60. Ithaca, N.Y.: Cornell University Press.

Pearson, Hugh. 1994. *The Shadow of the Panther: Huey Newton and the Price of Black Power in America.* Cambridge, Mass.: Perseus.

Perretz, Harriet, ed. 1978. *The Gray Panther Manual: Vol. I Organizing.* Philadelphia: Gray Panthers.

Piven, Frances Fox and Richard Cloward. 1979 [1977]. *Poor People's Movements: Why They Succeed, How They Fail.* New York: Vintage.

——— 1982. *The New Class War: Reagan's Attack on the Welfare State and Its Consequences.* New York: Pantheon.

———. 1988. *Why Americans Don't Vote.* New York: Pantheon.

Polletta, Francesca. 2002. *Freedom Is an Endless Meeting: Democracy in American Social Movements.* Chicago: University of Chicago Press.

Posner, Prudence. 1990. Introduction. In *Dilemmas of Activism: Class, Community, and the Politics of Local Mobilization*, ed. Joseph Ling and Prudence Posner, 3–20. Philadelphia: Temple University Press.

Pratt, Henry. 1976. *The Gray Lobby.* Chicago: University of Chicago Press.

Quadagno, Jill. 1988. *The Transformation of Old Age Security: Class and Politics in the American Welfare State.* Chicago: University of Chicago Press.

Roszak, Theodore. 2001. *Longevity Revolution: As Boomers Become Elders.* Berkeley, Calif.: Berkeley Hills.

Sahlins, Marshall. 1976. *Culture and Practical Reason.* Chicago: University of Chicago Press.

———. 2000. *Culture in Practice: Selected Essays.* New York: Zone.

Sanjek, Roger. 1977. *A Profile of Over 60 Health Services Users: A Report and Recommendations.* Berkeley, Calif.: Over 60 Health Clinic Geriatric Health Services Program.

———. 1982. *Federal Housing Programs and Their Impact on Homelessness.* New York: Coalition for the Homeless.

———. 1984. *Crowded Out: Homelessness and the Elderly Poor in New York City.* New York: Coalition for the Homeless and Gray Panthers of New York City. Reprinted in *Homeless Older Americans: Hearing before the Subcommittee on Housing and Consumer Interests of the Select Committee on Aging, House of Representatives, 98th Congress*, Comm. Pub. No. 98–461, 119–184. Washington, D.C.: Government Printing Office.

———. 1986. "Federal Housing Programs and Their Impact on Homelessness." In *Housing the Homeless*, ed. Jon Erickson and Charles Wilhelm, 315–21. New Brunswick, N.J.: Rutgers University Center for Urban Policy Research.

———. 1987. "Anthropological Work at a Gray Panther Health Clinic: Academic, Applied, and Advocacy Goals." In *Cities of the United States: Studies in Urban Anthropology*, ed. Leith Mullings, 148–75. New York: Columbia University Press.

———. 1990. "On Ethnographic Validity." In *Fieldnotes: The Makings of Anthropology*, ed. Roger Sanjek, 385–418. Ithaca, N.Y.: Cornell University Press.

———. 1998. *The Future of Us All: Race and Neighborhood Politics in New York City*. Ithaca, N.Y.: Cornell University Press.

Savishinsky, Joel. 2000. *Breaking the Watch: The Meanings of Retirement in America*. Ithaca, N.Y.: Cornell University Press.

Skocpol, Theda. 2003. *Diminished Democracy: From Membership to Management in American Civic Life*. Norman: University of Oklahoma Press.

Shield, Renée Rose and Stanley M. Aronson. 2003. *Aging in Today's World: Conversations between an Anthropologist and a Physician*. New York: Berghahn.

Shields, Laurie. 1981. *Displaced Homemakers: Organizing for a New Life*. New York: McGraw-Hill.

Sigelman, Daniel. 1981. *Your Money or Your Health: A Senior Citizens' Guide to Avoiding High Charging Medicare Doctors*. Washington, D.C.: Public Citizen Health Research Group.

Starr, Paul. 1982. *The Social Transformation of American Medicine*. New York: Basic Books.

Stevens, Susan. 1992. *Growing Up Nonprofit: Predictable Stages of Nonprofit Growth and Development*. St. Paul, Minn.: Stevens Group.

Strelnick, Hal. 1983. "Maggie Kuhn: 'All of Us Are in This Together.' " *Health/PAC Bulletin* 14(1): 19–26.

TeSelle, Eugene. 2003. *"A Network of the Concerned": The Witherspoon Society and Its Challenge to the Church*. Albuquerque, N.M.: Witherspoon Society.

Thomas, William. 2004. *What Are Old People For? How Elders Will Save the World*. Acton, Mass.: VanderWyk and Burnham.

Townsend, Claire. 1971. *Old Age: The Last Segregation*. New York: Grossman.

Trupin, Sophie. 1984. *Dakota Diaspora: Memoirs of a Jewish Homesteader*. Lincoln: University of Nebraska Press.

Van Tassel, David and Peter Stearns, eds. 1986. *Old Age in a Bureaucratic Society: The Elderly, the Experts, and the State in American History*. New York: Greenwood.

Waitzkin, Howard and Barbara Waterman. 1974. *The Exploitation of Illness in Capitalist Society*. Indianapolis: Bobbs-Merrill.

Wallace, Anthony. 1956. "Revitalization Movements." *American Anthropologist* 58: 264–81.

Weber, Max. 1947 [1925]. *The Theory of Social and Economic Organization*. New York: Free Press.

Weiner, Tim. 2007. *Legacy of Ashes: The History of the CIA*. New York: Doubleday.

Index